THE

Media

READER

THE

Media

READER

Edited by

Manuel Alvarado and John O. Thompson

BFI Publishing

First published in 1990 by the
British Film Institute
21 Stephen Street, London W1P 1PL

Designed by Julia King
Set in Plantin by
Fakenham Photosetting Limited, Fakenham, Norfolk
Printed in Great Britain by
Courier International Ltd, Tiptree, Essex

British Library Cataloguing in Publication Data
   The media reader.
   1. Society. Role of mass media
   I. Alvarado, Manuel *1948–*   II. Thompson, John O. *1947–*
   302.2'34

   ISBN 0–85170–258–9
   ISBN 0–85170–259–7 pbk

Remembering
Bill Bonney, Eric Michaels and Gillian Skirrow

ACKNOWLEDGMENTS

The editors owe a particular debt of gratitude to Tana Wollen who was involved with this project at an early stage. We would also like to thank Ed Buscombe, Geoffrey Nowell-Smith and Roma Gibson.

The publishers gratefully acknowledge the following for permission to reprint material:

The author, editors and Lawrence and Wishart for 'The Whites of their Eyes – Racist Ideologies and the Media' by Stuart Hall, © Stuart Hall; the author and MIT Press for 'Diaspora Culture and the Dialogic Imagination: The Aesthetics of Black Independent Film in Britain' by Kobena Mercer, © Celebration of Black Cinema, Inc., Boston, Mass.; *Framework* and the authors for ' "Typical Aussies": Television and Populism in Australia' by Noel King and Tim Rowse, 'Parody and Marginality – The Case of Brazilian Cinema' by João Luiz Vieira and Robert Stam, 'Review of John Hill, *Sex Class and Realism – British Cinema 1956–1963*' by Paul Willemen, 'Gandhiana and Gandhiology' by Ashish Rajadhyaksha, 'The Classic TV Detective Genre' by Michael Westlake; the authors and Ablex Publishing Corporation for 'On Counting the Wrong Things' by Brian Winston and 'Toward a Workers' History of the US Film Industry' by Michael Nielsen, © Ablex Publishing Corporation; *Screen* and the authors for 'Sex and Address in *Dynasty*' by Mark Finch, 'Broadcasting Politics: Communications and Consumption' by Kevin Robins and Frank Webster, 'Individualism Versus Collectivism' by Janet Staiger, 'Melodrama, Serial Form and Television Today' by Jane Feuer; *Art & Text* for 'Aboriginal Content: Who's Got It – Who Needs It?' by Eric Michaels; the authors and Macmillan for 'Advertising and the Manufacture of Difference' by Bill Bonney and Helen Wilson; the authors and Frances Pinter for 'The Valorisation of Consciousness: The Political Economy of Symbolism' by Sut Jhally; the author and the *International Journal of Advertising* for 'Editorial' by Jules Goddard; the author, the International Association for Audio-Visual Media in Historical Research and Education, and the copyright-holders (K.R.M. Short and S. Dolezel) for 'The Problem of "Authenticity" in the German Wartime Newsreels' by Karl Stamm; Sage Publications Ltd, *Media, Culture and Society* and the author for 'Visions of Instability: US Television's Law and Order News of El Salvador' by Robin Andersen; the author and *Mediamatic, The European Art/Media Magazine* (Binnenkadedijk 191, NL–1018 ZD Amsterdam, Holland) for 'The *Moonlighting* Story' by Philip Hayward; the author and Indiana University Press for 'Clinical Eyes: The Medical Discourse' by Mary Ann Doane; the author and Pantheon Press, a division of Random House, Inc./Alfred A. Knopf, Inc. for 'Prime Time – Deride and Conquer' by Mark Crispin Miller; Manchester University Press for 'Hellivision: An Analysis of Video Games' by Gillian Skirrow; the author and Methuen for 'Video Replay: Families, Films and Fantasy' by Valerie Walkerdine.

CONTENTS

NOTES ON
CONTRIBUTORS

Manuel Alvarado is Head of Education, British Film Institute.

Robin Andersen lectures at the Department of Communications, Fordham University, New York.

Bill Bonney was Associate Head of the Faculty of Humanities and Social Sciences, NSW Institute of Technology (now University of Technology, Sydney). He died in 1985.

Mary Ann Doane teaches in the Modern Culture and Media Centre at Brown University. She is author of *The Desire to Desire*; *The Woman's Film of the 1940s* and co-editor of *Revision: Essays in Feminist Film Criticism*.

Jane Feuer is Associate Professor at the University of Pittsburgh. Articles on television have appeared in *Screen, Harper's Cultural Studies, South Atlantic Quarterly* and various anthologies. She is a co-editor (with Paul Kerr and Tise Vahimagi) of *MTM 'Quality Television'* (BFI, 1984). She is currently working on a book about television in the Reagan era.

Mark Finch is currently with Frameline, a lesbian and gay Distribution company based in San Francisco. He is also a film programmer and freelance writer who still laments the passing of *Dynasty*.

Jules Goddard was the editor of the *International Journal of Advertising*.

Stuart Hall helped found the Centre for Cultural Studies at Birmingham University and was its Director (1968–79). He is now Professor of Sociology at the Open University. He has written extensively on the media, culture theory and politics.

Philip Hayward lectures in Drama and Mass Communications at Macquarie University, Sydney. He has contributed to journals such as *Screen, Block, Mediamatic* and *Marxism Today* and has edited a critical anthology entitled *Picture This: Media Representations of Visual Art and Artists*.

Sut Jhally is Associate Professor of Communication at the University of Massachusetts at Amhurst. He is the co-author, with William B. Leiss, of *Social Communication in Advertising*.

Noel King is a lecturer in Screen Studies at the University of Technology, Sydney.

Kobena Mercer has lectured and written widely on the cultural politics of race, ethnicity and media representation and is currently working in the Television Unit, British Film Institute.

Eric Michaels lectured in Media Studies at Griffith University, Queensland and was a frequent contributor to *Art & Text*. His book-length studies include *The Aboriginal Invention of Television* and *For a Cultural Future*. He died in 1988.

Mark Crispin Miller, who heads the Film Study programme at Johns Hopkins University, is the author of *Boxed In: the Culture of TV*. He has also written on other aspects of mass culture for the *New Republic*, the *Atlantic*, the *Nation* and other publications. He edited the forthcoming collection of essays, *Seeing Through Movies*, which Pantheon will be publishing in Spring 1990.

Michael Nielsen lectures at Wesley College, Dover, Delaware and has written widely on labour and the film industry.

Ashish Rajadhyaksha is a freelance journalist, art and film critic working in Bombay. He has published books on the work of Ritwik Ghatak, contributes to *Framework* and is currently working on an encyclopaedia of Indian cinema.

Kevin Robins is Research Associate at the Centre for Urban and Regional Development Studies (CURDS) at the University of Newcastle. With Frank Webster, he is the co-author of *Information Technology: A Luddite Analysis* (1986) and *The Technical Fix: Computers, Education and Industry* (1989).

Tim Rowse is the author of *Australian Liberalism and National Character* (Kibble, 1977) and *Arguing the Arts* (Penguin, 1987) and many papers on Australian history and cultural policy. He is completing a PhD in Aboriginal history at the University of Sydney.

Gillian Skirrow was a Lecturer in Film and Television Studies at the Universities of Strathclyde and Glasgow and a founding member of the John Logie Baird Centre. She was a member of the *Screen* editorial board and published articles on television and on women and technology. She died in 1987.

Janet Staiger is an Associate Professor, teaching Critical and Cultural Studies at the University of Texas at Austin. She is co-author with David Bordwell and Kristin Thompson of *The Classical Hollywood Cinema: Film Style and Mode of Production to 1960*.

Robert Stam is Associate Professor of Cinema Studies at New York University and is the author of *The Interrupted Spectacle*, *Reflexivity in Film and Literature* and *Subversive Pleasures: Bakhtin, Cultural Criticism and Film*.

Karl Stamm is Director of the Art and Museum Library of the City of Cologne and a Lecturer at the University of Bonn.

John O. Thompson is Lecturer in Charge, Department of Communication Studies, University of Liverpool. He is the editor of *Monty Python: Complete and Utter Theory of the Grotesque* and co-author, with Ann Thompson, of *Shakespeare, Meaning and Metaphor*.

João Luiz Vieira teaches at the Federal University of Rio de Janeiro and is currently Curator of the Rio de Janeiro Cinemateque. He is the author of *Espacos do Sonho* (Space of Dreams), a book about the architecture of movie palaces, and co-author of *D. W. Griffith*.

Valerie Walkerdine is Professor of Psychology at the Institute of Art and Design, Birmingham Polytechnic.

Frank Webster is Chair of Sociology at Oxford Polytechnic. He is the author of *The New Photography* (1980) and, with Kevin Robins, of *Information Technology: A Luddite Analysis* (1986) and *The Technical Fix: Computers, Education and Industry* (1989).

Michael Westlake taught film studies at Manchester University. He is currently a freelance writer and lecturer. His writings include *Film Theory: an Introduction* (with Robert Lapsley; Manchester University Press, 1988) and the novels *Imaginary Women* and *The Utopian* (Carcanet Press, 1987 and 1989).

Paul Willemen has published books on the work of Tashlin, Pasolini, Ophuls and on Indian cinema. Co-editor (with Jim Pines) of *Questions of Third Cinema*. Editorial board member of *Screen* in the 70s and editor of *Framework* in the 80s.

Helen Wilson is Senior Lecturer in the Faculty of Humanities and Social Sciences at the University of Technology, Sydney. She is the co-author (with Bill Bonney) of *Australia's Commercial Media* (Macmillan, 1983) and edited a collection of essays in memory of Bill, who died in 1985, called *Communication and the Public Sphere* (Macmillan, 1989).

Brian Winston is Dean of the School of Communication at Penn State University, Pennsylvania. He has published several books on the media and is currently writing a book about documentary film for the Cambridge University Press.

General Introduction

The essays collected in this Reader, diverse though they are, all fall within the category of Critical Media Theory. *Theory* here simply means that they contain more than factual information: they are informative-*plus*, and the added value consists in attempts to make broader sense of the facts, to give explanatory accounts rather than lists or gossip. But what *Critical* means, for writing produced in the 80s that will be worth reading in the 90s, may be worth spelling out at greater length.

In everyday speech, to criticise someone is to suggest that he or she could do better, even that he or she is doing harm. Criticism in this sense isn't necessarily an unfriendly or a hurtful act, but it has, one might say, an edge to it. For complicated historical reasons, 'criticism' in literary and other textual studies has come to mean something more neutral: indeed, literary criticism is more often than not a matter of demonstrating how splendid the text in front of the critic is. In what follows, we would like our readers to continue to hear the edge in 'Critical'; Critical Media theory is a subdivision of Social Criticism rather than of Literary (or indeed Film or Television) Criticism. It can be contrasted, as a mode of orientation toward its objects, with a yea-saying attitude which we might call the Celebratory.

Economic growth and technological innovation, the latter particularly proceeding at a tremendous pace, make media development currently a genuinely exciting area even when the hype is discounted. As new forms of contact amongst people nationally and globally develop, and new outlets for the creativity of individuals and collectivities open up, ought we not to be working in Celebratory rather than in Critical mode, by and large?

We hope the essays we have brought together here testify to the continuing instruction and pleasure which are to be had from recent, lively work in a Critical tradition attuned to certain real difficulties facing both media practitioners and their audiences at the onset of a new decade. Liveliness has been a key criterion for selection. A *mechanically* Critical reflex in this field, as in any other, can indeed become tedious. Mechanical or merely dutiful Criticism is produced when its practitioners lose touch with any real reason to Criticise; it amounts to laziness on the part of writers who would often write more authentically in Celebratory mode but who have picked up the Critical as a set of tricks of thought or unexamined 'progressive' dogmas.

Perhaps this is today a greater danger than the surviving impulses from the earlier tendency (flourishing from the 20s into the 60s) to be Critical from a fundamentally reactionary perspective, to deplore the media as Mass hence Crass. That tradition was elitist and unfair, but rarely consolidated itself as received doctrine or curricular dogma. Or perhaps it did, but we have moved forward: we all now recognise the great beauty of classical Hollywood studio production, do we not? We are all conscious – are we not? – of the skill and love that go into media production now, and which will guarantee that our media artefacts will look even more interesting in the future (where, with digital recording techniques, nothing need ever be lost) than they do now.

It is not a residual contempt for Mass Culture that hangs heavily over the institutionalised Media Studies curriculum today so much as an unexamined underestimation of the staying-power of Market Culture.

Without a doubt, the global integration of a market in images and sounds will continue and indeed intensify in the foreseeable future. A lack of realism about this infected a great deal of the Critical Media theory we have inherited from the 70s and earlier. Much of the shrewd and adventurous writing produced in Britain in that decade, whether in the journals *Screen* and *Screen Education*, at the Birmingham Centre for Contemporary Cultural Studies or elsewhere, now reads unsatisfyingly, at least around the edges, because of its hidden reliance on the utopian notion that an end to the market economy was around the corner (*somehow* – the politics and the economics tended to be left to others). Events unfolding in the latter half of the 80s in the USSR, China and Eastern Europe, combined with the post-oil-crisis prosperity of the USA, Japan and Western Europe, have shifted our perceptions of what is possible and indeed what is desirable in the economic sphere. The command-economy dream is dead: long live markets! Or, more sensibly, long live one's favoured version of a balance between markets and regulation.

The mark of mechanical Criticism now is that it has not noticed any of this. It continues to operate on the assumption that, just over the next hill, a post-market economic order awaits – or at least it *should*, and if it doesn't we can nevertheless carp about anything less, to an unlimited degree. This way lies, evidently, tedium and irrelevance. But giving the market its due means that we need to justify Critical Media Theory in somewhat different terms from those used heretofore.

There is indeed a great deal to celebrate about the flexible, self-regulating, information-pooling, libertarian, permanent-revolutionary aspects of market organisation, and this is no less true where the media are concerned than in other areas of the economy. But the market is itself perfectly capable of producing perverse effects or of perpetuating ancient wrongs. We are becoming more aware, precisely as the inevitability of global market logic is driven home, how much real difference particular institutions and histories make within that over-arching logic.

What we want the market to deliver, over and above the literal goods, must be a society in which the enlightenment ideals of Liberty, Equality and Fraternity are, so far as it is possible, promoted rather than frustrated. If the orienting function of post-market ideals has waned, the same cannot be said of these three: market thought and socialist thought equally have drawn their vitality from them, and the various liberation struggles of our time are all heirs to the 18th century's fundamental intellectual break with traditional defences of deference, hierarchy and domination. Our readers will duly find that the Criticism in the following essays of past, current and proposed media practices concentrates on their anti-Enlightenment tendencies.

In a global media economy, it becomes ever more important that *all* people, and peoples, should have rights of faithful and respectful representation. The essays in Part I examine battles over this. Access to the means of representation for the oppressed and the marginalised *can* be won within a market/market-plus-regulation framework, but such access isn't gained without struggle. Equally, the market mechanism can favour the profitable recycling of the stereotypes and cliches in the representation of groups of all sorts that make for Smooth Viewing, at the expense of those groups' dignity or even of their visibility. Agreeing on this as a general point leaves the key question still to answer, case by case: how, short of a quasi-command-economy and the centralised provision of corrective, 'progressive' images – where the progressiveness, as with Stalinist 'Socialist Realism', is fatally undermined by the bullying tone, and an even more oppressive stereotypy is soon instituted – can the cliches be challenged, subverted, by-passed?

Another problem which eternally threatens the market's own dynamic from within is that of too-great concentration of economic control. The monopoly tendencies within the global media field, especially given the capital investment necessary for market entry into technologies such as satellite or cable, threaten the very pluralism which is one of the market's proudest boasts. And, over and above the dominance of particular multinational enterprises, their general tendency to speak for the powerful nations that constitute their home base – notably the U S A, but foreseeably Europe – involves the perpetuation of the subordination of small, poorer nationals and peoples to the larger and the richer. The classic manner of dealing with anti-competitive aspects of capitalism remains regulation, and in one form or another this cannot but involve the state (which of course shows as few signs of withering away under capitalism as under communism). And here the opposite danger of a cosy, paternalist, protectionist, finally chauvinist regulatory regime emerges as equally real. Or, if the state so regulates as to insist that entry into the market be made maximally easy, do we risk losing Quality as the smaller, cheaper producers undercut organisations with the size and experience to provide broadcasting in the public service tradition? The essays in our second section, concentrating on question of organisation and control of the media, take up the dilemmas we face in this area.

How the media industries are owned and regulated clearly has implications for the democratisation-of-representation issues with which our first section is concerned. Equally, it bears on the theme of our third section, where it is the audience's investments in the pleasures on offer that come under scrutiny. Here the danger has always been, to put it bluntly, moralistic condescension on the part of the Critic: pleasure is suspect, only the Higher Pleasures are guiltless, the media provide Lower Pleasures and corrupt us accordingly. Against aggressive put-down moves of this sort, the 'anything goes' cheeriness of (one branch of) 'post-modernist' rhetoric has come as a breath of fresh air. Down with hierarchies dogmatically privileging one medium over another and with canons dogmatically privileging one work over another!

Keeping the Enlightenment ideals in mind helps greatly in sorting out what nevertheless is open to Critique on the pleasure side (or, in an older phrase, the 'uses and gratifications' side) of media reception. Whatever the ultimate status of psychoanalysis as a human science, the process of reflection initiated by Freud has reminded us of how the human subject can give himself or herself, and others, a bad time in the course of seeking for the good. Feminist work on the cinema and other media has brought home to us dramatically how an unequal treatment of gender relations lurks at the heart of great and not-so-great film and television texts alike. A pleasure thus seems open to Critique – with due tentativeness and sensitivity to what positively it affords its fans – to the extent that it involves the viewer/listener/reader in one or more of the following difficulties:

– *de-skilling*: abilities, know-hows, sensitivities are subtracted rather than added to the audience-members' repertoire (leaving them with less Liberty to act than they might have had);
– *self-denigration*: the audience-members' pleasure is made dependent on thinking systematically less well of themselves, and of those like themselves, than Equality and Fraternity considerations would suggest was desirable;
– *contempt for others*: pleasure derives from fictional resolution of audience worries via some sort of scapegoating or 'containment' of worry-inducing groups, thus imposing upon them an un-Equal and un-Fraternal status.

Some such checklist as this seems to be emerging as basic to any non-moralistic, non-backward-looking attempt to identify the aspects of current media practice that have a limiting rather than an enhancing effect on audience-members' abilities to act for themselves and alongside others.

So much for the overview. Perhaps it imposes too much order on the irregular landscape. Basically, we have assembled essays that we enjoyed and that taught us something. We wish the readers of this Reader no less good fortune.

Manuel Alvarado and John O. Thompson
October 1989

Please note that ellipsis points inside square brackets are used to indicate the omission of parts of an article.

PART

one

CULTURAL

IDENTITY

1

The Whites of their Eyes
Racist Ideologies and the Media

STUART HALL
From *Silver Linings: Some Strategies for the Eighties*, edited by George Bridges and Rosalind Brunt (London: Lawrence and Wishart, 1981)

This paper was presented in 1980 very much in response to the substantial Conservative electoral victory of 1979 which first brought Mrs Margaret Thatcher to power as the British Prime Minister. As indicated in his opening paragraph, Stuart Hall used this opportunity to develop both a more complex conceptual understanding of the 'common sense' basis of racism and at the same time a strategic analysis of how to build alternative media practices in order 'to bend the twig of racist common sense which currently dominates popular thinking'.

Due to reasons of space we have cut this second strand, for while being of historical interest it nevertheless focuses on a debate – about a programme made by the Campaign Against Racism in the Media (C A R M) in 1979 for the B B C's 'access television' slot *Open Door*, entitled *It Ain't Half Racist, Mum* – which has subsequently moved on.

The bulk of the article, however, continues to provide a valuable conceptual base for the introduction of a number of key issues which are unfortunately still pertinent. Firstly, Hall introduces for a wider, and largely white, audience the black notion that the concept of race is a 'white' rather than a 'black' problem. Secondly, he establishes the crucial and useful distinction between *overt* and *inferential* racism – a distinction which has since influenced much writing in this area. Thirdly, Hall offers a typology of different racial stereotypes which provide what he calls the 'base images of the "grammar of race"', that is the *slave figure*, the *native*, and the *clown* or *entertainer*.

Fundamentally what Hall carefully and persuasively argues is that racism in general – and the racism of the media in particular – has to be understood in terms of structures, practices and discourses and not as simply something which emanates from certain individual human beings: 'What defines how the media function is the result of a set of complex, often contradictory, social relations; not the personal inclinations of its members'.

M.A./J.O.T.

In this essay I want to address two, related, issues. The first concerns the way the media – sometimes deliberately, sometimes unconsciously – define and construct the question of race in such a way as to reproduce the ideologies of racism. The second is concerned with the very difficult problems of strategy and tactics which arise when the left attempts to intervene in the media construction of race, so as to undermine, deconstruct and question the unquestioned racist assumptions on which so much of media practice is grounded.

We need to think about both these questions together: the often complex and subtle ways in which the ideologies of racism are sustained in our culture; and the equally difficult question as to how to challenge them in the practice of ideological struggle. Both form the basis of a wider anti-racist strategy which – I argue here – neglects the ideological dimensions at our peril.

For very complex reasons, a sort of racist 'common sense' has become pervasive in our society. And the media frequently work from this common sense, taking it as their base-line without questioning it. We need, urgently, to consider ways in which, *in addition* to the urgent and necessary political task of blocking the path to power of the openly organised racist and right-extremist organisations, we can also begin to construct an anti-racist common sense. This task of making anti-racist ideas popular is and must be part of a wider democratic struggle which engages, not so much the hard-line extremists of the right, or even the small numbers of the committed and converted, but the great body of common sense, in the population as a whole, and amongst working people especially, on which the struggle to build up an anti-racist popular bloc will ultimately depend.

Questions of strategy and tactics are not easy, especially when what is at issue is the winning of popular positions in the struggle against racism. There are few short cuts or ready-made recipes. It does not follow that, because our hearts are in the right place, we will win the struggle for 'hearts and minds'. And even the best analysis of the current situation provides few absolute guidelines as to what we should do, in a particular situation. Neither passionate left-wing convictions nor the immutable laws of history can ever replace the difficult questions of political calculation on which the outcome of particular struggles ultimately turns. This essay is written in the firm conviction that we need to be better prepared, both in our analysis of how racist ideologies become 'popular', and in what are the appropriate strategies for combatting them. Both, in their turn, depend on a more open, less closed and 'finalist' debate of positions among people on the left committed to the anti-racist struggle. [. . .]

[. . .] We begin by defining some of the terms of the argument. 'Racism and the media' touches directly the problem of *ideology*, since the media's main sphere of operations is the production and transformation of ideologies. An intervention in the media's construction of race is an intervention in the *ideological* terrain of struggle. Much murky water has flowed under the bridge provided by this concept of ideology in recent years; and this is not the place to develop the theoretical argument. I am using the term to refer to those images, concepts and premises which provide the frameworks through which we represent, interpret, understand and 'make sense' of some aspect of social existence. Language and ideology are not the same – since the same linguistic term ('democracy' for example, or 'freedom') can be deployed within different ideological discourses. But language, broadly conceived, is by definition the principal medium in which we find different ideological discourses elaborated.

Three important things need to be said about ideology in order to make what follows intelligible. First, ideologies do not consist of isolated and separate concepts, but in the articulation of different elements into a distinctive set or chain of meanings. In liberal ideology, 'freedom' is connected (articulated) with individualism and the free market; in socialist ideology, 'freedom' is a collective condition, dependent on, not counterposed to, 'equality of condition', as it is in liberal ideology. The same concept is differently positioned within the logic of different ideological discourses. One of the ways in which ideological struggle takes place and ideologies are transformed is by articulating the elements differently, thereby producing a different meaning: breaking the chain in which they are currently fixed (e.g. 'democratic' = the 'Free' West) and establishing a new articulation (e.g. 'democratic' = deepening the democratic content of political life). This 'breaking of the chain' is not, of course, confined to the head: it takes place through social practice and political struggle.

Second, ideological statements are made by individuals: but ideologies are not the product of individual consciousness or intention. Rather we formulate our intentions *within ideology*. They pre-date individuals, and form part of the determinate social formations and conditions in which individuals are born. We have to 'speak through' the ideologies which are active in our society and which provide us with the means of 'making sense' of social relations and our place in them. The transformation of ideologies is thus a collective process and practice, not an individual one. Largely, the processes work *unconsciously*, rather than by conscious intention. Ideologies produce different forms of social consciousness, rather than being produced by them. They work most effectively when we are not aware that how we formulate and construct a statement about the world is underpinned by ideological premisses; when our formations seem to be simply descriptive statements about how things are (i.e. must be), or of what we can 'take-for-granted'. 'Little boys like playing rough games; little girls, however, are full of sugar and spice' is predicated on a whole set of ideological premisses, though it seems to be an aphorism which is grounded, not in how masculinity and femininity have been historically and culturally constructed in society, but in Nature itself. Ideologies tend to disappear from view into the taken-for-granted 'naturalised' world of common sense. Since (like gender) race appears to be 'given' by Nature, racism is one of the most profoundly 'naturalised' of existing ideologies.

Third, ideologies 'work' by constructing for their subjects (individual and collective) positions of identification and knowledge which allow them to 'utter' ideological truths as if they were their authentic authors. This is not because they emanate from our innermost, authentic and unified experience, but because we find ourselves mirrored in the positions at the centre of the discourses from which the statements we formulate 'make sense'. Thus the same 'subjects' (e.g. economic classes or ethnic groups) can be differently constructed in different ideologies.

When Mrs Thatcher says, 'We can't afford to pay ourselves higher wages without earning them through higher productivity', she is attempting to construct at the centre of her discourse an identification for workers who will cease to see themselves as opposed or *antagonistic to* the needs of capital, and begin to see themselves in terms of the *identity of interests* between themselves and capital. Again, this is not only in the head. Redundancies are a powerful material way of influencing 'hearts and minds'.

Ideologies therefore work by the transformation of discourses (the disarticulation and re-articulation of ideological elements) and the transformation (the fracturing and recomposition) of subjects-for-action. How we 'see' ourselves and our social relations *matters*, because it enters into and informs our actions and practices. Ideologies are therefore a site of a distinct type of social struggle. This site does not exist on its own, separate from other relations, since ideas are not free-floating in people's heads. The ideological construction of black people as a 'problem population' and the police practice of containment in the black communities mutually reinforce and support one another. Nevertheless, ideology is a practice. It has its own specific way of working. And it is generated, produced and reproduced in specific settings (sites) – especially, in the apparatuses of ideological production which 'produce' social meanings and distribute them throughout society, like the media. It is therefore the site of a particular kind of struggle, which cannot be simply reduced to or incorporated into some other level of struggle – for example, the economic class struggle, which is sometimes held to govern or determine it. It is the struggle over what Lenin once called 'ideological relations', which have their own tempo and specificity. It is located in specific practices. Ideological struggle, like any other form of struggle, therefore represents an intervention in an existing field of practices and institutions; those which sustain the dominant discourses of meaning of society.

The classic definition of ideology tends to regard it as a dependent sphere, which simply reflects 'in ideas' what is happening elsewhere, for example, in the mode of production, without any determinacy or effectivity of its own. This is a reductive and economistic conception. Of course, the formation and distribution of ideologies have determinate conditions, some of which are established outside of ideology itself. Messrs Murdoch and Trafalgar House command (through *The Times*, *Sunday Times* and the *Express* group) the resources of institutionalised ideological power in ways which no section of the left could currently aspire to. Nevertheless, ideologies are not fixed forever in the place assigned to them by 'the economic': their elements, as Laclau has argued,[1] have 'no necessary class belongingness'. For instance, 'democracy' belongs *both* to ruling-class ideology, where it means the Western system of parliamentary regimes, *and* to the ideologies of the left, where it means or refers to 'popular power', against the ruling power bloc. Of course, though the heads of small shopkeepers are not necessarily filled exclusively with 'petty-bourgeois thoughts', certain ideological discourses *do* have or have acquired, historically, well-defined connections with certain class places. (It is easier for a small shopkeeper, than for an assembly line-worker in British Leyland, to think of his or her interests as equivalent to those of an independent self-employed small capitalist). These 'traces', as Gramsci called them, and historical connections – the terrain of past articulations – are peculiarly resistant to change and transformation: just as it is exceedingly hard, given the history of imperialism, to disinter the idea of 'the British people' from its nationalistic connotation.

New forms of ideological struggle can bring old 'traces' to life, thus Thatcherism has revivified liberal political economy. Even in such well-secured cases, transformations *are* possible ('the people' coming to represent, not the 'nation, unified under the ruling class', but the *common* people *versus* the ruling class – an antagonistic relation rather than an equivalent and unifying one). The corollary of this is that there is no fixed, given and necessary form of ideological consciousness, dictated exclusively by class position. A third of the British working class has regularly seen itself, in terms of how it votes, as 'rightfully subordinate to those who are naturally born to rule over others'. The famous working-class deference Tory vote shows they do not necessarily see themselves as their class position would lead us to suppose: e.g. as the 'majority exploited class which ought to supplant the class which rules over us'.

At the last (1979) election, Mrs Thatcher clearly had some success in getting skilled and organised workers to *equate* (articulate together) their own opposition to incomes policies, wage control and the demand for a 'return to collective bargaining', with her own, very different, conception of 'letting market forces decide wage levels'. Just as the working class is not impervious to reactionary or social-democratic ideas, so it is not *a priori* impervious to racist ideas. The whole history of Labour socialism and reformism is a refutation of the idealistic hope (rooted in economism) that the economic position of the working class will make it inevitable that it thinks only progressive, anti-racist or revolutionary ideas. Instead, what we have seen over the past two decades is the undoubted penetration of racist ideas and practices, not only into sections of the working class, but into the very organisations and institutions of the labour movement itself.

Let us look, then, a little more closely at the apparatuses which generate and circulate ideologies. In modern societies, the different media are especially important sites for the production, reproduction and transformation of ideologies. Ideologies are, of course, worked on in many places in society, and not only in the head. The fact of unemployment, as the Thatcher government knows only too well, is, among other things, an extremely effective ideological instrument for converting or constraining workers to moderate their wage claims. But institutions like the media are peculiarly central to the matter since they are, by definition, part of the dominant means of *ideological* production. What they 'produce' is, precisely, representations of the social world, images, descriptions, explanations and frames for understanding how the world is and why it works as it is said and shown to work. And, amongst other kinds of ideological labour, the media construct for us a definition of what *race* is, what meaning the imagery of race carries, and what the 'problem of race' is understood to be. They help to classify out the world in terms of the categories of race.

The media are not only a powerful source of ideas about race. They are also one place where these ideas are articulated, worked on, transformed and elaborated. We have said 'ideas' and 'ideologies' in the plural. For it would be wrong and misleading to see the media as uniformly and conspiratorially harnessed to a single, racist conception of the world. Liberal and humane ideas about 'good relations' between the races, based on open-mindedness and tolerance, operate inside the world of the media – among, for example, many television journalists and newspapers like the *Guardian* – alongside the more explicit racism of other journalists and newspapers like the *Express* or the *Mail*. In some respects, the line which separates the latter from the extreme right on policies, such as, for example, guided repatriation for blacks, is very thin indeed.

It would be simple and convenient if all the media were simply the ventriloquists of a unified and racist 'ruling class' conception of the world. But neither a unifiedly conspiratorial media nor indeed a unified racist 'ruling class' exist in anything like that simple way. I don't insist on complexity for its own sake. But if critics of the media subscribe to too simple or reductive a view of their operations, this inevitably lacks credibility and weakens the case they are making because the theories and critiques don't square with reality. They only begin to account for the real operation of racism in society by a process of gross abstraction and simplification.

More important, the task of a critical theory is to produce as accurate a knowledge of complex social processes as the complexity of their functioning requires. It is not its task to console the left by producing simple but satisfying myths, distinguished only by their super-left-wing credentials. (If the laws and tendencies of the capitalist mode of production can be stated in a simplified form because they are essentially simple and reducible, why on earth did Marx go on about them for so long – three uncompleted volumes, no less?) Most important of all, these differences and complexities have real *effects*, which ought to enter into any serious political calculation about how their tendencies might be resisted or turned. We know, for example, that the broadcasting institutions are not 'independent and autonomous' of the state in the way suggested in the official wisdom. But if we neglect to ask why the question of 'independence' and the media's 'relative autonomy' are so important to their functioning, and simply reduce them to what we think of as their essential nature – pure instruments of ruling-class or racist ideology – we will not be able to deconstruct the credibility and legitimacy which they, in fact, carry (which depends, precisely, on the fact that 'autonomy' is not a pure piece of deception). Moreover, we will have an over-incorporated conception of the world, where the state is conceived, not as a necessarily contradictory formation, but as a simple, transparent instrumentality. This view might flatter the super-radical conscience, but it has no place in it for the concept of class struggle, and defines no practical terrain on which such struggle could be conducted. (Why it has passed so long for 'Marxism' is a mystery.) So we must attend to the complexities of the ways in which race and racism are constructed in the media in order to be able to bring about change.

Another important distinction is between what we might call 'overt' racism and 'inferential' racism. By *overt* racism, I mean those many occasions when open and favourable coverage is given to arguments, positions and spokespersons who are in the business of elaborating an openly racist argument or advancing a racist policy or view. Many such occasions exist; they have become more frequent in recent years – more often in the press, which has become openly partisan to extremist right-wing arguments, than in television, where the regulations of 'balance', 'impartiality and neutrality' operate.

By *inferential* racism I mean those apparently naturalised representations of events and situations relating to race, whether 'factual' or 'fictional', which have racist premises and propositions inscribed in them as a set of *unquestioned assumptions*. These enable racist statements to be formulated without ever bringing into awareness the racist predicates on which the statements are grounded.

Both types of racism are to be found, in different combinations, in the British media. Open or overt racism is, of course, politically dangerous as well as socially offensive. The open partisanship of sections of the popular press on this front is an extremely serious development. It is not only that they circulate and popularise openly racist policies and ideas, and translate them into the vivid populist vernacular (e.g. in the tabloids, with their large working-class readership) it is the very fact that such things can now be openly said and advocated which *legitimates* their public expression and increases the threshold of the public acceptability of racism. Racism becomes 'acceptable' – and thus, not too long after, 'true' – just common sense: what everyone knows and is openly saying. But *inferential racism* is more widespread – and in many ways, more insidious, because it is largely *invisible* even to those who formulate the world in its terms.

An example of *this* type of racist ideology is the sort of television programme which deals with some 'problem' in race relations. It is probably made by a good and honest liberal broadcaster, who hopes to do some good in the world for 'race relations' and who maintains a scrupulous balance and neutrality when questioning people interviewed for the programme. The programme will end with a homily on how, if only the 'extremists' on *either side* would go away, 'normal blacks and whites' would be better able to get on with learning to live in harmony together. Yet every word and image of such programmes are impregnated with unconscious racism because they are all predicated on the unstated and unrecognized assumption that the *blacks* are the *source of the problem*. Yet virtually the whole of 'social problem' television about race and immigration – often made, no doubt, by well-intentioned and liberal-minded broadcasters – is precisely predicated on racist premises of this kind. This was the criticism we made in the CARM programme, *It Ain't Half Racist, Mum* and it was the one which most cut the broadcasters to their professional quick. It undermined their professional credentials by suggesting that they had been partisan where they are supposed to be balanced and impartial. It was an affront to the liberal consensus and self-image which prevails within broadcasting. Both responses were, in fact, founded on the profound misunderstanding that racism is, by definition, mutually exclusive of the liberal consensus – whereas, in inferential racism, the two can quite easily cohabit – and on the assumption that if the television discourse could be shown to be racist, it must be 'because the individual broadcasters were intentionally and deliberately racist. In fact, an ideological discourse does *not* depend on the conscious intentions of those who formulate statements within it.

How, then, is race and its 'problems' constructed on British television? This is a complex topic in its own right, and I can only illustrate its dimensions briefly here by referring to some of the themes developed in the two programmes I was involved in. One of the things we tried to show in *The Whites Of Their Eyes* was the rich vocabulary and syntax of race on which the media have to draw. Racism has a long and distinguished history in British culture. It is grounded in the relations of slavery, colonial conquest, economic exploitation and imperialism in which the European races have stood in relation to the 'native peoples' of the colonised and exploited periphery.

Three characteristics provided the discursive and power-coordinates of the discourses in which these relations were historically constructed. (1) Their imagery and themes were polarised around fixed relations of subordination and domination. (2) Their stereotypes were grouped around the poles of 'superior' and 'inferior' natural species. (3) Both were displaced from the 'language' of history into the language of Nature. Natural physical signs and racial characteristics became the unalterable signifiers of inferiority. Subordinate ethnic groups and classes appeared, not as the objects of particular historical relations (the slave trade, European colonisation, the active underdevelopment of the 'underdeveloped' societies), but as the given qualities of an inferior *breed*. Relations, secured by economic, social, political and military domination were transformed and 'naturalised' into an order of *rank*, ascribed by Nature. Thus, Edward Long, an acute English observer of Jamaica in the period of slavery wrote (in his *History of Jamaica*, 1774) – much in the way the Elizabethans might have spoken of 'the Great Chain Of Being' – of 'Three ranks of men [sic], (white, mulatto and black), dependent on each other, and rising in a proper climax of subordination, in which the whites hold the highest place'.

One thing we wanted to illustrate in the programme was the 'forgotten' degree to which, in the period of slavery and imperialism popular literature is saturated with these fixed, negative attributes of the colonised races. We find them in the diaries, observations and accounts, the notebooks, ethnographic records and commentaries, of visitors, explorers, missionaries and administrators in Africa, India, the Far East and the Americas. And also something else: the 'absent' but imperialising 'white eye'; the unmarked position from which all these 'observations' are made and from which, alone, they make sense. This is the history of slavery and conquest, written, seen, drawn and photographed by The Winners. They cannot be *read* and made sense of from any other position. The 'white eye' is always outside the frame – but seeing and positioning everything within it.

Some of the most telling sequences we used was from early film of the British Raj in India – the source of endless radio 'reminiscences' and television historical show-pieces today. The assumption of effortless superiority structures every image – even the portioning in the frame: the foregrounding of colonial life (tea-time on the plantation), the background of native bearers. . . . In the later stages of High Imperialism, this discourse proliferates through the new media of popular culture and information – newspapers and journals, cartoons, drawings and advertisements and the popular novel. Recent critics of the literature of imperialism have argued that, if we simply extend our definition of nineteenth-century fiction from one branch of 'serious fiction' to embrace popular literature, we will find a second, powerful strand of the English literary imagination to set beside the *domestic* novel: the male-dominated world of imperial adventure, which takes *empire*, rather than *Middlemarch*, as its microcosm. I remember a graduate student, working on the construction of race in popular literature and culture at the end of the Nineteenth Century, coming to me in despair – racism was so *ubiquitous*, and at the same time, so *unconscious* – simply assumed to be the case – that it was impossible to get any critical purchase on it. In this period, the very idea of *adventure* became synonymous with the demonstration of the moral, social and physical mastery of the colonisers over the colonised.

Later, this concept of 'adventure' – one of the principal categories of modern *entertainment* – moved straight off the printed page into the literature of crime and espionage, children's books, the great Hollywood extravaganzas and comics. There, with recurring persistence, they still remain. Many of these older versions have had their edge somewhat blunted by time. They have been distanced from us, apparently, by our superior wisdom and liberalism. But they still reappear on the television screen, especially in the form of 'old movies' (some 'old movies', of course, continue to be made). But we can grasp their recurring resonance better if we identify some of the base-images of the 'grammar of race'.

There is, for example, the familiar *slave-figure*: dependable, loving in a simple, childlike way – the devoted 'Mammy' with the rolling eyes, or the faithful field-hand or retainer, attached and devoted to 'his' Master. The best-known extravaganza of all – *Gone With The Wind* – contains rich variants of both. The 'slave-figure' is by no means limited to films and programmes *about* slavery. Some 'Injuns' and many Asians have come on to the screen in this disguise. A deep and unconscious ambivalence pervades this stereotype. Devoted and childlike, the 'slave' is also unreliable, unpredictable and undependable – capable of 'turning nasty', or of plotting in a treacherous way, secretive, cunning, cut-throat once his or her Master's or Mistress's back is turned: and inexplicably given to running way into the bush at the slightest opportunity. The whites can never be sure that this childish simpleton – 'Sambo' – is not mocking his master's white manners behind his hand, even when giving an exaggerated caricature of white refinement.

Another base-image is that of the 'native'. The good side of this figure is portrayed in a certain primitive nobility and simple dignity. The bad side is portrayed in terms of cheating and cunning, and, further out, savagery and barbarism. Popular culture is still full today of countless savage and restless 'natives', and sound-tracks constantly repeat the threatening sound of drumming in the night, the hint of primitive rites and cults. Cannibals, whirling dervishes, Indian tribesmen, garishly got up, are constantly threatening to over-run the screen. They are likely to appear at any moment out of the darkness to decapitate the beautiful heroine, kidnap the children, burn the encampment or threatening to boil, cook and eat the innocent explorer or colonial administrator and his lady-wife.

These 'natives' always move as an anonymous collective mass – in tribes or hordes. And against them is always counterposed the isolated white figure, alone 'out there', confronting his Destiny or shouldering his Burden in the 'heart of darkness', displaying coolness under fire and an unshakeable authority – exerting mastery over the rebellious natives or quelling the threatened uprising with a single glance of his steel-blue eyes.

A third variant is that of the 'clown' or 'entertainer'. This captures the 'innate' humour, as well as the physical grace of the licensed entertainer – putting on a show for The Others. It is never quite clear whether we are laughing with or at this figure: admiring the physical and rhythmic grace, the open expressivity and emotionality of the 'entertainer', or put off by the 'clown's' stupidity.

One noticeable fact about all these images is their deep *ambivalence* – the double vision of the white eye through which they are seen. The primitive nobility of the ageing tribesman or chief, and the native's rhythmic grace, always contain both a nostalgia for an innocence lost forever to the civilised, and the threat of civilisation being over-run or undermined by the recurrence of savagery, which is always lurking just below the surface; or by an untutored sexuality, threatening to 'break out'. Both are aspects – the good and the bad sides – of *primitivism*. In these images, 'primitivism' is defined by the fixed proximity of such people to Nature.

Is all this so far away as we sometimes suppose from the representation of race which fill the screens today? These *particular* versions may have faded. But their *traces* are still to be observed, reworked in many of the modern and up-dated images. And though they may appear to carry a different meaning, they are often still constructed on a very ancient grammar. Today's restless native hordes are still alive and well and living, as guerilla armies and freedom fighters in the Angola, Zimbabwe or Namibian 'bush'. Blacks are still the most frightening, cunning and glamorous crooks (and policemen) in New York cop series. They are the fleet-footed, crazy-talking under-men who connect Starsky and Hutch to the drug-saturated ghetto. The scheming villains and their giant-sized bully boys in the world of James Bond and his progeny are still, unusually, recruited from 'out there' in Jamaica, where savagery lingers on. The sexually-available 'slave girl' is alive and kicking, smouldering away on some exotic TV set or on the covers of paperbacks, though she is now the centre of a special admiration, covered in a sequinned gown and supported by a white chorus line. Primitivism, savagery, guile and unreliability – all 'just below the surface' – can still be identified in the faces of black political leaders around the world, cunningly plotting the overthrow of 'civilisation': Mr Mugabe, for example, up to the point where he happened to win both a war and an election and became, temporarily at any rate, the best (because the most politically credible) friend Britain had left in that last outpost of the Edwardian dream.

The 'Old Country' – white version – is still often the subject of nostalgic documentaries: 'Old Rhodesia', whose reliable servants, as was only to be expected, plotted treason in the outhouse and silently stole away to join ZAPU in the bush . . . Tribal Man in green khaki. Black stand-up comics still ape their ambiguous incorporation into British entertainment by being the first to tell a racist joke. No Royal Tour is complete without its troupe of swaying bodies, or its mounted tribesmen, paying homage. Blacks are such 'good movers', so *rhythmic*, so *natural*. And the dependent peoples, who couldn't manage for a day without the protection and know-how of their white masters, reappear as the starving victims of the Third World, passive and waiting for the technology or the Aid to arrive, objects of our pity or of a *Blue Peter* appeal. They are not represented as the subjects of a continuing exploitation or dependency, or the global division of wealth and labour. They are the Victims of Fate.

These modern, glossed and up-dated images seem to have put the old world of Sambo behind them. Many of them, indeed, are the focus of a secret, illicit, pleasurable-but-taboo admiration. Many have a more active and energetic quality – some black athletes, for example, and of course the entertainers. But the conno-tations and echoes which they carry reverberate back a very long way. They continue to shape the ways whites see blacks today – even when the white adven-turer sailing up the jungle stream is not *Sanders Of The River*, but historical drama-reconstructions of Stanley and Livingstone; and the intention is to show, not the savagery, but the serenity of African village life – ways of an ancient people 'unchanged even down to modern times' (in other words, still preserved in econ-omic backwardness and frozen in history for our anthropological eye by forces unknown to them and, apparently, unshowable on the screen).

'Adventure' is one way in which we *encounter* race without having to *confront* the racism of the perspectives in use. Another, even more complex one is 'entertain-ment'. In television, there is a strong counterposition between 'serious', informatio-nal television, which we watch because it is good for us, and 'entertainment', which we watch because it is pleasurable. And the purest form of pleasure in entertain-ment television is *comedy*. By definition, comedy is a licensed zone, disconnected from the serious. It's all 'good, clean fun'. In the area of fun and pleasure it is forbidden to pose a serious question, partly because it seems so puritanical and destroys the pleasure by switching registers. Yet race is one of the most significant themes in situation comedies – from the early Alf Garnett to *Mind Your Language*, *On The Buses*, *Love Thy Neighbour* and *It Ain't Half Hot, Mum*. These are defended on good 'anti-racist' grounds: the appearance of blacks, alongside whites, in situation comedies, it is argued, will help to naturalise and normalise their presence in British society. And no doubt, in some examples, it does function in this way. But, if you examine these fun occasions more closely, you will often find, as we did in our two programmes, that the comedies do not simply include blacks: they are *about race*. That is, the same old categories of racially-defined characteristics and qualities, and the same relations of superior and inferior, provide the pivots on which the jokes actually turn, the tension-points which move and motivate the situations in situation comedies. The comic register in which they are set, however, protects and defends viewers from acknowledging their incipient racism. It creates disavowal.

This is even more so with the television stand-up comics, whose repertoire in recent years has come to be dominated, in about equal parts, by sexist and racist jokes. It's sometimes said, again in their defence, that this must be a sign of black acceptability. But it *may* just be that racism has become more normal: it's hard to tell. It's also said that the best teller of anti-Jewish jokes are Jews themselves, just as blacks tell the best 'white' jokes against themselves. But this is to argue as if jokes exist in a vacuum separate from the contexts and situations of their telling. Jewish jokes told by Jews among themselves are part of the self-awareness of the community. They are unlikely to function by 'putting down' the race, because both teller and audience belong on equal terms to the same group. Telling racist jokes across the racial line, in conditions where relations of racial inferiority and superiority prevail, reinforces *the difference* and reproduces the unequal relations because, in those situations, the point of the joke depends on the existence of racism. Thus they reproduce the categories and relations of racism, even while normalizing them through laughter. The stated good intentions of the joke-makers do not resolve the problem here, because they are not in control of the circumstances – conditions of continuing racism – in which their joke discourse will be read and heard. The time *may* come when blacks and whites can tell jokes about each other in ways which do not reproduce the racial categories of the world in which they are told. The time, in Britain, is certainly *not yet arrived*.

Two other arenas [. . .] relate to the 'harder' end of television production – news and current affairs. This is where race is constructed as *problem* and the site of *conflict* and debate. There have been good examples of programmes where blacks have not exclusively appeared as the source of the 'problem' (ATV's *Breaking Point* is one example) and where they have not been exclusively saddled with being the aggressive agent in conflict (the London Weekend Television *London Programme* and the Southall Defence Committee's *Open Door* programme on the Southall events are examples). But the general tendency of the run of programmes in this area is to see blacks – especially the mere fact of their existence (their 'numbers') – as constituting a problem for English white society. They appear as law-breakers, prone to crime; as 'trouble'; as the collective agent of civil disorder.

In the numerous incidents where black communities have reacted to racist provocation (as at Southall) or to police harrassment and provocation (as in Bristol), the media have tended to assume that 'right' lay on the side of the law, and have fallen into the language of 'riot' and 'race warfare' which simply feeds existing stereotypes and prejudices. The precipitating conditions of conflict are usually *absent* – the scandalous provocation of a National Front march through one of the biggest black areas, Southall, and the saturation police raiding of the last refuge for black youth which triggered off Bristol – to take only two recent examples. They are either missing, or introduced so late in the process of signification, that they fail to dislodge the dominant definition of these events. So they testify, once again, to the disruptive nature of black and Asian people *as such*.

The analysis of the media coverage of Southall contained in the NCCL Unofficial Committee of Inquiry *Report*,[2] for example, shows how rapidly, in both the television and press, the official definitions of the police – Sir David McNee's statement on the evening of 23 April, and the ubiquitous James Jardine, speaking for the Police Federation on the succeeding day – provided the media with the authoritative definition of the event. These, in turn, shaped and focused what the media reported and how it explained what transpired. In taking their cue from these authoritative sources, the media reproduced an account of the event which, with certain significant exceptions, translated the conflict between racism and anti-racism into (a) a contest between Asians and the police, and (b) a contest between two kinds of extremism – the so-called '*fascism*' of left and right alike.

This had the effect of downgrading the two problems at the centre of the Southall affair – the growth of and growing legitimacy of the extreme right and its blatantly provocative anti-black politics of the street; and the racism and brutality of the police. Both issues had to be *forced* on to the agenda of the media by a militant and organized protest. Most press reports of Southall were so obsessed by embroidering the lurid details of 'roaming hoardes of coloured youths' chasing young whites 'with a carving knife' – a touch straight out of *Sanders Of The River*, though so far uncorroborated – that they failed even to mention the death of Blair Peach. This is selective or tunnel-vision with a vengeance.

A good example of how the real causes of racial conflict can be absorbed and transformed by the framework which the media employ can be found in the *Nationwide* coverage of Southall on the day following the events. Two interlocking frameworks of explanation governed this programme. In the first, conflict is seen in the conspiratorial terms of far-left against extreme-right – the Anti-Nazi League against the National Front. This is the classic logic of television, where the medium identifies itself with the moderate, consensual, middle-road, Average viewer, and sets off, in contrast, extremism on both sides, which it then equates with each other. In this particular exercise in 'balance', fascism and anti-fascism are represented as *the same* – both equally *bad*, because the Middle Way enshrines the Common Good under all circumstances. This balancing exercise provided an opportunity for Martin Webster of the National Front to gain access to the screen, to help set the terms of the debate, and to spread his smears across the screen under the freedom of the airwaves: 'Well,' he said, 'let's talk about Trotskyists, extreme Communists of various sorts, raving Marxists and other assorted left-wing cranks.' Good knockabout stuff. Then, after a linking passage – 'Southall, the day after' – to the second framework: rioting Asians *vs* the police. 'I watched television as well last night,' Mr Jardine argued, 'and I certainly didn't see any police throwing bricks . . . So don't start making those arguments.' The growth of organised political racism and the circumstances which have precipitated it were simply not visible to *Nationwide* as an alternative way of setting up the problem.

In the CARM programme *It Ain't Half Racist, Mum*, we tried to illustrate the inferential logic at work in another area of programming: the BBC's 'Great Debate' on Immigration. It was not necessary here to start with any preconceived notions, least of all speculation as to the personal views on race by the broadcasters involved – though one can't expect either the BBC hierarchy or Robin Day to believe that. You have simply to look at the programme with one set of questions in mind: Here is a problem, defined as 'the problem of immigration'. What is it? How is it defined and constructed through the programme? What logic governs its definition? And where does that logic derive from? I believe the answers are clear. The problem of immigration is that 'there are too many blacks over here', to put it crudely. It is *defined* in terms of *numbers of blacks* and what to do about them. The *logic* of the argument is 'immigrants = blacks = too many of them = send them home'. That is a rcist logic. And it comes from a chain of reasoning whose representative, in respectable public debate and in person, on this occasion, was Enoch Powell. Powellism set the agenda for the media. Every time (and on many more occasions than the five or six we show in the programme) the presenter wanted to define the base-line of the programme which others should address, Mr Powell's views were indicated as representing it. And every time anyone strayed from the 'logic' to question the underlying premiss, it was back to 'as Mr Powell would say . . .' that they were drawn.

It certainly does not follow (and I know of no evidence to suggest) that Robin Day subscribes to this line or agrees with Mr Powell on anything to do with race. I know absolutely nothing about his views on race and immigration. And we made no judgment on his views, which are irrelevant to the argument. If the media function in a systematically racist manner, it is not because they are run and organised exclusively by active racists; this is a category mistake. This would be equivalent to saying that you could change the character of the capitalist state by replacing its personnel. Whereas the media, like the state, have a *structure*, a set of *practices* which are *not* reducible to the individuals who staff them. What defines how the media function is the result of a set of complex, often contradictory, social relations; not the personal inclinations of its members. What is significant is not that they produce a racist ideology, from some single-minded and unified conception of the world, but that they are so powerfully constrained – 'spoken by' – a particular set of ideological discourses. The power of this discourse is its capacity to constrain a very great variety of individuals: racist, anti-racist, liberals, radicals, conservatives, anarchists, know-nothings and silent majoritarians.

What we said, however, about the *discourse* of problem television was true, despite the hurt feelings of particular individuals: and demonstrably so. The premiss on which the Great Immigration Debate was built and the chain of reasoning it predicated was a racist one. The evidence for this is in what was said and how it was formulated – how the argument unfolded. If you establish the topic as 'the numbers of blacks are too high' or '*they* are breeding too fast', the opposition is obliged or constrained to argue that 'the numbers are not as high as they are represented to be'. This view is opposed to the first two: but it is also imprisoned by the same logic – the logic of the 'numbers game'. Liberals, anti-racists, indeed raging revolutionaries can contribute 'freely' to this debate, and indeed are often obliged to do so, so as not to let the case go by default: without breaking for a moment the chain of assumptions which holds the racist proposition in place. However, changing the terms of the argument, questioning the assumptions and starting points, breaking the logic – this is a quite different, longer, more difficult task.

[. . .]

Is it true that ideologies work exclusively by their forms? This position depends on an anti-realist aesthetic – a fashionable position in debates about ideology in the early 1970s. In its absolute form, it needed to be, and has been, quite effectively challenged and qualified. It represented at the time a certain justified 'formalist' reaction to the over-preoccupation with 'content' and 'realism' on the traditional left. But it was and is open to very serious criticism. For one thing it was founded on a rather loony and quite a-historical view of the narrative and presentational forms in television. They were said *all* to belong to the same type of 'realism' — *the* realism of *the* realist text, was the phrase – which, apparently, was introduced in the fourteenth century and had persisted, more or less, right up to *Man Alive*. This highly specious account was sealed – quite incorrectly – with the signature of Brecht. In this absolutism form, the thesis has proved quite impossible to defend, and many of those who first proposed it have since either backed away from its excesses or fallen into an eloquent silence.

The view that lumps together the latest, banal, T V documentary and the T V drama documentary on the General Strike of 1926, *Days Of Hope*, is so historically naïve and simplistic, and so crude politically, as to give it the status of a blunderbuss in a war conducted by missile computer. This is not to deny the importance of form in the discussion of ideology. Nor is it to deny that programmes which simply reproduce the existing dominant forms of television do not sufficiently break the frames through which audiences locate and position themselves in relation to the knowledge which such programmes claim to provide. But the argument that *only* 'deconstructivist' texts are truly revolutionary is as one-sided a view as that which suggests that forms have no effect. Besides, it is to adopt a very formalistic conception of form, which, in fact, accepts the false dichotomy between 'form' and 'content'; only, where the left has traditionally been concerned exclusively with the latter, this view was concerned only with the former. There were other calculations to be made. For example, that using the existing format of the typical programme which viewers are accustomed to identify with one kind of truth, one could undermine, precisely, the credibility of the media by showing that even this form could be used to state a different kind of truth.

A second consideration is this: if all the dominant television forms are 'realist' and realist narratives are bad, does it follow that all avant-garde or 'deconstructivist' narratives are good? This is also a rather loony position to take. The history of culture is littered with non-revolutionary 'avant-gardes': with 'avant-gardes' which are revolutionary in form only; even more, with 'avant-gardes' which are rapidly absorbed and incorporated into the dominant discourse, becoming the standard orthodoxies of the next generation. So, 'breaking and interrupting' the forms is no guarantee, in itself, that the dominant ideology cannot continue to be reproduced. This is the false trail along which some of the French theorists, like Julia Kristeva and the *Tel Quel* group, tried to drive us, by a species of polite intellectual terrorism, in the 1970s. In hindsight, the left was quite right to resist being hustled and blackmailed by these arguments.

This is no abstract debate, restricted to intellectuals of the left bank exclusively. It relates to political choices – harsh ones, to which there are no simple solutions, but which confront us every day. In any left bookshop today, one will find the imaginatively-designed, style-conscious, frame-breaking, interrogative avant-garde 'little journals' of the left: interrupting the 'dominant ideologies' in their form at every turn – and remorselessly restricted to a small, middle-class, progressive audience. One will also find the traditionally-designed, ancient looking, crude aesthetics of the 'labour movement' journals (*Tribune*, the *Morning Star*, *Socialist Challenge*, for example) – remorselessly restricted to an equally small and committed audience. Neither appears to have resolved the extremely difficult problem of a truly revolutionary form *and* content: or the problem of political effectiveness – by which I mean the breakthrough to a mass audience. This is not simply a problem of the politics of popular communication on the left: a burning issue which no simple appeal to stylistic aggressiveness has yet been able to solve. If only the social division of labour could be overcome by a few new typographical or stylistic devices!

Actually, however, it would be wrong to end this piece with a simple defence of what was done, which simply mirrors by reversal the criticisms levelled. We knew we had an exceedingly rare opportunity – not something the left can afford to squander. We knew the programme could have been better, more effective – including using more effectively ideas we did or had to jettison. These are genuinely matters of debate and properly the subject of criticism. I want, instead, to draw a different lesson from this episode. It is the degree to which the left is unable to confront and argue through constructively the genuine problems of tactics and strategy of a popular anti-racist struggle. To be honest, what we know collectively about this would not fill the back of a postage stamp. Yet, we continue to conduct tactical debates and political calculation as if the answers were already fully inscribed in some new version of Lenin's *What Is To Be Done?* Our mode of political calculation is that of the taking of absolutist positions, the attribution of bad faith to those genuinely convinced otherwise – and thereby, the steady advance of the death-watch beetle of sectarian self-righteousness and fragmentation.

It somehow enhances our left-wing credentials to argue and debate as if there is some *theory* of political struggle, enshrined in the tablets of stone somewhere, which can be instantly translated into the one true 'correct' strategy. The fact that we continue to lose the key strategic engagements and, in the present period, have lost very decisive terrain indeed, does not dent, even for a moment, our total certainty that we are on the 'correct line'. My own view is that we hardly begin to know how to conduct a popular anti-racist struggle or how to bend the twig of racist common sense which currently dominates popular thinking. It is a lesson we had better learn pretty rapidly. The early interventions of the Anti-Nazi League in this area, at a very strategic, touch-and-go moment in the anti-racist struggle was one of the most effective and imaginative political interventions made in this period by groups other than the already-engaged groups of black activists. It is an experience we can and must build on – not by imitating and repeating it, but by matching it in imaginativeness. But even that leaves no room for complacency – as we watch the racist slogans raised on the soccer stands and listen to racist slogans inflect and infect the chanting of young working-class people on the terraces. Face to face with this struggle for popular advantage, to fight on only one front, with only one weapon, to deploy only one strategy and to put all one's eggs into a single tactic is to set about winning the odd dramatic skirmish at the risk of losing the war.

Notes

1 Ernesto Laclau, *Politics and Ideology in Marxist Theory* (London: New Left Books, 1977).
2 *Southall: Report of the Unofficial Committee of Inquiry* (London: National Council for Civil Liberties, 1980).

▌▌
Diaspora Culture and the Dialogic Imagination
The Aesthetics of Black Independent Film in Britain

KOBENA MERCER

From *Blackframes: Critical Perspectives on Black Independent Cinema*, edited by Mbye B. Cham and Claire Andrade-Watkins (Cambridge, Mass.: MIT Press, 1988)

▌n 1981 Marcia Lloyd founded the 'Celebration of Black Film' which is held in Boston, Massachusetts. The principle of the Festival is encapsulated in her founding statement – 'For the independent film-maker, the hurdles of production are followed by the uncertainties of distribution and exhibition. For the black film-maker, patterns of under-representation or exclusion continue to prevail. The fact that there is a dynamic community of black, independent film-makers despite these obstacles presents good reasons to celebrate.'

The fifth festival held in 1988 saw the presentation of a number of papers by critics and scholars of African descent examining the 'particularities as well as the commonalities of the history, the context and the aesthetics of black independent film practice in "Anglophone" Africa, the United States and Britain'. In this paper, Kobena Mercer identified two main tendencies – the 'monologic' and the 'dialogic' – in his analytic account of the recent work of black British film-makers.

The monologic tendency in black British film-making refers to those productions which, adopting the styles and conventions of mainstream cinema, attempt to offer only a different content. The critical view of such films is that they provide a 'dependent expressivity', a 'cultural mimicry and neo-colonial surrender'. The dialogic tendency refers to films which not only contest racist stereotypes through changing the story, but also interrogate the dominant language and codes of mainstream cinema. This dual concern with the politics of racism and representation generates a critical dialogue with both the practices of film-making and the containing culture.

This distinction, at one level, would seem to be merely echoing theoretical debates which took place in the 1970s over the film-making practices of Costa Gavras (*Z*, *State of Siege*) and Gillo Pontecorvo (*Battle of Algiers*, *Queimada*) on the one hand and Jean-Luc Godard and Nagisa Oshima on the other. However, the project of, and commitment to, a 'critical dialogism' which attempts to de-territorialise and de-colonise the historical and cultural situation of, in particular, third generation black British people is one which shares features more closely allied to the struggle over and for a 'Third Cinema'.

As Mercer writes: '. . . the issue is not the expression of some lost origin or some uncontaminated essence in black film language, but the adoption of a critical "voice" that promotes consciousness of the collision of cultures and histories that constitutes our very conditions of existence.'*

M.A./J.O.T.

> Our imaginations processed reality and dream, like maniacal editors turned loose in some frantic film cutting room . . . we were dream serious in our efforts.
>
> Ralph Ellison[1]

The question of aesthetics arises today as a crucial issue for black film-making practices in Britain for two important reasons. First, significant changes in the material conditions of black politics since the early 80s have enabled a creative and prolific upsurge in black film-making activity in recent years. The emergence of a new generation of cinematic activists – Ceddo, Sankofa, Retake, Black Audio Film Collective – symbolises a new threshold of cultural struggle in the domain of black cinema and image-making. Their work deepens and extends the narrative and documentary frameworks for black film-making established by Horace Ové, Lionel Ngakane, Menelik Shabazz and others in the 1960s and 70s. And the emergence of a new 'experimental' approach has also widened the parameters of black film prac- tice, bringing a new quality of diversity to black film-making.

Until now, black film in Britain has emphasised the radical content of its political message over the politics of representation inherent in the medium. Certain aesthetic qualities generated by self-consciously cinematic strategies at work in new forms of black film-making today indicate significant shifts and critical differences in attitude to the means of representation. In this context it becomes necessary to think through the political implications of choices and decisions made at the level of film-form. If such shifts and changes within black film-making may be momentarily grasped as an accentuation of the expressive over the referential, or as an emphasis on the complexity rather than the homogeneity of the black experience in Britain, what is at issue is not a categorical 'break' with the past but the embryonic articulation of something 'new' that does not fit a pre-given category.

Second, insofar as aesthetics concerns the conceptual criteria for evaluating

---

* For an interesting and recent examination of the debate surrounding the proposal for a 'Third Cinema', see Paul Willemen's article 'The Third Cinema Question: Notes and Reflections' originally published in *Framework* no. 34 (1987) and reprinted in Jim Pines and Paul Willemen (eds.) *Questions of Third Cinema* (BFI, 1989), which responds to a proposition first argued by Octavio Getino and Fernando Solanas, after having made the film *La Hora de los Hornos*, in their highly influential polemic 'Towards a Third Cinema', published in *Tricontinental* no. 13 (October 1969) and re-printed in translation in *Afterimage* no. 3 (Summer 1971) and in Michael Chanan (ed.) *Twenty-five Years of the New Latin American Cinema* (BFI/Channel 4, 1983).

artistic and cultural practices, it now becomes necessary to reflect more rigorously on the role of critics and criticism. This need arises with urgency not simply because the increase in quantity at the point of production necessitates clarification of qualitative distinctions at the point of reception, but more importantly because of the bewildering range of conflicting responses provoked by new work such as *Handsworth Songs* (Black Audio Film Collective, 1986) and *The Passion of Remembrance* (Sankofa, 1986).

I would like to be able to use a word like 'modernist' to describe the 'shock of the new' here, as responses among audiences, critics and institutions have ranged from hostile impatience to the awarding of prestigious prizes. It is precisely this dissensus that indicates something important is going on! It would be useful to note some of the terms of dissensus to grasp what is at issue. White audiences and critics have commented on the 'influence' of Euro-American avant-garde cinema and film theory, which is not in itself a criticism, but nevertheless suggests an underlying anxiety to pin down and categorise a practice that upsets and disrupts fixed expectations and normative assumptions about what 'black' films should look like.[2] Black audiences and critics have been similarly bemused by the originality of a practice that explicitly draws on a dual inheritance from both Third World and First World cultures, but it is interesting to note that the most vociferous critiques here concern a dispute over the political content of the films.

In particular, I want to highlight the brief debate initiated by Salman Rushdie's singularly unconstructive critique of *Handsworth Songs*, as it implicitly reveals a crisis of criticism for black cultural politics.[3] Rushdie's disdainful and dismissive response – 'There's more to life in Handsworth than race riots [sic] and police brutality' – betrays a closed mind which assumes, as Stuart Hall pointed out in reply, that '*his* [Rushdie's] songs are not only different but better'. What makes Rushdie's position all the more worrying is not that the conservative literary-humanist criteria he adopts are so at odds with the open-ended textual strategies performed in his own work, but that he uses his literary 'authority' to delegitimate the film's discourse and disqualify its right to speak.

As with the unfavorable review in *Race Today*[4], Rushdie enacts an appallingly authoritarian practice of 'interpretation' which assumes *a priori* that one version of reality, his political analysis of Handsworth, has more validity, legitimacy and authority than another, the version articulated by the film. What is at stake here is the fact that there is no shared framework for a viable practice of black cultural criticism, a fact both acknowledged and disavowed by Darcus Howe's defense of Rushdie's polemic which claimed that it '[lay] the foundations of a critical tradition'. To argue that a few columns of newsprint 'lay the foundations' for black film criticism is to recognise that such a 'tradition' does not yet exist, which itself could be read as an indictment of the kind of legitimating authority Howe arrogates to himself as 'an activist in the black movement for over 20 years, organising political, cultural and artistic thrusts . . . from our black communities'.

At one level, the lack of an ongoing discourse of radical black film criticism is one unhappy legacy of the marginalisation and underdevelopment of black film-making in Britain. This must be understood as a consequence of material conditions. Previously we had to wait so long to see a black-made film that we didn't really 'criticise': there wasn't enough space to 'theorise' aesthetics; we were simply 'thankful' the films got made in the first place. Moreover, we encounter a double absence here, as the 'professionalisation' of critical film theory in journals like *Screen* in the 70s effectively 'screened out' black and Third World film practices, confining itself to a narrowly Euro-centric canon. At this critical conjuncture we cannot afford to merely 'celebrate' the achievements of black film-makers or act as 'cheerleaders' for the so-called 'ethnic arts'. As Stuart Hall remarks on black cultural production generally, 'We have come out of the age of innocence [which] says, as it were, "It's good if it's there"', and are now entering the next phase in which 'we actually begin to recognise the extraordinary complexity of ethnic and cultural differences'.[5]

In the thick of this difficult phase of transition, my concern is to explore whether a more adequate model of criticism might not be derived from the critical practice performed in the films themselves. To the extent that what is at issue is not a struggle between one person and another but between different ways of thinking and talking about black film-making, a more useful and viable criterion for criticism comes from the concept of 'interruption', which 'seeks not to impose a language of its own [as does the practice of "interpretation"] but to enter critically into existing configurations [of discourse] to re-open the closed structures into which they have ossified'.[6]

To articulate the past historically does not mean to recognise it 'the way it really was'. It means to seize hold of a memory as it flashes up at a moment of danger. . . . Only that historian will have the gift of fanning the spark of hope in the past who is firmly convinced that *even the dead* will not be safe from the enemy if he wins.

Walter Benjamin[7]

A cursory survey of the work of black film-makers in Britain will reveal the preponderance of a 'realist' aesthetic in films made within both documentary and narrative genres. This insistent emphasis on the real must be understood as the prevailing mode in which independent black film has performed a critical function in providing a counter-discourse against those versions of reality produced by dominant voices and discourses in British film and media. Thus, the substantive concern with the politicising experience of black youth in films such as *Pressure* (dir. Horace Ové, 1974) and *Step Forward Youth* (dir. Menelik Shabazz, 1977) demonstrates a counter-reply to the criminalising stereotypes generated and amplified by media-led moral panics in the 70s.[8] Similarly, *Blacks Britannica* (1979) – although not a black British film, it is read, used and circulated as such – 'gives voice' to those excluded and silenced by the discourse of media racism. This oral testimony combines with the political analysis advanced by the activists/intellectuals featured in the film to present an alternative 'definition of the situation'. And as *Struggles for the Black Community* (dir. Colin Prescod, 1983) shows, the historical emphasis in this counter-discourse is an overdetermined necessity to counteract the *de*historicising logic of racist ideology.

There is significant continuity at the level of thematic concern with the politics of racism in new documentaries such as *Handsworth Songs* (dir. John Akomfrah, 1986) and *Territories* (dir. Isaac Julien, 1984). Yet important differences in the articulation of a counter-discourse on the real reveal distinct approaches to the politics of representation.

The 'reality-effect' produced by realist methods depends on the operation of four characteristic values – transparency, immediacy, authority and authenticity – which are in fact aesthetic values central to the dominant film and media culture itself. By adopting a 'neutral' or instrumental relation to the means of representation, this mode of black film practice seeks to redefine referential realities of race thro⸱ ⸱h the same codes and forms as the prevailing film language whose discourse of racism it aims to contest. Clearly we need to clarify the contradictions involved in this paradox.

By presenting themselves as transparent 'windows on the world' of racism and resistance, such films emphasise the urgency, immediacy and 'nowness' of their message. In the case of the 'campaigning' documentary, such as *The People's Account* (dir. Milton Bryan, 1986), this is a contextual necessity, as such films perform a critical function by providing an alternative version of events so as to inform, agitate and mobilise action. However, such communicative efficacy in providing counter-information exhausts itself once the political terrain changes. Further, although it is always necessary to document and validate the authority of experience ('who feels it, knows it'), the selection of *who* is given the right to speak may also exclude others: the voices and viewpoints of black women, for example, are notable by their absence from films such as *Blacks Britannica*. Finally, the issue of authenticity, the aspiration to be 'true to life' in narrative drama especially, is deeply problematic, as a given 'type' of black person or experience is made to 'speak for' black people as a whole. Not only does this reduce the diversity of black opinions and experiences to a single perspective assumed to be 'typical', it may reinforce the tokenistic idea that a single film can be regarded as 'representative' of every black person's perception of reality.

In short, black film practices which incorporate these filmic values are committed to a mimetic conception of representation which assumes that reality has an objective existence 'out there', and that the process of representation simply aims to correspond to or 'reflect' it. Certain limitations inherent in this conception become apparent once we contrast it to the semiotic concept of signification at work in new modes of black film discourse. My aim is not to polarise different approaches in black film-making, but to argue that this latter mode offers new perspectives on the real-politics of race by entering into a struggle with the means of representation itself. Foregrounding an awareness of the decisions and choices made in the selection and combination of signifying elements in sound and image, these new films are conscious of the fact that the reality-effect is constructed by the formal tendency to regulate, fix, contain and impose closure on the chain of signification. By intervening at the level of cinematic codes of communication, they interrupt the ideological purpose of naturalistic illusion and perform a critical function by liberating the imaginative and expressive dimension of the filmic signifier as a material reality in its own right.

Territories is not 'about' Notting Hill Carnival[9] so much as it documents the problems of trying to 'represent' the complex multifaceted aesthetic and political meanings of this phenomenon of diaspora culture. Its fragmentary collage of archival and original material interrupts the transparency necessary for an 'objective' account to achieve a quality of *critical reverie*. By this I mean that the openness of the film text hollows out a cognitive and affective space for critical reflection on the polyvocal dimension of Carnival – an event/process in which social boundaries and hierarchical power relations are momentarily dissolved and upended. So, rather than passively 'reflect' this (which risks neutralising the subversive potential of Carnival), the text enacts or embodies the critical spirit of Carnival with 'the sense of the gay relativity of prevailing truth and authority' (Bakhtin) that itself 'carnivalises' codes and conventions such as space-time continuity in editing. In this way the film destabilises fixed boundaries, precisely what happened in Carnival 1976 when black youth massively reveled in the pleasure of political resistance to the policing of black culture where the state attempted to literally impose closure and containment.

Carnival breaks down barriers between active performer and passive audience. *Territories* does something similar by emphasising its performance and reflexive mode of address to enlist the participation of the spectator. Discontinuous gaps between sound and image-tracks create a rhythmic homology between the deconstructive aesthetic of dub-versioning – which 'distances' and lays bare the musical anatomy of the original song through skilful re-editing which sculpts out aural space for the D J's talk-over[10] – and the jump-cut montage principle of the film.

Its phatic mode of enunciation, highlighted by images which show two women examining footage on an editing machine, also questions the univocal captioning role of the voice-over within the documentary genre. The choral refrain – 'we are struggling to tell a story' – underlines the fact that its story does not arrive at a point of closure, and this deferral of any authoritative resolution to the issues it raises implies that the spectator shares active responsibility for making semantic connections between the multiaccentuated perspectives of the image-flow. This is important because by pluralising the denotative value of given signs such as the Union Jack flag, the surplus of connotations engendered by multiple superimposition of imagery does not lead to the 'infinite regression' of formalism. Of the many readings the film allows, I feel it can be said that it's a film about 'self-image' because the ambivalence of its images – such as the two men entwined in an intimate embrace – is directional: its multiaccentuality is strategically anchored to raise questions about the dialectics of race, class and, especially, gender and sexuality as they cut across the public/private division in which social identities are constructed in the first place.

Handsworth Songs engages similar carnivalising strategies at the level of montage and dissonant reverberation between sound and image. The juxtaposition of actuality footage of civil disorder, on the one hand, and images drawn from 'official' archive sources and 'family-album' photographs, on the other, interrupts the amnesia of media-representations of the 1985 conflict in Birmingham and London. Instead of 'nowness', the film reaches for historical depth, creating a space of critical reverie which counteracts the active ideological forgetting of England's colonial past in media discourses on Handsworth to articulate an alternative 'archeological' account.

A female narrator tells of a journalist pestering a black woman on Lozell's Road for a news story: in the poetry of resistance, she replies, 'There are no stories in the riots, only the ghosts of other stories.' This reflexive comment on the intertextual logic of the film marks out its struggle to excavate and reclaim a creole counter-memory of black struggle, itself always repressed, erased and made invisible in the dominant 'popular memory' of British film and media discourse. Against divisive binary oppositions between Asian/Afro-Caribbean and between first and third generations, the interweaving of the past-in-the-present through oral testimony and poetic re-encoding of archive imagery seek to recover a 'sense of intimacy'; the film itself moves to 'seize hold of a memory as it flashes up at a moment of danger'. It talks back to the disparaging view of our foreparents as 'naive' and 'innocent' by invoking the dreams and desires that motivated migrations from the Caribbean. In this way it 'rescues the dead' from that amnesia and collective forgetfulness that haunt the English collective consciousness whenever it thinks of its crisis-ridden 'race-relations'.

History is not depicted in a linear novelistic narrative – which would imply that our stories of struggle are 'over'. Rather, the presence of the past in the absences of popular memory is invoked through multiple chains of association. Retinted images of chains in an iron foundry, overlaid by the eerie intonation of an English working-men's song, powerfully evoke not only the connection with the chains of slavery that made the industrial revolution possible, but the legacy of the imperial past in England's contemporary decline. Again, the spectator is enlisted as active discursive partner, sharing subjective responsibility for making connections between the latent nuclei of meanings inscribed beneath the manifest 'racial' forms of social conflict. What *Handsworth Songs* does is activate the reality of 'social fantasy' in shaping our cognition of the real world: the metaphorical and metonymic logics that cut across the signifying chain of the film-work operate at an unconscious level along the lines of condensation and displacement which Freud identified in the symbolic mechanisms of the dream-work.

'In dreams begin responsibilities,' wrote Delmore Schwartz. It seems to me to be crucially important to recognise the multiaccentuated quality of the voices that speak in these new modes of black film-writing because, as Volosinov/Bakhtin pointed out,

The social multiaccentuality of the ideological sign is a very crucial aspect [of 'class' struggle] . . . [as] each ideological sign has two faces, like Janus. This *inner dialectic quality* of the sign comes out fully into the open only in times of social crisis or revolutionary changes.[11]

To the extent that this re-echoes Fanon's insight that the fixed meaning of the signs of colonial authority become increasingly unstable, uncertain and ambivalent at the point where struggles for national/cultural liberation reach a new moment of intensity,[12] the emergence of this quality in black film discourse today implies a qualitative intensification of the struggle to decolonise or de-territorialise cinema as a site of political intervention. The liberation of the imagination is a precondition of revolution, or so the surrealists used to say. Carnival is *not* 'the revolution', but in the carnivalesque aesthetic emerging here we may discern the mobility of what Bakhtin called the 'dialogic principle' in which the possibility of *change* is prefigured in collective consciousness by the multiplication of social dialogues.[13] What is at issue can be characterised as the critical difference between a *monologic* tendency in black film which tends to homogenise and totalise the black experience in Britain and a *dialogic* tendency which is responsive to the diverse and complex qualities of our black Britishness and British blackness – our differentiated specificity as a diaspora people.

They will be intimately related to the British people, but they cannot be fully part of the English environment because they are black. Now that is not a negative statement . . . Those people who are in western civilisation, who have grown up in it, but made to feel and themselves feeling that they are outside, have a unique insight into their society.

C. L. R. James[14]

It has been said that the films of Sankofa and the Black Audio Film Collective are influenced and informed by ideas from European artistic practices. Indeed they are, but then so are those films made on the implicit premise of a mimetic theory of representation, whose 'neutral' aesthetic dimension bears traces of the influence of the prevailing codes and 'professional' ideology of the capitalist film industry, which, of course, is centred in the West. There is no escape from the fact that as a diaspora people, blasted out of one history into another by the 'commercial deportation' of slavery (George Lamming) and its enforced displacement, our blackness is thoroughly imbricated in Western modes and codes to which we arrived as the disseminated masses of migrant dispersal. What is in question is not the expression of some lost origin or some uncontaminated essence in black film-language, but the adoption of a critical 'voice' that promotes consciousness of the collision of cultures and histories that constitute our very conditions of existence.

We return therefore to confront the paradox, which is that the mimetic mode of cinematic expression is a form of cultural mimicry which demonstrates a neo-colonialised dependency on the codes which valorise film as a commodity of cultural imperialism.[15] The problem of imitation and domination was confronted in literary debates around aesthetics in the African, Caribbean and Afro-American novel in the 1940s, which highlighted the existential dilemma of dependent expressivity: how can the 'colonised' express an authentic self in an alien language imposed by the imperial power of the 'coloniser'?[16]

There is, however, another response to this problematic, inscribed in aesthetic practices of everyday life among black peoples of the African diaspora in the 'new world' of the capitalist West, which explores and exploits the creative contradictions of the clash of cultures. Across a whole range of cultural forms there is a 'syncretic' dynamic which critically *appropriates* elements from the mastercodes of the dominant culture and 'creolises' them, disarticulating given signs and re-articulating their symbolic meaning otherwise. The subversive force of this hybridising tendency is most apparent at the level of language itself where creoles, patois and Black English decentre, destabilise and carnivalise the linguistic domination of 'English' – the nation-language of master-discourse – through strategic inflections, reaccentuations and other performative moves in semantic, syntactic and lexical codes.[17] Creolising practices of counter-appropriation exemplify the critical process of dialogism as they are self-consciously aware that, in Bakhtin's terms,

The word in language is half someone else's. It becomes 'one's own' only when . . . the speaker appropriates the word adapting it to his own semantic and expressive intention. Prior to this moment of appropriation the word does not exist in a neutral or impersonal language . . . but rather it exists in other people's mouths, serving other people's intentions: it is from there that one must take the word and make it one's own.[18]

Today, the emergence of this dialogic tendency in black film practice is important, as it has the potential to renew the critical function of 'independent' cinema. Since former generations of black intelligentsia have now entered the media marketplace and broadcasting institutions, and some appear to have happily assimilated common-sense notions of 'artistic excellence',[19] the creole versioning and dialoguing with critical elements from Euro-American modernism is infinitely preferable to the collusion with the anti-cinematic conservatism inherent in such conformist positions (which continue in the great British tradition of anti-intellectualism).

There is, on the other hand, a powerful resonance between the aspirations of the new work, which seeks to find a film language adequate to the articulation of our realities as 'third-generation' black people in Britain, and the critical goals advocated by the concept of Third Cinema which combats the values of both commercialism and 'auteurism'.[20] Aware of the pernicious ethnologocentric force which Clyde Taylor[21] has shown to be inherent in the very concept of 'aesthetics' as such, my aim has been precisely to avoid the construction of a monolithic system of evaluative criteria (itself neither useful nor desirable). Rather, by appropriating elements of Bakhtin's theory I have tried to differentiate relational tendencies in the way black films perform their critical function. Evaluating this function is always context-dependent. The lucid immediacy of *We are the Elephant* (Ceddo, 1987), for instance, not only articulates an incisive account of South African realities of repression and resistance, but in doing so it strikes a dialogic blow against the censorship of image and information-flows imposed by apartheid and the alienating spectacle of money-making epics like *Cry Freedom*. This is to say that if there are dialogic moments within films conceived in a conventional mode, there are also profoundly monologic moments in some of the new work, such as the 'speaker's drama' in Sankofa's *Passion of Remembrance* and the remorseless repetition of Black Audio's earlier tape-slide *Signs of Empire*. We are dealing not with categorical absolutes but the relative efficacy of strategic choices made in specific contexts of production and reception.

I would argue that new modes in black British film-making are instances of 'imperfect' cinema, in Julio Garcia Espinosa's phrase:[22] conducting research and experiments, adopting an improvisational approach and hopefully learning from active mistakes through trial and error. In this sense Stuart Hall's comment that the originality of the new work is 'precisely that it retells the black experience as an

English experience', must be amplified. In place of reductionist tendencies in the monologic single-issue approach which creates a binary 'frontier-effect' in its political analysis of reality, as if black subjects confront white society as our monolithic Other, critical dialogism gestures towards a counter-hegemonic perspective which assumes that questions of race cannot be isolated from wider social policies. In Hall's terms,

The fact of the matter is that it is no longer possible to fight racism as if it had its own, autonomous dynamic, located between white people or the police on the one hand and blacks on the other. The problem of racism arises for *every single political development* which has taken place since the New Right emerged.[23]

Critical dialogism overturns the oppositional relations of hegemonic boundary maintenance by multiplying critical dialogues *within* particular communities and *between* the various social elements of the general 'imagined community' of the nation. At once articulating the personal and the political, it shows that our 'other' is already inside each of us, that black identities are plural and non-unitary and that political divisions of gender and sexual identity are to be transformed as much as those of race and class. Moreover, critical dialogism questions the monologic exclusivity on which dominant versions of national identity and belonging are based. Paul Gilroy shows how the sense of a mutual and logical exclusivity between the two terms 'black' and 'British' is an essential condition for the hegemony of racism over the English collective consciousness.[24] New ways of interrupting this hegemonic logic are suggested by the dialogic movement of creolising appropriation.

Fully aware of the creative contradiction, and the 'cost', of our outside-in relation to England, cultural work based on this strategy gives rise to the thought that it is possible to turn dominant versions of Englishness inside-out. Gramsci argued that a political struggle enters its hegemonic phase when it goes beyond particular economic interests to make alliances between different classes of the 'people' so as to re-direct the 'collective will' of the nation ('state + civil society'). On this view, counter-hegemonic strategy depends on the struggle to appropriate given elements in the common sense of the people and to re-articulate those elements of consciousness into a radical democratic direction, which used to be called 'equality'. At a micro-level, the textual work of creolising appropriation activated in new forms of black cultural practice awakens the thought that such strategies of dis-articulation and re-articulation may be capable of transforming the 'democratic imaginary' at a macro-level by 'othering' inherited discourses of English identity.

Aware that 'there is a Third World in every First World and vice versa' (Trin T. Minh-ha), the diaspora perspective has the potential to expose and illuminate the sheer heterogeneity of the diverse social forces always repressed by the monologism of dominant discourses – discourses of domination. In a situation where conservative forces have deepened their hold on our ability to apprehend reality and would have us believe that 'it's great to be Great again' (1987 Tory election slogan), we must encourage and develop this critical potential. It might enable us to overcome reality.

Notes

1 Introduction, *Shadow and Act* (New York, Vintage/Random House, 1964), p. xvi.
2 Reviewing *Passion*, Judith Williamson discerned the influence of Godard, Duras, Mulvey and Wollen; *New Statesman*, 5 December 1986. On *Territories*, Colin MacCabe found its 'visual flair . . . limited by its adherence to the bankrupt aesthetics of that narrow modernism advocated by much of the film theory of the 70s'; *Guardian*, 4 December 1986. Problems of 'Eurocentrics' in contemporry English critical film-theory are discussed in Robert Cruz, 'Black Cinemas, Film Theory and Dependent Knowledge', *Screen* vol. 26 nos. 3–4 (May–August 1985).
3 Novelist Salman Rushdie, born in India and living in Britain, is the author of *Midnight's Children* (winner of the 1981 Booker Prize) and *The Satanic Verses* (1988). Rushdie's polemic, 'Songs doesn't know the score', *Guardian*, 12 January 1987, was followed by letters from Stuart Hall (15 January) and Darcus Howe (19 January).
4 See Michael Cadette, 'Contrived Passions and False Memories', *Race Today Review '87* vol. 17 no. 4 (March 1987).
5 Cited in David A. Bailey, Introduction, *Ten. 8* no. 22 ('Black Experiences') (Summer 1982), p. 2.
6 David Silverman and Brian Torode, *The Material Word: Some theories of language and its limits* (London: Routledge & Kegan Paul, 1980), p. 6.
7 'Theses on the Philosophy of History', *Illuminations* (London: Fontana, 1973), p. 257.
8 See Stuart Hall and others, *Policing the Crisis* (London: Macmillan, 1979), and Stuart Hall, 'The Whites of their Eyes: Racist Ideologies and the Media', in Bridges and Brunt (eds), *Silver Linings – Some Strategies for the Eighties* (London: Lawrence & Wishart, 1981), reprinted in the present volume.
9 The Notting Hill Gate neighbourhood in the London Borough of Kensington was an area of mass Caribbean settlement in the 1940s and 50s and the scene of the white-initiated 'race-riots' of 1958; the first carnival was organised by activist Claudia Jones, and the event has subsequently developed as one of the largest street festivals in Britain, held annually on August Bank Holiday Weekend.
10 See Paul Gilroy, 'Stepping out of Babylon – race, class, and autonomy', in Centre for Contemporary Cultural Studies, *The Empire Strikes Back* (London: Hutchinson, 1982), p. 300.
11 V. N. Volosinov, *Marxism and the Philosophy of Language* (New York and London: Seminar Press, 1973), p. 19.
12 See 'On National Liberation', in *The Wretched of the Earth* (Harmondsworth: Penguin, 1967), and see also Homi Bhabha's introduction, 'Remembering Fanon', in the reprint of *Black Skin/ White Masks* (London: Pluto, 1986).
13 See 'Discourse in the Novel', *The Dialogic Imagination*, trans. C. Emerson and M. Holquist (Austin: University of Texas, 1981), and see also Tvetzan Todorov, *Mikhail Bakhtin: The Dialogical Principle* (Manchester and Minnesota: Manchester University Press, 1984).
14 'Africans and Afro-Caribbeans: a personal view', *Ten. 8* no. 14 ('Black Image/Staying On') (Spring 1984).
15 The imitation of Hollywood form in initial development phases of various 'national' cinemas is discussed in Roy Armes, *Third World Film-making and the West* (London and Berkeley: University of California Press, 1987). The transfer of professional ideology is discussed in Peter Golding, 'Media Professionalism in the Third World', in James Curran and others (eds.), *Mass Communication and Society* (London: Edward Arnold, 1977).

16 See Homi K. Bhabha, 'Representation and the Colonial Text' in Frank Gloversmith, *The Theory of Reading* (Brighton: Harvester Press, 1984). These debates have been recently revived in Ngugi wa Thiong'o, *Decolonising the Mind: The Politics of Language in African Literature* (London: John Currey/Heinemann, 1986).

17 On creolisation and interculturation, see Edward K. Braithwaite, *The Development of Creole Society in Jamaica* (Oxford: Oxford University Press, 1971), *Contradictory Omens* (Mona, Jamaica: Savacou Publications, 1974) and on linguistic subversion of the formation of 'nation-language', *The Story of the Voice* (London: New Beacon Publications, 1983).

18 *The Dialogic Imagination*, pp. 293–4.

19 Farrukh Dondy (Commissioning Editor for Multicultural Programming, Channel Four Television) on the BBC 'ethnic minority' magazine *Ebony*, transmitted November 1986. Darcus Howe and Tariq Ali edit *The Bandung File*, a black/Third World current affairs programme on Channel Four.

20 The concept of Third Cinema proposed by Latin American independent film practice in the 60s – see F. Solanas and O. Getino, 'Towards a Third Cinema' in Bill Nichols (ed.), *Movies and Methods* (London and Berkeley: University of California Press, 1976), and subsequently developed with reference to African cinema by Teshome Gabriel, *Third Cinema in the Third World: The Aesthetics of Liberation* (Ann Arbor: UMI Research Press, 1982) – was the focus of the conference held at the 40th Edinburgh International Film Festival (EIFF), 1986. For two versions of this event see my reflections on 'Third Cinema at Edinburgh', *Screen* vol. 27 no. 6 (1986) and David Will's account in *Framework* nos. 32–3 (1986).

21 Clyde Taylor's paper 'Black Cinema/White Aesthetics' was presented at the EIFF conference 'Third Cinema: Theories and Practices' (organised by Jim Pines, Paul Willemen and June Givanni). Elucidation of Taylor's argument is provided in his counter-reply to Will in 'Eurocentrics vs. New Thought at Edinburgh', *Framework* no. 34 (1987).

22 See 'Meditations on Imperfect Cinema . . . Fifteen Years Later', *Screen* vol. 26 nos. 3–4 (May–August 1985).

23 'Cold Comfort Farm' (on the Tottenham and Handsworth 'riots'), *New Socialist* no. 32 (November 1985).

24 See *There Ain't No Black in the Union Jack* (London: Hutchinson, 1987), especially chapter 2. Chapter 5, 'Diaspora, utopia and the critique of capitalism', provides further clarification of Bakhtin's relevance for thinking a diasporan aesthetic.

III
'Typical Aussies': Television and Populism in Australia

NOEL KING AND TIM ROWSE
From *Framework* nos. 22–23 (Autumn 1983)

Australian television offers a uniquely fascinating area of study for the media analyst. One particularly striking aspect of the system is the fact that three versions of the same game show format can be transmitted, for example the British, USA and Australian versions of the *Price is Right*, *Blind Date* or *Blankety Blanks* (the title is intriguingly pluralised in the Australian version). Similarly both the British and USA versions of the same popular situation comedies are screened, for example *'Till Death Us Do Part* and *All In The Family*. The price of speaking approximately the same language and apparently sharing cultural similarities with two other disparate cultures, has led to an interesting and uniquely (albeit related to the Canadian experience) Australian set of anxieties and problems about cultural identity.

In their account of the relationship between Australian television and the populist politics of the country, Noel King and Tim Rowse focus on a type of advertisement which is also possibly unique to Australia – the 'humanity ad'. Even when the 'humanity ads' are financed by commercial enterprises they look and function far more like community or public utility advertisements because what they would primarily seem to be 'selling' is 'Australianism'. Thus instead of encouraging 'the collision of cultures and histories' for which Kobena Mercer is calling in film-making practices of a minority community in Britain, these ads function in the diametrically opposed way in order to, as King and Rowse describe, '*identify* a product, a sentiment or a service with an imagined community, diverse but essentially unified'.

It is this 'television project' of attempting to construct an ideologically unified culture out of a heterogeneously drawn amalgam of peoples (and on the back of the near extermination of the indigenous peoples – cf. Eric Michaels later in this section) which provides the authors with the basis for a political analysis of television as a social institution. Their account of these advertisements enables them to identify four significant characteristics of the social institution of television which suggestively provide a structure for a wider-ranging analysis of how the culture of television functions ideologically across a range of programmes.

Thus, according to the analysis offered by King and Rowse, television provides '. . . the articulation (in both material practice and symbolic representation) of a three-way relationship between viewers, the world depicted or *implied*, and those doing the depicting'. They provocatively propose an analysis of television which equates its operations with those of a populist party, that is a party, according to Nicos Mouzclis' analysis, 'with a minimal organisational mediation between leaders and base'.

M.A./J.O.T.

It's a typical Aussie morning
On a typical Aussie day
And I love this place I was born in
In a typical Aussie way
And I'd sure hate to lose our sunshine
But I can feel it slippin' away
And we all have to wake up sometime
That everything is not OK
Have a go, you can do it
Have a go, you'll come through it
That's how we got the country started
Boots and all and not half-hearted . . .
'Have a Go' ad.

Much of the analysis of the political discourse of television has argued that the viewer is given the position of concerned but neutral onlooker picking her way through the possible allegiances to this or that side by means of the 'neutral' terms of reference provided by broadcasting professionals. This account evokes an active, interested citizenry addressed as such by newscasters, discussion moderators and interviewer. But this diligent public might well be a minority of the actual or potential audience; clearly 'a lot of people don't follow politics and won't choose to watch public affairs programming'. In liberal democracies (and this is certainly true of Australia) there are traditions of apathy, suspicion and cynicism towards Politics. The persistent smell of corruption together with recurring instances of sheer incompetence reinforce, in Australian political culture, a populist strain which defers to political managers in order not to bother with them. The post-war prosperity of Australia and the speed with which individuals could materially improve their lot have under-written such attitudes and it is clear that television provides places for viewers with these dispositions.

In developing this argument in relation to some contemporary television advertisements we hope to outline some of the main features of Australian populism and to make some remarks about television in general. In Australia the political discourse of television is not only about politics, it is about the relationship between 'Politics' and 'ordinary life', duty and enjoyment, artifice and authenticity, Public Affairs and its public.

The 'Humanity' Advertisement

Australia has a dual television system – government networks (The Australian Broadcasting Corporation and the Special Broadcasting Services 'multicultural' station) and private networks of which three (Channels 7, 9, and 10) are national in scope. Plainly, both parts of the system strive for wide appeal, but whereas the government stations are committed to serving some minority audiences in at least some of their programming, the commercials are financed solely by their advertising revenue. The two sides of the system constitute audiences with significantly different profiles; the government stations' audiences are more affluent and 'educated'. Programming too resembles the A and B pattern found in the USA by Williams.[1] The commercial stations buy more American programmes, have developed 'personalities' sooner, show more movie re-runs, fewer one-act plays and 'educational' shows. Most importantly for the purposes of this paper, about fifteen minutes of every broadcast hour consists of Australian-made advertisements. Prominent among these in the last five years are advertisements whose principal ideological work is not to constitute viewers as distinct individuals but as members of a (distinctively Australian) common humanity. Indeed in the trade they are known as 'humanity ads'. The characteristics of this genre are easy to list.

First, they portray a large number of people, shot singly or in groups who are manifestly 'ordinary people' (as opposed to actors). Secondly, a high proportion of the people (sometimes all of them) are shot responding directly to the gaze of the camera, either smiling, raising a beer glass or making some similarly standardised gesture. In Channel 7's ads it takes the form of raising seven fingers (in two distinct gestures of five and two). In 'Have a Go' it is both thumbs upraised, facing the camera. In 'Do the Right Thing' it consists of putting litter in a bin – although, in this ad, the participants often don't face the camera. The third characteristic is that in each case, the narrative is a loose mosaic, made up of the juxtaposition of a series of similar, but diverse, human images. In some of the ads each image could itself be taken as a mini-narrative. In the 'Project Australia' ads each scene depicts a person performing a task and in most of the ads the effect is of a series of actions and activities fleetingly caught. None of the ads is unified by the presence of a continuous character nor cohered by a strong linear story (as, for instance *is* the case in the 'I'm a Soldier' army recruiting ads) but rather are mosaics of simultaneous, similar but individuated actions and gestures. The ads thus exhibit (at one remove) the assumed diversity (yet similarity and simultaneity) of the viewing audience.

One of the crucial strategies for cohering these series of images is contained in the presence of the jingle which functions both to carry the overall message of the ad and, at various moments via individual lines or couplets, to anchor a meaning for the particular image with which it coincides. So in the *Daily Mirror* ad, the image of an old man sitting beside the El Alamein Fountain (at Kings Cross in Sydney) *could* be very ambiguous, perhaps signifying some of the poverty so common in a large city. The jingle 'captions' the image by saying 'And Bruce is just taking some sun', thereby providing a positive, optimistic reading of the scene. Occasionally the jingle has a punch-line, as in Project Australia's 'We're all in the same boat' where the camera draws back from the ensemble of individual cartoon images to reveal them as a map of Australia.

Finally, those ads which exhibit the structure outlined above tend to be about a wide range of products and ideas. If it is a commodity then the ad says very little about it, since the ad is calculated not to *describe* a good but to *identify* a product, a sentiment or a service with an imagined community, diverse but essentially unified. A newspaper (*The Daily Mirror*), or television station (Channel 7) and a building society (Newcastle Permanent) are all well-served by being represented as common property. (This would not be so with, say, Chivas Regal, Volvos or Arpege perfume, which depend on senses of distinction). The theme, so prominent in these ads, of unity in diversity or of a plural community, is one of the most important discursive figures in the ideology of the nation-state where the common or national interest is conceived as an ensemble of discrete individual wills given collective expression by representative institutions.[2] It is an ideology which cannot accommodate (and continually seeks to demobilise) antagonistic senses of difference in which blocs of social forces are ranged against each other, or in which 'the people' is constructed as the opposite of another term – 'the ruling class' or 'imperialist forces'. Clearly this non-antagonistic mobilisation of a sense of community is quite different from, say, Nazi populism which identified as the Other, Jews or West European treachery. It means that the 'patriotism' that some critics identify in 'Project Australia' and 'Have a Go' is not a chauvinism mobilised against alien cultures. Indeed the 'Project Australia' ad tends towards inclusiveness, a 'melting pot' of multi-ethnicity, while the 'Have a Go' ad does not indulge in 'union bashing' but instead mobilises a sense of collective disquiet, calculated to make each viewer feel equally responsible for the economic malaise.

Clearly, then, the great 'strength' of these humanity ads is that they are inclusive of a wide variety of points of identification with a common interest. The most obvious example of this general practice is contained in the words of the 'Have a Go' ad (quoted in the epigraph to our paper), an ad which opens with images of 'typical' Australian activities: lugging sacks of potatoes, fishing, the racetrack, children on beaches.

In the Project Australia animated ad, similar appeals to typicality and a shared history are made. The ad opens with an over-weight 'Norm' figure sitting in a chair watching T V and saying 'I *want* to come on Aussie, I want to have a go, I don't want Australia to be a failure', a statement joined on the soundtrack by a chorus of emphatic 'No!s'. The main jingle then begins, sung by alternating male and female voices saying 'Australians came from everywhere to give this nation soul' and assuring us that 'by rolling up our sleeves and working harder for our quids, we'll make the lucky country rich and free for all our kids'. The anachronistic 'quids' is used to invoke a timeless Australian colloquial speech (given free reign in another encyclopaedic line 'have a bash, have a shot, beauty Norm and have a go'): 'come on Aussie' alludes to the enormously popular song promoting World Series Cricket and 'the lucky country' mobilises Donald Horne's phrase in a way which ignores its ironic meaning. What these ads have in common, across their diverse range of reference, is the consistent invocation of an earlier tradition of Australianness, of work and service in the national interest. A proud inheritance is at risk, a point emphasised by the fact that the ads close with a 'real' *spoken* repetition of a significant phrase from the jauntily-sung jingle (e.g., 'because if we don't it'll be too late').

The sense of responsibility implied in these two advertisements is duty to ourselves – a benign sense of fellowship rather than of obedience to some authoritative expression of the national will. As part of the New World recently settling at an exhilarating place Australians indeed 'came from everywhere to give this nation soul', where this 'soul' is the shared sense of responsibility, open to all who will roll their sleeves up and work. The symbol of Australia is thus the Australians themselves, various in origin but united in enterprise. The nation is not given any symbolic expression (apart from flags) other than images of the people who make it up. Perhaps another way of making this point would be to say that a sentence like 'your country needs you' would be syntactically at odds with these ads in separating as subject and predicate the unity of 'we'.

It is quite incidental to the structure and imagery of the humanity ad that 'the people' is co-extensive with 'the nation'. Among other ads there are a number of other communities addressed and represented.

For instance, media institutions can define themselves as embodying a quasi-community of viewers, as was the case in the Channel 7 'colour machine' series. This was done all the more convincingly by the *Daily Mirror* ad. The 'Patch of Blue' is Sydney Harbour and the jingle is a eulogy of sunny, aquatic, enjoyable Sydney – the very place of leisure and simple enjoyment that is 'reflected' in the *Mirror* (which, being a Murdoch evening tabloid, is much less about political news than it is about sport, competitions readers can enter, and human interest stories). With images of leisure, not work, the ad evokes a sense of their city of which Sydney-siders are fond – a relaxed, sun-filled place of leisure whose symbols are the harbour and the Opera House (and less, these days, The Bridge, with its overtones of triumphant work). The final words of the jingle change the address to the viewer. 'We'd just like to add, at the end of our ad, Sydney's a nice place to be'. (Images of children). Acknowledging the world outside the advertisement, these words speak to the viewer simply as another Sydney-sider. The coy admission of the artifice of the ad contained in the concluding pun works to secure an identification between the viewer and the 'content' of the commercial. The earlier pun, 'You can see it all in the mirror' – as the viewer watches the T V screen fill with post-card images of Sydney – had begun the work is then completed by the tacit statement that no deceptions could possibly be wrought on a true Sydney-sider about his/her city. To this extent the ad (for the paper) and the television screen on which it appears are presented as 'undistorting' mirrors, neutral transmitters of an agreed truth (contained in the false humility of 'Sydney's a nice place to be').

The series of three Newcastle Permanent Building Society ads similarly mobilise a geographical as well as a civic community with the addition that in this case a sense of community is represented in terms of class and region. These two senses of apartness (from capital cities – Newcastle is the largest Australian city outside the capitals and is larger than Hobart) and potential inferiority (stemming from the usual identification of Newcastle with steelworks and dockyards, heavy industry and dirt) are catered to in the lines 'make it (the Building Society, the town) grow with the people you know, the people who won't put you down'.

These ads evoke a battler's past and a defensive pride in Newcastle. The ownership of a home, insofar as it signifies a life in this particular community, is the common aspiration implied by the advertisement. And, as was the case with the other ads, this life must be made in terms which understand a common heritage. In this case, a heritage of industrial conflict is alluded to briefly by the image of locked gates on a wharf and is followed immediately by an overhead shot of a billowing spinacre as the accompanying jingle says 'been through the rough times, know about the rough times, lookin' for the good times ahead'. A significant feature of the history of the town (one which could have prompted a different kind of remembrance) is thereby elided while the ad sets about extolling an investment in the future. Any specific, properly historical sense of class is dissolved into images of rough masculinity (pubs and sport), family aspirations and community enjoyment.

Two of the ads begin with voice-overs from old working-class people, one male and one female. Each sequence connects with the recent *genre* of oral labour history documentaries; their function is similarly to provide the effect of the veridical. They are repositories of *the* (rather than a) history of Newcastle.

The other one of the three Newcastle Permanent Ads begins by reflecting on its own status as an ad, on the possibility of its own lack of truthfulness. The opening image is of an elegantly dressed, glamorous young couple drinking champagne at a 'piazza' table. The shot widens to reveal them posing for a camera and into the shot comes, 'unscheduled', a council water truck manned by rowdy employees in singlets. The couple are showered and the jingle says:

> Life's not like a commercial
> It's not like they make it seem
> everything funny, everything sunny
> Just pie-in-the-sky-high dream.

This evokes a sense of a real Australia full of unpretentious, ordinary people, outside the artificiality of the media and politics, and this is apparent across all of the humanity advertisements. They appeal to and deepen a sense of the separateness of civil society from politics, of day-to-day personal realities from the 'public' world of politicians and media personalities whose codes of dress, speech and conduct are held to be artificial, distant.

The consistent appeal to endorse the ordinary as authentic and shared is the theme common to the humanity ads. The more patriotic advertisements described above avoid politics and go straight to the people as the source and addressee of their messages. Several of the others reflexively draw attention to the possibility of television artifice – and so authenticate themselves. In all of them, it is the public which speaks to itself, powerfully implying a less authentic public world of politics and media hype that is elsewhere, and ultimately unnecessary.

The Post-war Revision of Australianism

The historical context of these historically and culturally self-conscious advertisements stretches back to the 1940s. In the decade of anti-fascist triumph and Labour rule at the federal level (1941–9) a sense of popular destiny was mobilised, by official initiatives, towards the objectives of victory in war and reconstruction in peace. The themes of Australianism were social-democratic and even, for some, socialist. Looking back to the forties in 1959, one socialist historian, writing of the discovery that he and his comrades had made then, said:

Aggressive militant democracy was not only a function of the international labour movement, but was deep-rooted in Australian popular history; that fraternity existed not only in the popular front but in the Australian tradition; that 'comrade' had much in common with 'mate'.[3]

Much of the cultural history of Australia since the forties should be written as the erosion of precisely that vision of Australian people. It was not until 1972 that a Labour government regained power in the Federal sphere and by then it projected a rather different sense of destiny – that of modernising and humanising. A different constituency mandated it – an educated and critical middle class, marginalised regions (the unsewered outer suburbs), and marginalised social interests – women, migrants and Aborigines, were consciously added to the traditional Labour movement base. The ideological struggle over the content of Australianism had displaced a workerist populism. It became a matter of celebration by Australian social critics in the sixties that Australia was a nation of suburbs in which peoples' aspirations went no further than enjoying their friends and family on the weekends. The proponents of Left Australianism regarded these suburban anti-heroes as the lost constituency of socialism – the outcome of embourgeoisement. But the optimistic assessment of right-wing populists outflanked the pessimism of left-wing observers: the former sold more books.

In any case it was necessary for Left Australianism to reassess their faith in the intrinsically radical instincts of ordinary Australians. The revisionist left historians of the seventies pointed out the modest aims of Australian labourism, the depth of worker's loyalty to British civilization and their consequent racism, xenophobia and nationalism. Such reassessments were complementary to other arguments (since the late 1950s) that Australian history was a story of businessmen, bureaucrats and middle-class leaders, as well as a story of workers. To this list historians have recently added women and Aborigines.

While Left Australianism became historiographically outmoded it was also demographically dated by the 1970s. In 1976 one Australian resident in five had been born overseas. The rhetoric of nationality and the assumptions of policy-makers were only just yielding to a critique of Australia's ethnocentric response to its immigrants (many of whom were Southern European and Asian). 'Multiculturalism' has been the most powerful alternative to a unitary sense of Australians – 'The ideal of one Australian family, devoid of foreign communities, thus preserving our homogeneity and solidarity as a nation,' to quote the Labour Prime Minister who initiated the post-war migration program.

The image of Australians in the humanity advertisements registers the impact of these two struggles over the definition of Australianism – the victory of an optimistic account of popular consumerism over the despair of socialist critics, and the displacement of an ideal of homogeneity by one of diversity. There is a specific political context which gives appeal to an image of Australians as diverse peoples with a playful zest for life. From 1968 until 1975 some cultural norms of political action were disrupted. Protests against the Vietnam War made the boundaries of legitimate forms of political action controversial. In the period of Whitlam's Prime Ministership (1972–75), the purpose and adequacy of the instruments of government were made to be an issue. The conservative media's coverage of politics of the Whitlam era focused on 'scandal' and 'incompetence'. The constitutional crisis of 1975 broke the seemingly obvious convention that the party with the most members in the lower house forms the government. Conventions were manipulated until they came apart in people's hands, or so it seemed. If we add to this the 'scandalous' entry into public affairs of the politics of sexuality, and the rise of a popular politics of the urban environment, then it becomes an enlivened but, for some Australians, disturbing period, in which the meaning and methods of politics became disputable. An imagery which played off a distaste for politics, a feeling of its remoteness and endemic treachery, could flourish because it offered something unequivocal and certain – people themselves. As a medium replete with such imagery, a medium presenting itself as the people talking to themselves, television begins to resemble a populist party.

Television as a Populist Party

In Ernesto Laclau's work 'populism' refers to those interpellations, made necessary by popular-democratic institutions, which posit the 'people' as the opposite term of some entity which is hostile to their interests and that entity is specified within the populist discourse itself.[4] In those humanity ads to which we have referred, the non-popular entity remains unnamed and the 'popular' remains plural and inclusive. Insofar as the people are 'ordinary' (not actors) there is one inference the viewer can always draw, namely that television fare usually is artifice, people paid to dress up and say things, and this is opposed to the popular. This is made explicit in the Newcastle Permanent Building Society ad. The invocation of 'Newcastleness' as something resistant to the blandishments and reputation of other places is given expression in the opening fable of the elegant actor and actress upstaged by the council water truck. This scene and the close of the *Mirror* ad, mentioned above, refer to the possibility of their own lack of good faith only to self-reflexively guarantee their lack of artifice. With the circulation of such images and with the prominence of the theme of leisure and enjoyment in daily life we can see a pointing out of the non-popular term. What the people are not is: the official world of well-rehearsed speeches, of scripts and sets and contrived images, of remote and staged politics – the Public sphere where the spontaneity of the public would be found to be awkward.

The humanity ad must be seen as an example of broadcasting's ability to imply or constitute a plebiscitary relation between itself and the public. This relation, although not concrete, enables the construction of an impression of immediacy. In an important critique of Laclau's theory, Nicos Mouzelis has argued that if we are to describe a political party as populist we should take note of more than its rhetoric and imagery: the organizational relationship between leaders and base is also important.

Neither parties with well developed bureaucratic structures (like the Italian Communist Party or the Australian Labour Party) nor parties with a network of local patron-client relationships (such as the inner city A L P) should be included as populist, argues Mouzelis. A populist party is one with a minimal organizational mediation between leaders and base. 'Any intermediaries, whether of the clientelistic or the more bureaucratic type, are distrusted. They are seen as preventing the direct immediate rapport between the populist leader and "his people".' It is a relationship effected in rallies and plebiscites.[5]

The relationship between broadcasting personnel and viewers is similarly 'plebiscitary' in that the commercial imperative to amass the largest possible audience requires at least an approximate responsiveness to ratings. Television 'professional' talk is saturated with the rhetoric of pleasing people, being for the people, giving the people what they want. Of course this is the traditional and unsurprising rhetoric of any entertainer, but broadcasting organisations have taken on many more functions than simply those of amusing and diverting an audience. They are also influential in setting and providing the terms of the agenda of political discussion. They not only please the people, but they (and the print media) stand in place of the people, talk *for* the people to those whom they select as key political actors. In both pleasing and informing they consistently imply a complicity with the public in their critical detachment from The Public.

Television has material characteristics which make that implication possible and here we identify four significant characteristics of television as a social institution. The first two are drawn from the work of Raymond Williams.

Broadcasting, as it has developed to this point, brings transmitting groups and a receiving public into a social relationship which is as much determined by the re-existing structures of industrial societies as it is by broadcast technology itself. Transmission is highly centralised and is in the hands of political-economic elites. Reception, on the other hand, is dispersed and simultaneous, taking place within the family/household, the site of most acts of consumption and the focus of much of our individual aspirations.

The second feature of television identified by Williams is contained in the concept of 'flow'. If viewers watch television for a general period rather than switch from programme to programme in specific choices, and if the function of the shift from one programme to the next has become rare or non-existent, then viewers experience 'flow'. 'Flow' refers to the tendency for firm distinctions between different kinds of programmes to become blurred. In Williams' descriptions, 'though the items may be various the television experience has in some important ways unified them'.[6]

Thirdly, television's selective use of direct address to camera encourages an inscription of 'the viewer as public', aligned with and represented by the directly gazing moderator or interviewer. It is a convention that any interviewee address not the television viewer but rather the presenter who acts as a mediator, functioning as 'our' representative, putting the questions 'we' want answered. One of the effects of the presenter's functioning as a representative of the public is that his/her address works to unify the viewing public. When a news-reader begins a report on a petrol strike with the words 'the news is still not good' the implication is that 'the public' is unified in its interest in the strike. It does not want this or that result but merely and commmonly the restoration of supplies. It is an addressing of the public and one or other side of the dispute. The presenter's address unifies the public as victim, as if his/her own position were that of the detached observer of the state of that public's affairs, reporting impartially while the two sides bicker.

Television's tendency to signify the ordinary, the human and the familiar is the fourth feature of the medium we wish to mention. The economics of production express themselves in the everyday 'ordinariness' of much of what is shown.[7] The public itself is an ever-ready subject-matter of television; it is cheap to telecast (in news, sport, quiz and variety) the doings of audiences and crowds. Witness the place of live audiences, quiz shows and the Don's Wheel section of *The Don Lane Show*. Familiarity and ordinariness are also produced in dramatic series and serials in which the economics and logistics of cheap, rapid output often result in a small familiar group of actors performing in standard sets; that is, the *milieux* of dramatic narratives tend to become quasi-familial if they are not already depicting the families so common to situation comedy.[8]

Considering these four characteristics we can start to observe the ideological work of the humanity advertisements in the context of a culture of television – the articulation (in both material practice and symbolic representation) of a three-way relationship between viewers, the world depicted *or implied*, and those doing the depicting. That the first and third terms are often unspoken does not mean they can be ignored.

The humanity ads derive some of their characteristics from a culture which television, as an institution, has developed; namely, a repertoire of plebiscitary actions. The telethon, for instance, is a 'show' in which the 'stars' are the individual donors whose names are read out as the total of the public's collective generosity rises on a graph, which is the site of the programme's 'narrative'. 'Stars' and 'personalities' adopt a more self-effacing demeanour when they appear, not to perform, but to give encouragement to the public, for it is *they* who really are the centre of attention. The public is also a performer in shows which use a live audience. Live audiences feature differently from show to show, but in *The Don Lane Show* they are frequently addressed separately from Don's address to the camera; they are allowed to seem part of the studio team, just as Don and Bert make a practice of featuring the production crew and orchestra. Don Lane makes the presence of the studio audience (who can see how the show is contrived/artificed) the occasion for being an 'up front' sort of guy, whose relationship with the audience is a kind of friendly partnership. Don and Bert's clowning, and especially Bert's (American) slapstick and rude attempts to destabilise the slickness of (American) Don, stand in contrast to the more conventionally 'showbiz' acts in the show.[9] The continual disarming and exposure of the artifice of performance is the hallmark of Australia's most successful variety show.

It is the exposure and critical mediation of the Public world to a private audience which also characterises recent developments in public affairs television. The commercial network's recent promotion of their own news programmes has highlighted the integrity and familiarity of the news presenters. In the case of the Nine Network's Brian Henderson the slogan was 'Brian told me'. (Channel Seven has stayed closer to the traditional – and B B C/ A B C – selling point of the professionalism of the News Service, shooting the newsreader against the background of the news work-room. News as the outcome of newswork is implied to be more trustworthy). Channel 10 and Mike Willesee have developed an image of the newsreader/investigator as a public advocate and consumer ombudsperson.

The television genre featuring 'the public' from which the humanity advertisements derive most directly is 'voxpop' – the interview with a person in the street, an easy way to get visually interesting footage on a news item about something controversial. A variation of the-popular-as-genuine was evident in those ads in which 'real housewives' were interviewed about margarine or detergent. The humanity ads have eliminated the questioner and the question and have stylised the encounter into a series of rapid and standardised 'answers' delivered straight to the viewer. Lastly, as John Langer has noted, sincerity and familiarity in television personalities has become a feature which different television genres have in common. Personalities, unlike stars, are 'real people' who mediate the programme flow to the viewer.[10]

The Party of Non-Partisanship

Although it is the area in which television's practices of signifying politics have been most fully elucidated, and in which the most assertive political critique of television has been made, there are dangers in allowing news and current affairs to become the implicit model of television's signification of political and social life. News/current affairs is only one portion of television culture. 'Entertainment' and advertising are much more prominent in the percentage of programme time they occupy, and they too put forward a subtle account of politics. Public affairs programmers seem to address viewers in a way that is quite specific – the viewer as 'concerned citizen'. It is an address to which many respond with a Great Refusal – switching to a lighter programme. Corrigan and Willis point to the otherness of entertainment, the implicit populism of commercial calculation.[11] There is a necessary heterogeneity among television's addresses to the 'serious' or 'light-hearted' viewer which makes viewer choice possible. For the pleasure-seeking, leisure-oriented viewer, politics is, for a time at least, the business of another kind of viewing; it is for now a confusing or laughable bore.

David Morley has recently reminded us that in audience decodings of television the modes in which the audience is addressed should be thought of separately from the explicit content of what is said on T V and should be related instead to the genre of show being watched.[12] A genre-specific account of television must come to terms with the concept of flow, however, if that concept is taken to refer to the eliding of the distinctions between television programmes. (Langer's essay on the ubiquity of the 'personality' throughout television is more at ease with 'flow'). In depicting the humanity advertisement as a crystallisation of a plebiscitary rhetoric found in a number of different kinds of programme our argument is also more an account of television than of a particular genre. A prominent theme of the television we watch in Australia then, is the immediacy, diversity and basic optimism of 'the people'. Television mobilises a sense of the common (but individually differentiated) detachment of the daily life of ordinary people from the official duties and formally-defined institutional life of society. The idea of citizenship has been enlarged to encompass the vast republic of domestically-based consumption. The humanity advertisements which best capture consuming as a collective and symbolically-affirmed citizenship are the *Life: Be In It* series. Conceived as a health promotion campaign by the Victorian State Government in 1977 in response to the climbing costs of health care 'for such problems as obesity, heart disorders and psychological trauma', market research convinced the planners of this campaign that 'fitness' was a hard concept to sell and that 'fun' and 'doing your own thing' were better themes. The animated ads show people doing a variety of things – from touching their toes to flying a balloon. The images and the jingle are comic and include an 'everyman' figure called 'Norm' – a model of Australian indolence who finally gets active in phase two of the campaign. The creator of the *Life: Be In It* series, Phillip Adams, was explicitly opposed to trying to communicate any sense of duty. Indeed this kind of health promotion is politically alternative to the re-introduction or strengthening of the 'user-pays' principle, which financially penalises profligate citizens. Adams said:

It is one thing for Chairman Mao to require his six hundred million acolytes to indulge in daily exercise. It is quite another for a government in our laconic, ironic society to attempt the same thing. The Chinese are very willing to sublimate their egos in a national effort. The Australian has a strong anti-authoritarian streak and far prefers to offer irreverent advice from the outer than participate in physical activity.[13]

We can gloss Adam's point as saying that television, reaching into the private world, away from the pressures of work and politics, must not speak with the voice of duty but with the voice of relief from it, a voice of leisure and fun.

It is neither surprising nor stretching an analogy to see the institution of broadcasting as resembling a populist party. The question is rather – what kind of party with what kind of programme? Bob Connell has related press and party in the following way. He argues that one of the historic reasons for the weakness of the organisational structures of the non-Labour parties is that the press functioned as the mobiliser of non-Labour voters by articulating the same sense of the public interest as the non-Labour leadership. It is only the parties with an alternative political programme, a counter hegemonic ideology, that need an organised structure, linking leaders and rank and file in a continuing effort of counter-education and mobilisation.[14] This insight is valuable in suggesting a degree of functional equivalence between party and a mass medium, but it may overlook the genuineness of media non-partisanship. Television stations do not seek to take power, only to articulate the relation between the powerful and the powerless from a 'neutral' position. The coverage of industrial relations may consolidate a conservative constituency by identifying one side as reasonable and the other as refractory, or it may merely adopt as its principal terms of reference the necessity of settlement, and an end to disputation whose motives it does not try to characterise or judge. A position can be created for the consumer, disdainful of either side. This address to the bothered consumer, as someone beyond politics, whose side the telecast is taking, is perhaps an even more secure neutrality than an account which addresses the viewer as someone who potentially was interested enough to take sides.

So the neutral position could be rendered, as it is in some studies[15] as a partisanship with the proper and legitimate framework of dispute – Parliament, Arbitration – which prescribe formats of reasonable action. Or broadcasting can be for its audience a 'non-partisan party', one which expresses a dimension of social life that is outside of politics, outside the contrived worlds of appearance, polish, professional artifice; that world 'outside politics' is a world of 'people' who are continuous with television's public. There is an address in entertainment, in advertisements, in talk shows which implies the viewers' estrangement from the Public world. In constructing 'the public' as a characteristic protagonist of TV shows, television is constructing definitions of public space. Public space is, like 'the public', an ensemble of conventional fictional images wherein the actions of 'us' – the 'public' – take place. While it is true that any space can be made the place of public assembly, some public spaces come to signify 'the public', or various publics. Town halls signify civic action, churches piety, playgrounds children in good hands, and beaches leisure. Television imagery can feature an infinite number of possible 'public spaces' yet there is a striking uniformity in the imagery of public spaces in the humanity advertisement – the street, the park, the beach, the harbour, all sites of enjoyment. Television also gives us sporting venues as visualised public spaces. Parliament, court-rooms, factories, offices, school-rooms are rarely depicted yet each is arguably a public space. The home is rarely visualised as a real place, but is constantly before our eyes as an idealised one which we have in common, in acted dramas and advertisements. On Australian television visualised public spaces are sites of consumption and leisure. There is an egalitarian theme in this: leisure is the great leveller, or, in Donald Horne's words 'the genteel have been vulgarised, the vulgar made more gentle. People now enjoy themselves more in the same kind of ways'.[16]

Broadcasting's rhetoric of being an ordinary person's medium, of being on the side of the public against a Public World of political jobbery, forced respectability and transparent artifice, has a strong basis in the material conditions of the audience's life. For they are spectators whose lack of power is no illusion. Moreover they are characteristically at home, in leisure time, and consuming rather than producing (apart from wives/mothers who are doing both). The public is thus a hedonistic spectator, addressed as having certain needs, expectations and attitudes – a viewer relaxed and thankfully detached from the Public world. The humanity ad, and the idioms of television which it so thoroughly embodies, confirms and celebrates the gap between a signified ordinary peoples' world and a signified Public

World. What detaches this implied public from partnership with a particular party programme is the strength of this separation and the construction of the public as knowing hedonists.

Hedonism is a problem ideology for Capitalism in so far as it works *for* consumption but *against* notions of duty and work. Television expresses this tension by constructing its audience in contrasting ways, favouring the hedonistic. The pressure to strive for ratings (a pressure from which non-commercial broadcasters are not immune), leads television as an institution to project itself more as a community of leisure and enjoyment than as a community of duty. In 1980, for example, Malcolm Fraser's anti-Soviet stance was partly undermined by the Seven Network's televising of the Moscow Olympic Games. Seven was able to present itself as the protector of everybody's enjoyment of sport against the marauding intrusion of 'politics'. It insisted on its right and obligation to please the public rather than take sides in a Public dispute. Responding to the market's consumption to give 'the people' what they want, will sometimes disengage the media from their support for particular political and moral conservatisms. But, by the same token, the populism of television seems to have strict limits in its mobilisation against elements of the Public. It is rooted in a partisanship with an affluent disaffection from the political, a resolute preference for the world lived and consumed in private.

Notes

1 Raymond Williams, *Television: Technology and Cultural Form* (London: Fontana, 1974). See also S. Kippax and J. P. Murray, *Small Screen – Big Business* (Sydney: Angus and Robertson, 1979).

2 N. Poulantzas, *Political Power and Social Classes* (London: New Left Books, 1973).

3 I. Turner, 'Life of the Legend', *Overland* no. 16 (December 1959).

4 Ernesto Laclau, *Politics and Ideology in Marxist Theory* (London: New Left Books, 1977).

5 N. Mouzelis, 'Ideology and Class Politics', *New Left Review* no. 112 (1979), pp. 43–59.

6 *Television: Technology and Cultural Form*, p. 95.

7 Stuart Hall, 'Television as Medium and its Relation to Culture' (stencilled occasional paper, Centre for Contemporary Cultural Studies, Birmingham University, 1975).

8 Horace Newcomb, *TV – The Most Popular Art* (New York: Doubleday, 1974).

9 See J. Langer and J. Goldlust, 'Don Lane's Electronic Sideshow', *Cinema Papers* no. 24 (1979–80), pp. 605–7.

10 J. Langer, 'Television's Personality System', *Media, Culture and Society* vol. 4 (1981).

11 Paul Corrigan and Paul Willis, 'Cultural Forms and Class Mediations', *Media, Culture and Society* vol. 2 (1980), pp. 297–312.

12 David Morley, 'The Nationwide Audience: a Critical Postscript', *Screen Education* no. 39 (1981).

13 Phillip Adams, 'Advertising Rationale', *Australian Journal for Health, Physical Education and Recreation* no. 84 (1979), pp. 11–15.

14 R. W. Connell, *Ruling Class, Ruling Culture* (Melbourne: Cambridge University Press, 1977).

15 For example Stuart Hall, Ian Connell, Lidia Curti, 'The "Unity" of Current Affairs Television', *Cultural Studies* no. 9 (1976).

16 Donald Horne, *The Lucky Country*, 3rd ed. (Ringwood: Penguin, 1971).

IV
On Counting the Wrong Things

BRIAN WINSTON

From *The Critical Communications Review I*, edited by Vincent Mosco and Janet Wasko (Norwood, N.J.: Ablex, 1983)

Content analysis, and more generally the application of quantitative social-science methodologies to the study of the media, has suffered both from thoughtless acceptance on the part of funding bodies and a public only too willing to believe that Science Has Spoken, and from thoughtless rejection by many of us on the basis of 70s High Theory. (Quantitative work was perceived as empiricist, and North American, and boring; that the justified distrust was mixed up with some snobbery and laziness, it is hard to deny.) Brian Winston's sardonic essay is notable for uniting a lethal attack on the stupid side of content analysis (the sort of attack that mere distant disdain doesn't allow you to mount) with a realistic sense that 'counting things' and empirical work generally will remain an important investigative and argumentative tool in the analysis of media bias.

Winston's chief target is a study, emanating from the USA's Right, suggesting that North American television's portrayal of businessmen [sic] is regularly hostile. Winston scrupulously points out that the substantive point may have some truth in it (see fn. 2); presumably this could be explained in terms of the traditions of North American populism, which might render network TV's love-affair with business a love that dare not speak its name. But the way the point is upheld is open to serious criticism, which is worth mounting not only as an attack on these particular much-publicised 'scientifically-established' results but as a warning to other groups who probably do have cases against the media: beware of trying to make your case thus! The moral drawn by Winston is not that counting things is a hopelessly-flawed enterprise, but that quantitative methods must be employed thoughtfully and self-critically in the context of a wider analytical, and political, project.

M.A./J.O.T.

> In content analysis, safety is in thought, not in numbers; like any method, it can be abused.
>
> John Waite Bowers

It is one thing to perceive misrepresentation, bias, cultural skewedness, distortion, on the television screen and quite another to document that perception. The technique available for such work is content analysis, a methodology with a long tradition and an equally long history of criticism. In order to illustrate the difficulties of applying content analysis to television, specifically to delineate systematic traits in the representation of particular groups, we shall examine an extensive (and expensive) recent study of the image of businessmen on the screen, place the techniques used (and abused) in that study in the context of the more academic tradition of content analysis, and offer some suggestions as to how such techniques might be developed for the purposes of determining the image of labor on American television.

I

Crooks, Conmen and Clowns: Businessmen in T V *Entertainment* is a study of prime-time television in which a sample of two hundred shows was made.[1] A number of characters within these programs were identified as 'working in a business-related occupation' and coded as businessmen. The characters' actions were then determined as being business, personal, or a combination of the two. This categorization gave a context to any action taken by the character. The characters were classified according to their occupations into five groups:

1. the heads of big businesses,
2. managers and executives,
3. owners of small businesses,
4. salespersonnel, and
5. infrequent portrayals of other types of businessmen.

On occasions when the programs indicated overtly by reference, setting, or props the economic status of the character, this too was noted. Also marked was the television network on which the characters appeared and whether they were either a continuing major or minor figure in the series or just a 'one shot'.[2]

The main work of the study was to categorise the actions taken by this group of characters as being either positive, negative, or neutral. Positive actions were coded into three subcategories: charitable/philanthropic, sympathetic/helpful, or those which contribute to the larger society in an economically helpful way. Negative actions were encompassed by illegal behavior, malevolent acts, foolish acts, and greedy or self-centred actions. Finally, 'neutrally coded businessmen are identified as businessmen but have no discernible positive or negative function'.[3]

Eighty-eight of the 200 programs analysed yielded characters definable as 'businessmen'. Of the 118 characters so identified, 46 per cent were major continuing characters, 12 per cent minor continuing characters, and 42 per cent one-shots. Twenty-four per cent were heads of large corporations, 14 per cent were executives and managers, 40 per cent owned small businesses, and 9 per cent were salespeople. Thirteen per cent of the characters represented all other businessmen. Economically, 80 per cent of this population could be identified as either upper ('very rich')[4] or middle-class in a ration of three to two.

Analysing the behavior of these characters revealed that overwhelmingly they acted positively in the realm of personal rather than business relations. In fact, 94 per cent of all positive actions involved 'interpersonal help or sympathy, while only 3 per cent concern charitable activities, and another 3 per cent involve socially productive behavior'.[5]

(There were in fact 29 positive actions in all, and the 3 per cent figures both refer to single incidents in a single segment of *Hart to Hart*.) This positive group of actions, however, was only one-quarter of those taken by the characters. A further 8 per cent were classified as neutral, and 67 per cent of the actions noted were negative. This last percentage involved 43 per cent illegal acts, 13 per cent malevolent acts, 24 per cent foolish acts, and 20 per cent greedy acts.

The study notes that the pattern of positive and negative acts was maldistributed across the classification of characters by appearance. An overwhelming percentage – 84 per cent of the one-shot business figures – were involved in negative actions. Major regular series figures achieved greater equilibrium, behaving negatively 52 per cent of the time and positively 43 per cent of the time. Within the negative behavior category, one-shot characters were engaged in illegal (as opposed to malevolent, foolish, or greedy) acts 72 per cent of the time. Major continuing characters, on the other hand, tended to be foolish (55 per cent) rather than illegal (11 per cent) when behaving negatively.

The results of the positive–negative analysis were equally maldistributed across the occupational categories. It was found that the heads of big businesses, who were never foolish, behaved illegally in exactly three-quarters of the actions noted. Such characters were generally found to be behaving negatively (71 per cent) as against positively (29 per cent). This leads to the most salient conclusion of *Crooks, Conmen and Clowns*:

Fully three-quarters of those corporate leaders portrayed in a negative light engage in illegal activity. . . . *Over half of all business leaders on these prime time shows (15 of 28 characters) are portrayed as criminals.* [italics in original][6]

If this finding is familiar, it is because it was placed before the public in a series of op-ed public series advertisements late in 1981 by United Technologies, Kaiser Aluminium, and Mobil Oil, among others. Of course, for the purposes of the advertising copywriter, the sociological cast of the work was simplified. The finding quoted above, for instance, became (in the words of the 'executive summary' thoughtfully provided in *Crooks, Conmen and Clowns* for those too busy to read the entire thirty-eight pages):

The majority of characters who run big business are portrayed as criminals.[7]

It might be thought that such media amplification clearly distinguishes the work of the Media Institute (the publisher of *Crooks, Conmen and Clowns*) from the normal practice of social science. But although most sociology receives nowhere near so extensive a press, such is not the case. Indeed the findings of the Institute are suitable for amplification by exactly the measure that the work conforms to the normal practices of content analysis. As it itself points out:

The purpose of the Media Institute's study is not to render moral judgements or dictate how businessmen should be portrayed on television. Rather, it is concerned with systematically investigating how businessmen appear in television entertainment by using a content analysis system. ... The Institute is simply explaining, in a systematic fashion, what viewers see when presented with Hollywood's version of businessmen.[8]

All the advertisements relied on the findings as facts, as the proof of a case. Such proof is deemed to emerge, then, from 'the objective, systematic and quantative description of the manifest content of communication' (to quote the classic definition of the function and purpose of content analysis)[9] which the Media Institute provided. The sociological quality of the work validates its methods and conclusions.

The effects of this sociological strategy are two-fold. First, the arguments as to systematic misrepresentation of the business world are placed on a level above the simple self-serving claims of opinion presumably to the point at which broadcasters, always adept at ignoring complaints other than libel, will be forced to take notice and modify their output. The second effect reinforces the first. The chief advertising officer of at least one of the above companies has stated that, because of the report, he will not place his company's advertising dollars in hostile television program environments.[10] Such is the power of positivism in the culture. Although *Crooks, Conmen and Clowns*, as we shall now show, is methodologically extremely poor, it is not thereby ruled out of court – unfortunately. Much legitimate academic work in the content analysis tradition is little better.

In order to count content it is basically necessary to formulate an hypothesis, select a sample, generate categories, encode the sample according to the categories, tabulate the encoding, and reach conclusions.[11] Two major problems are involved in such work, and the Media Institute has surmounted neither. The first of these is in the generation of categories.

Content analysis stands or falls by its categories. ... Since the categories contain the substance of the investigation, a content analysis can be no better than its system of categories.[12]

Crooks, Conmen and Clowns brings an insouciance to this difficult task. 'The Institute's content analysis system uses standard coding categories ...'.[13] Unfortunately, beyond standardised computing procedures and computer dictionaries (none of which is cited and none of which seems readily able to encompass the image of businessmen), no such coding categories exist. The Media Institute therefore created *a priori* categories. The targeted group of characters was defined as follows:

A character is defined as a businessman if he is identified in a business-related occupation, either through information he or another character supplies or through the televised work setting.[14]

Here the problem of establishing criteria whereby a 'business-related occupation' can be determined is totally ignored. This vagueness is then compounded because the Media Institute is not concerned with workers except, it would seem, by implicit contrast to business-related occupations. Behind this confusion, it might seem, lies a vulgar Marxist notion involving the employment or supervision of labor as a crucial criterion. Thus, business-related occupations seem to include the owner and sales director of *WKRP in Cincinnati* but not, it is to be presumed, the disc jockeys or the receptionist. The study does not state whether or not the station's manager is in a business-related occupation. Similarly the newspaper owner in *Lou Grant* is included, but the categorization of the other levels of management is left vague. One assumes that the reporters and photographers, as employees without supervisory roles, are not in business-related occupations. (Printers and other technical workers, it should be noted, seldom appear in *Lou Grant*. The paper is produced automatically, by reporter-operated video display units.)[15]

Given the fairly arbitrary class of 'businessmen', it is not surprising that the subcategories (owner of large business, small business, and so on) are equally flawed. Louie, the obnoxious dispatcher in *Taxi*, is a businessman in the 'executive or managerial' subcategory. Stockbrokers, however, are not executives or managers but come within the residual fifth category. *Archie Bunker* is an owner of a small business, but a rancher apparently is not.

To this must be added the consideration that the initial determination of character was dependent on the entirely haphazard 'information he or another character supplies'. It is entirely possible, given the content analysis system being used, that a stream of unidentified businesspeople constantly did good deeds that went unnoticed by the Media Institute because the characters worked at home and nobody said, 'This is a businessperson.'

The system, such as it was, broke down completely with the determination of economic status:

Distinctions are made among the rich or wealthy businessmen, those who are middle class and those whose economic status is not clearly defined. Although inferences must be made in some cases, it is usually easy to distinguish among such general economic categories. For example, it is reasonable to assume that a businessman who has a chauffeur-driven limousine is wealthy.[16]

In fact, it is not at all easy to distinguish anything of real economic status on television since the coded representation of reality that television uses virtually excludes in fictional areas any realistic representation of anything other than a middle-class milieu. Look only at the palatial apartment inhabited by those two prime-time prime representatives of labor, America's best loved working girls, *Laverne and Shirley*. This is a tradition of gentrification, if you will, dating back through *Life of Riley et al.*, to the tinsel world of Hollywood. It is an essential element in the upbeat optimistic social agenda television sets. It is so dominant that even the authors of *Crooks, Conmen and Clowns* are forced to notice it without understanding the significance of what they report: 'Archie Bunker lives in the same house he owned in his previous incarnation as an archetypical hard-hat.'[17]

Against this dream world background, perhaps only the presence of servants has any social meaning at all. The example of the chauffeur was therefore neatly chosen. But such an indicator is insufficient to justify the statement that 'over half the businessmen portrayed enjoy lifestyles that must be supported by incomes that run well over six figures'. This betrays a literal and subjective reading of the sample comparable to the belief exhibited by some heavy watchers (of daytime soaps, for example) in the fully independent reality of their heroes and heroines.

It should be noted that the above deals with the problems of identifying the targeted group of characters, and it should involve less judgmental work (and less inferential leaps) than the determination of positive, negative, and neutral acts. These last might be the sort of 'standard coding categories' that the Institute had in mind, but that consideration in no way lessens their extremely vexed nature. A series of rhetorical questions serves to define these central terms, culminating thus:

In short in the world of simplistic television plots, do businessmen usually wear the white hats or the black hats.[18]

In the world of simplistic social science, the 'white hat' is divided into three parts (charity, sympathy, and social good) and the 'black hat' into four (illegality, malevolence, foolishness, and greed). The rationale for all this is nowhere given.

Let us take the clearest subcategory, and the only one with any external established codified reference points: illegality. (This subcategory, as we have seen, was highlighted as a major result of the study.) 'Illegal' means against the law, i.e. passing a stopped schoolbus, smoking a joint, buying beer in a New York supermarket on Sunday morning, and so on. An assumption might be made that there was no complete isomorphism between the boundaries of legality in fact and in the television audiences' minds. It could be that one character's illegality will be applauded or admired by the audience. It is a little like the equally clear and commonsensical category of violence. Custard pies and banana skin slips are violent, but they are not necessarily perceived in the same way as fist fights and gun battles. *Crooks, Conmen and Clowns* is based entirely on a strict reading of legality and of malevolence, benevolence, and so on – though what these look like systematically is difficult to know.

The size of the sample and how it was limited are pertinent here. The Media Institute took what it described as a 'conservative' approach to coding:

If a character is defined as a businessman in one episode of a series, but his business connection is not made explicit in another segment, he is coded only in the first episode.[19]

Thus, the already small sample of two hundred programs (four episodes of each series) was reduced to eighty-eight. The unwarranted assumption justifying this reduction is that audiences cannot remember from one week to another who is who in a series, which, if true, would necessitate the restructuring of vast areas of television culture. Every conclusion reached by this study should be prefaced with a remark, to the effect that 'Among characters who said, "I am engaged in a business-related occupation", or who were told, "You are engaged in a business-related occupation", or who were seen in a setting that proclaimed it a place of business-related occupation, X was noted.' This means that single incidents can be transformed into significant percentages, as the 3 per cent figures for charity and social good reveal. It could well be that one illegal parking ticket by one chauffeur-employing character contributes substantially to the 75 per cent figure of illegal acts by this class. One wonders, in fact, what percentage of negative image making, as defined by *Crooks, Conmen and Clowns*, can be laid at the door of J. R. Ewing or other Iago-like embodiments of evil.

Furthermore, it is arguable that any one of the examples given in the study can be read differently, and different inferences drawn from those given with such authority by the Media Institute. Mr Carlson, the owner of *W K R P in Cincinnati*, is given to playing with toys and avoiding work of all kinds, a tendency that could look like very attractive and shrewd behavior to many whose work situation is less privileged. And it cannot be argued that he is simply a fop because, as any regular watcher of the series can attest, the character acts at crucial moments as the final line of support to all the other characters in an approved nineteenth-century paternalistic fashion. The fact that he is a practising Christian whose faith is dealt with sympathetically cannot, we would suggest, mean that he must always be perceived as 'foolish' by the audience. (We assume that the episodes in which Mr Carlson exhibits these traits were episodes in which nobody referred to him as the boss, in which he was not seen in his office, and which were therefore not noted in the study.)

Ambiguities of this sort can be given endlessly. For instance, the distinction drawn between private and business acts offers as an example the private activities of Mrs Pynchon, the newspaper owner in *Lou Grant*, as a volunteer following a fire or as a helper to a reporter in re-establishing a relationship with her mother. The assumption that plot functions can be 'purely personal having nothing to do with their role as businessmen' is applied here. But again the distorted world of the television addict comes to mind, for in what sense does Mrs Pynchon have *any* role function in *Lou Grant* except as the owner of the paper, whether she is seen in that particular circumstance or not? She is only a television character, and she must be defined by her television reality. Thus everything she does, including the two examples given, she does as the head of a large corporation, because she perceives herself as a benevolent capitalist acting in the name of civic duty and employee management – for the good of the Trib. The converse would be equally true. Characters casually referred to as businesspeople, whose prime function in a domestic situation is to act domestically, would continue to so act despite the business allusion.

At this point, the Media Institute enters the world of inferences. The problem of inferences lies behind the problem of establishing categories, and of itself it constitutes the second major area of difficulty in the content analysis tradition. We have already seen how the work of the Media Institute relies heavily on an analysis based on Judeo-Christian ethics to an extent that mocks its statement of purpose, with its denial of intended moral judgment. What is more interesting are the inferences made about the audience. Not only does the Institute believe characters cannot be remembered from week to week, but the authors also hold that the audience cannot distinguish between comedy and drama. As a result, characters like Mrs Pynchon count for the same as comedy characters like Mr Jefferson and Mr Carlson. They assume that the audience makes no distinction as to realism, so that the fantastic worlds of *Fantasy Island*, *Charlie's Angels*, and even *Dallas* are treated as being the same as the realistic worlds of *The White Shadow* or *Lou Grant*. They also assume that the audience cannot tell the past from the present and future. Consequently, characters are to be found creating identical effects regardless of the date of the show's setting. In *Little House on the Prairie*, for example, Mrs Olsen plays a Iago-type character in a stylized and pantomimic fashion, unlike anybody else in the show, and this nineteenth-century figure is said to exemplify 'the greedy businessman [sic].' (There are no businesswomen in *Crooks, Conmen and Clowns*.) The audience is deemed to have identical responses to shows with a contemporary setting like *Barney Miller* and the futuristic *Buck Rogers in the 25th Century*.

Perhaps the best summation of this total failure to infer an understanding of common performance codes is to be found in references to a since-deceased situation comedy series *One in A Million*, in which a Black woman cab driver becomes the head of a large corporation. Despite its title and plot, the show is used by the Media Institute as a general mold for the audience's view of reality in general and for businessmen in particular.

Crooks, Conmen and Clowns seeks to demonstrate the hypothesis that business-men (whatever they might be) are treated badly by prime-time television. We have shown that, whether or not such is the case (and there is some evidence that it could be),[20] *Crooks, Conmen and Clowns* in no way proves it. Since the work is so poor, it might be thought that it could be dismissed more succinctly; but there are two justifications for not so doing. First, the findings have been given such wide and prestigious publicity that they could well enter public consciousness as received facts. Second, our contention is that, despite its manifest faults, *Crooks, Conmen and Clowns* was nevertheless recognisable as sociology and usable as an example of content analysis in a tradition to which we now turn.

2

The Songs of Zion is a collection of ninety hymns first published by Moravian Pietists in Sweden in 1744 and published again amid controversy in unlicensed editions two and three years later. An orthodox Lutheran subjected this work to analysis and demonstrated that the language of the hymns privileged Jesus at the expense of the Father and the Holy Ghost and that it used un-Biblical, un-Lutheran terms. The Pietists responded with their own content analy-sis, which demonstrated that the words were to be found in the *Bible* and in Luther's writings and that the mentions of Christ had been counted without reference to their context.[21] Echoes of this argument reverberate through the content analysis literature.

The counting of newspaper column inches began nearly a century ago, and each new medium has been subjected to similar scrutiny (with a significant bias against visual material of any kind). Modern content analysis begins in the 1940s with the work of Lasswell and his associates on political 'symbols', defined as terms of the political myth, such as rights, freedom, democracy, and the like, which could then be counted in particular contexts (as in Soviet May Day slogans from 1918–1943).[22] But during the same period this definition was formulated, Cartwright commented:

One of the most serious criticisms that can be made of much of the research employing content analysis is that the 'findings' have no clear significance for either theory or practice. In reviewing the work in this field, one is struck by the number of studies which have been apparently guided by a sheer fascination with counting.[23]

In quoting this excerpt, the authors of *The General Inquirer* state that 'a large proportion of studies bearing the label of content analysis have been mechanical, superficial tabulations of who says how much of what to whom'.[24] They offer a revised definition:

Content analysis is any research technique for making inferences by systematically and objectively identifying specified characteristics within a text.[25]

By making inference central, this definition implicitly denies the validity of Berelson's comment that 'In a great many studies there is no problem of inference at all.'[26] Berelson sees the possibility of 'content analyses in which the description of content itself is a primary objective'. (So, too, does the Media Institute.) But others insist on 'the inferential leaps analysts will make from their descriptions of messages to the antecedents and consequences of those messages'.[27] Without such leaps, one is confronted by simple-minded countings – in television, studies of character behavior for instance – of how many cigarettes are lit, of drinks drunk, or of illicit acts of sex consummated on the daytime soaps. This strand is still prominent in the literature. Inferential leaps compromise 'objective, systematic and quantative description'. It is arguable that they are unavoidable if work of any meaning is to be accomplished.

The General Inquirer introduced computing techniques to content analysis and thus advanced the tradition in the 1960s. But despite the greater awareness of the inference problem, it was still not solved. It is possible to make an ethnomethodological critique of most of the computing dictionaries that have been created. The following is an example:

an investigator concerned with self-image may well be interested in identifying the number of self-references within documents written by different individuals, and so construct a category, S E L F, composed of the following signs: I, me, mine, myself.[28]

Such an investigator might well then infer that all documents of the type designated curricula vitae and the Book of Isaiah were lacking in S E L F.

The difficulties of establishing the relationship between 'intent and content' specifically in the matter of determining sample and categories is matched by the relationship between 'content and effect'.[29] How this later stage can be done systematically and objectively, unless some 'map' of the terrain around the communication is produced, remains largely unanswered. One map-making device has been to apply (where possible) the results of techniques such as semantic differentiation to the content analysis count.[30] As a technique for determining semantic space, it appears to have greater validity for social scientists and statisticians than it does for nonspecialists like broadcasters, to whom it can look like nothing so much as a Pelion atop an Ossa, both composed solely of subjectivities.[31]

It can be seen how close *Crooks, Conmen and Clowns* is to this tradition. The claims of objectivity and systematic analysis, the procedures of sampling and categorisation are all part of content analysis. Not 'all the relevant context' was 'analysed in terms of all the relevant categories' so that unbiased information was not revealed. But does this compare all that badly with the following deliberately eclectic, random (save only for an avoidance of the violence index) and short selection of academic work?

The continued problem of dealing with inferences can be found in most contemporary content analysis. Take as typical an analysis of the 1976 Presidential Election. The traditional judgmental categories of favorable, unfavorable, and neutral are used to categorise news references to the candidates, but nowhere are the meanings or rationale of these terms explained.[32] An interesting example of applied content analysis can be found in *Television Violence and the Adolescent Boy* (a $300,000 study funded by C B S but undertaken for obscure reasons in Britain).[33] As part of this work, which involved extensive interviews with working-class teenage boys, a determination was made as to the violence level of British television programs. This determination was then used to gauge the violent quality of the boys' viewing diet. In this study, 231 separate television programs were rated by ex-members of the B B C's television panel. This panel is a group of the public charged with diary-keeping functions; it is a somewhat narrowly based group in terms of class. The scope of the Panel was further reduced by selecting only 'persons who had been educated to the age of 16 or over – the view being taken that the rating task was intellectually demanding and hence likely to be better done by people with more advanced education behind them'. These people then graded the programs according to thirty-one predetermined dimensions of television violence, which had been created by another panel of thirty schoolteachers. Schoolteachers were chosen for this preliminary task for the following reason:

because of their contacts with children and young people the teachers' concepts of violence were expected to be closer to those of young people generally than might be the case for some other intellectually competent set of judges.[34]

The net result of all this work was that *Match of the Day*, a round-up of soccer games (themselves the stated venue of much teenage violence) that was edited to highlight violent action on the field, was classed as being one grade of violence away from 'not violent at all' on a scale of 0 to 10.[35]

All too often, in the literature, one discovers such things as the following: a group of researchers, having determined that the contents of newspapers could fit within 284 'problem categories' (such as unemployment or crime), states: 'To reduce the complexity of studying the data for illustrative purposes, the 284 problem categories were reduced to 28. The collapsing of content codes was based upon conceptual groupings of categories, but some information was obviously lost.'[36] One can assume that 'conceptual grouping' is what led the Media Institute to 'malevolence, foolishness, social good', and the rest. Here it led to one of the 28 clusters involving 'recession' and 'unemployment' while another contained the category 'labor' (in the sense of management-union relations).[37] The information lost was obviously balanced by the ideology gained.

Our purpose is not to offer a content analysis of the content analysis literature (which would be as superogatory a task as could be envisaged). It is rather to offer some easily obtained evidence to show a continuity between *Crooks, Conmen and Clowns* and academic work. A tradition that includes the content analysis of military and nationalistic illustrations on German stamps from Weimar to the Second World War can easily accommodate the work of the Media Institute.[38]

3

Regrettably, the tradition can equally easily embrace *Television: Corporate America's Game*.[39] The statistical and judgmental work is far sounder than that of the Media Institute, but the Union's careful monitoring has to exist, as does *Crooks, Conmen and Clowns*, in a hostile world, and unlike *Crooks, Conmen and Clowns*, there are no dollars to place the findings of *Television: Corporate America's Game* on every influential op-ed page in the nation. The answer has to be that the positivist tools of content analysis have to be applied to such good purpose that they finally deliver on their promise and compel attention. *Television: Corporate America's Game* is a good beginning, but in the area of dramatic programs its findings can be too easily discussed. 'A network wag pointed out that Shakespeare's plays had more kings than fools,' reported the *TV Guide* in its account of *Television: Corporate America's Game*, thereby discounting all the laborious analysis of occupational prevalence done by the union monitors.[40]

This comment is made without prejudice to the crucial work of sensitising workers to the problem of their television image, which has to be a prime and justifiable function for the I A M and other unions concerned with this issue. Rather what we seek to address is the issue of the usefulness, in a radical sense, of content analysis as a technique. For content analysis remains the only available tool for establishing maps, however faulty, of television's output. The positivist characteristics of content analysis suit the purposes of researchers like those involved in *Crooks, Conmen and Clowns* well enough; so the problem is then how to adapt those techniques so that they lose nothing of their empiricist force and, at the same time, work to explicate the true nature of the picture of social relations that television presents.

As a first step, the willingness to be disengaged that some academics exhibit as a badge of purity, as it were, must be discarded.

Another wrong reason for content analysis is to prove an accusation. The analyst is already convinced, for example, that television news is 'left' or 'right' biased and to 'prove' it produces an empirical study.[41]

The willing self-emasculation implied here unpacks as an injunction to set only hypotheses that are irrelevant. A favorite one in this area is to plot network differentiation when their homogeneity is what is most socially significant.[42] What if the analyst has an hypothesis that television news (or indeed any other part of the output) is producing social meanings hostile to any one group of the population, labor, say. There is no reason why a researcher with such a pertinent hypothesis (once 'hostile' is satisfactorily determined) should be 'already convinced' of its validity, any more than a researcher who believes A B C, more than its rivals, favors beef over lamb, is therefore the embodiment of scientific detachment.

Having then discarded this ideologically charged neutral social science stance in favor of a commitment to relevance, which in no way impinges on the independent validity of one's hypotheses or on the rigor of one's empiricism, it is possible to delineate – at least in a preliminary way – some features of this critical content analysis of television.

First, all the relevant contexts must be studied in terms of all the relevant categories. This requirement means that the traditional justifications for reducing samples – limiting the area to be studied or any other abridgement of work, however soundly argued for methodologically – cannot be accepted. In effect, findings must be based on a sufficiently large body of output – a whole season of a dramatic series or a period of months for news broadcasting – so that the true regularities of ideological production can be described without the distortions of particular news incidents or dramatic episodes skewing the results.

Second, inferences as to intent should be kept to a minimum. Categories should therefore not be helped into life by 'conceptual groupings' and the like. Much television production is formulaic, and it is possible to isolate production points or patterns similar to the 'desks' of a newspaper or the limited 'roles' in the *comedia dell'arte* or early grand opera. Such an ethnomethodological procedure capitalises on whatever explicit manifestations of intent are contained organisationally in the production process. If categories are of this sort, rather than those created however painstakingly on *a priori* basis, the resultant analysis is likely to mesh with the data of the sample in a more self-evident and relevant way. Of course, by this procedure one is in danger of blindly accepting the preferred professional readings and ideology of the broadcasters, which are encoded in these production points and patterns. But *a priori* categorisation systems are in practice just as likely to fall into this trap. Television is a manufactured artifact, and its processes of production relate to the patterns and practices that exist inside the industry, not to some abstract analytic.

Third, inferences as to effects should be predicated on the existence of other 'maps' or accounts of the phenomena in hand, or on linguistic or other semiological techniques that minimize the excesses of positivism. What is proposed is a relativism that clothes the analyst in something more substantial than assertions that the research is simply explaining, in a systematic fashion, what viewers see. Critical television content analysis should make its inferences on the basis of comparison between television's structurings of the same reality. This much done, the importance of the researchers' own ideological position is reduced, as is also their reliance on conceptions like positive, negative, neutral, or the Protestant work ethic.

[. . .]

The crucial work in critical content analysis must be in the development of hypotheses. It is valuable to demonstrate that newsrooms do not select news items, even within the limitations of normative news practices, according to their stated procedures for making such selections. But it is only valuable because newsrooms do have such stated procedures. In their case, the requirements governing the processes of selection are laid down by law or other regulations. Conversely, it is less valuable to count the population of dramatic programs by occupation, say, because, as 'the network wag' implicitly suggests, there is nothing in our dramatic culture that requires social reality to be reflected in that way. Further, as *Crooks, Conmen and Clowns* haphazardly notes, the presence of a character is no guarantee of his or her treatment.

As specialized academic techniques seep down into more general consciousness, they are more than likely to suffer sea changes which leave them at best travestied and at worst distorted beyond recognition. But it is in the nature of the case that the susceptibility of any given technique to either of these fates is not equal. Some techniques are less able to withstand the descent into common knowledge than others. It is here suggested that content analysis, 'a procedure of deliberate simplification'[43] is peculiarly fraught in this regard. Its debasement, it can be argued, is in-built as it were, and, as classically practised even in the hands of the most skilled sociological exponent, it it unlikely to yield the 'objective, systematic and quantative description of the manifest content of communication' that it promises.

The objective, systematic and quantative description of communication, certainly of mass communication and especially of television, is nevertheless a thing to be sought after. If we cannot have such a description of television's content, then how, in any real sense, can we know what it is? And how can we plot its effects on audiences, or the uses and gratifications that such audiences have in viewing it? Or, finally, how can we understand the processes of production without knowing what is produced?

Content analysis is the logical center of broadcasting research, and that, in terms of volume and effect, it has not been so is a clear measure of its limitations hitherto. But if the academy fails to provide a 'map' of television content, it is difficult to see how effective social requirements can be generated for broadcasting. It is no surprise that broadcasters take such little cognizance of their constituents, for they can defend their output against all comers. Without the 'map', no case can be sustained as to any kind of cultural skewedness except on the basis of one-off examples of misrepresentation or libel (which are not the norm). And if no case can be made, then there is none to answer.

There is a widespread perception that television is seriously misrepresenting the society of which it is a part, with implied damage to the social fabric. Almost any group will from time to time voice concerns similar to those contained in *Crooks, Conmen and Clowns*. For instance, it was recently reported that farmers in Omaha believed the television image made 'farmers look slow-witted, straw-chewing, full-time coffee drinkers' who all 'like country music' and who have 'low to average intelligence'.[44] Often broadcasters will take comfort from the contradictory nature of such perceptions and argue that this is proof enough of their impartiality, accuracy, or what you will – as if two wrongs did indeed make a right.[45]

The function of content analysis within critical communications studies is therefore clear. It is to provide an account of the content of television and other media output that can be used to raise consciousness as to the nature of the output, as well as to demonstrate the underlying ideology governing its production.

Notes

1 L. J. Theberge, *Crooks, Conmen and Clowns: Businessmen in TV Entertainment* (Washington, D.C.: The Media Institute, 1981).

2 Theberge, p. 18.

3 Theberge, p. 6.

4 Theberge, p. 11.

5 Theberge, p. 15.

6 Theberge, p. 23.

7 Theberge, p. ix.

8 Theberge, p. 1.

9 B. Berelson, *Content Analysis in Communications Research* (Glencoe, IL: The Free Press of Glencoe, 1952), p. 18.

10 M. Pollan, 'The businessman on the box', *Channels* vol. 1 no. 4 (1981), p. 47.

11 J. Bowers, 'Content Analysis', in P. Emmert and W. D. Brooks (eds.), *Methods of Research in Communications* (New York: Houghton Mifflin, 1970), p. 293.

12 Berelson, *Content Analysis*, p. 147.

13 Theberge, p. 3.

14 Ibid.

15 The absence of workers in *Lou Grant* has regrettably not been noticed by the Union Media Monitoring Project where the presence of unionized reporters is generously praised.

16 Theberge, p. 15.

17 Theberge, p. 12.

18 Theberge, p. 13.

19 Theberge, p. 3.

20 Analysis of how heavy viewers regard society undertaken at the Annenberg School suggests that such persons, although in general favorably inclined to institutions, nevertheless distrust business *and* science. (Personal communication.) It was also found that 'of the three most common professional types portrayed on television, it was the businessman whose image was the blackest'. (Pollan, 'The businessman on the box'.)

21 K. Dovring, 'Quantitative semantics in 18th century Sweden', *Public Opinion Quarterly*, vol. 18 no. 4 (1954), p. 393.

22 H. D. Lasswell, *Language of Politics: Studies in Quantitative Semantics*, rev. ed. (Cambridge: MIT Press, 1965).

23 D. Cartwright, 'Analysis of qualitative material', in L. Festinger and D. Katz (eds.), *Research Methods in the Behavioral Sciences* (New York: Holt, Rinehart and Winston, 1953), p. 24.

24 P. Stone, *The General Inquirer: A Computer Approach to Content Analysis* (Cambridge: MIT Press, 1966), p. 5.

25 Ibid.

26 B. Berelson, 'Content analysis', in G. Lindzey, *Handbook of Social Science* vol. 1 (Reading: Addison-Wesley, 1954), p. 516.

27 Bowers, p. 291.

28 Stone, p. 134.

29 See Berelson, *Content Analysis* (1952) and 'Content analysis' (1952).

30 C. E. Osgood, *The Measurement of Meaning* (Urbana: University of Illinois Press, 1957).

31 A television debate in Britain in October of 1975 had the then editor of BBC television news

simply denying that 'militant' had any negative connotations not solely placed there by the academic he was debating. See B. Winston, 'Making the news', *The Listener*, 23 October 1975.

32 L. Lichty and G. Bailey, 'Reading the wind: Reflections on content analysis of broadcast news', in W. Adams and F. Schreibman (eds.), *Television Network News: Issues in Content Research* (Washington, D.C.: George Washington University, School of Public and International Affairs, 1978), p. 118.

33 W. Belson, *Television Violence and the Adolescent Boy* (Farnborough, England: Saxon House, 1978), p. 110.

34 Belson, p. 102.

35 Belson, p. 109.

36 S. Greendale and E. Fredin, 'Exploring the structures of national issues: Newspaper content and reader perception', in P. Hirsch, P. Miller, F. Kline (eds.), *Strategies for Communication Research* vol. 6 (Beverly Hills: Sage, 1977), p. 171.

37 Greendale and Fredin, p. 177.

38 P. Warchol, 'Stamp illustrations and militarism in Nazi Germany' cited in G. Gerbner (ed.), *The Analysis of Communication Research* (New York: John Wiley, 1969), p. 321.

39 Union Media Monitoring Project, *Television: Corporate America's Game*, n.d.

40 Union Media Monitoring Project, p. 8; *TV Guide*, 19 December 1981, p. A2.

41 Lichty and Bailey, p. 112.

42 Many studies, including *Crooks, Conmen and Clowns* and *Television: Corporate America's Game*, do network breakdowns. But more pertinently see R. Frank, *Message Dimensions of Television News* (Lexington, MA: Lexington Books, 1973), where 'The only rudimentary hypothesis is a postulated variance among the three network news broadcasts, which the analysis does substantiate, but why this is important or even interesting is not explained.' (D. Paletz and R. Pearson, 'The way you look tonight: A critique of television news criticism', in Adams and Schreibman op. cit., p. 75). The findings of the Glasgow Group would suggest that the differences noted by Frank could be attributed to different organizational deployments of reportorial resources rather than meaningful ideological differences between the networks. (Glasgow University Media Group, *Bad News* (London: Routledge & Kegan Paul, 1976), p. 236).

43 Lasswell, *Language of Politics*.

44 *Variety*, 20 January 1982, p. 43.

45 See for instance the juxtapositioning of reports on *Crooks, Conmen and Clowns* and *Television: Corporate America's Game* in Pollan, 'The businessman on the box'.

V
Sex and Address in 'Dynasty'

MARK FINCH

From *Screen* vol. 27 no. 6 (November–December 1986)

Mark Finch provides here an account of some of the ways in which gay men in the U K, as in the U S A, have been able to have some fun with one of the great 80s international television phenomena, *Dynasty*. His essay is rich in detail, both in evoking the weird and wonderful contents of the serial and in documenting its relationships to other cultural artefacts, from Joan Collins' autobiography to the 1984 Hippodrome *Dallas* and *Dynasty* Ball. But underpinning all this is a distinction between Liberal Gay Discourse (itself the product of an reconciliatory overlap between 'traditional gay culture' and 'radical gay culture', made possible by the latter's cultural-political successes) and Camp Discourse.

Liberal Gay Discourse seeks for gay people, as for any other group, the liberty and equality promised by Enlightenment ethics. It does so, not necessarily solemnly, but *seriously*. Camp Discourse, on the other hand, brings together a range of seriousness-subverting devices; while these need not be oppositional (and obviously will run into a degree of self-contradictoriness if they present themselves as *seriously* oppositional), the raw material which they invert, parody, deflate is that of Mainstream Seriousness, the seriousness of patriarchal, heterosexual values for instance. Finch sees *Dynasty* as answering to the demands of Liberal Gay Discourse to a real, if limited, extent; but it is precisely at one of those limits, the series' commitment to flamboyantly unserious narrative and characterisation, that Camp Discourse emerges as a second, and perhaps more convivial, focus for gay viewing pleasure.

It is impossible to read Finch's essay – whatever one thinks about *Dynasty* – without being impressed by the complexity of the phenomena it addresses. Against the classic picture of the work of art as one in which the text, embodying the unitary intention of the artist, determines a meaning bringing together audience-members into a single Ideal Reading, we have here a text produced collectively, facing a set of 'many different social groups', the internal identity of *each* of which is maintained under great and contradictory pressures.

M.A./J.O.T.

Gay culture means something more specific than it pretends: a discursive system developed out of a metropolitan, white, middle-class and male gay community. Gay culture speaks from and to this position; it describes a socially-defined audience and an attendant cluster of texts. Derek Cohen and Richard Dyer distinguish four key roles for culture in constituting an audience: as identity, knowledge, propaganda, pleasure. Thus culture

has a role that necessarily precedes any self-conscious political movement. Works of art express, define and mould experience and ideas, and in the process make them visible and available.[1]

In other words, gay culture is the prerequisite of political formation; it admits to our existence, interprets that fact in relation to the rest of the world, and provides us with pleasure in the process. Cohen and Dyer write about traditional and radical gay culture, and the consequent result of their collision. Traditional gay culture is neither necessarily produced by nor addressed to gay people: it is high straight culture or showbiz, and always an identification with the 'feminine': *Madame Butterfly*, Judy Garland and E.M. Forster. Radical gay culture is clearly allied to the expansion of gay liberation and women's movement, and sets up new terms of difference in, for example, *Word Is Out*, *Fag Rag* and Gay Sweatshop's plays. The overlap has resulted in a new 'gay mainstream culture, operating in neither the alternative modes of the radical gay culture nor the subcultural language of the traditional'.[2] But Cohen and Dyer hesitate to describe, or confuse, the distillation of gay discourse into mainstream culture. Whereas traditional gay culture historically involves a grabbing at elements in straight culture, the latter now self-consciously claws back gay cultural terrain. It is no longer helpful to describe male pin-ups and coffee table books on camp in terms of a distinction between gay and straight culture; what has to be unravelled is the text's exact investment in either social group. What has the incorporation of gay discourse meant for contemporary mainstream texts? The weekly television serial *Dynasty*, 'seen on one hundred networks throughout the free world',[3] represents a significant moment in this recuperative strategy, when the (ostensibly) most-watched mass media text becomes the latest addition to British and North American gay culture.[4]

Address (1): Form and Gender

It is a well-known fact that *Dynasty* makes more American women happy than any other show on American television. According to the A.C. Nielson Company, the series is consistently the viewing favourite of women aged from 18 to 54.[5]

Like their North American counterparts, British women are assumed, in the absence of gendered demographics, to be pleased with *Dynasty*'s role models for real lives: 'Mature women everywhere have at last found a heroine their own age'.[6] It is this representational terrain, allied to the serial's association with soap opera form, which constitutes the popular assumption that *Dynasty* is more attractive to women than men. But single gendered address is complicated by conflicting contextual determinants.

My husband Richard and I are asked often these days . . . what we think the phenomenal appeal of *Dynasty* is based on. . . . We yearned for something we remembered from the movies we grew up with in the forties: stories where the audience pulled for men and women to fall in love and walk off in the sunset holding hands; stories with characters who dreamed of, pursued, and found their romantic ideal. . . . There seemed to be a renewed need for romance. Perhaps it had never left but was merely neglected in the necessary reevaluation of more complex times. And so we set out to create the ultimate American fantasy family.[7]

Producer Esther Shapiro turns the women's picture into a genre for both genders, by asserting her own married status (see also Aaron and Candy Spelling, producers, and Eileen and Robert Pollock, script-writers) and by forgetting the narrative problems which sustained those romantic texts. Shapiro remembers exactly the part that melodramatic continuous serials can never duplicate: the happy end. Certainly, *Dynasty* hinges upon heterosexual romance, centrally through Blake and Krystle; like the byline for the Perfume 'Forever Krystle', it is a 'Love That Lives Forever'. But if that love is to live forever, if *Dynasty* is to reach its silver anniversary, there must always be a struggle to maintain that love. Romance fiction survives on this struggle, and Shapiro has picked upon a particularly complex example: 'It's the story of Daphne du Maurier's *Rebecca* retold with the wicked first wife still alive and kicking high and hard'.[8] As Alison Light recalls, *Rebecca* is hardly an innocent text. For the unnamed heroine, Max De Winter's first wife presents, originally, an idea of a successful marriage which has room for female sexual desire, and, finally, the failure of this ideal and denial of a unified self. For Light, *Rebecca* is 'the crime behind the scene of Mills and Boon'.[9] Two aspects of her model unravel *Dynasty*'s investment in gender: an unwillingness to read romance fiction as solidly oppressive, and a psychoanalytic frame which allows her to understand the textual construction of gendered subjectivity – a feminine point of view. The first aspect attends to the ambiguity of *Dynasty*'s response. In the serial form's perpetual postponement of closure, Krystle and Blake will always have problems about their relationship. In the first four series, Krystle left Blake four times, once each series; but if we always expect her to return, Blake is constructed with much less certainty. Linda Evans and John Forsythe previously appeared together in an American sitcom, *Bachelor Father*, the former playing the latter's adolescent niece. In *Dynasty*, Blake's role as father takes narrative and visual precedence over his role as husband; and the inflection is very often monstrous, if not incestuous. Forsythe's performance (Blake's mouth curls sarcastically, he moves abruptly, shouts, and 'stares through' characters) compounds a narrative which has him wilfully excluding his second wife in favour of Alexis, or threatening maniacally to keep the family together. In episode 7 he rapes Krystle when he finds she has been using birth control pills, an event that music and camera position register as traumatic. Of course, Blake's violence has been most pronounced with his son, Steven: they fight each other, physically (episodes 12 and 62) and in court (episodes 13, 63 and 64). In *Dynasty*, the struggle to maintain heterosexual romance and the family is articulated through forms of violence, particularly a *mise en scène* and soundtrack that generically codify emotional anguish.

Women's pictures are the only Hollywood texts regularly to explain the world (which becomes the domestic sphere) from an inscribed feminine perspective. Laura Mulvey, arguing from the same position as Light, and against auteurism, describes these melodramas in terms of a model which does not search 'beneath the surface' for authorial irony, but instead finds subversion in the practice of feminine exposition within a masculine cinema: 'Ideological contradiction is the overt main-spring and specific content of melodrama'.[10] Henry Fenwick, in his *Radio Times* column, states a preference for *Dynasty*'s 'fragmented storylines, conspiracies and revelations, disappearances, reappearances, and reversals of fortune' compared to the 'stronger narrative thrust ... more butch storyline' of *Dallas*.[11] Are male viewers all occupying feminine subject positions? Address has to be understood – not in content study, like Ellen Seiter's listing of television melodrama's male-centred stories[12] – but in the negotiation between textual subject place and specta-torial social position.

Address (2): Looking at Men

Clearly, *Dynasty* is a cross-addressed text. A key location of this confusion is in the construction of desirable male bodies, a confusion which becomes coherent in a male gay context.

If *Dynasty*'s women are Cosmo Girls[13] one decade on –

The women of *Dynasty* would have lives and purposes. They would engage men competitively in business and with equal passion in bed. They too would be strong and goal-orientated.[14]

– the serial's men are *Playgirl* pin-ups, with all the problems of diegetic dimensiona-lity that implies. Mark Jennings is the best example, an opportunity for Alexis to declare how 'cute' he looks in tennis shorts. American television censorship reverses traditions of Hollywood cinema; women cannot be naked, but men can be seen in next to nothing. Of course, there are ways in which television can eroticise women, narratively and through editing, but women are differentiated, principally, in *Dynasty*, by costume. The familiar cinematic devices for eroticising women are used for male characters. Jeff, Dex, Adam, Steven and certain guest stars are shown in states of undress, whereas Blake, his lawyer and majordomo are not; the men available for romantic liaisons with characters are also available for *Dynasty*'s audience. This would seem to be a female audience, because undressed men are mostly introduced in the same shot as a female character (as in episode 86, where Sammy-Jo enters the gymnasium to find Adam there, in shorts), and because Steven's periods of homosexuality find him removed from this strategy, as if his gayness takes him away from the realm of desirable men. But an assumption that men can be constructed as sexual spectacle for women, using the same codes that have transformed women into spectacle for men, is a naive one. When Mark steps out of the shower (episode 57), there is a play upon his near-nudity, transformed into total nudity by close-ups which cut off the towel around his waist; this device is 'commented upon' by Alexis' pretence of being nude in his bed, when the camera has shown that the quilt conceals her shoulderless dress. Laura Mulvey's vocabul-ary of fragmentation and fetishisation[15] is appropriate for describing a visual strategy (white towel/tanned skin, disorientating close-ups of Alexis' pale hand on Mark's back and chest) but not, here, for mapping pleasure. It seems to me that the pleasure for female spectators is in seeing men treated like women, rather than the pleasure of seeing nudity in itself: a textual equality to match representations of strong women.

Mulvey's use of pleasure here is psychoanalytically-based; she neither engages with the distinct address of women's genres (though she addresses this in a later article),[16] nor allows for extra-textual construction of the spectator, especially the determination of sexuality. Usually, when women are eroticised in a text, lesbian and heterosexual male spectators are most easily accommodated; the former's transgression is blurred by the fit of conspiring in the eroticisation of heroines. For female heterosexual spectators, a non-masculine position is an impossible one; along with gay men, they have to work to convert the hero's actions into spectacle. But women are not trained to objectify bodies as men are,[17] which implies that *Dynasty*'s codification of men along a *Playgirl/Cosmopolitan* discourse enables a gay erotic gaze at men through the relay of a woman's look.

A further problem with Mulvey's account is whether it is applicable to television at all, a medium which 'engages the look and the glance rather than the gaze'.[18] Yet the system of spectacle is something *Dynasty* takes from cinema, even if, in a hierarchy of erotic pleasure, the gay male spectator who occupies a culturally-constituted feminine position is perhaps the only one to make the system work. In the same way, gay discourse 'makes sense' of aspects uncontainable within a dominant reading – like wit and representations of the male body – at the same time as *Dynasty* struggles to recuperate homosexuality.

By 'wit' I do not mean to ascribe a textual self-consciousness to *Dynasty*'s makers; I am interested in the conditions of its manifestation, and how it informs popular readings. Wit is primarily evident in dialogue, but in *Dynasty*, music is of more importance than in other genre serials. A musical narrative is constructed for the events leading to Fallon's car crash (episode 86), mixing elements of a familiar 'love theme', unusual (but easily understood) screeching strings, carousel music (referring back to episode 82), *Dynasty*'s frequent fast-paced dramatic theme, and ending on a repeated echo of her scream, teasingly over a black screen. For *Dynasty*'s regular viewers, this soundtrack makes sense without an accompanying image; together, they amount to a circuit of certainty about what is happening. Music sometimes makes the image ironic. An establishing shot of the mansion, from an unfamiliar angle (west wing in long shot, through trees) is coupled with an instrumental version of Michael Jackson's 'Thriller' – which turns out to be diegetically justified by Sammy-Jo's use of personal hi-fi (episode 85). And Sammy-Jo's seductions, of which there are two in episode 86, are underscored by a parodic jazz theme, as men declare (through lustful expressions and dialogue) their desire for her; that is to say, it's all an act. Dialogue is more frequently witty, but this is most often interpretable as characterisation, contained within conventions of mimetic drama: yet there are moments which sustain an uncertainty about *Dynasty*'s project, especially in a play upon viewer's knowledge of a diegetic history (Alexis often retorts, 'but that's all in the past!', as in episode 82), other serials (especially *Dallas*), and the actors' futures.

An example of the latter unfolded when Pamela Sue Martin left the series. For ten episodes before the season's end we were allowed to speculate on how her character, Fallon, would disappear, almost each one offering a different reason. She becomes engaged to Peter (episode 76) and they plan a long honeymoon. Thirty minutes later, Peter has deserted, and Fallon is knocked down by a drunk driver. She isn't dead though, just paralysed (episode 77). Fallon completely recovers, only to suffer sudden blackouts (episode 79). Her doctor tells her it isn't a brain tumour, there is no danger (episode 81). Happy at last, Fallon accepts Jeff's proposal, but in the midst of her wedding she is seized with another migraine, drives away and collides with a truck (episode 86). That is still not the end: in the following series she is still alive (episode 87), and Jeff interviews someone who gave her a lift after the accident (episode 88); he discovers that she eloped with Peter after all (episode 89), only to be killed in a plane crash (episode 90). This playfulness is sealed when the female corpse cannot be positively identified, leaving a way for continued involvement, although Pamela Sue Martin has retired. The text flirts with our knowledge, prolonging the pleasure of speculation beyond the conventions of British soap opera and other melodramas (compare the death of Pam's fiancé in *Dallas*, drawn-out by that serial's standards, yet only involving an incurable disease and a plane crash).

Of course, the play upon Pamela Sue Martin's departure is partly determined by Fallon's immense structural importance as a central character (the exits of Tracy and Kirby, in episodes 85 and 86, are far less elaborate). But it is as if the text takes this opportunity to be witty about conventions of television melodrama. A similar strategy announces the change of actor who plays Steven, and shows how this is constructed by many formal aspects. The play around Fallon prioritises the part of plot development, melodrama's characteristically sudden narrative transformations. Steven's reappearance is primarily invested in visual codes. Before the accident, he is filmed from behind, in silhouette; as the camera moves to a frontal shot, he turns his head away, so we just miss seeing his (new) face (episode 44). This strategy is not to disguise the new actor, but declares the opposite by acknowledging that we are curious to see him. For a further six episodes he is filmed in full-face bandages, and the opening credit sequence refuses to name Jack Coleman (which would mean picturing him). The bandages come off (episode 50) and the camera looks over Steven's shoulder, but cannot see his reflection in the mirror he holds; finally, the camera pulls back and Steven stands to face us. *Dallas* has shown how the replacement of actors in order to continue with the same character can be constructed without explanation and without play. Viewers are not confused, of course, but they are not given any pleasure in the actual change: it is quickly asserted. *Dynasty* allows badinage, articulated textually and in conjunction with the special conditions of media gossip that the transatlantic time-lag facilitates.

Liberal Gay Discourse (I): The Ordinary and Individual Homosexual

Dynasty is the site of competing discourses, two of which construct opposed homosexualities; these are the textual articulations of camp, and of the modern gay movement – or liberal gay discourse. Whereas with straight readings of *Dynasty* there is an overwhelming amount of popular documentation, the status of the British gay community allows little access to the same machinery, so that what evidence there is of *Dynasty*'s importance exists primarily in the unrecorded gestures and dialogue of gay men. Within this terrain, there is scant evidence that the liberal discourse has been picked up, which suggests that it is not addressed to gay people at all.

Richard and Esther Shapiro are award-winning writers of 'social issue' television movies for P B S: *Sarah T, Portrait of an Alcoholic* (1975), *Intimate Strangers* and *The Cracker Factory*, about wife-beating and insanity (both 1979). Their liberal project is most clear in statements about *Dynasty*:

> If I had wanted to write a story from the point of view of a homosexual, there is no way that a mass audience would have taken it. But by using one ninth of the show to deal with Steven . . . over a number of years, I can deal with that thing, and that will become familiar to an American audience, without having to beat everybody over the head and say 'this is socially significant'.[19]

Textually, this ambition translates into a notion of balance, informed by the message of the gay movement to straight America. Specifically, this is the gay movement at its most consumerist and acceptable after Stonewall (1968) but before A I D S (1980), and its message is that we are individuals, just like you.

Blake	Steven, I'm about as Freudian as you could hope for in a capitalistic exploiter of the working classes. When I'm not busy grinding the faces of the poor, I even read a little. I understand about sublimation. I understand how you could try to hide sexual dysfunction behind hostility toward a father. I – I'm even prepared to say that I could find a little homosexual experimentation . . . acceptable – just as long as you didn't bring it home with you. Don't you see, son, I'm offering you a chance to straighten yourself out?
Steven	Straighten myself out? I'm not sure I know what that means. I'm not sure I could if I wanted to. And I'm not sure I want to.
Blake (sarcastic)	Of course! I forgot the American Psychiatric Association has decided that it's no longer a disease. That's too bad. I could have endowed a foundation – the Steven Carrington Institute for the Treatment and Study of Faggotry. (angry) Now if you'll excuse me, I've got to go and get married.

This exchange, from episode 2, establishes some of the signifiers of the liberal discourse: the invocation of psychoanalysis, Steven's tentative assertiveness, the dissemination of 'facts' about homosexuality (it's not a disease). Conversely, the liberal project is upset by the suggestion, however parodic, of a political base to prejudice, and by Blake's sudden change of mood. I want first to expand upon the construction of liberal gay discourse, and then show how it suffers under the weight of contradiction.

One key way in which the text constructs balance is through dialogue. If someone (usually Blake or Sammy-Jo) says 'faggot', someone else in the same episode will say something tolerant (exceptionally, in the above example, Blake says both). Liberal gay discourse is maintained by opposition to these illiberal characters, rather than by residing in a single fixed source. Andrew can say 'There is no evidence that a child raised by a gay will turn out gay himself' (episode 62), not because this is his conventional position but because he is saying it to Blake, the consistent face of homophobia. Other non-regular characters who represent (what the text declares to be) anti-gayness are undermined by *mise en scène* or performance: the social worker who testifies in court that all homosexuals are 'antagonistic and over-emotional' (episode 63) is played by – in *Dynasty*'s terms – a physically unattractive woman. The notation of Blake's homophobia, though, is particularly complex, since he also has to be a credibly charismatic man. At the gay parenting trial (episode 63 and 64) he continually loses his temper and attacks a reporter; yet by episode 69 he has been sufficiently recovered by the text so that his proposal of remarriage will seem irresistable to Krystle.

The point is that what *Dynasty* finds unlikeable is prejudice, not Blake Carrington. With regard to 'social issues' the text constructs two sides, and shows both. In episode 12, Blake is depicted as the drunken master of an old dark house – two uncommon exterior shots coupled with ominous music establish that he is up (light on) late at night. But we have been prepared for this by scenes which illustrate his frustration at his failing marriage. So when he discovers that Steven is entertaining Ted in his bedroom, his anger is justified as 'the last straw'. Through parallel editing, the text offers both sides of what ends in murder. Travelling shots from Blake's point of view are coupled with dialogue which explains that Steven is saying goodbye to Ted, as Krystle has just done to Matthew (previous scene), a sad moment affirmed by a repeated musical theme. Blake's view of the embracing men is understandable, but mistaken. But so is Steven when he cries 'murder'. For the fight, the camera position keeps rapidly returning to the doorway, where Fallon, who is the only one to see what actually happens, stands; finally, we share her view of the incident. Thus, soap opera's subject position, 'a sort of ideal mother . . . who possesses greater wisdom than all her children',[20] becomes one of an ideal juror. 'Do you consider yourself a prejudiced man, Mr Carrington?' asks the defence lawyer (episode 63); prejudice is on trial, not homosexuality or homophobia (a specific form of prejudice). There is an insistence on free speech ('Opinions should be heard') set against the problem of human rights ('I won't change the way I live or my beliefs just to make life easier for Blake Carrington'). Therefore the hearing can only be concluded by Steven's sudden marriage (episode 65), an evasion of the issue of gay parenting which proclaims that the issue never was gay parenting.

The text has greater problems with the appearance of Steven, a central signifier of liberal gay discourse. He is what the gay movement in North America argues gay men are like, and the sort of media representation the movement wishes for. He stands as a realist strategy to avoid stereo-typing, but exactly because *Dynasty*'s form is melodrama and because of the cultural centrality of 'types',[21] this strategy is confounded at almost every stage. According to *The Authorized Biography of the Carringtons*, Steven is 'a study in contradictions'.[22] Steven may conform to the serial's criteria of male attractiveness, but his association with literature and opera – his biography trails references to Ben Jonson, Emily Dickinson, Winston Churchill; his first love token to Claudia is a book; he quotes Robert Louis Stevenson at his wedding (episode 65); he remembers Pavarotti's 'nine high Cs' at the Metropolitan Opera (episode 2) – ties in, however faintly, with a tradition of homosexual aesthetes. Traditional gay culture's equation of the aesthetic with the feminine is also signalled by location and music: Ted and Steven go to a French restaurant, the soundtrack exploits the classical connotations of slow, 'melancholy' violins. Physiognomically, Al Corley contained this melancholy in features best described as 'brooding' (heavy brow, deep-set eyes, protruding lips); he played the part with his head down, and sometimes stammered. Similarly, Steven's past is used to explain his homosexuality; in court (episode 63), Alexis exclaims,

> Blake banished me from my own children! He deprived them of my own guidance, depriving them of everything a mother should give. . . .

At which point, Blake contests:

> Guidance! It was your guidance that did it! You had seven years to turn [Steven] into what he is. I've been fighting to make him into a man ever since!

Constant remarks that Steven is Alexis' favourite child sometimes amount to an incestuous competition with his romantic partners; in episode 66, Alexis phones Steven on his wedding night and has him check her apartment for intruders. A psychoanalytic explanation is thus proposed.

The prolongation of revealing Steven's new face is determined by its importance as the erasure of Al Corley's melancholy features and the substitution of Jack Coleman's far less troubled physiognomy. But this coup for liberal discourse's avoidance of stereotyping is sabotaged by the problem of how to involve Steven in stories that do not comment upon his sexuality. At the moment of recuperating homosexuality within the family, *Dynasty*'s generic requirement – that individuals are characterised by their transgression, like Fallon's promiscuity or Claudia's neurotic obsession, which become the sites for narrative problems – means that homosexuality will always be disruptive to the family's happiness and solidarity.

Liberal Gay Discourse (2): Going off Balance

The most recuperable part of the gay movement's message is that gay people are individuals who happen to be gay. When Steven forces his family to say out loud 'Steven is gay' (episode 34), the text is complexly acknowledging a personal issue that has to be defined socially. *Dynasty*'s liberal discourse is complicated by signifiers of a socially and politically defined homosexuality.

In episode 2, Steven and Claudia have individual liberationist speeches which disrupt (through pace and duration) preparations for Blake and Krystle's wedding. As representatives for what in *Dynasty*'s liberal frame are two easily elided discourses, the women's movement and gay movement, Claudia and Steven are perfect romantic partners. Claudia faces her husband with her sexual dissatisfaction ('What I'm trying to say is that women have sexual fantasies too'); Steven's confession of gayness is equally signalled as courageous, through performance and camera distance. This political alliance is heightened by Steven's accusations that oil companies like his father's have 'sold America out' by not developing alternative energy resources; 'Bolshevik', his sister jokes. Although Steven has lost this leftist inflection by *Dynasty*'s third series, in which he works as a controlling executive at rival Colbyco, episode 58 has Chris, his lawyer, come out as gay: 'Do you want to hear the story of my life? It's the same as yours.' Chris synopsises his gay romance, sham marriage, divorce and loneliness 'in the closet'; 'Are you surprised?' Steven answers for the viewer: 'I don't know. . . . I don't look for these things', but his astonished smile suggests he has been taken by surprise. Similarly, a man appears from out of a crowd in a New York bar and reminds Steven that they were college friends, flirtatiously proposing a dinner date (episode 85). *Dynasty*'s gay characters suggest a shared history and anonymity.

Steven's surprise on both meetings is partly the celebration of a liberal discourse which has, by repressing stereotypes, caught us off guard. At the same time, the text problematises the iconography of homosexuality. *Dynasty* foregrounds television's censorial inability to depict gay intimacy within realist codes by showing, melodramatically, how Steven's gayness is defined by a heterosexual gaze. Any display of affection is seized upon and translated into violence from other (straight) characters. Ted touches Steven's hand in a restaurant and is seen by a co-worker who later starts a fight (episode 5). Blake finds Chris in Steven's apartment and assumes they are lovers, initiating an argument (episode 62). Claudia, from a doorway, sees Luke adjusting Steven's tie and assumes they have made love (episode 94), causing her to sleep with another man. The diegetic spectator is wrong in assuming that Steven is sexually involved with these men. Chris insists that Steven tell his father that they are just friends (episode 63), but Steven will not do so 'on principle'. His implication is that this – Blake's misinterpretation and consequent custody trial – is a test case for all gay people. The catalogue of abrasions to liberal gay discourse suggest opposition to the concept that homosexuality is a personal issue, and opens up an area for gay address – not just in considering how we are identified by straight society, but in asking how we can be banished. This is central to a social group aware of its capacity for self-effacement.

Steven	You know what Oscar Wilde said, 'Work is the curse of the drinking classes'.
Jeff (laughs)	Clever man, Oscar Wilde. Shame he was a homosexual.
Steven	Yeah, kind of makes you long for the good old days when they used to burn them at the stake.
Jeff	You know, I think that's a little rough, Steven – I mean, even for a joke.
Steven (intense)	Oh, you mean 'Gay is Good'? 'Give a Cheer for a Queer'?
Jeff	No, I mean different strokes for different folks.
Steven	But you wouldn't want your brother to marry one?

When Steven moves from duplicity (episode 2) to fierce declaration (episode 34), the text attempts to extinguish his 'gay voice' by sending him to Singapore, or marrying him to Sammy-Jo and Claudia. Ted's death, Steven's facial reconstruction and Chris' inexplicable disappearance foreground the problem of erasing homosexuality from the text. Peter Buckman argues that, when dealing with 'social issues', continuous serials have the virtue of duration;[23] *Dynasty* has, at the time of writing, had 84 episodes in which to discourse homosexuality, compared to a film melodrama like *Making Love* (directed by Arthur Hiller, 1982) or *Lianna* (directed by John Sayles, 1982). This is not to collapse into Shapiro's claim about using 'one ninth of the show', but to argue that in the other eight ninths, when *Dynasty* does not wish to deal with homosexuality and instead passes for straight, gaps and evasions in liberal discourse constitute an enquiry into the conditions of textual acceptance. This is complex enough to shore up a gay address also facilitated by representational problems about the male body; however, camp circulates as a second gay discourse, and has a more successful investment in a male gay audience.

Camp Discourse (1): Cultural Contexts

Introducing *Dynasty*'s third season, *Radio Times* refers to 'dramatic death-dodging and dynamic derring-do';[24] at the same time, the voice-over announcement before *Dynasty* prepares us for something less than serious, actually using the term 'camp' before episode 87. But British newspaper reviews noted *Dynasty*'s camp long before this, with the entrance of Joan Collins in episode 14. The *Guardian, Observer* and *The Times* particularly use the serial to assert critical superiority, inflected differently from the tabloid papers' 'so funny, it's awful'. A two-paragraph review in the *Observer*[25] name-drops Wagner, Strauss, Jean Harlow, Lady Bracknell and Handel. *Dynasty* is employed to signal the reviewer's willingness to camp; this is a class-based discourse, an aspect often disregarded in attempts to define camp. The *Mirror* would never call *Dynasty* camp. The *Observer*'s reviewer also shows how camp is only a game, the end result of Susan Sontag's intellectual reclamation[26] and the mainstreaming of camp in texts like *The Rocky Horror Show* (1972) and *Hi-De-Hi* (1980). Two recent examinations of camp are marketed as chic gift books.[27] Today, 'camp is not necessarily homosexual. Anyone or anything can be camp. But it takes one to know one.'[28] And this is camp's problematic: neither a consistent theoretical perspective, nor a certain group of artefacts.

Arguments for camp's subversiveness, specifically in questioning culturally-constituted gender roles, are themselves questionable:

Being essentially a mere play with given conventional signs, camp simply replaces the signs of 'masculinity' with a parody of the signs of 'femininity' and reinforces existing social definitions of both categories.[29]

Furthermore, the subversive argument is formalist in that it assumes a fixed relation between camp and gay culture, disregarding the historical specificity of that relation. When Richard Dyer defines camp as

a characteristically gay way of handling the values, images and products of the dominant culture through irony, exaggeration, trivialisation, theatricalisation, and an ambivalent making fun of and out of the serious and respectable[30]

he is actually describing pre-gay movement culture. Camp becomes important when it speaks to that historical experience. Bruce Boone,[31] for example, shows how Frank O'Hara's poetry uses camp discourse to oppose language colonised by liberal intellectuals, invested in an address to readers familiar with 1960s urban gay slang. Similarly, if camp is considered subversive in *Dynasty*, it is to the extent that it displaces liberal gay discourse as the site for gay address; central in this operation is Joan Collins/Alexis, who – at specific instances – signifies a different level of enunciation from other figures in the text.

Dynasty's camp is most evident in conversation within the gay community, or in the paraphernalia of the community's bastions, gay clubs – particularly, in Britain, between June and December 1984.[32] The Hippodrome Club (gay for one night each week) held a *Dallas* and *Dynasty* Ball on 16 July 1984, with over sixty look-alike contestants, mostly dressed as Alexis. The same club had been screening scenes from the two serials, giant-size, above the dance floor, since early June. When Krystle and Alexis fought in the lily-pond (episode 58), this was immediately and frequently screened in Heaven, 'Europe's largest gay discotheque'. Norma Lewis' Hi-Energy single, 'Fight for the Single Family', was accompanied by a video which pixillated and repeated images of the pond battle and studio fight (from episode 29), still screened in both clubs. These venues are pivotal in defining British gay culture: they are predominantly used by salaried, white 18–30 year old men.

In the gay press, the Hippodrome Ball was considered one of 1984's 'highlights'; a disco single was released in November, marketed solely through the club and – like the venue itself – seemingly addressed to gay men who had enjoyed the Ball, while also accessible to a lesbian or straight audience. 'Dyna-Dall', 'a dream of *Dallas* and *Dynasty*', peculiarly conflates the two serials, and largely disregards the particular differences of each; it is most successful in reiterating melodrama's compression, inconsistency and (for the spectator) compulsiveness, in a fast beat, multiple percussion and actual lyrics:

> *Dallas* and *Dynasty* playing on my mind you see,
> I'm always thinking of you.
> *Dallas* and *Dynasty*, keep on taking over me,
> Don't want to watch but we do. . . .
>
> *Dallas* and *Dynasty*, you provide the fantasy,
> That's why we're so hooked on you.
> Characters of different size disappear before my eyes,
> And fade right back into view. . . .
>
> Is he with she or she with he?
> I'm so confused it's hard to see
> Just who is living with who.
> And as we try to work it out
> They change the storyline about,
> Now that's not a nice thing to do!

The song goes on to imagine the excesses of mixing characters from each serial. Of course, Hollywood melodrama – and especially the women's picture – has always been the material of camp. 'Dyna-Dall' only articulates this interest as due to narrative incoherence and improbability. But *Dynasty* references the women's picture, like *The Women* (directed by George Cukor, 1939), through formal signifiers like costume (*Dynasty* designer Nolan Miller is 'in love' with Adrian's gowns for Crawford and MGM)[33] and geography (confrontations take place in powder rooms, beauticians', boutiques). Other aspects of *Dynasty*, catalogued under 'excess', amount to 'irony, exaggeration, trivialisation, theatricalisation', which circulate about the figure of Joan Collins/Alexis.

Camp Discourse (2): Alexis, the Enunciator

Of all *Dynasty*'s regular characters, Alexis is most closely matched by the performer's star persona. There are two key signifiers of this image: Britishness and bitchiness. From her work in the 1950s and 60s (especially *Land of the Pharaohs* 1955, *The Opposite Sex* 1956, *Seven Thieves* 1960) Collins acquires the connotations of British Beauty, like Diana Dors. Joan Collins is 'our Joanie'.[34] *Past Imperfect*, her autobiography, and *The Stud* (both 1978) confirm the signifiers of promiscuity and hardness that are deployed in earlier films (again *Land of the Pharaohs* and some of her 1970s horror films). Finally, she is indelibly associated with *The Bitch* (1979), a film which works to problematise that equation. *Dynasty* plays upon this image:

I'm the best thing that *Dynasty* has got. It's because of me that the show became a hit.[35]

There are endless signs which work to sustain 'that bitch'.[36] She need no longer be referred to by name; when Krystle fights back, 'The Bitch is Ditched'.[37] A more innocuous version of this is the perfume, *Scoundrel* – but Joan is a bitch for refusing to join in *Dynasty*'s merchandising campaign, instead promoting a cheaper fragrance than *Forever Krystle*. Endlessly, the comparison is with Linda Evans, the serial's only other performer to be involved in a kind of fit between role and star image. Good-hearted Linda, has 'inner beauty';[38] Joan is hard, exterior. Gay culture responds to this hardness and innuendo: bitch becomes a term of endearment. Bradley and The Boys have recorded a special 'Bitch version' of 'Dyna-Dall': 'Dance, You Evil Witch!'. Collins has played the witch in *Hansel and Gretel* for cable television,[39] and at Heaven's Christmas party an inverted fairy tale pantomime of insipid heroes and vivacious villains was brought to an end by video excerpts from *Dynasty*. Alexis is not far from a Wicked Witch of the West whose actions are directed against the happy monogamous couple – she originally arrived out of nowhere (a narrative surprise) to avenge her gay son's dead lover (episode 13).

Underneath it all, she is a woman capable of great love, whose devotion to her children can result in a fierce protectiveness, which is often misinterpreted as cold brutality. Her toughened and guarded facade is merely armor for a core of vulnerability that lies deep within her.[40]

Shapiro locates a final aspect which conflates role and star, but which works (ostensibly) against signifiers of bitchiness. Collins' daughter was close to death after being hit by a car in 1979:

'No!' I heard myself scream. 'No, no, no!'. . . . This was a nightmare. It must be a nightmare. 'Not my baby, not Katy!' I started to scream and thrash about. All my reason went. I became like an animal. I had no control – just unbearable agony and the frustration of being away from our beloved little girl at this dreadful time.[41]

Like many parts of Collins' autobiography, this corresponds precisely with a scene from *Dynasty*. Fallon is hit by a car, and is in hospital, close to death; episode 78 ends, unusually, not with a new revelation of dramatic incident, but on a shot of Alexis' hysterical grief as she proclaims how much she loves Fallon, and the 'unbearable agony' of not being near her (she has been forbidden to see Fallon). *Dynasty* frequently constructs images of Alexis as an anxious mother.

The Alexis/Joan Collins conflation casts her as an outstanding figure. Rebecca Bailin describes how narrative is always enunciated 'by' a cluster of discourses and that, exceptionally, in *Marnie* (1964), one diegetic character becomes associated with the level of (hegemonic, patriarchal) enunciation.[42] Similarly, Alexis' irony can be read as referring outside the diegesis. This is organised around two of Joan Collins' frequent claims: that she is really an actress who has her mind on better things than *Dynasty*, and that it was she who made the serial the success it is.

The close alliance of star and character biography implies that Collins is not acting, but playing out a role familiar to her. 'Men have used women for centuries. So why shouldn't it be our turn now?' she asks Tracy (episode 84), quoting from her autobiography.[43] And yet, despite the idea that this really is not acting, the way she plays Alexis emphasises performance; she completes her line to Tracy by grandly lighting a cigar. Often, Alexis ends her speeches with a deliberate gesture, like biting into a grape or turning her head away from the character she has been talking to (as in episode 59); these gestures are in excess of the non-naturalist performance melodrama demands. Alexis is at the centre of ambiguity about *Dynasty*'s project, re-cast as her intention: she asks Adam to defend her at the murder trial, and he consequently demands her utter honesty, to which she smilingly inquires (in medium close-up): 'When have I been anything but honest?' (episode 87). Alexis is always plotting. Characters are always reacting to her plots. Whether or not she succeeds, narrative change is brought about – sensationally, in the merger of Colbyco and Denver-Carrington (episodes 50–67) and Blake's bankruptcy (episodes 83–92). Frequently, Alexis is on the telephone to a private detective, discovering what we want to know. (Where is Krystle's first husband? Who was Kirby's mother?) She knows more than other characters. When Mark shouts 'You can't get rid of me', Alexis replies 'Just watch' (episode 84): he is dead in the next scene, although Alexis had nothing to do with it. Her 'knowledge' extends outside the diegesis.

Joan Collins/Alexis' irony is also directed at formal conventions. She is informed of Mark's death and insists, but casually, that it cannot be true: 'I left him only hours ago, and he was very much alive' (episode 84). The joke is that generic and serial conventions have conspired in his death. Equally, Alexis' retort to Dominique's 'Would you say these are the clothes and jewels of a journalist?' (episode 85) is 'Well . . . anything can be rented nowadays', a joke about *Dynasty*'s expansive wardrobe. Of course, there is a fine distinction between irony within and without the diegesis. Other characters have witty dialogue; it is Collins' persona, performance, camera strategy and reactions of other characters which construct the special meaning of her words and gestures. Alexis of all characters comes closest to direct address; she has more lines to deliver as soliloquy. Krystle, Claudia and others are placed in reaction shots to her wit, threats and insults; they are shown to smile more often than look threatened or insulted – in admiration of Alexis' audacity, and also of her role.

I am not claiming that Alexis' irony consistently ruptures the diegesis, nor that the only spectator to understand this is a male gay one. But Alexis' construction (role as enunciator) makes sense of the text's wit, claims it for her own, and this is appreciable from a gay subject position. That Alexis is often allied to the level of enunciation is asserted by those moments when she is without knowledge. In scene four of episode 86, Alexis dares Kirby to shoot her – 'Go ahead, pull the trigger and watch me die' – calling on our knowledge of conventions which disallow Kirby to do exactly that. Yet scene 21 reverses her and our certainty: Alexis is arrested for murder. The police command to 'cuff the lady' enforces the loss of diegetic control.

Conclusion: The Discursive Battleground

According to Umberto Eco, mass media texts are most often closed texts. Unlike the fixed textual relations concealed by high art's seeming ambiguity, closed texts

are in fact open to any possible aberrant decoding. . . . They seem to be structured according to an inflexible project. Unfortunately, the only one not to have been 'inflexibly' planned is the reader.[44]

But Eco does not show how 'aberrant decodings' are facilitated by specific textual strategies; he implies that they are little more than the consequence of perverse readers. Furthermore, Eco's formalism fails to account for the specific investments of mass media texts in both their own media and an inter-textual domain. Janet Wolff finds Eco's model to be entirely relativist: a text can mean whatever the reader wants. Wolff attempts to describe the reader's part in producing meaning without collapsing into relativism:

The way in which the reader engages with the text and constructs meaning is a function of his or her place in ideology and society. . . . The role of the reader is creative but at the same time situated.[45]

A media text has to address itself to many different social groups in order to sustain its mass appeal. *Dynasty*'s contradictions and complexity allow the reader's 'creativity'. Of course, a male gay reading is constructed within the serial's preferred reading, but this is the discourse of a gay movement which inscribes a liberal heterosexual subject position.

While entertainment is responding to needs that are real, at the same time it is also defining and delimiting what constitutes the legitimate needs of people in this society.[46]

The 'legitimate needs' of gay men within gay culture are circulated within an oppositional discourse. Gay culture trains us to be alert to a particular conception of homosexuality which involves signifiers of 'femininity'. 'If there is such a thing as a gay sensibility', argues P.F. Grubb, '. . . it is to be found in a preparedness to find certain sign-material relevant for perception-forming processes related to homosexuality'.[47] Aspects of *Dynasty*'s excess and compromised address cohere as camp discourse, which, through referencing Hollywood's melodramas/women's pictures, touches on camp historical alliance with homosexuality. Camp is what the liberal gay discourse/modern gay movement represses. This does not mean that camp is necessarily radical (any potential for subversion depends on the fixing of a contextual moment, and at least the questioning of its class specificity), but that it does enable Joan Collins/Alexis – in a supreme fit between character and star – sometimes to disrupt the diegesis (by plotting, joking, 'acting') and thus usurp the liberal discourse. The latter is itself insecure in that its notion of balance, avoidance of stereotyping, and affirmation of the individual is splintered by recognition that gayness is a political, collective issue; that definitions of homosexuality must be social; and that gayness keeps returning as potential disruption to the bourgeois family. In other words, when the text wants to pass for straight – turn its balancing act into a vanishing trick – camp discourse, associated with a different level of enunciation, draws out 'tell-tale' gaps and ruptures, just as if (and this was one of the sights at the Hippodrome's *Dallas* and *Dynasty* Ball) Steven Carrington, still in bandages and a dressing gown, had donned a tiara and drop ear-rings.

Mark Finch's guide to Channel 4's 1986 gay cinema season, *In the Pink*, is available for £1.50 in cheque or postal order payable to Channel 4 Television from: In the Pink, PO Box 4000, London W3 6XJ.

Notes

1 Derek Cohen and Richard Dyer, 'The Politics of Gay Culture' in Gay Left Collective (ed.), *Homosexuality, Power and Politics* (London: Alison and Busby, 1980), p. 172.

2 Ibid., p. 184.

3 Esther Shapiro, *The Authorized Biography of the Carringtons* (London: Comet, 1984).

4 Cohen and Dyer also establish the terms of my argument in their emphasis on male gay culture, which has a specificity apart from lesbian culture. As I go on to describe, *Dynasty*'s investment is exclusively in male gay culture. I can find no evidence that *Dynasty* addresses a lesbian audience to the same degree.

5 *Glasgow Herald*, 12 December 1984.

6 *Daily Mail*, 25 August 1984.

7 Shapiro, p. 2.

8 *Radio Times*, 21–7 July 1984.

9 Alison Light, 'Returning to Manderley: Romance Fiction, Female Sexuality and Class', *Feminist Review* no. 16 (Summer 1984), p. 22.

10 Laura Mulvey, 'Notes on Sirk and Melodrama', *Movie* no. 25 (1977), p. 53.

11 *Radio Times*, 15–21 September 1984.

12 Ellen Seiter, 'Men, Sex and Money in Recent Family Melodramas', *Journal of the University Film and Video Association* no. 35/1 (Winter 1983), pp. 17–27.

13 See Charlotte Brunsdon, 'A Subject for the Seventies', *Screen* vol. 23 no. 3–4 (October 1982), pp. 20–9.

14 Shapiro, p. 3.

15 See Laura Mulvey, 'Visual Pleasure and Narrative Cinema', *Screen* vol. 16 no. 3 (Autumn 1975), pp. 6–18.

16 Laura Mulvey, 'Afterthoughts on "Visual Pleasure and Narrative Cinema" inspired by *Duel in the Sun*', *Framework* nos. 15–17 (Summer 1981), pp. 12–15.

17 Rather than justify this argument with 'sociological' evidence (like the preponderance of 'sexual objectification' in the male gay community), I would want to point to textual evidence like *Saturday Night Fever* or *American Gigolo*, that is, films which pose the problem from a masculine perspective: the difficulty, for men, of being objectified.

18 John Ellis, *Visible Fictions* (London: Routledge & Kegan Paul, 1982), p. 128.

19 Esther Shapiro, quoted in the *Sunday Express*, 1984.

20 Tania Modleski, *Loving With a Vengeance: Mass Produced Fantasies for Women* (Hamden, Conn.: Shoe String Press, 1982), p. 92.

21 See Richard Dyer (ed.), *Gays and Film* (London: British Film Institute, 1977), pp. 27–39.

22 Shapiro, p. 73.

23 Peter Buckman, *All For Love* (London: Secker and Warburg, 1984), p. 69.

24 *Radio Times*, 4–11 April 1984.

25 *Observer*, 24 February 1985.

26 Susan Sontag, 'Notes on Camp', *Against Interpretation* (New York: Dell, 1967), pp. 292f.

27 Mark Booth, *Camp* (London: Quartet, 1983) and Philip Core, *Camp: The Lie That Tells the Truth* (London: Plexus, 1984).

28 Core, p. 7.

29 Andrew Britton, 'For Interpretation: Notes Against Camp', *Gay Left* no. 7 (1978), pp. 11–14.

30 Richard Dyer, 'Judy Garland and Gay Men', in *Heavenly Bodies* (London: Macmillan/British Film Institute, 1986).

31 Bruce Boone, 'Gay Language as Political Praxis: The Poetry of Frank O'Hara', *Social Text* vol. 1 no. 1(1982), pp. 59–92.

32 Contemplating the determinants which act upon this lessening of interest would make an interesting aside: I'm not sure that it can be located in actual episodes, but it may have more to do with: a) the BBC's continued promotion of *Dynasty* through Fenwick's column in *Radio Times* and its now settled place in the schedule – i.e. bringing the serial far more visibly into the mainstream; b) the British launch of *Dynasty* merchandising, directed, fundamentally, at wealthy married women; c) the decline in London club attendance and the first wave of media panic about AIDS – i.e. dividing the gay community and eroding opportunities for gay cultural concretisation.

33 Nolan Miller interviewed by Russell Harty, *Harty Goes to Hollywood*, BBC2, 10 August 1984.

34 *Daily Star*, 23 June 1983.

35 Joan Collins in *Nine to Five*, 16 July 1984.

36 *Sunday People*, 27 August 1984.

37 *Sun*, 14 March 1983.

38 *Woman's Own*, 8 December 1984.

39 Joan Collins, *Past Imperfect* rev. ed. (London: W.H. Allen, 1984), p. 303.

40 Shapiro, p. 39.

41 Collins, p. 307.

42 Rebecca Bailin, 'Feminist Readership, Violence, and *Marnie*', *Film Reader* no. 5 (1982), pp. 24–36.

43 Collins, p. 323.

44 Umberto Eco, *The Role of the Reader* (Bloomington: Indiana University Press, 1979), p. 8.

45 Janet Wolff, *The Social Production of Art* (London: Macmillan, 1982), p. 115.

46 Richard Dyer, 'Entertainment and Utopia', *Movie* no. 24 (1976), p. 7.

47 P.F. Grubb, 'You Got It from All Those Books: A Study in Gay Reading', paper delivered at Gay Studies Conference, Amsterdam, 1982.

VI

Parody and Marginality
The Case of Brazilian Cinema

JOÃO LUIZ VIEIRA AND
ROBERT STAM
From *Framework* no. 28 (1985)

With a cinematic history stretching back to the birth of film, Brazilian movies have frequently flourished despite huge economic problems, government censorship and political repression. Similarly, with an internationally ambitious television organisation (TV Globo) which has become the world's fourth largest commercial TV company (after the three USA Networks), Brazil and its culture figures significantly on the world's screens.

Having said that, outside Latin America little is still known about the important strand in the world's history of film which Brazilian cinema offers. This piece, then, by João Luiz Vieira and Robert Stam provides valuable information about a neglected area, offering a theoretically imaginative and stimulating account of the relationship between a fascinating body of films and their containing culture.

The essay provokes further thoughts about the concept of cultural identity, sharing with earlier pieces in this collection an anti-essentialist position in terms of the inevitability of intertextuality in the production of cultural artefacts: 'Since there can be no nostalgic return to pre-colonial purity, no unproblematic recovery of national origins undefiled by alien influences, the artist in the dominated culture cannot ignore the foreign presence but must rather swallow it and recycle it to national ends'.

Drawing in particular on the theoretical writings of Mikhail Bakhtin – a body of work which proved to be increasingly influential in the late 1980s – the authors deploy the concepts of the 'carnivalesque' (ironically appropriate for a culture which enjoys one of the world's largest annual carnivals) and of the parodic to understand both Hollywood cinema in its dominance and the three 'layers' which constitute Brazilian cinema in its 'marginality'. As the authors write: 'Thus, parody stands at the point of convergence of multiple contradictions, serving at times a negative aesthetic based on self-derision and servility, and at other times becoming an instrument of carnivalised revolt against hegemony'.

The result is a politically intriguing aesthetic which could hardly be more different from those predominantly discussed in the other essays in this volume – one which might provide a valuable basis upon which to build alternative film and television making practices in other cultural situations. In the meantime it is to be hoped that a group of films which, in Paul Willemen's words, 'evince a freewheeling attitude towards questions of realism, verisimilitude, historical-temporal conventions within narrative genres . . . within a "popular-commercial" format', are made more easily available around the world.

M.A./J.O.T.

Contemporary critical discourse has shown a remarkable fascination with the concept and practice of marginality, a phenomenon theorised by thinkers as diverse as Bakhtin – in his conception of the carnivalesque; by Foucault – in his historic-theoretical empathy for the mad, the criminal, the 'perverse'; and by Derrida – with his affinity for all that is eccentric, parasitic, all that belonging, so to speak, to the borderline. Our focus here will be on the rôle of a 'marginal' artistic practice – carnivalesque parody – within a 'marginal' context, that of a Third World country. More specifically, we will investigate parodic strategies within commercial as well as avant garde Brazilian cinema, seen as a creative response to its own marginalisation due to hegemonic structures of production, distribution and exhibition. Parody, we shall argue, both reflects these structures and, potentially, affords a means of resistance to them.

While focusing on the specific case of Brazilian parodies, we will also implicitly be advancing a more general argument, hopefully of relevance to other marginal practices, be they third world, feminist, or avant garde. This general argument has to do with the usefulness of the critical categories developed by Mikhail Bakhtin and the Bakhtin Circle for transcending puristic dichotomies and exhausted methodologies. These critical categories include not only the widely disseminated notion of the 'carnivalesque', but also less well-known concepts such as 'polyphony', defined as multiple voices co-existing within the same text, along with more linguistically-oriented tropes such as 'dialogism' and 'heteroglossia'. Unlike many other critical approaches, Bakhtin's thought does not have to be 'stretched' to make room for opposition practices; rather, it has a built-in affinity for the marginal. Artistic texts, for Bakhtin, are the site of conflict between centrifugal and centripetal forces, the meeting place of multiple languages (heteroglossia) competing for ascendancy. Bakhtinian categories, therefore, are appropriate to both metropolitan and peripheral texts, for they are appropriate wherever competing class, racial, or gender discourses scrape against each other within the same text.[1]

We must begin, however, by clarifying our essential terms. By parody, first of all, we refer to a reflexive mode of discourse which renders explicit the processes of intertextuality through distortion, exaggeration, or elaboration of a pre-existing text or body of texts. Bakhtin's re-reading, with Rabelais as point of departure, of the history of modern European literature, showed that what had been considered marginal and eccentric – the parodic sport of Sterne or the overheated polyphonic madness of a Dostoyevsky – was, in fact, the paradigm of a new kind of 'dialogic' literature. Far from being a marginal sub-genre, then, parody can be seen as an ever-present tendency with perennially fecund and paradigmatic importance. But parody has an even more special rôle in a context of asymmetrical arrangements of power. By appropriating an existing discourse but introducing into it an orientation oblique, or even diametrically opposed to that of the original, parody is especially well-suited to the needs of the oppressed and the powerless, precisely because it *assumes* the force of the dominant discourse, only to deploy that force, through a kind of artistic jujitsu, *against* domination. Within a context of hegemony, parody, at its best, becomes a privileged instrument within a struggle for aesthetic and political power.

Parody, for Bakhtin, forms part of the larger universe of the carnivalesque. The carnivalesque represents the transposition into art of the spirit of carnival – popular festivities which offer the people brief entry into a symbolic sphere of utopian freedom. Carnival crowns and uncrowns, it inverts rank and redistributes rôles, turning sense into nonsense according to the 'logic of the turnabout' and of the 'world upside down'. Carnival institutes a ludic relation to official discourses, whether political, ecclesiastical, or literary. Liberatory mechanisms such as the donning of costumes (or *fantasias*, as they are suggestively called in Portuguese) divorce individuals from their ordinary position within the social formation and project them into a playful *communitas*. Bakhtin's theory of carnival arose not only out of his literary studies, but also out of a vital oral culture in some respects marginal to mainstream European culture. Many Latin American literary critics, not surprisingly, have seen the notion of the carnivalesque as a key to the specificity of Latin American cultural production.[2] Since Latin America has been economically, politically and culturally marginalised, its best artists and critics have made this marginalisation, this ironic consciousness of simultaneously belonging to two cultures – one's own and that of the metropolitan centers of power – absolutely central to their work.

The category of carnival has even more special relevance to Brazil, however, in the sense that in carnival there is not only a textual entity but also a dynamic cultural manifestation. While European carnivals have degenerated into the ossified repetition of perennial rituals, carnival in Brazil remains a vibrant, protean cultural expression crystallising a profoundly mestizo and polyphonic culture. Brazilian anthropologist Roberto da Matta describes present-day carnival, in its literal denotation, in terms strikingly reminiscent of those of Bakhtin, as a time of festive laughter and gay relativity, a collective celebration which serves as a means of symbolic resistance on the part of the marginalised majority of Brazilians against internal hegemonies of class, race and gender.[3] Carnival, for da Matta, is the privileged locus of inversion. All those who have been socially marginalised – the poor, the black, the homosexual – take over the symbolic center of the city. The business district, usually synonymous with serious productive labor, becomes the irradiating center of playfulness. Black *favelados* dress up as queens and kings, while men dress as women and women as men. The festival, at least in the central thrust of its symbolic system – we are not suggesting that three days of carnival *literally* overturn class and gender rôles reinforced throughout the year – is profoundly democratic and egalitarian. As a moment of integration and collective catharsis, a profoundly social and interactive form of *jouissance*, carnival offers a transindividual taste of freedom in which costumed revellers play out imaginary rôles corresponding to their most utopian desires.

The carnivalesque, then, forms an especially apt instrument for the investigation of Brazilian cinema, which has always been deeply impregnated by the cultural values associated with carnival. The forms of this carnivalesque presence range from the pro-filmic incorporation of actual carnival activities – a feature of the first 'views' at the turn of the century through Rocha's *Idade da Terra* (Age of the Earth, 1980) and more diffuse allusions via music or costume, to the use of strategies of travesty and inversion unaccompanied by any direct allusion to carnival. The very word 'carnival' figures prominently in the titles of a disproportionate number of Brazilian films, from early views such as *O Carnaval de 1908* (1908 Carnival) through sound-era chanchadas such as *Alô Alô Carnival* (1936) to post-Cinema Novo productions such as *Quando o Carnaval Chegar* (When Carnival Comes, 1971). The *chanchadas*, the musical comedies popular through the 30s, 40s and 50s, were not only released at carnival times but were also designed to promote carnival songs. They were designated, as if in anticipation of a Bakhtinian analysis, *'filmes carnavalescos'* – 'carnivalesque films'. The 70s have witnessed a 'recarnivalisation' of Brazilian cinema, not only as a key trope orienting the film-makers' conception of their own production, but also as a means of renewing contact with the popular audience. Film-maker Carlos Diegues conceived both *Xica da Silva* (1976) and his most recent *Quilombo* (1984) as *'samba-enredos'* (samba-plots), i.e., as structurally analogous to that popular narrative form, combining songs, dances and costumes, called a samba school pageant. The marginal heroes of Fernando Cony Campos' *Ladrões de Cinema* (Cinema Thieves, 1977), meanwhile, steal film-making equipment from American tourists visiting Rio's carnival, and conceive the film they plan to make – concerning an historical rebellion against Portuguese colonialism – as a kind of samba school narration.

Brazilian carnivalesque strategies must be seen within the context of neo-colonial hegemony, i.e., in the light of the central reality of a political and economic dependency that conditions Brazilian cultural production. According to the perspective adopted by 'dependency analysis', a world capitalist system encompasses much of the Third World; countries like Brazil are not 'lagging behind' the advanced industrial countries, but are rather locked into the negative dialectic of a global system which simultaneously generates both development at the center and under-development on the periphery.[4] The consequences of hegemony are particularly visible within the film industry, where the Hollywood film has been a strong presence ever since 1903, when the Casino Nacional, a vaudeville beer-hall in Rio de Janeiro, announced the exclusive engagement of the films of American Biograph and Mutoscope Company. After a brief period of control of its internal market, known to Brazilian film historians as the 'Bela Epoca', or 'Golden Age', Brazilian Cinema lost that control with the arrival of North American distribution firms in Brazil during and after the First World War. During the 20s and 30s, Hollywood consolidated its domination. The 'cinema' came to be equated with one of its specific modes; a 'dialect', that of classical Hollywood fiction film, came to be posited as a universal language. This model was internalised by film-makers (fascinated by the high production values and narrative fluidity of the American film), by exhibitors (who for economic reasons favored the foreign product), by spectators (enthusiastic consumers of imported entertainment), and by that 'third industry', the press (which demonstrated a subtle predisposition toward the foreign film and a less subtle prejudice against the national product).[5]

Carnival and the Chanchada

In the face of foreign domination, the visible presence of Brazilian cinema was guaranteed in the post-sound era only by the incessant production of *chanchadas*, the most popular genre ever produced in Brazil. A derogatory epithet created by hostile mainstream critics, '*chanchada*' refers to a body of films (made between the early 30s and continuing in modified form up to the present) featuring predominantly comic plots interspersed with musical numbers. The *chanchada* was from its inception intimately linked to the world of carnival. The '*Alô, Alô*' in the titles of early *chanchadas* such as *Alô, Alô Brasil* (1935) and *Alô, Alô Carnaval* (1936) – the latter featuring an already famous Carmen Miranda – alludes to the common salutation by radio speakers to carnival revellers. But even those *chanchadas* not marked by the diegetic presence of carnival are still linked to the larger universe of carnival in that they incorporate the social inversions typical of carnival and develop, like carnival itself, an implicit social critique. Many *chanchadas*, for example, aim satirical barbs at the political life and administration of Rio de Janeiro, spoofing galloping inflation and populist politics. Thus, Brazilian culture and popular desire infiltrated the genre; the on-screen presence of marginal characters drawn from daily urban life paralleled the physical incorporation of the urban masses into the movie theaters themselves.

The frequent parodic strategies of the *chanchadas* are premised on the fact of hegemony; they assume that the audience, given the asymmetrical nature of informational exchange between North and South, has already been inundated by North American cultural products. But artistic products are inscribed in a multiform web of mediations which defy simplistic analogy to more conventional commodities, and the Brazilian conjuncture offers an extremely complex situation, not reducible to any mechanical dependency schema, in which assertive national self-pride co-exists with idealisation of the foreign. The *rapports de forces* between idealisation and critique varies from film to film. In some films, Brazilian cinema itself becomes the object of attack, the scapegoat for the incapacity of an underdeveloped country to copy, within the standards dreamed of by both film-maker and public, the powerful technological efficiency of American films. In others, parody becomes a means of subversion of canonised codes. Thus, parody stands at the point of convergence of multiple contradictions, serving at times a negative aesthetic based on self-derision and servility, and at other times becoming an instrument of carnivalised revolt against hegemony.

One *chanchada* especially encapsulates these ambiguities. In 1952, amidst much negative criticism of the *chanchada* and its major producer, the Atlântida Studio, a film appropriately entitled *Carnaval Atlântida* responded to such charges by defending a model of cinema based on sublime debauchery and carnivalesque irony. The subject of *Carnaval Atlântida* is film-making itself and, more specifically, the inappropriateness of Hollywood-style super-productions in Brazil. In *Carnaval Atlântida*, film director Cecilio B. De Milho (Cecil B. de Corn) abandons his plan for an epic super-production of Helen of Troy in the implicit recognition that the conditions of national cinema are not propitious for a serious film on a grand scale. The Hollywood-dictated standards for the genre, with ostentatious sets and the proverbial cast of thousands, were simply not feasible in an under-developed country. Against the ambitious De Milho, other characters argue for a more popular, less lofty 'adaptation' of the story of Helen of Troy, recommending that he discard the proposed epic in favor of a carnival film. De Milho cedes to popular pressure, but insists on the right to make the epic version 'later', i.e. when Brazilian cinema will have acquired the technical means and financial resources to produce such films. For the present, however, Brazilian cinema is presumed capable only of dealing with carnival; Helen of Troy can only appear in carnivalesque guise.

One sequence, in which De Milho explains his conception of *Helen of Troy*, demonstrates the Brazilian internationalisation of Hollywood standards: the set, a precariously-constructed studio garden in a Greek palace decor, is heavy and artificial, and the actors' gestures are theatrical. The producer's elitist vision is then contrasted with the point-of-view of two studio janitors, interpreted by black actors Colé and Grande Otelo. Through their look we move from the academic 'scene' to the scene as they imagine it, as the celebrated black singer Blecaute (Blackout) appears dressed in Greek costume singing *Dona Cegonha*, a song written for the carnival celebration, accompanied by Grande Otelo tripping over his toga. Serious themes, then, had to be relativised and relocated within the context of carnival. '*Helen of Troy* won't work,' De Milho is told, 'the people want to dance and move'. *Carnaval Atlântida* thus traces the fecund inter-relationships between parody, *chanchada* and carnival, offering a compensatory mechanism which guarantees popular success in a foreign-dominated market.

In the wake of *Carnaval Atlântida*, another *chanchada*, *Nem Sansão nem Dalila* (Neither Samson nor Delilah, 1954) parodies the Cecil B. De Mille blockbuster, an enormous financial success in Brazil in the early 50s. The film's dream structure has the protagonist, an employee in a barber shop, thrust by a time machine into the city of Gaza in the year 1153 B.C., where he turns into the Biblical Samson. The film offers an exemplary metaphor for the relation between American and Brazilian cinema, and the mediating rôle of parody, in the form of a prop. In contrast to the original, where the strength of Samson (played by Victor Mature) derives from his natural hair, in the parody it derives from a wig. Brazilian parody, it is implied, is to Hollywood super-production as a wig is to the natural hair of the American actor. The natural strength of the hair aptly metaphorises the might of a developed film industry linked to the internal mechanisms of a powerful economy, in opposition to the simulated strength of an accessory, derivative cinema. At the same time, the wig, as one of the favored costume devices of carnival revellers, evokes an organic element of the language of carnival.

The double negation of the title – *Neither* Samson *nor* Delilah – already designates the film as parody, thus establishing a kind of teasing intertextual dialogue with the public through the shuttling interdependency between the two texts. The music by Lirio Panicelli is strikingly reminiscent of the original score by Victor Young, as is the overall design of the temple, with the enormous statue in the background. The decor retains, however, the characteristically impoverished black-and-white look of the Atlântida studios, which becomes the pretext for spoof. At one point, Samson, as he dances with the ladies of the palace, burns his hands in the flames of one of those inevitable unquenchable urns of fire, usually placed symmetrically along doors and staircases, that habitually decorate the interiors of Hollywood palaces. Within this decor, meanwhile, the film stages an anachronistic melange of over-coded generic clichés, from spectacular, pseudo-Biblical dance numbers to Medieval swashbuckling.

In the same year, Carlos Manga directed another parody, this time taking the Western as object of scrutiny and elaboration. The film, *Matar ou Correr* (To Kill or to Run, 1954), spoofs Fred Zinneman's *High Noon* (1952), which in Portuguese bore the title *Matar ou Morrer* (To Kill or to Die). *Matar ou Correr* respects the integrity of the Western in general, and *High Noon* in particular, locating its parody exclusively in the comic *chanchada* figures of Grande Otelo and Oscarito, treated as two ridiculous Brazilians lost in a heroic world. All the other characters act according to the classical patterns of the conventional Western; their types, costumes and behavior perfectly fit the determinate generic codes. The ingenue is romantic in her traditional, puritanical long dress, while the saloon singer is the blonde, naked-shouldered *femme fatale*. The villain, similarly, respectably conforms to the emblematic demands of his type, including black color code for dress. It is only the 'Brazilian' characters, visitors from the carnivalesque world of the *chanchada*, who refuse to conform to the conventions of realistic and serious representation. The character impersonated by Grande Otelo, Ciscocada (a play in Portuguese on Cisco Kid and Coconut Candy), is made instantly laughable by his ridiculous western clothes – large, rounded furry calfskin pants (similar to those worn by Mickey Rooney in *Babes in Arms*), visibly and grotesquely disproportionate to his modest stature. It is the figure of Oscarito, as Kid Bolha, the appointed sheriff of City Down, however, who forms the real target of criticism. After a career as a charlatan (he tries to sell grasshoppers as shrimp), he is appointed sheriff by mere chance rather than through legitimate strength or intelligence. He is a complete *tabula rasa* in terms of his knowledge of the survival codes of the western, such as fighting, shooting, and even mounting a horse. In direct and demeaning contrast with the heroism and strength displayed by Gary Cooper, Kid Bolha is a clumsy and cowardly clown. When he learns that the notorious villain Jesse Gordon will be arriving on the two o'clock train, Kid Bolha collapses in fear and prayerfully invokes the aid of his departed mother. In the climactic duel, the sheriff is unable properly to draw his pistols and ultimately hits the villain through sheer chance.

Matar ou Correr, unlike the critical satire of *Nem Sansão nem Dalila* and *Carnaval Atlântida*, more closely approximates Alfred Leide's notion of parody as a special form of conscious imitation, an exercise in mastering a technique or style.[6] *Matar ou Correr* offers conclusive proof of mastery of Hollywood codes of film-making and thus serves as a demonstration of cinematic competence on the part of a fledgling director. Not only does the general look of the film correspond to that of any authentic vintage Western, but certain shots make the Brazilian spectator doubt that the film was actually shot in the Rio suburb called Jacarepaguá. (One long shot of a stagecoach traversing the landscape, for example, bears a striking resemblance to countless similar shots from Hollywood Westerns.) Manga successfully elaborates the familiar formulaic motifs: saloon encounters between hero and villain, rooftop chases, stagecoach robberies, rearing horses, fist fights, crashing furniture and horse-borne bandits vanishing into the prairie landscape. Painstaking editing skilfully exploits associative processes, juxtaposing the rhythmic criss-crossing of moving horses, for example, with the legs of can-can dancers in the saloon. The film never exposes, however, the meaningless nature of these hackneyed formulae.

Matar ou Correr does introduce occasional deconstructive devices. The film's initial intertitles, for example, alert us to imminent anachronisms. A text, superimposed over a simplified drawing of Rio's celebrated cityscape, reads:

This picture was shot at a certain place in the West, at an unspecified time. In order to make our work easier, and to facilitate the work of the actors and the public's understanding, the language spoken in the film is doubtless Portuguese. We have maintained, however, the local expression Waltzung meaning everything is fine, O K, wonderful.

This Jarryesque foregrounding of the linguistic improbability of the text anticipates other reflexive devices in the film, the most telling of which is Kid Bolha's desperate attempt to delay 'High Noon' by pulling back the hands of the clock. This direct citation of a powerful distinctive feature of the original – its posited equivalence between fictional (story) and screen (discourse) time – marks an attempt by the parody's main character to halt the momentum of the narrative, even as it functions to deconstruct the spatio-temporal coordinates of mimetic representation.

Parody, as that artistic mode which mingles affectionate imitation and mordant critique, is both hostile and sympathetic to its 'target'. *Matar ou Correr* navigates uneasily between mockery and mimicry, and in this sense exemplifies the ambivalence which characterises colonised discourse. Carlos Manga's clear resentment at Hollywood domination, expressed in interviews and occasionally evoked by the film, co-exists with his overwhelming desire successfully to imitate the generic codes of a beloved original.[7] The problem with the film lies in its failure to recast critically the internalised codes of a canonised genre. Its ultimate effect, consequently, is less to bury obsolete forms or demonstrate their irrelevance to the Brazilian context, than to reinforce the myth of Hollywood superiority. Rather than operate a deconstruction or transvaluation, the film ultimately leads the audience to direct its laughter at the paradoxically 'alien' Brazilian characters, unable to master the codes of 'City Down'.

Parody and Self-Denigration

Continuing the tradition begun by the *chanchadas*, a disproportionate number of Brazilian films in the 70s and 80s have chosen to parody

American films or television programs. A thoroughgoing study of parody in this period would include such films as: *A Banana Mecanica* (The Mechanical Banana, 1973), a partial parody which took commercial advantage of the furore created by the anticipated Brazilian censorship of Kubrick's *A Clockwork Orange*, entitled 'The Mechanical Orange' in Portuguese; *Nos Tempos da Vasolina* (Back in the Time of Vasoline, 1979), a parody of *Grease*, called in Portuguese 'Back in the Time of Brilhantine'; and *Sabada Alucinante* (Hallucinating Saturday, 1979), which mingled parodic references to both *Saturday Night Fever* (1977) and *Thank God It's Friday* (1979). Although more concerned with marketing strategies capitalising on the success of a foreign original than with parody as such, these films do dramatically signal the ubiquitous penetration of the American film in Brazil. At the same time, four comic actors known as *Os Trapalhões* (roughly translatable as the 'Four Stooges' or the 'Four Morons') have devised a successful formula by transposing literary-film heroes into twentieth-century Brazil: *Simbad, O Marujo Trapalhão* (Sinbad, the Moron Sailor, 1976); *O Trapalhão na Ilha do Tesouro* (The Moron on Treasure Island, 1975); *Robin Hood: O Trapalhão Floresta* (Robin Hood, Moron of the Forest, 1977) and *Cindarelo Trapalhão* (The Moron Cindarello, 1980). The box-office appeal of the group, attracting a large audience of teenagers and children, has enabled *Os Trapalhões* gradually to displace Disney productions within the children's market. American television has also provided the Trapalhões with material for parody: *O Incrivel Monstro Trapalhão* (The Incredible Moron Monster, 1981) and *O Homem de Seis Milhões de Cruzeiros contre as Panteras* (The Six-Million Cruzeiro Man Against Charlie's Angels, 1978), this last a hypertextual elaboration of *two* television series, and another demonstration of relative technical poverty analogous to the disproportion in monetary power between the enfeebled Cruzeiro and the mighty Dollar.

More interesting for our purposes, however, are those recent parodies which take as their object Hollywood 'high-tech' super-spectacles. Unlike other arts such as literature or painting, which are only indirectly affected by neo-colonial hegemony, cinema, by its very nature, entails direct involvement with an advanced technology which tends to be monopolised by the metropolitan countries. The fascination that these high-tech productions exert on Brazilians can be measured not only in staggering gross box-office receipts, but also in the production of parodies of such films. Many of the most successful high-tech Hollywood films of the past 15 years have attracted the parodic interest of Brazilian film-makers. *Planet of the Apes* (1968), *The Exorcist* (1973), *Jaws* (1975), *King Kong* (1976), *Star Wars* (1977) and *E.T. The Extraterrestrial* (1982) have all spawned tropical offspring: *Os Trapalhões no Planalto dos Macacos* (The Morons on the Plateau/Planet of the Apes, 1976); *O Jeca contra o Capeta* (The Country Bumpkin Against the Devil, 1976); *Bacalhau* (Codfish, 1976); *Costinha e o King-Mong* (Costinha and King Mong, 1977); *Os Trapalhões na Guerra dos Planetas* (The Morons in the Planet Wars, 1978) and *E Téia a Mulher do Extraterrestre em Sua Aventura no Rio de Janeiro* (Mrs E.T. and her Adventures in Rio de Janeiro, 1984).

Another indication of the powerful appeal of these exhibitions of omnipotent technology is the fact that other successful Hollywood films, such as *Love Story*

(1970) and *Kramer vs. Kramer* (1980), have *not* been parodied. The aim of the high-tech parodies, in any case, is to seize the box-office leftovers of dominant cinema, which immediately places them in a subserviently parasitic and 'shadowy' position in relation to their prototypes. Their secondary aim, at least potentially, is to direct cathartic laughter against dominant cinema, resulting in a kind of purifying practice or aesthetic exorcism similar to that achieved by the rituals of inversion described by Victor Turner or those depicted in Jean Rouch's *Les Maîtres Fous*.[8]

We may begin our discussion of the parody of high-tech super-spectacles with a close look at the poster advertising the Brazilian parody of *Jaws*. The poster of *Bacalhau* (Codfish, 1976) leaves little doubt in the mind of the curious spectator that the film in question is a spoof of the Hollywood horror film *Jaws* (1975), then in the process of becoming the 'all-time box-office hit' in Brazil. The sensational image of the original poster was likely to be fresh in the spectator's mind, thus facilitating the necessary mental links between original and parody. The formal structure of the *Bacalhau* poster directly evokes the narrative image developed by the *Jaws* proto-type. In both, a realistic painted rendition shows a huge fish, in a deep blue sea, moving upwards toward a swimming woman. In both posters, the upward move-ment is implied not only by the vertical position of the fish but also by the bubbles emerging from the mouth. The graphic design recapitulates the same overall composition with the bold lettering of the title occupying the upper central position. But instead of the threatening 'Jaws' (or 'Tubarão' – 'shark' – in the Portuguese translation), which anchored the polysemy of the original poster and defined the species of fish depicted, the parody poster announces the more innocuous '*Bacal-hau*' – codfish. While both posters hermeneutically point to the same enigma – will the fish attack the helpless woman swimming on the surface? – the Brazilian poster actually evokes the contrary of risk and danger. The American title synecdochically evokes the aggressive king of the seas, while 'bacalhau', for the Brazilian, evokes domesticity, less the fish devouring than the fish being eaten on a plate, since 'bacalhau' is the name of a popular dish in Brazil, a cultural heritage from Portuguese traditional cuisine. It bears, furthermore, a specific connotation asso-ciated with sexuality, since it is also popularly associated with the scent of sexual activity.

While the two images share the notion of 'eating the victim', the implied devouring is motivated by sharply contrasting impulses. The smaller, more uniformly rounded teeth of the codfish are considerably less menacing than the terrifyingly long and sharply irregular fangs of the American shark. More strik-ingly, the anthropomorphically lascivious tongue projects itself outside the wide-open mouth, stretching up toward the woman's body, its phallic form reiterating that of the fish and designating the poster's central point of interest, the loose bottom part of the woman's bikini. A closer look at the woman shows her looking directly into the (presumably male) spectator's eyes with a regard implying excite-ment and 'secret knowledge'. The explicit sexual suggestiveness of the poster anchors the film in the '*pornochanchada*' genre, that wave of sexist soft-core comedies which flourished in the 70s. The parody poster, in conformity with the codes of *pornochanchada*, discards the suspenseful narrative invitation of the original *Jaws* poster ('She was the first . . . and so it all began') in favor of a promise of comic closure and erotic fulfilment ('And that's the way it always ends.')

Bacalhau Brazilianises its prototype according to a principle of comic degradation. The American police-chief Brody (Roy Scheider) becomes the distinctly unheroic Breda, grotesque in his Bermuda shorts and striped sox, and more interested in ogling women at the beach than in watching over the community's safety. The Matt Hooper (Richard Dreyfus) of *Jaws* becomes the Portuguese oceanographer Matos. His nationality makes him the immediate object of mockery, since the Portuguese, as Brazil's former colonisers, are a frequent satiric scapegoat for Brazilians, to the point that a Portuguese *scientist* would strike many Brazilians as a kind of oxymoron. Matos arrives from Portugal in a parcel post package, dressed in a diving suit and reading the *National Geographic*. The American fisherman Quint becomes the Brazilian Quico. Remarkably inept, constantly entangled in lines and hooks, Quico dresses in faded blue in order to 'disguise himself as the sea', and attempts to kill the codfish with an archaic bow and arrow. Instead of the heroism of the three men who confront the shark in *Jaws*, Breda, Matos and Quico are ultimately cowards, frightened of the final duel with the codfish, much in the same way that Sheriff Kid Bubble is terrified by the duel in *Matar ou Correr*. During the climactic confrontation, the police chief faints at the sight of the fish's open mouth and, contrary to *Jaws*, it is the fish, finally, who chases the boat and the men. The codfish is captured, ultimately, through sheer luck.

The Brazilian version adds one personage to the original gallery of characters – the homosexual fashion designer Ceci – thus further anchoring the film in the *pornochanchada* genre, where such characters proliferate. Ceci is associated with all the stereotypical indices of homosexuality: a 'suspect' profession, falsetto voice, transvestite manners, and devotion to domestic activities. Speaking more generally, *Bacalhau* consistently sexualises what was non-sexual or only latently sexual in the original. Playing on the Portuguese word *'comer'* (to eat), which has a sexual as well as culinary connotation, *Bacalhau* portrays a situation in which the codfish's 'victims' ardently desire to be 'devoured'. Quint's rage at the shark in *Jaws*, similarly, is given a more explicitly sexual etiology in *Bacalhau* (and by distant implication for Captain Ahab as a possible intertextual prototype for Quint); Quico's vindictive fury against the codfish, it is implied, stems from the past loss of a penis to the fish.

The comedy of *Bacalhau* assumes knowledge of the original. Throughout the film, the spectator is engaged in a process of comparative decoding with constant reference to the American prototype. *Bacalhau*'s initial sequence, for example, carefully reproduces the narrative action and even the filmic decoupage of the first sequence of *Jaws*. As the credits fade, a long shot reveals fun-loving teenagers gathered around a night-time beach fire. The following shot shows a young couple kissing. As the girl leaves the boy, the camera follows her as she undresses and moves toward the sea. But unlike the boyfriend in *Jaws*, here the boy does not follow the girl, but rather continues kissing the sand. (Alternating montage juxtaposes his misplaced kisses with her entry into the water.) Since the spectator familiar with *Jaws* is aware of the danger the girl is in, he/she regards the boy as something of an imbecile. And since Brazilian cinema lacks the technical resources for night-time underwater shooting and spectacular camera tricks, the codfish's first attack is eliminated. Instead, we are given a long shot of the beach, presumably on the following day. Instead of the horrifying close-up of a crab moving around the sandy bones of a hand, a long shot depicts the first appearance of an unexpected character, Ceci, swaying his hips and singing softly until he screams in horror at the sight before him – a blanched skeleton.

Bacalhau's complete structural dependence on the original differentiates it from the *chanchada*'s more liberated adaptations of whole genres and styles as well as of specific films. While *Matar ou Correr* mocks the Brazilian element only in characterological rather than technical-cinematic terms, *Bacalhau* ultimately re-inforces the prejudice against Brazilian cinema *as cinema*, by emphasising, through a constant process of derogatory comparison, the long-taken-for-granted technological superiority of dominant cinema. When the memory of the original is evoked, what is negated is the Brazilian film itself, rather than the original. *Bacalhau* highlights the discrepancies between parody and original in a self-destructive manner, not as a weapon against domination. In a vicious circle, both author and public share and stimulate an attitude of self-contempt based on the alleged Brazilian incompetence in imitation. The climactic moment of *Bacalhau* crystallises this self-contempt through a reflexive device involving the codfish's first full appearance on the screen. The same public that had been dazzled by the persuasive mimesis achieved by the design and engineering of the mechanical shark of *Jaws* suddenly observes its poor Brazilian relative under the water, first through a close-up of the eyes and then, as the immobile body passes before the camera, the mocking insignia on the tail – 'Made in Ribeirão Preto' – a provincial city in the state of São Paolo. Unlike the made-in- U S A shark, the Brazilian fish is made of cheap fiberglass and propelled by a highly visible nylon cord. Retroactively, the audience realises that only the eyes and the mouth were endowed with any motor capacity. Amused but also feeling cheated, the public responds with ambiguous laughter.

The spectator of *Bacalhau* passes through distinct stages, resulting in two separate but complementary attitudes: a parodic first laugh at dominant Hollywood cinema gives way to a 'last laugh' at Brazilian cinema. The film-makers regard themselves as aliens in the 'higher' world of true Cinema; the laughter provoked by the parody rebounds against themselves and the audience. Rather than question spectatorial identification with the foreign model, *Bacalhau* fosters uncritical ad-miration. Rather than satirise the mindless consumption of high-tech super-spec-tacles, the spectators are made to see themselves as 'strangers' to Brazilian cinema. One remark in the film encapsulates this attitude. Police Chief Breda, typing his report on the codfish's first attack, writes that the attack was by a 'very big fish', but then muses to himself that *'tubarão de verdade . . . só mesmo naquele filme . . .'* (a real shark . . . only in that other film). This reflexive reminder urges the spectator in the direction of a 'correct' but humiliating reading, involving both film-maker and spectator in a ritual of self-denigration. Breda's meta-commentary critiques the factitiousness of the parody while implying, by a kind of associational boomerang, the nobler truth of the other fiction which is as reality to its shadow. Thus, the film renders homage to the 'other' (the ideal ego of both film-maker and spectator) and the repressed desire of *becoming* the dominant cinema of high technological proficiency. *Bacalhau*'s apparent comedy, in the end, masks a melancholy cinematic consciousness.

In the following year, another parody, *Costinha e o King Mong* (1977), adopted similar strategies but for a distinct public. The film's signal achievement was to materialise the long-sought ideal of Brazilian parody: simultaneous release with the original, in this case the Dino de Laurentiis version of *King Kong*. The Paramount production had been widely publicised in Brazil even while still in production, with the press giving wide stress and photographic coverage to the 'revolutionary' visual effects engineered by Carlos Rambaldi's giant mechanical ape. Anticipating easy profits in the wake of the expected box-office success of *King Kong*, the Brazilian producer took advantage of the advertising apparatus of the film and prepared his Brazilian version. This parasitic strategy proved successful, partially because the 14-and-over rating of the American film limited its audience in a youthful country like Brazil. Aware of this favorable circumstance, the producers of *Costinha e o King Mong* adopted a strategy opposite to that of *Bacalhau*, de-eroticising the original in favor of a 'family-oriented' spectacle. The two films were ultimately released not only simultaneously but also side-by-side in neighboring first-run theaters in downtown Rio de Janeiro.

The poster of *Costinha e o King Mong* re-elaborates the original poster in what seems like a deliberate attempt to deceive unattentive spectators (mostly children) who were already familiar with the narrative iconography of *King Kong*, not only through advance publicity stills of the De Laurentis film, but also through frequent television re-runs of the 1933 version. Apart from the phonetic similarity in the apes' names, the graphic composition of the bold red lettering of *King Mong* carefully hides, behind the figure of the ape's face, the letter 'M', the only character distinguishing it from the original title. The buildings depicted on the poster, depicting landmarks drawn from the architectural landscape of Rio de Janeiro, effectuate proximity with the original by alluding to climactic narrative moments of *King Kong*. The Brazilian poster suggests a possible fall of the ape from the top of Rio's modern Metropolitan Cathedral, graphically treated so as to emphasise the verticality of its lateral perspective, thus forcing similarity with the World Trade Center in New York.

Costinha e o King Mong aims at proximity with the original more by striving to reproduce special visual effects than by closely following the narrative line as in *Bacalhau*. The producers emphasise precisely those points of contact which throw up a special challenge to the Brazilian producer attempting to equal the original's illusionistic powers. Although crowded with local cultural references (of which Costinha's farcical persona, familiar from stage, screen and television, is the strongest), the parody integrates most of the original's spectacular moments: the ape's first appearance followed by the cupping of Costinha in its paw; the fight with the prehistoric animal; the destruction of the tribe's great wall; the breaking out of the cage at the show; and the final scenes involving chaotic crowds and a great city.

The results, predictably, are frustrating. The textural surface of the film is shabby and impoverished. Despite color and a relatively high budget, the character-isation of the leopard men and the great wall, for example, seems undeniably crude. Roughly-painted masks and a profusion of cheap shields try to compensate for the absent 'cast of thousands', while the fragile logs scarcely seem plausible reason for intimidation on the part of the ape. The mysterious atmosphere of the remote locale is largely achieved through rudimentary lighting effects and an abundance of smoke, and the spectator easily perceives the photographic panels providing back-drop for what is transparently a man in a gorilla costume. But it is King Mong himself who is the object of the film's most derisive laughter. His mask, like that of the dinosaur, is rigid and, except for the eyes and mouth, lacks all mobility. The hand, meanwhile, reveals a black cover more reminiscent of a bargain-basement couch than of the convincing mechanical hand of the original.

With *Costinha e o King Mong*, the reinforcement of an attitude of self-contempt toward the national film industry reached a young audience already accustomed via television to the presence of dominant cinema, thus leaving the Hollywood supers-pectacle untouched as a canonised system. Parodies such as *Bacalhau* and *Costinha e o King Mong* might play an important creative role if their film-makers managed to articulate a distanced critique of the model being parodied. They might provide a space for reflection on the cultural and economic conditions faced by Brazilian cinema and effectively expose the powers of infiltration of the foreign film in molding and alienating the Brazilian spectator. Parodies might exercise their pedagogical vocation by revealing with clarity and irony the ideological significa-tions embedded in the entertainment values of Hollywood high-tech spectacles. *Bacalhau*, for example, might have tellingly exposed the final victory of the police apparatus in *Jaws* (represented by police chief Brody), allied with science (the oceanographer) over the people (represented in grotesque form by Quint) as the victory of repressive technocratic and scientific knowledge over the fisherman's empirical intuition. Similarly, such films might expose the patriarchal structures and sexist attitudes which disfigure both the foreign and the national cinema. A film like *O Cangaceiro Trapalhão* (1983), inspired by the fast-paced action of *Raiders of the Lost Ark* (1981), might have paradoxically highlighted the neo-colonial ideology promoted by dominant cinema in general and by the Spielberg film in particular. It might critique the representation of the supposedly 'natural' right to plunder national treasure in 'remote' areas of the globe in the name of Science (Professor Anthropologist-Archaeologist Indiana Jones). The gold statue at the beginning of the Spielberg film might be revealed as a metaphor for the resources constantly being shipped to the developed world. Rather than emulate the illusionism of Hollywood cinema, parodies such as *Costinha e o King Mong* might have been the springboard for a devastating critique of the shallow factitiousness ultimately conveyed by the increasingly sophisticated mimesis of contemporary dominant cinema. Such parodies would contribute not only to the renovation of film language, but also to the formation of a new audience which would be able ideologically to penetrate and critically re-work the canonised forms of spectatorial fascination.

Anthropophagy and the Avant Garde

Commercial Brazilian films, while perhaps marginal in relation to Hollywood, constituted the mainstream in terms of Brazil. In the early 60s, the Cinema Novo directors declared their opposition both to the dominant foreign model and to commercial Brazilian cinema. Seeing itself as an avant gardist expression of Third World otherness, Cinema Novo discarded the carnivalesque good humor of *chanchada* in favor of a didactic practice that attempted to transform a negative condition – peripheral under-development – into a positive source of signification, by integrating into its very language the indices of scarcity. If early Cinema Novo was 'parodic', it was so only in what Genette would call the 'metatextual' sense, i.e., in its cinematic critique of an anterior text (the dominant model taken as a system) not explicitly cited.[9] The Hollywood model is present in early Cinema Novo only *in absentia* through a series of strident refusals – of dramatic density, heroes, subjectification, continuity editing. Instead of the pleasurable indulgences of carnival, early Cinema Novo proposed an 'aesthetic of hunger' and displeasure in the service of political consciousness. In its wish to make a definitive break with Hollywood alienation, however, Cinema Novo at times threw out the baby of pleasure with the bathwater of dominant ideology.

It was only in its third, or 'cannibal-tropicalist', phase that Cinema Novo rediscovered carnival and parody.[10] The cultural movement called Tropicalism, which emerged in the late 60s, drew partial inspiration from the Brazilian Modernist avant garde of the 20s – a Modernism which, unlike its European counterpart, fused political nationalism with aesthetic internationalism – and especially from Oswald de Andrade's notion of 'anthropophagy' as metaphorically applied to cultural products. For Modernists like Oswald, cannibalism formed part of a strategy of national resistance toward cultural colonialism. Brazilian artists were to digest imported cultural products and exploit them as raw material for a new formulation, thus turning the imposed culture back, transformed, against the coloniser. (Modernism, in this sense, used Europe to liberate itself from Europe.) Within this new formulation, parody takes on a new and strategic rôle. The notion of 'anthropophagy' assumes the inevitability of inter-textuality. Since there can be no nostalgic return to pre-colonial purity, no unproblematic recovery of national origins undefiled by alien influences, the artist in the dominated culture cannot ignore the foreign presence but must rather swallow it and recycle it to national ends. Anthropophagy implied as well a transcendance of early Cinema Novo's Manichean opposition between 'authentic Brazilian cinema' versus Hollywood alienation. Tropicalism rejected the dualism which contrasted pure rural folklore with the imperialised mass-culture of the cities. Tropicalism aggressively mingled the folkloric and the industrial, the native and the foreign; its favored technique was the aggressive collage of discourses, the result of an anthropophagic devouring of the variety of cultural stimuli in all their heterogeneity.

Joaquim Pedro de Andrade's *Macunaíma* (1969), based on a landmark novel from the Modernist period, develops anthropophagy as theme and strategy. In diegetic terms, *Macunaíma* exploits the cannibalist motif in order to expose the predatory Social Darwinism of class society in the Third World. In terms of aesthetic strategy, however, *Macunaíma* renews contact with the world of *chanchada* and carnival. The renewed contact with the *chanchada* takes many forms in the film, most notably through the casting of key *chanchada* actors like Grande Otelo and Zeze Macedo, but also through the inclusion of songs popular from the *chanchada* period. This socially-conscious recycling of *chanchada* strategies enabled *Macunaíma* to realise a goal long inaccessible to Cinema Novo directors – the reconciliation of political and aesthetic avant-gardism with popular appeal.[11] Like the source novel, the film also offers many features associated with carnivalisation and Menippean satire: the miraculous birth (a 'woman', played by a man, gives birth to a 60-year-old baby); the oxymoronic protagonist (whose very name means 'great evil' and who is simultaneously black/white/Indian); sexual inversions (men dressed as women, women with men's voices, reversal of conventional sex roles); marginal characters (hustlers, prostitutes); contemporary allusions (satire of racism and political repression); grotesque image of the body (urination, defecation); and a comic approach to death (the capitalist Pietro-Pietra dies with a joke on his lips).[12]

At the same time that Cinema Novo entered its tropicalist phase, there emerged an alternative Underground cinema. If Brazilian cinema is by definition on the margins of hegemonic cinema, and if Cinema Novo was on the margins of mainstream Brazilian commercial cinema, the Underground was, so to speak, on the outskirts of the margins. Not only were the Underground films made in a 'marginal' area of the city – the low-life district of São Paulo known as *Boca do Lixo* (literally, 'mouth of garbage') – they also featured marginal characters. The Underground movement constituted both a rejection and a renovation of a Cinema Novo now seen as *embourgeoisé* and paternalistic, overly cautious in both thematics and cinematic language. As Cinema Novo moved toward relatively big-budget, 'quality' films, the Novo Cinema Novo (The New New Cinema) demanded a radicalisation of the 'aesthetic of hunger', rejecting a well-made cinema in favor of a 'dirty screen' and 'garbage aesthetics'. Unlike Cinema Novo's more active metaphor of 'hunger', as Ismail Xavier points out, the metaphor of garbage expressed an aggressive sense of marginality, of surviving within scarcity, condemned to recycle the materials of dominant culture: ' "Hunger" evoked the dignified victim that redeemed itself through violence; "garbage" evokes devalued waste matter, a passive element subject to decay and oblivion.'[13] A garbage style, for the Underground, was the style most appropriate to a Third World country picking through the leavings of an international system dominated by First World monopoly capitalism.

The first indisputably Underground film, Osualdo Candeias' prophetically titled *A Margem* (In the Margins, 1967), thematises marginality in all the diverse overtones of that word. It is set, first of all, along the margins of São Paulo's irredeemably polluted Tietê river, where diverse 'marginals' improvise their daily survival by begging, prostitution and junk collecting. Along the river a highway, known in Portuguese as 'the Marginal', also generates its gallery of marginal characters. *A Margem* treats these characters with great warmth and respect, suggesting, to paraphrase a revolutionary slogan from May 1968, that '*nous sommes tous des marginaux*'. The film denounces as a cruel mystification the notion that marginals are somehow 'outside' society. In fact, they are its product and distorting image, the repressed other that reflects the truth about the larger social body.[14] At the same time, Candeias hints at an analogy to cinema itself. There is no single valid cinema, in relation to which all other cinemas are to be belittled as marginal and inferior. Within Candeias' quiet but radical egalitarianism, all cinemas are created equal as all human beings are created equal.

Our purpose here, however, is not to survey the development of alternative cinema since Cinema Novo, but rather to examine strategies of parodic intertextuality in a few representative films. Rogério Sganzerla's *Bandido da Luz Vermelha* (Red Light Bandit, 1968), a seminal independent production, outlines the rise and fall of a famous outlaw mythologised by the mass-media in a milieu peopled by marginals: thieves, drug addicts, smugglers, prostitutes and artists. Sganzerla shows an anthropophagic openness to all intertextual influences, including those of Hollywood and the mass-media. Unlike Cinema Novo's radical rejection of dominant cinema, Sganzerla deploys Hollywood against Hollywood through tactics of generic conflation and discursive collage. Sganzerla was himself quite explicit about this tactic, calling *Red Light Bandit* a 'film-summa, a western, a musical documentary, detective story, comedy *chanchada*, and science fiction'. The director's desire was to weld 'the sincerity of documentary (Rossellini), the violence of the gangster film (Fuller), the anarchic rhythm of comedy (Sennett, Keaton), the brutal narrative simplification of the western (Hawks)'.[15] Such an improbable collage of incompatible genres makes the film inevitably anti-illusionistic, turning it into a compilation of *pastiches*, a kind of cinematic writing in quotation marks.

At the same time, *Red Light Bandit* posits a homology between a red-light district in a Third World country as a 'realm of garbage' and the text itself as a collection of film and mass media refuse. The film draws on the degraded material of the mass media, both in its local forms (sensationalist press, radio broadcasts) and its imported forms (American T V serials, B-films, science fiction). The collage principle works both 'horizontally', through the forced contiguity of heterogeneous and mutually relativising discourses, and 'vertically', through the superimposition, at the same syntagmatic point, of multiple elements, for example through overlaying voice-over narration along with three or four kinds of music playing simultaneously. The film's soundtrack typifies this strategy, mingling a veritable anthology of Hollywood programmatic music, classical and symphonic pieces, and Brazilian and American camp materials. Beethoven's Fifth Symphony coincides with the Brazilian Folksong '*Asa Branca*' in a provocative polyphonic levelling of high classical and 'low' folkloric art. Thus *Red Light Bandit* modifies, transforms and re-elaborates one of the primary narrative and aesthetic procedures of Cinema Novo – the erudite elaboration of Brazilian popular culture – by promiscuously mingling, in a chaotic hetero-glossia, the languages of city and country, metropolis and periphery, resulting in a carnivalesque overturning of hierarchies, a condensation of modes of discourse usually thought to be separate.

In the 80s, other independent films offered telling demonstrations of the creative power of Brazilian parody for generating fiction through meta-fiction. Consciously influenced by *Red Light Bandit*, Ivan Cardoso's *O Segredo da Múmia* (The Secret of the Mummy, 1982) throws together prototypical characters from diverse films from the same genre as an economical means of recycling generic materials. Here the intertextual references – to the *chanchada*, *Red Light Bandit*, American B-film, Andy Warhol pop horror, Mel Brooks (especially *Young Franken-stein*), Val Lewton, Boris Karloff – serve not as homage but as structural armature for an attack on Hollywood illusionism. The collage appropriates not only the coded diegetic residue of genre films but also the left-overs of other films, reportedly picked up directly from editing-room trash cans in what amounts to a literalisation of the 'garbage-can' aesthetic. This spliced assemblage, of heteroclite materials, includes clips from Atlântida newsreels, shots of lightning and thunderstorms, segments of B-films, emphasises the artificiality of the process of narrative construction. The assemblage calls attention to the wide range of archival material available in Brazil, material often thought to be non-existent, thus demonstrating the many ways such material might be artistically recuperated. These images include the landing of an old airplane from the now extinct Brazilian Royal Airlines, and the election of Martha Rocha as Miss Brazil in 1954 with an homage paid to her by the celebrated poet Manuel Bandeira. They constitute, in short, cherished images for the Brazilian popular unconscious. The minimalist approach of the film is also exhibited in the deployment of stills and postcards. The title 'Cairo 1954' appears over a postcard image, while on the soundtrack, a clichéd piece of 'exotic' orchestral music evokes a stereotypical Egypt. The flagrant intention is to deploy such hackneyed strategies as part of a parodic defamiliarisation which 'lays bare the device'. *The Secret of the Mummy* thus renews the norms of quotation to recreate and recontextualise them, making them the subject of a new deconstruction.

The same method of ironic hybridisation serves equally well in Julio Bressane's *Tabu* (Taboo, 1982), a film which continues the author's project, initiated in *Rei do Baralho*, of 'transvaluating' the codes of the *chanchada*. Bressane posits a hypothetical meeting between popular 20s composer Lamartine Babo and a modernist poet and dramatist, Oswald de Andrade, played by Colé, the *chanchada* veteran familiar from *Carnaval Atlântida*. Lamartine Babo here invokes the spirit of popular culture and carnival (a point underlined by the casting of popular singer-composer Caetano Veloso to incarnate the role), while de Andrade embodies the erudite avant garde elaboration and theorisation of popular culture. This suggestive structural mechanism allows Bressane to place in correlation, through a kind of retrospective rapprochement, the popular carnival music of Rio and the erudite literary vanguardism of São Paulo. At the same time, the film elegiacally celebrates the Rio of the 30s as a utopian tropical paradise by associating it with interpolated footage from Murnau's *Tabu*. One remarkable audio-visual montage superimposes a carnival song about the daily chores of fishermen, delivered by *chanchada* star Emilinha Borba, on Murnau's images of natives dancing in Tahiti. By spreading the spirit of carnival to the South Pacific, in a kind of joyful heterotopian contamination, Bressane demonstrates, once again, the inexhaustible suggestiveness of a tradition rooted in anthropophagic Modernism and its latter-day incarnation, Tropicalism.

Intertextual parody in Brazil has not been limited to the foreign or even to the fiction film. Sergio Bianchi's documentary *Mato Eles?* (Should I Kill Them?, 1983) treats a subject – the desperate situation of the last surviving remnant of certain indigenous tribes in Brazil – scarcely amenable, at first glance, to satiric or parodic treatment. Yet the film completely deconstructs the conventional approach, in Brazil and elsewhere, to this kind of topic. Instead of the customary realistic depiction of the local habitat, interspersed with talking heads and disembodied voice-over (expressing the enlightened consciousness of the author), Bianchi satirically questions not only the official discourse concerning the Indian, but also the traditional *bonne conscience* of the 'denunciation documentary'.

Mato Eles? constitutes a relentless assault on the assumptions and sensibility of the middle-class spectator accustomed to documentaries which flatter his/her narcissistic sense of humanist compassion. *Mato Eles?* as its question mark implies, is a filmic reflection on the nature of asking questions, which itself questions the right of white film-makers to 'speak for' the Indians. The film is structured around a series of apparently whimsical multiple-choice questions, addressed to the spectator at regular intervals. The Brechtianism of these title-questions, in their implicit call for spectatorial collaboration and the 'rendering of a verdict' is tinged here with bitter irony, for the questions and proposed answers tend to the mutually contradictory and the absurd. One question reads: 'Very few Indians remain from the once-numerous Xeta tribe. What happened to the others? Choose one of the following: 1) They all intermarried with the white population and are now living in the cities. 2) They all died due to infectious diseases and litigation concerning land rights. 3) They are all on vacation in Europe. 4) The Xeta Indians never existed. This documentary is false. 5) All the above answers are correct.' Another question poses three unpalatable alternatives: 'The extermination of the Indians should be: 1) immediate; 2) slow; 3) gradual.' The questions and answers leave no comfortable space for the progressive spectator, rather, they confront the spectator with the reality of extermination, in a manner which initially provokes laughter but subsequently elicits reflection and self-doubt.

Mato Eles? also deconstructs the official 'Indianist' discourse predominant in Brazil since the romantic movement of the 19th century. For the romantics, the Indian was the prized locus of national specificity, the symbol of Brazil's uniqueness. But this idealisation of the Indian coincided historically with an ongoing process of physical and cultural annihilation. The heroic fighters celebrated in countless songs, poems and novels, the film suggests, are now imprisoned in a dreary cycle of disease and impotence. Bianchi mocks the heroicising vision of the Indian by announcing a film-within-the-film, an Indianist epic entitled, in transparent homage to James Fenimore Cooper, 'The Last of the Xetas'. The romantic music of *O Guarani*, an Indianist opera by Brazilian composer Carlos Gomes, soars lushly on the soundtrack, swelling our expectations for an epic-heroic spectacle. Instead, Bianchi shows us the sole surviving member of the tribe, quite literally the 'last of the Xetas', presented in a series of photographs strongly reminiscent of police mug shots. The 'brave warrior' of romanticism has become the despised object of the official discourse of police photos coldly registering the reality of genocide.

Nor does Bianchi exempt himself from criticism. At one point, a venerable guarani Indian surprises the film-maker by asking exactly how much money he was paid to make the film. This inconvenient question, which normally would have made its way into the editing-room trashcan, segues to a directorial voice-over in which he speculates about other avenues for financially exploiting the Indian – anthropological scholarships, photograph albums, arts and crafts shops, showing films in Europe. Thus the 'voice-of-God' offscreen narration is used, against the grain of conventional practice, to mock the film-maker himself. The condescending voice of monologic Truth here deconstructs itself, thus closing the film's circle of multiple ironies directed at the power structure, at the film, at the film-maker, and at the canonised formulae of the meliorist documentary.

Conclusion

We have examined a historically evolving constellation of possible strategies for a marginal cinema, in this case the Brazilian, in search of a language at once accessible, innovative and deconstructive. The challenge for such film-makers is, while acknowledging the scarcity of means generated by economic under-development, to offer an aesthetic strategy appropriate to this reality and congenial to the culture, so as to make the work a critical response rather than a mere symptom of under-development. Virtually all the films here discussed can be seen as, in Ismail Xavier's poignantly apt phrase, 'allegories of under-development'. The *chanchada* parodies, for example, allegorise a cruel proportion of power. Scarito's wig to Victor Mature's hair (in *Nem Sansão nem Dalila*), Carlos Manga's parodic cat (in the logo of *Matar ou Correr*) to M G M's lion; Cape Carnival (in Victor Lima's *Os Cosmonautas*/The Cosmonauts) to Cape Canaveral; codfish to shark (*Bacalhau*); cruzeiro to dollar (*The Six Million Cruzeiro Man*). At their best, the parodies challenge this proportion, suggesting that it is neither inevitable or eternal.

The avant garde films, meanwhile, also take as their point of departure the widespread penetration of dominant cinema within Brazil, orchestrating an orgy of clashing allusions and citations not in a spirit of reverential homage but rather in an impulse of creative disrespect and irreverence. Their hybridisation of incompatible materials produces a textual heterotopia in which antagonistic generic strands mutually critique and relativise one another. Within this textual polyglossia, to employ Bakhtin's term, dominant cinema is made to war against itself, while the Brazilian *magister ludi* stands aside and ironises. Tropicalism simply assumes the presence of international intertextuality. A double consciousness, that life on the periphery passes both 'here' and 'elsewhere' undergirds the modernist trope of anthropophagy, of devouring the foreign in order to affirm the national. At the same time, these artists do not portray a situation of cultural passivity. They are deeply aware of a resistance culture rooted in what Cuban writer Alejo Carpentier called 'lo real maravilloso americano' (the marvellous real of Latin America). Many of the critical phrases associated with the contemporary Renaissance within Latin American art – 'magical realism', 'quotidian surreality' – not only assert an alternative culture but also suggest the inadequacy of the high mimetic tradition for the expressive needs of an oppressed but polyphonic and polyrhythmic culture.

Parody, Hegel argued, emerges when artists outgrow conventions and are ready to dissociate themselves from the past. To this temporal historicising critique inherent in parody, Latin American artists add a spatial, even geographical dimension emphasising the inappropriateness, the out-of-placeness of metropolitan models which are nonetheless omnipresent. (The trope of marginality, in the end, is a eurocentric misnomer, since life is lived *centrally* wherever there are human subjects.) Brazilian cinema, for its part, has often been most effective when it has been most outrageous, when it draws on the vital taproot of Brazilian irony and humor and on the deep traditions of Carnival's 'gay relativity'. A retrospective glance at the history of Brazilian film history reveals that carnivalesque comedy has repeatedly 'saved' the national industry by touching something deep in the Brazilian popular unconscious. At three crucial junctures, Brazilian cinema has suffered a redemptive 'fall' into comedy. The Atlântida Studio, after its initial attempt to make serious dramatic films, reverted to *chanchada* with its third production, the appropriately titled *Tristezas Não Pagam Dividas* (Sadness Pays no Debts, 1944). The Vera Cruz Studio, after a problematic flirtation with high-art seriousness, was forced in the 50s to return to the comic mechanisms and even the stars of the *chanchada*. And Cinema Novo, while impressing international critics with its aesthetic and political sophistication, only made substantial contact with the Brazilian mass public with *Macunaíma*, rooted in carnival, the *chanchada* and anthropophagy. And in the wake of *Macunaíma*, as we have seen, a number of other films developed a carnivalesque model combining political coherence, commercial viability and popular appeal.

The kinds of films we have been discussing here have historically been the object of a multiplicity of superimposed prejudices – against comedy as an 'inferior' form (a prejudice traceable at least as far back as Aristotle): against parody (seen as parasitic and derivative); against punning (as the 'lowest form of humor'); against generic impurity and levelling (seen as portending, for the conservative critic, an ominous levelling within society itself); against physicality and what Bakhtin calls the 'material bodily stratum'; against sexuality (seen as animalist and degrading); and, more subtly, against the lower-class popular audience. These prejudices have in common the notion of higher/lower, superior/inferior; a complex set of homologies linking parallel hierarchisations traversing issues of corporality, class and genre. In this sense, our argument is itself carnivalesque, operating a dislocation in the analysis away from what has been considered paradigmatic in favor of marginal or critically devalued forms. Thus, in a typically carnivalesque gesture, we have relegated the established center to the margins of our concern and enthroned what was regarded as marginal, making it the critical center.

Notes

1 See Mikhail Bakhtin, *Problems of Dostoevsky's Poetics* trans. P. W. Rotself (Ann Arbor: Ardis, 1973); *Rabelais and His World* trans. Helene Iswolsky (Cambridge, Mass.: MIT Press, 1968); *The Dialogic Imagination* ed. Michael Holquist (Austin: University of Texas Press, 1981); and V. N. Volosinov, *Marxism and the Philosophy of Language* (New York: Seminar Press, 1973).

2 See, for example, Emir Rodrigues Monegal, 'Carnival, Antropofagia, Paródia', in *Paródia* (Rio de Janeiro: Paz e Terra, 1981).

3 See Roberto Augusto da Matta, 'O Carnaval como um Rito de Passagem', in *Ensaios de Antropologia Estrutural* (Petropolis: Vozes, 1977) and *Carnavais, Melandros e Heróis* (Rio de Janeiro: Zahar, 1978).

4 For expositions of dependency analysis, see A. G. Franck, *Capitalism and Underdevelopment in Latin America* (New York: Monthly Review Press, 1966); and James Cockroft, A. G. Franck and Dale Johnson, *Dependence and Underdevelopment: Latin America's Political Economy* (New York: Anchor Books, 1971). For a later, more critical view of the literature on dependency, see Fernando Henrique Cardoso, 'The Consumption of Dependency Theory in the United States', in *Latin American Research Review* (1977), pp. 7–24.

5 Brazilian film magazines such as *A Scena Muda* and *Cinearte* promoted American films and American stars through synopses of forthcoming releases, news items and gossip concerning the stars' careers and lifestyles, and reader response contests concerning 'best female star', 'best male actor' and so forth.

6 See Alfred Liede, 'Die Parodie', *Reallexikon* (Berlin) vol. 3 (1966), p. 14.

7 In interviews with us, Carlos Manga was quite explicit about his ambivalence, claiming that he had intensely admired the craft of the Western and had seen *High Noon* scores of times; at the same time he deeply resented Hollywood domination of the Brazilian film market.

8 See Victor Turner, *The Ritual Process: Structure and Anti-Structure* (Ithaca: Cornell University Press, 1977). The Rouch film (1954–5) concerns the annual ceremonies of the Hauka cult from the Upper Niger region, in which the initiates become possessed by powerful spirits and, in a state of trance, impersonate the roles of the white colonial authority figures, including a parodic representation of a 'changing of the guard'. Rouch's thesis in the voice-over commentary is that the ritual plays a therapeutic role in the lives of these marginalised and oppressed people, allowing them to accommodate the psychological disjunctions caused by colonialism.

9 In *Palimpsestes* Genette defines metatextuality as the critical relation between one text and another, even when the commented text is not explicitly cited (Genette offers the example of Hegel's *Phenomenology of Mind* as a metatext in relation to Diderot's *Rameau's Nephew*). Metatextuality, for Genette, is just one of five types of 'transtextuality'; the others are intertextuality, paratextuality, architextuality, and hypertextuality. See Gérard Genette, *Palimpsestes: La littérature au second degré* (Paris: Seuil, 1982), pp. 7–13.

10 Carnival is present in some 'second-phase' Cinema Novo films, but only in its negative dystopian mode. Rocha's *Terra em Transe* (*Land in Anguish*, 1967), for example, thematises what the director called 'the tragic carnival of Brazilian politics', and often uses an allegorical style of representation associated with the samba school pageants from the Rio carnival. But in *Land in Anguish*, made in the afterwash of a coup d'état which left in ruins decades of left-liberal illusions, the apparent movement of carnival (and of populist politics) is shown as a dead-end frenzy. Implicit in the symbolic utopia of carnival, within a context of repression and alienation, is the 'morning after' that comes with renewed contact with ambient social reality.

11 Joaquim Pedro de Andrade's filmic recuperation of the values of the *chanchada* helped pave the way for a revaluation of the *chanchada* on the part of the intellectuals, the highest expression of which is Paulo Emilio Salles Gomes' 'Cinema: Trajectory within Underdevelopment' (1973), where he lauds *chanchada* as a legitimate expression of the culture of the oppressed. Whereas the Cinema Novo directors, for example Rocha in his 1963 *Revisão Crítica do Cinema Brasileiro*, had stressed historical discontinuity – Cinema Novo as a fundamental break – Salles Gomes stressed Brazilian cinema as a continuum. See Paulo Emilio Salles Gomes, 'Cinema: Trajectory within Underdevelopment', in Randal Johnson and Robert Stam, *Brazilian Cinema* (East Brunswick: Associated University Presses, 1982) and Glauber Rocha, *Revisión Crítica del Cine Brasileño* (Madrid: Editorial Fundamentos, 1971, originally published in Portuguese in 1963).

12 For a thorough and illuminating textual analysis of *Macunaíma*, see Randal Johnson, 'Cinema

Novo and Cannibalism: *Macunaíma*', in Randal Johnson and Robert Stam, *Brazilian Cinema*, as well as Robert Stam, 'The Carnival of Modernism', in *Reflexivity in Film and Literature: From Don Quixote to Jean-Luc Godard* (Ann Arbor: U M I Press, 1984).

13 See Ismail Xavier, 'Allegories of Underdevelopment: From "the Aesthetics of Hunger to the Aesthetics of Garbage"' (New York University doctoral dissertation; Ann Arbor: University Microfilms, 1982). Xavier's study constitutes the most thoroughgoing investigation of Brazilian underground cinema to date, and is itself a model of sophisticated textual and contextual analysis. Xavier focuses his discussion on the following films: Rocha's *Black God, White Devil* and *Land in Anguish*; Sganzerla's *Red Light Bandit*; Bressane's *The Angel is Born*; and Tonacci's *Bangue-Bangue*.

14 In Brazil, a full-blown social theory was developed to justify the repression and displacement of the 'marginal' populations of Rio de Janeiro and other Brazilian cities – 'marginality theory'. This theory branded favela squatters as deviant, criminal, perverse and basically outside the charmed circle of 'civilisation'. Janice Perlam, in *The Myth of Marginality*, argues that the marginals in fact are the product of the central society and intimately related to it. See *The Myth of Marginality* (Berkeley: University of California Press, 1976).

15 Johnson and Stam, *Brazilian Cinema*, p. 316.

VII
Review of John Hill, 'Sex, Class and Realism – British Cinema 1956–1963'

PAUL WILLEMEN

From *Framework* no. 35 (1987)

We have included this review not so much to draw attention to John Hill's excellent book (published by the British Film Institute, 1986) as to put before our readers the broader reflections on developments in 80s media theory that Paul Willemen provides here. Willemen puts his finger on a real problem facing critical media analysis in the wake of the development of techniques for close reading of film and television 'texts' over the last twenty years. As texts are revealed to be more and more multi-layered, ambiguous, ironic, and as their viewers concurrently emerge to be similarly hard to pin down, there is a strong temptation to move into a celebratory mode: 'Isn't popular culture wonderful! it's so *complicated*!' Willemen succinctly points out that it was never central to one's objections to dominant media practices that they be thought of as semantically impoverished: micro-level analysis of pretty well anything discloses a plethora of patterning, all very nice in its way, but not of great relevance to issues of power and excluded perspectives. If the complexity of the message and its uptake is taken to justify it, we are dangerously close to declaring that 'Whatever is, is right'. (Or, 'Whatever *means* . . .'.)

M.A./J.O.T.

[. . .] The exciting part of Hill's enterprise resides in the way he shows the way out of the main impasse currently incapacitating Anglo-Saxon criticism: the impossible choice between textual analyses according to a variety of deconstructivist protocols usually claiming that the film in question throws up stimulating contradictions and is thoroughly plural, and, on the other hand, the abdication of critical responsibilities in favour of the celebration of existing patterns of consumption based on a principled refusal to countenance the possibility that vast sectors of the population have come to derive pleasure from conservative orientated media discourses.

Hill begins by mapping the dominant forces shaping the social formation along with the discourses which offer ways of making sense of lived experience. He discusses the main motifs (neurotic knots) organising those discourses: juvenile delinquency, consumerism, changing gender roles, racism, urbanisation, etc., locates them within a political dynamic which defines the presentation of these motifs and suggests particular solutions to the problems raised. In that way, he is able to discern in which political direction certain types of discursive arrangements seek to move the viewers. He then talks about developments in an industry programmed by the need for spectacle and sensationalism, and in need of innovation in a period of sharp decline:

> ... in the last instance it was economic self-interest which was determinant. The strategy of the majors was thus to adapt and incorporate ... innovations [in methods of production and subject matter] by making them their own. Thus, it was not long before Rank had jumped on the social problem/realism bandwagon ... It should be remembered that while innovations did occur it was still by and large against a backdrop of 'business as usual' ... A year after *Room at the Top* it was *Doctor in Love* which topped the British box office, with *Sink the Bismarck* not far behind.

At the time, independence was resolutely confined within the structures of combine control, if not at the point of production, then by the distribution and exhibition structures.

Having set the scene within which film-makers wove their discursive networks, Hill then tackles the way the texts function in that context. He ranges across a large number of social problem and working-class/realist films, fully sensitive to the plurality and contradictoriness of individual texts, faithfully noting their points of tension and fissures where excess threatens to pull the film in surprising directions. But having charted the shifting spectrum within which the films produce meanings, he is able to show how they raise problems, define them and propose solutions to them. Solutions which almost invariably are aligned with at worst rabid conservatism or at best with timid and confused forms of vacuous humanism. Hill carefully avoids suggesting these films were pernicious simply because they propagandized on behalf of conservative positions: their real effectivity is in the kinds of sense they ruled out of court, i.e., which types of understanding of social experience they systematically precluded.

The breath of fresh air thus introduced by Hill's book concerns the demonstration that texts may be as plural and contradictory as you please (all texts are anyway). What matters is how they define issues and above all within which constraints and boundaries they locate the range of 'thinkable' solutions. Hill thus again raises the question of what a socialist cultural practice might be: what kind of practices or products could induce viewers to experience pleasures conducive to a socialist culture; which types of formal innovation and organisational arrangements are required to enable issues to be raised within socialist frameworks of understanding?

In so doing, he identifies – although he doesn't do so explicitly in the book – a crucial failing in contemporary leftist media culture. In the late 60s and throughout most of the 70s, socialist film theory discredited the notion that texts were homogeneous statements with transparent meanings and a direct effect on the viewer's beliefs. That there were important connections between text, the social and subjectivity was taken for granted: the problem was to determine the precise nature of these connections. These efforts were not successful and often wrongheaded, but at least they implied an image of what a socialist cultural practice might be, for producers as well as for consumers. These theoretical writings operated with a socialist ideal ego as something yet to be attained. This ideal ego was a puritanical one, to be sure, but at least there was an image to move towards, perhaps best summarised by Brecht's often invoked 'fighting' conception of popularity.

However, since the installation of a Conservative government in the U K, large sectors of the apparently left-inclined intelligentsia have devoted themselves, under the guise of criticising the shortcomings of 70s theory and its puritanical ideal ego which has to work for its gratifications, to the total elimination of any kind of socialist ideal ego. Suddenly, there was no longer any need to argue for a move towards a socialist cultural practice since that practice was deemed to exist already and could be found in the way working-class people (and black people, and women, and gays, etc.) made sense of/with the material provided for them by the established media multinationals and our existing television regimes. At best, that cultural practice was said to manifest itself in the way particular social groups resisted these media offerings or consumed them in erratic ways. At worst (and predominantly) existing patterns of consumption were legitimised and even celebrated. This profoundly demobilising and destructive development appears to be based on the (innocent?) misuse of certain aspects of 70s theory, such as the notion of textual plurality, combined with a belief in the socialist essence of the ideologies of oppressed consumers (an oppressed person likes *Rocky* . . . and that can only be because s/he recognises socialist elements in the film . . . and it is up to the left cultural critic to draw attention to this fact by finding the socialist elements within the film in question). The debilitating thrust of such an approach is usually cloaked in an aggressively populist rhetoric aimed against intellectuals at a time when we need to keep our critical wits more than ever.

Hill's approach, on the other hand, implies a fundamental critique, regrettably not elaborated in the book, of the way the gap between textual meaning-effects and the reader's meaning constructions has been exploited in recent left writing on the media, especially television. Contrary to the celebrants of textual plurality, Hill takes on board the pertinent aspects of Adorno's cultural industry argument which acknowledges that cultural production under capitalist conditions is necessarily implicated in a capitalist logic, and that assertions about the way people consume cultural objects float in thin air unless they are put into the context of an analysis of that logic.

It is true that the plurality of meaning is inherent in any form of discourse production, but this plurality is produced under specific social conditions which cannot be reduced to the variants in the viewing situation (family, cinema, classroom, etc.). These viewing conditions, together with the cultural products (films, T V programmes) and with the viewers themselves (taking into account that social existence determines consciousness) are all overdetermined and constrained by the general logic of capitalist production within which and by which they are located.

Adorno's persuasive argument concludes that the overriding capitalist logic at issue in cultural production is the process of commodification: the relentless pressure to replace use value by exchange value. However, it is a contradiction within capitalism that in order for exchange value to be enthroned as emperor, it is also necessary to ensure a degree of adherence to the requisite imperial ideologies and to discredit or, if possible, to eradicate from memory the discourses which could threaten the rule of commodity fetishism. That is the context within which the current references to 'pleasure' must be seen. As Adorno predicted:

> The more inexorably the principle of exchange value cheats human beings out of use values, the more successfully it manages to disguise itself as the ultimate object of enjoyment.
>
> (in *Gesammelte Schriften*, vol. 14, Suhrkamp, 1973, p. 20)

Capitalism also requires cultural products to have a use value: a use value for capitalism. In the words of Andreas Huyssen:

> If cultural products were commodities through and through and had only exchange value, they would no longer even be able to fulfil their function in the process of ideological reproduction. Since they do preserve this use value for capital, however, they also provide a locus for struggle and subversion.
>
> (*After the Great Divide*, Indiana U.P., 1986, p. 22)

What must be remembered in the discussion about pleasure, struggle and subversion in relation to textual plurality is precisely that it is a capitalist logic which creates and defines the sites of possible contestation. Merely to play around within those spaces with the material offered is to consent to that process of definition, not to challenge it.

There are, of course, powerful forces at work within capitalism to confine those spaces even more rigorously, even to try and abolish them altogether. The latest manifestations of this ruthless pressure to intensify the process of commodification emanate from the European banking sector as well as from Jack Valenti of the Motion Picture Association of America. Bart de Haas, director of the Amsterdam bank Pierson, Heldring and Pierson which is to head a syndicate of European banks aiming to set up a European media industry in conjunction with the E E C, publicly stated earlier this year:

> We have an overwhelming misunderstanding of the word 'culture' . . . There is no way to finance a risky industry like the film business if it is regarded as culture . . . The reason we are against culture is because without a purely business approach we cannot raise enough money to produce a viable product. The production of a Mercedes or a B M W is not regarded as a cultural activity, so why should film be considered as culture?

Valenti put the American perspective on the issue in more warlike terms befitting current U S Government rhetoric (and actions), labelling as 'the enemy' countries which

> refuse admission or restrict entry of U S film properties under the guise of Cultural Sovereignty. We are very much in favor of taking a tough stand. I am determined that we are not going to allow foreign countries that have free access to the American market with films and tv programmes and in every aspect of trade, to battle our entry into their countries.
>
> (quoted in *Variety*, 14 May 1986, p. 7)

Although it makes sense to argue for the total commodification of cultural products such as films in a multinational and a global context, which is where de Haas and Valenti speak from, national *bourgeoisies* have to acknowledge the (use) value of cultural production if only to bolster their own sense of legitimacy. Hence the potential conflict between Valenti and national film industries. It may happen, of course, as it has in the UK, that a Government may regard the use value of film as marginal or irrelevant and to concentrate on ensuring the capitalist use value of television instead, abandoning film to the forces of commodification or to control film through the regulation of television, given the increasing subordination of film to television's production and dissemination capacities. This is Britain's contribution to the forces of multinational commodification.

The tragic mistake of many left cultural commentators and academics is to connive with these forces, wittingly or not. The way questions of pleasure are discussed in relation to 'popular' films or TV programmes helps the commodity disguise itself as the ultimate object of enjoyment and thus contributes to the process whereby the stress on exchange value inexorably cheats human beings out of use values. This is not to say that the pleasure question is not important. Merely that it should be argued on totally different grounds, as is done, for example, in Ashish Rajadhyaksha's contribution on popular Indian cinema to *Framework* no. 32/33. The lack of attention to the capitalist logic overdetermining cultural production is also one of the most serious shortcomings of, for example, Dave Morley's work on the way audiences/viewers use television. His work tends to construe the site of plurivocality, the space for resistance, as a space only invested by the power relations that obtain within family or peer group situations. He thus undervalues the fact that media discourses are constructed within the boundaries of capitalism's need to perpetuate itself and its need for profit. What 'play' there is for individuals to resist or struggle is thus already severely constricted and pre-shaped. Individuals may very well not adhere to the meanings preferred by television, but these meanings will nevertheless remain the only material most audiences have to work with (newspapers can be ruled out as alternative sources since they appear to be given even less credence than TV). This is not simply a matter of agenda setting: the terms in which the agenda is to be discussed have been set at the same time. When seen in that light, it is perhaps not surprising that Morley's work tends to pay more attention to the way the TV as a piece of sound-and-image emitting furniture is used in interpersonal relations, that is, the immediate commodity aspect of the use of TV. It is possible to see his discussion of the uses of TV-as-furniture as substituting for attention to the things people can and, more importantly, cannot do with TV discourses, caught themselves in a relentless commodification process to the point where scheduling is now reduced to the disposition in time of a range of commodities analogous to the way a supermarket displays its wares in space. This process of commodification has even invaded individual programmes themselves, such as *Hill Street Blues*, which now present a carefully market-researched alternation of generically codified commodities transforming the programme into a kind of shopping mall where a customer may walk past one shopwindow in order to be caught by another one a bit further on.

Hill's book should put paid to the illusion that with the recognition of textual plurality, matters can now safely be left to the consumer's consciousness. Instead of relying on a fantasy identification with 'the working class' and elevating this delusion into an ethical imperative, Hill examines the way films live in their social frameworks and he had to conclude that

What is significant . . . is not just the ideological homogeneity, or otherwise, of the views which the films displayed, but also the range of views and the *boundaries* [Hill's emphasis] in which these operated.

[. . .]

VIII
Aboriginal Content:
Who's Got It – Who Needs It?

ERIC MICHAELS

From *Art & Text* nos. 23/4 (March–May 1987)

At a time when all the governments of Europe, and the European Community, faced with the establishment of Direct Broadcasting by Satellite (DBS), are filled with anxiety about the potential destruction of the complex of languages and cultures which constitute the European heritage, this article by Eric Michaels offers an intriguing and timely account of the media problems faced by the Aboriginal peoples of Australia. To the European and North American reader the production and exhibition situations he outlines, and the institutions to which he refers, may be unknown, but the problems and solutions he discusses are all too depressingly familiar and pertinent.

This is one of a number of articles Michaels wrote about the use of electronic media by aboriginal communities in Australia. There are many interesting aspects to this work stemming from the fact that it is about largely oral cultures encountering television through the new technologies of video and satellite without necessarily having experienced the earlier media 'stages' of printing, cinema and terrestrially broadcast television.

Thus in a related article★ he outlines how the Warlpiri peoples' reading of televisual narrative fiction revealed their unfamiliarity with the major television genres and conventions, leading to levels of understanding strikingly different to those intended by the producers. This difference, which arose from the very different way in which the Warlpiri use video as offering a basically mnemonic, evocative, symbolic system, posits the need, Michaels suggests, for a new theory of interpretation which requires the reconsideration of television as a type of writing system.

In this piece Michaels expands on this notion by describing in some detail the way in which 'alternative' media practices and aesthetics he considers to be 'Brechtian', are adopted by the Warlpiri people involved in television production at Yuendumu. Intriguingly, such work largely results in what he assesses to be a rather pure form of verité documentary.

★ See Eric Michaels, 'Hollywood Iconography: A Warlpiri Reading' in Phillip Drummond and Richard Paterson (eds.) *Television and its Audience – International Research Perspectives* (BFI: 1988), pp. 109–24.

However, the author's main concerns in this article are to question the concept of Aboriginal 'content', and the role and function the Australian state and the key media and Aboriginal institutions fulfil in their attempt to solve the complex of issues surrounding the establishment of 'Aboriginal media'. In a powerful concluding section, Michaels locates the discourses and debates about Aboriginal media taking place among the institutionally powerful and legitimated operations, outside the communities themselves, and uses this analysis to make a compelling case for localism as the key concept in 'Aboriginal content':

If we take 'community' rather than 'aboriginality' to be the subject and make 'local' the qualifier, only then do we avoid the traps of racism and paternalism in our rhetoric and practice. . . .

Warlpiri Media Association programmes only become 'Aboriginal Content' when they are exported from Yuendumu, and perhaps only when they are expropriated from Aboriginal Australia. In the context of their transmission at Yuendumu they are simply local media.

This article presents a provocative and stimulating argument providing a number of disturbing resonances for the analysis of broadcasting problems currently being faced in Europe. Certainly this paper could be used to argue strongly against many of the pan-European T V initiatives currently being considered and lobbied for. As may be imagined, in Australia the paper was more than provocative, in that it represented a challenging and contentious analysis to the institutions involved in these debates. Nevertheless, for the record, it must be stated that despite his criticisms of some aspects of the work of the Central Australian Aboriginal Media Association, Eric Michaels was a public defender of the organisation.

M.A./J.O.T.

Introduction

During a telephone conversation with an executive of a television company licenced to begin direct broadcasting to one of the remote satellite footprints next year, I was asked, somewhat plaintively, if I could help him to identify precisely what would constitute 'Aboriginal Content', and if perhaps I might help get him some. This category is evolving as a criterion for judging the suitability of program services by the Australian Broadcasting Tribunal when evaluating applications where a significant component of the intended audience will be Aboriginal. The Tribunal may in fact be extending its criteria for suitability, within the policy context of localism, by analogy to the 'Australian Content' requirement it imposes on radio and television licence holders. The notion of Australian content has proved problematic in some respects, which may have contributed to the difficulty of enforcement. But, as I intend to indicate, compared to 'Aboriginal Content', Australian content is a piece of cake. Presumably, an

Aboriginal content requirement will encourage a considerable market for documentary and ethnographic film production, and as such could prove to be of general interest to students of Australian cinema.

I could do little more than commiserate with the T V executive; he indeed had a problem. Would the Tribunal accept programs made by Europeans about Aborigines; a *Country Practice* episode with an Aboriginal character; or only programs made by Aborigines themselves? And if the Central Australian Aboriginal Media Association (C A A M A) makes a video clip of Midnight Oil, what is that? In fact, this typology of possible Aboriginal content would have to be expanded still further, and perhaps some earnest taxonomists might offer their services to the Tribunal to develop a discussion paper on the matter. Instead, I want to take this opportunity to attempt to develop a response to what seems an eminently fair question, without, I suspect, ultimately coming up with an answer that will do the T V executive much good. The matter intrigues me because the problematic of Aboriginal content expands in a number of interesting directions which allow us to consider not just the media text, in its narrow sense, but the production contexts and institutional practices which ultimately reach into the much broader social and cultural facts of the ascription and inscription of Aboriginality in Australia. Indeed, I will begin by noting my own genetic lack of Aboriginal – or even Australian – content, and admitting that the topic excites me partly because it requires a reflexive posture if I intend to develop this any further at all.

My own interest in coming to Australia was not Aborigines *per se*, in whom I had no specialist background, but in their experience of coming to the media as a test and an analogy to questions posed within the modern Western tradition. Ultimately, I wanted to understand our, not their, media revolution. To accomplish this, I undertook three years of field studies in remote central Australia, involved with the introduction of T V and video mostly at the remote community called Yuendumu. Somewhere along the line, the distinction between 'our' media revolution and 'theirs' may have blurred as the particularity of the Australian situation engaged me during my fieldwork. But now, even as the field recedes in some sense and I become more reflective, I remain impressed with just how important the Aboriginal experience of television is proving to be for Australian media as a whole.

For that reason, these matters of Aboriginal media policy, practice and law arise in the more general context of documentary cinema. It might be argued, of course, that these are interesting if peripheral issues to the central enterprise of Australian media production, and proceed with an admittedly specialist concern. But I prefer to suggest that the issues which arise around the practice of Aboriginal media will eventually inform the construction of diverse mass-mediated images from documentary resources, the raw materials of peoples' lives and lived experiences. By putting it this way, I am rejecting here a generic definition of documentary as a particular expository convention which presumes some privileged relationship to the real (a definition still useful in much textual analysis) – because assumed there is a transparency of opposition between truth and fiction (actuality and imagination) which, I think, obscures the significant issues for theory and practice.

I am proposing a more utilitarian, processual definition, geared more to media practitioners, subjects and viewers. Such a definition would be based not on the properties of the text, but on the conditions of its production and use. These may or may not be easily identifiable in that text itself, especially if we are not trained to look for them. This requires that we expand the critical analysis to consider evidence of the conditions of making, transmitting and viewing, and to acknowledge that texts come into existence, and must be described, in terms of social relations between institutionally situated audiences and producers, and that meanings arise in these relationships between text and context in ways that require a precise description in each case.

The impetus for an altered definition is not merely theoretical: it has an industrial basis as well. The new availability of home video cameras and other inexpensive imaging machines, and the proliferation of channels for display and transmission, means that we are seeing more and more media (and a proliferation of genres) constructed from lived events in non-fictive modes. Aboriginal video is one of the examples which has received special attention and analysis, but I suspect it heralds a general expansion of a class of texts which we will be involved in producing and criticising increasingly over the next few years.

Let me turn now to three items, which I will associate later with particular texts, to describe a locus of contradictions for my consideration of 'Aboriginal Content'. My analytical bias throughout will remain on remote 'traditional' communities, not because I want to argue that they are somehow more 'really' Aboriginal, but because their former isolation from mass media triggered the debate on Aboriginal air rights. Thus, they form a particularly important piece in the puzzle of Aboriginal content.

Cases
Item 1
The Warlpiri-speaking people of Yuendumu, in the remote Northern Territory, between 1982 and 1986, archive over three hundred hours of video tape essentially produced – photographed, directed and edited – by community members themselves. These productions are first circulated around camp VCRs, and later are transmitted over a pirate low-power transmitter. A researcher (myself) and certain educationalists in the community assist in training and in some phases of production. Similar video production and distribution systems emerge, over this period, in as many as a dozen separate remote communities. They can be distinguished by the degree to which their products are accessible (either by content or distribution) to non-local, non-Aboriginal audiences. They can also be distinguished, as the non-Aboriginal assistants working in support functions for these video units tend to do, by the degree of European intervention. Or, as Penny MacDonald, Executive Producer of the 'First feature-length video made entirely by traditional Aborigines' and I have debated it: 'My Aborigines are more self-managed than yours.'
Item 2
The Central Australian Aboriginal Media Association (CAAMA) expands from radio broadcasting to video production in 1983. Arguing that imported satellite-

delivered television may present certain dangers for traditional Aboriginal language and culture (24 distinctive language communities exist in the service area), it mounts a successful bid for the Central Zone Commercial Television Licence. CAAMA's television production unit, which will supply the original programming for the licenced service, is headed by an exclusively European direction and production staff managing a trainee group of town-based Aborigines, none of whom speak any Aboriginal languages or practice traditional custom. CAAMA's subsidiary television company, Imparja, enters negotiations with the West Australian Zone licence holder, 'Golden West Network', which will effectively extend the West Australian Service to Central Australia with perhaps three hours a week reserved for CAAMA-produced transmissions – which means perhaps six minutes per language group per week, not counting commercials or English language.

Item 3

The Task Force on Aboriginal and Islander Broadcasting and Communications publishes its recommendations in 1984, which are accepted, mostly, by Cabinet late in 1985, and are poised for implementation in 1987, following consultation with a Department of Aboriginal Affairs (DAA) determined Aboriginal broadcasting 'consultative' committee. The Task Force recommendations are far-ranging, but a number of themes emerge in close reading. Of particular interest is a notion ascribed to the Chairman, Aboriginal bureaucrat and educator Eric Willmot, called 'embedding'. In its simplest sense, embedding means the interpellation of Aborigines, Aboriginal issues or themes, in programs which are not otherwise identifiable as Aboriginal in content or production particulars. Significantly, Professor Willmot recommends that such programming will constitute the majority of Aboriginal television content. It is more likely to be produced by, and appear on, public service television (ABC, SBS) than in any specialised commercial or Aboriginally-organised context. The task force appears to endorse the embedding concept, with recommendations for a major role for ABC television in the production and transmission of such materials. In response, there has been an upsurge of activity within the ABC around the opportunities seen to flow from the Task Force's recommendations.

Discussion

Each of these items abstracts circumstances at a pivotal site in the recent struggle for Aboriginal media access. Taken as a whole, they pose not merely contradictions, they suggest a complete fragmentation of the discourse on Aboriginal media. Not only doesn't DAA seem to be talking about what CAAMA is talking about, and CAAMA in turn fails in its dialogue with the remote communities, but they don't seem to be talking to each other very much.

Examples are not difficult to find. The Task Force policy for regional and remote broadcasting was based on the assumption that no Aboriginal media group would have direct access to a satellite transponder, and worked its distribution policy around what now CAAMA – and the Tribunal – have disproved. But no revision of policy to consider this fundamental shift, and the possibilities it poses, have been discussed, so that CAAMA's situation becomes isolated and encapsulated in government thinking. Even so, the government can claim that the problems in the remote central Australian communities are now solved by the CAAMA licence.

CAAMA, meanwhile, its resources and attention largely diverted by Darwin, Canberra and the demands of its commercial licence, has no dedicated resources for supporting, assessing or even communicating with the remote Aboriginal producing stations, who in turn are kept in fair ignorance of all of the policy and planning whose first cause, it was said, is in the interests of 'traditional language and culture'. And the DAA seems to have an almost pathological fear of actually communicating with the bush. No remote producers were invited to the recent consultative committee meeting, even though an agenda item was a major, multi-million dollar scheme for licencing and hardware supplies for remote stations.

These, however, are familiar contradictions of Australian Aboriginal Affairs in their neo-colonial manifestation, and perhaps only seem more grotesque because the subject of these miscommunications is, in this case, communication itself. Equally alarming are the contradictions within sites, identified by each of the items above:

1. the government (via an Aboriginal bureaucrat) recommending that Aboriginals 'embed' themselves in the ABC;

2. CAAMA, in the service of Aboriginal cultural maintenance, undermining the very sense of the remote satellite licencing scheme by proposing a networking system which will probably dump extensive America media via Perth into Central Australia;

3. the apparent contradiction of self-determined and self-managed television broadcasting in remote, traditional communities whose record in most other areas of development (e.g. health, literacy, management and essential services) has hardly been impressive.

Associated Texts

We are screening several videos in association with this address to provide examples of some of the kinds of programs which might qualify as Aboriginal content. Admittedly, the choice had as much to do with availability as any curatorial principle. But I think it becomes clear quite quickly what kinds of products are associated with what kinds of production systems.

It so happened that all of the tapes involved Aboriginal producers to varying degrees. The 'government' tapes, from the Institute of Aboriginal Studies and the Northern Territory government, involved Aborigines mostly in training capacities under the direction of Europeans. To my knowledge, none of the Aborigines involved speaks an indigenous language or maintains traditional customs. However, all feature 'traditional' subjects, often as not, doing European things. They are intended to present Aborigines in a positive light, positive in the sense of development, or even assimilation. In fact, the emphasis on technology and high production values (intended, rather than realised) seems part of a more general attempt to constitute Aborigines as 'world class, export quality' natives. They feature what the government sees to be 'good' Aborigines doing productive (i.e. non-Aboriginal) things.

There may be relatively few audiences which can be identified outside of bureaucracy (or perhaps Johannesburg) who will share this reading. There is some uncertainty in my mind, and I think in the tapes themselves, about just who the intended audience is in any case. The funding which produces these tapes usually instructs producers to aim them at diverse Aboriginal audiences, to whom the government wishes to transmit a message of its accomplishments. They are first vetted by bureaucrats who must be satisfied that they conform to the image the bureaucrats have of themselves (as well as of Aborigines). They are assuredly not meant to be controversial. But because Aborigines are likely to 'read' these tapes quite differently from European bureaucrats, and bureaucrats are unlikely to be able to anticipate Aboriginal readings, unanticipated meanings can emerge quite freely at different screenings. I have seen Aborigines double over with laughter at certain parts of these tapes not at all intended, I take it, to be funny. And I have seen them become livid with anger when traditional restrictions for the display of sacred information have been breached, as the Northern Territory government (and the A B C) does quite often. I suspect a Sydney audience reads these tapes with a certain dreadful irony, but I assure you they are not intended to produce that response.

The second group of tapes comes from regional Aboriginal media organis-ations. The model of this type is, of course, the C A A M A video magazine. These are distinguished by a quite different rhetorical style: they are culturally assertive, they feature translations in Aboriginal languages, and they take on controversial topics. But underneath this rhetorical surface, they seem to me surprisingly like the government tapes. They again have a similar mix of Aborigines succeeding at apparently European tasks, as well as inserts of a certain amount of 'traditional' material – indeed, a content analysis shows this may be even less than in the government tapes. Perhaps my processual definition of documentary will reveal that the means, if not the relations, of production are in some respects similar to the government video units, thus accounting for the similarity in product. Again, an Aboriginal trainee staff is under the direction of European specialists. There is an acceptance of basic western conventions of format, framing, narrative and episode, and an attempt at sophisticated production values. Part of the interest and charm of these tapes, for me, is the failure to achieve these production values, which in recent magazines is itself becoming conventionalised as a kind of folksy style which can be quite appealing. But it is difficult to detect anything uniquely non-western about the use of the medium here.

C A A M A is quite explicit about the relationship between producers and audience. A sign on the old radio station used to read, 'Aboriginal Radio in Aboriginal Country', and 'Aboriginal Radio for Aboriginal People'. I think the C A A M A radio service did achieve this in a number of remarkable ways. The unpalatable early experience of working at the Alice Springs A B C studios led them to an aggressive redesign of their first studio space, which featured considerable outdoor areas, breezeways and other camp-like features to make the space access-ible to local town campers and other Aborigines. The requirement to broadcast in three or four traditional languages meant creating a flexible production schedule and comfortable workplace for their interpreters – traditional people who were the heart of the on-air operation. The transmission range, which then was Alice Springs only, assured continual feedback from the audience which took an active and immediate interest in the station's operations. CAAMA radio, during 1983–85, exemplified local community access media. It was refreshing and, to the community's thinking, unarguably Aboriginal. This did not always show up in the content, which more often than not was American Country music, and imported Reggae. It was in the organisation of the workplace, and the relations of production, which emerged on-air mostly as format, announcing style and call-in cheerios which gave the station its authority and resonance for its Aboriginal audience.

With the expansion into television and the demands of a commercial licence, increased staff, higher technology and a more distant and less interactive audience, all these properties of the workplace may become compromised. The radio slogan now has been generalised at the new studios to 'Aboriginal Media for Aboriginal People'. But the more recent magazines and the ABC weekly broadcasts recognise that the more important audience at the moment may be the European public, the politicians and others, who now need assurances about Imparja television so they will cease their harassment and permit the service to proceed.

I do not mean by these criticisms to give support to the view current in some southern Aboriginal quarters that CAAMA is a whitefella organisation in league with the government, and that its massive funding base should be redirected to urban and more diverse Aboriginal organisations. I believe these charges are ill-considered, and have more to do with a too familiar struggle for limited resources in which 'Aboriginality' becomes an ascription to be negotiated more as a commodity than as a recognition of content or authority. Rather, if there is a charge to be made, it is to the government, or perhaps the structure of the broadcasting system, which may be beating CAAMA to death with its stick in return for a very questionable carrot: a licence to broadcast regional commercial television. To the extent the institutional demands of government alter the means by which Aboriginal media is produced, the Aboriginality of the content may suffer. CAAMA counters that these are early days, and that forward planning intends the redundancy of the European staff and increased Aboriginal management.

In all fairness, I should point to the videotape from the Torres Strait Islanders Media Association that is included in the video program under discussion. This tape was essentially shot and edited by me, under instruction from the TSIMA. In the end, this tape was rejected due to the poor signal quality, although the post-production at Metro Television provided a cleaner signal than we achieved in any of the Central Australian Tapes. TSIMA was happy with the production arrangement; if they can get a white PhD to do their camerawork and editing for them, this was acceptable. The tape was rejected because what was wanted was an even more 'professional' look, one which could compete with imported commercial programming.

Torres Strait culture and politics are quite different from their mainland counterparts. Of all indigenous Australians, they alone have charged the government with discrimination in its failure to import commercial television to their population. The question of Islander control of production may matter less here. I am uncomfortable exhibiting and describing this video, partly because an 'indigenous' tape made by me is not going to provide me with much interesting data about production (or is it?). For others, I believe that the contradictions of production compromise and confuse the product and its possible reading unless the situation is admitted. The final scene in this drama, of course, is telling you this. I prefer to move on to the area in which I feel more comfortable: remote, traditional production based on my more collaborative work at Yuendumu.

'Traditional' Aboriginal Television

The idea that 'traditional' oral societies might express themselves in unique and interesting ways using electronic technology has its roots in Sapir's[1] and Whorf's[2] formulations of the relationship between language and culture. This appears contradicted by McLuhan's[3] claim that the medium will cause the message, and was tested by Worth and Adair[4] in an experiment with Navajo Native Americans in the late sixties. The experimental and interventionist components of my own research among the Warlpiri arose from this tradition. I posed the question: 'What might television look like if it had been invented by Warlpiri Aborigines?' The answer is described in detail in my project report, purposely titled *The Aboriginal Invention of Television*.[5] Some matters treated more fully there command our attention in a discussion of documentary theory and practice.

The Warlpiri proved to be documentarians par excellence – specifically, practitioners of a 'verité' mode pioneered by Morin and Rouche in France, and developed in the United States as 'Direct Cinema' by Pennebaker, the Maysles, and Wiseman among others, emerging in Australia in films by the MacDougalls, MacKenzie, and Dunlop. The Warlpiri people of Yuendumu now prove to be the most doctrinaire practitioners of this style. The Warlpiri deny fiction, both in their oral tradition and now in video-making. Stories are always true, and invention, even when it requires an individual agent to 'dream' or 'receive' a text, remains social in a complex and important sense that assures truth. Rights to receive, know, perform or teach a story (through dance, song, narrative and graphic design) are determined by any identified individual's structural position and social-ritual history within an elaborately reckoned system of kin. Novelty can only enter this system as a social, not an individual invention. Not only is one's right to invent ultimately constrained, it is particularly constrained with respect to the kinship role, for it is the genealogy of an item – not its individual creation – which authorises it. In the most simple-minded sense we might say that this is a solution to the problem of continuity in oral tradition. The narrative imagination and memory are consumed by the requirement of preserving knowledge over time by encoding it as true stories collectively authored. There is little inducement to confound the matter with individuals' invented fictions.

When conformity to traditional values is encouraged in video training and production, Warlpiri video-makers respond by inventing a version of Direct Cinema in order to subsume the text under the general requirements of sociability and veracity required by Aboriginal orality. People did not 'make things up' for the camera; rather, they were careful to perform everything in a true and proper manner. Indeed, they proved quite sensitive to certain implications of this inscription process, and in particular instances took great care that the entire kin network necessary to authorise a ritual performance were involved in video performances as well. Otherwise, the camera preferred to find for itself a comparatively inconspicuous role in a variety of public performances.

The social and historical consequences of mass media are quite different from the consequences and conditions of oral traditions, which we can appreciate by contrasting the commodity form and the consequent exchange value of information in the two systems. Script, and especially print, tends to disassociate the author from his utterance. Indeed, complex conventions of signature, copyright, even the social construction of authorship – as a concept with legally enforced economic rights – emerge from the historically associated inventions of the printing press and modern capitalism. These conventions are required by the weakened links between speaker and speech in print and mass culture.

By contrast, oral transmission, where authors and their utterances remain linked in performance, does not emphasise elaborate social engineering to reinforce this linkage or assure the value of the utterance. Indeed, stories are attached in such a way to particular speakers that these stories are said to be owned. But I think the translation to English here is misleading, for the conditions of ownership in oral societies are, as I will discuss, quite distinct from what we mean by owning in materialist society. Probably ownership concepts for Aboriginal orality concern obligations to transmit and exchange rather more than to acquire and hoard in a capitalist sense. Instead of restricting use by signature and copyright, the social engineering required to assure value in oral traditions involves restricting access to performers and performances so that no one whom the social structure does not position in the correct kinship relationship can bear witness to any valuable speech or performance event. Indeed, kinship practice involves speech and associational restrictions which prescribe and proscribe interaction and styles so that what one says to whom, and in what way, is itself restricted.

Let me return to the problem the oral system poses for historiographic analysis: how does this system assure social reproduction of the cultural text over time without written archives? In fact, this problem is converted to possibility in Warlpiri orality by engineering a capacity for oral truths to respond to change without ever appearing to be changing. One means by which this is accomplished is by refusing to externalise inscription except in social discourses and performance. From within the oral system which stores information in specified authorities and reproduces it in socially regulated ritual, there is no contradiction possible to claim that Dreaming Law is and always was, as it is, eternal. From outside the system, we may observe that the law can change, without ever appearing to do so.

This is also managed by recourse to a spatial metaphor corresponding to identity with the land. By distributing information, as story, differentially throughout the society along the interlocking kinship matrix, the Warlpiri establish a network of information specialists, each maintaining some aspect – but never the whole – of the truth. Thus, important matters (such as ceremonies, authorisation, decision-making) require the assemblage of many people who will each contribute their piece of the puzzle. For example, for a whole song cycle to be performed may require many people (often from diverse locales) to collaborate in the performance. Thus, information is dispersed in time and space through a network that eventually encompasses the continent, and perhaps the world, in which each adult individual has particular, but constrained, speaking and knowing rights. Significantly, this system is not hierarchical, something extraordinarily difficult for people from class societies to appreciate, whether that society is British Colonial administration or a film crew.

Problems of Conduct for
European Producers

It may be helpful to deviate from the line of discussion at this point and identify some of the problems that my analysis of the traditional system implies for the conduct of European producers of Aboriginal subjects. Because one isn't allowed free access to events where information is displayed, traditional Aboriginal communities pose a particular problem for film-makers who wish to use these communities as sites for location shooting. One cannot film anybody, anywhere, at any time. Certain events and performances will always be off-limits, and responsible film-makers should take care to inform themselves of these facts by identifying the appropriate senior authorities and, minimally, securing permission for each take. This would be the minimal requirement; more extensive collaborative relationships would be preferred, as my points so far suggest. Of course if you are of the Albee Mengles adventure documentary school, venturing where no white man has ever gone before, you will instead take these limitations as challenges so that you can bag for your audience especially rare specimens of exotica. I suspect that there is a unique level of hell reserved for these film-makers, and would like to encourage the possibility that we will reserve a special section of our gaols for them just to make sure. But the problem is not always so clearly drawn.

Aboriginal information ownership obligates the owner to display that information, and to teach it to assure its value and continuity. Such display is understood to obligate the person so honoured and educated. In a face-to-face society (without print, electronic recording or mass distribution) the system operates as it is intended: to assure the continuing value of information. Not being especially racist, just ethnocentric, Aboriginal elders often include Europeans, even film-makers, in these displays, honouring them and obligating them at the same time. Unfortunately, film-makers (and journalists and anthropologists) do not always choose to understand the implications of this obligation. The transfer of knowledge here does not include the transfer of copyright; ownership still remains with the Aborigines.

In the past, when traditional Aborigines resisted literacy and remained outside the mass media distribution network, they rarely were aware of what happened to the words they allowed to be written and the images they permitted to be recorded. It could be argued, therefore, that there were no important consequences to this appropriation, although I would not take that position myself. But with the extension of the national media network to the outback and with Aborigines' new-found ability to see what Europeans make of them, the consequences become real and undeniable.

Aborigines who now are regarded by their 'countrymen' as having leaked information into the public network, are accused by their fellows as having 'sold their law'. Fights, social upheaval and elaborate paybacks can follow the desecration of a ceremony or even a design that occurs when it is broadcast. The problem is grave, serious, and 'culturecidal'. I would recommend that film-makers who intend to distribute their work on television should consider their conduct very carefully from now on. If not they are likely to find their access to Aboriginal communities wholly cut off in the near future, and possibly find the Aboriginal Heritage Protection Act[6] or even the laws governing obscenity and blasphemy extended retroactively to ethnographic films. The ABC, the most persistent offender, should be paying very close attention here if they plan to continue accessing Federal funds as the major site of appropriation and dissemination of Aboriginal images. Traditional people care not a whit what trendy and pro-Aboriginal rhetoric is used to frame these desecrations.

It is tempting to pursue this point further, to detail the rules and propose procedural guidelines for film-making in traditional communities. I demur, however, not just because any complete elaboration of Aboriginal information management traditions would result in far too prolonged a discussion. In fact, I could not undertake an exhaustive inventory for three reasons:

1. I don't know all of the components of this system;

2. I suspect that the system is emergent in some respects, so to treat the system as an inventory of static rules would always be misleading and inaccurate;

3. The point of these rules, I take it, is at the very heart of Aboriginal authority, orality and autonomy. If I succeeded in inscribing a 'Hamurabi's Code' in the stone of my text, I believe I would utterly subvert Aboriginal tradition, and in particular the essential rights, responsibility and definition of eldership in the lived Aboriginal tradition.

Or, to put it simply, if I had a complete understanding of this system, as a researcher-observer-European, I would disappear; I would have become 'Aboriginalised', and so might even refuse to tell you these things. But having argued that these rules exist as essentials of Aboriginal orality, that they subvert and contrast to 'print' culture, and that they are involved in the ways that traditional Aborigines constitute themselves in the making of video, I want to continue discussing what this means when people outside this tradition try to make films or television from the resources of Aboriginal people and events. And I want to address the very dangerous position in which this may place Aboriginal subjects, and finally, why Aborigines themselves judge the outcome of these efforts not as fictive but false – in fact, as lies – and judge the means of their production to be theft.

The Ethnographic Film-makers' Response

The idea that taking pictures of native peoples may be considered by them to be theft is now familiar enough to have become the point of a joke in *Crocodile Dundee*. Certainly, ethnographic film-makers have had the issue under consideration for over a decade. The ethics sessions at the Conferences on Visual Anthropology held in Philadelphia throughout the 1970s annually featured a certain amount of chest-beating and public displays of white guilt about the matter.[7] The discourse was imported to Australia in 1978 at the ethnographic film conference held at the Australian Institute of Aboriginal Studies.[8] I assumed these were ritual performances, intended, finally, to justify our practice, not to revolutionise it. A certain amount of stylish, and interesting, reflexivity did make its way into ethnographic conventions. It became usual, for instance, to show the results of field recording to the subjects, and insert their responses in the completed film itself. But in the end, the people who gave cameras to natives remained people who considered themselves researchers. Film-makers did not give up their cameras so easily. But in retrospect, I think some very important changes may have emerged from those sessions.

First, it was important to substantiate the charges of indigenous subjects, to demonstrate that the ethical problematic of image appropriation was not merely one of curious superstitions of backwards savages who misunderstood the technology. Our own analysis was leading to quite similar conclusions. There was a discourse on power here, signalled and enforced by the politics of positioning of people as either before or behind the camera.

Second, a limited defense was mounted by asking: 'What is the essential difference between taking pictures of people and writing about them?' Is it anything more than that the visual product proves more accessible to our subjects than our writing, so that it attracts their criticism first? The criticism might be one of ethnography as a whole, not just ethnographic film.

Third, raising these issues led into a new discourse, which found resonance in some of the more interesting criticial theories – particularly the newer marxisms and post-structuralist approaches. All of these return us to questions such as the relationship between subject and object, the problematic of authorship, and the linguistic character of representation. If it is not clear that this helped people make better films, I would claim that we became better at talking about our films. But this may be too cynical. If I fail to detect any important revolution in explicitly ethnographic film-making in the last decade which could pose an answer to these questions, I do detect a considerable change in what kinds of text we are willing to treat as ethnographic and to encompass in our considerations, as well as the kinds of roles we are willing to perform. Avant-garde and experimental film made by artists, home movies and videos, indigenous and third world production, have all been identified and treated for ethnographic interest. The interest is something more than Mead and Metraux's[9] 'Culture at a Distance' studies of texts; it is more immediate and reflexive.

There now may be far more willingness among a new generation of film-makers to act on the criticisms of appropriation and propose a radical, collaborative practice in film and video work with Aborigines. Cavadini and Strachan, Digby Duncan, David Woodgate, David Batty, Penny MacDonald and others are involved in a body of contemporary work in which their role as producers is no longer dominant, and where they seek to act as catalysts, providing conduits through which a more indigenous representation is possible. These relationships impose a new set of contradictions, as I suggested in my introductory examples of 'Aboriginal Content', and which I admitted with respect to my own work, particularly the T S I M A video. So I do not mean to suggest that handing the camera over to the subject automatically restores the subject and converts the process into a transparent act of auto-inscription. In fact, the working relationships between film-makers and Aboriginal subjects which result from the intention of media self-management, are diverse and have different success rates as judged from the perspective of either the participants or any given audience. Certainly, the results vary – in the case of the video product, in their interest and accessibility to Europeans.

Viewing this work can be a difficult experience for an urban audience. The pace is slow, the narrative difficult to grasp, and the work of 'reading' these forms can prove alienating to viewers, especially when these tapes are presented in a theatrical space. Yet some of these difficulties are precisely the qualities on which Aborigines judge these media to be positioned successfully in their own discourse. The matter is of theoretical interest, but may be even more important pragmatically.

Providing community media in locales with no productive economic base means that video expression here requires economic incentives and outside support. Media development could prove more successful in remote communities than has agricultural, industrial, or other material development projects, precisely because of the traditional interest and expertise in information management. My argument elsewhere has been that the Aboriginal world is an information society and as such offers something of particular value to the modern information age that can ultimately provide the basis of a reciprocal exchange.[10] But this goal is unlikely to be achieved within the dominant discourse on Aborigines and 'development'. The argument seems too subtle, and people remain unconvinced that Aborigines have anything unique to offer modern media. The emergent indigenous forms are vulnerable and likely to be destroyed precisely by the forces of media education, training and development. In that sector, I detect an 'official' rejection of indigenous production as clumsy or amateurish. The government, which sees the economic potential of these media mostly in terms of their suitability for export, despairs at the 'quality' of the local product in terms of these imposed standards. Much of its support will be directed at providing professional training to upgrade this quality. Certified professional film and television producers are likely to find themselves enlisted in this activity, which I argue may prove subversive of the emergent indigenous forms themselves, and so rob them of their ultimate exchange value in the western information economy. Rather than expand this theoretical argument, let me return to the ground with a last example, a description of how media is transmitted at Yuendumu, so that some further qualities of the communication system and its possible contribution to modern media can be demonstrated.

Yuendumu Television: Brechtian Theatre

Sometimes, on certain weekdays, perhaps around noon and again around 4 pm, Yuendumu T V may or may not go to air. The basic format is usually a kind of video D J: a compere selects pre-made tapes to show, and announces them along with any other news or commentary she or he thinks worthwhile. Sometimes kids come into the studio and read school stories, or old men tell stories live, but the D J format is the basic one.

Quite early on, the Warlpiri looked at the production system and decided that it really wasn't necessary to have several people in the studio to go to air. One person could turn on and focus the camera, do the announcements and switch over the tapes. This conforms to the Aboriginal work ethic, which demands maximum efficiency with no unnecessary waste of personnel or effort (especially when performing tasks for pay). The more difficult problem was finding a way to let people know when the station was broadcasting. The solution was to turn on some music (the signal is also received over A M radio), focus on a graphic and let that play for perhaps a half hour before beginning programming. Then, word of mouth would circulate through the camps and let people know to turn on their T V.

Jupurrula, one of the Warlpiri T V producers with whom I was most closely associated, is a big Reggae fan, so for his schedule he begins with Reggae music and focuses the camera on his Bob Marley T-shirt draped over a chair. After a while he refocuses on the compere's desk, walks around and into the shot, announces the schedule and any news, then walks out of the shot, turns off the camera and switches on the V C R. This procedure is repeated for each tape.

For me, the effect is almost an essay in Brechtian – or, more precisely, Beckett's – dramaturgy. The question that underlies a good deal of criticism of mass media seems to have its modern sources in these playwrights' work and that of Artaud. All proposed a different kind of involvement with the image than the 'willing suspension of disbelief', the conventionalised verisimilitude of both fiction and documentary narrative which lulled the nineteenth-century audience out of a critical posture and into a passive, receptive mood for entertainment. To the extent that today's mass media are entertaining, they now are also said to be anti-intellectual, drug-like, and politically oppressive. Critics of mass media, who are not simply elitist critics of proletariat culture, may in fact be asking: 'Can there be a Brechtian mass medium?' Can alienation and critical distance be preserved without losing the audience? The received wisdom is that this is somehow a contradiction in terms, although the A B C, unwittingly I think, nearly achieves this in its scheduling and program choices.

This is what fascinates me about Warlpiri T V. It could simply be argued that these forms emerge not from a mass society but a local one, and thus that the media it produces are not massified. Whatever the case, I am enthralled – as I am, say, at avant-garde film-makers' challenges to conventional forms. But I am forced to wonder if this was the point of the whole exercise, to satisfy my own quirky aesthetics, to satisfy my tastes for an alienating television. Indeed, the Warlpiri sometimes complain; they want to know why they can't also make Bruce Lee movies (which they dearly love) with Warlpiri language and characters. My response has been that we don't have the money or the equipment, that these are highly expensive entertainments, and that we need to stay with the things that only Warlpiri people can do, and therefore do best. We can use Bruce Lee films as training exercises, in a Frierian sense, and learn from a close reading just how they were made, how the special effects work, and why they're comparatively expensive. But I don't think this gets me off the hook entirely. There is a contradiction here.

As I have suggested, Warlpiri cosmology and expression imply a conservatism, a means of regulating social reproduction to obscure any influence of invention. This involves the identification of proper models for conduct as well as story, and only by encouraging an analogy to traditional expression could we in fact 'invent' a unique, Warlpiri T V. But Aborigines are entirely familiar with other kinds of T V, and want to know why they are restricted from access to other models. Indeed, they are well aware of the economic and prestige value of commercial cinema and T V, and there may be some fear that their own efforts are less prestigious and less valuable. Had the resources been available, a Warlpiri Kung Fu series would have been a fine idea; although I doubt that the Warlpiri production system could have succeeded here, I would have no problem being proved wrong. I suspect that the particular relationship between producer and audience which I am here reading as 'Brechtian' is actually a prerequisite for the authority of Aboriginal television, and that a Warlpiri Ninja adventure would either come out looking like this or result in a very different audience involvement.

I raise these points not because the Warlpiri (who are fiercely proud of their television as it is) think they are terribly important, but because they exist in a world that does. Australia as a whole, and the Department of Aboriginal Affairs in particular, places the highest value on 'professional standards', 'world class status', 'broadcast quality', and other imported credentials. The general aim of Aboriginal advancement seems to involve bringing Aborigines up to standard. And indeed, much of the Aboriginal Affairs media budget is directed at this goal in both the reception and production of media. Anything else would be less, and anything less could be discriminatory (a term which the mining industry has demonstrated can be perverted rather easily).

Aborigines who have positions of power in this bureaucracy are encouraged to see the media more and more in terms of the power of inscription; to occupy a gap created by the contact of cultures and the contrast with technology, and access the new media in ways that inscribe their own success as a model for others, as signatures drawn across that gap. As a result, they show little interest in distant developments such as the Yuendumu T V station, and are more involved in developing Aboriginal and even personal access to national and commercial media.

Culturecidal Content or Community Access

Edmund Carpenter, an anthropologist who was employed in the 1960s to advise the Australian government on the impact of modern media in traditional New Guinea culture, concluded that: 'We use media to destroy cultures, but first we use media to create a false record of what we are about to destroy.'[11]

The real difficulty with Carpenter's prediction is that it suggests only a protectionist agenda: quarantining Aborigines outside mass broadcasting. I think it fair to say that in Australia we have heard Carpenter's warning, and mean to find a more creative solution. But which solution will serve? The D A A's current support (at least in principle) of community production and other proposals to create 'balanced' services tailored to Aborigines, surely has this objective. I also take the sense of the Tribunal's encouraging 'Aboriginal Content' to be an attempt to prevent culturecide through media, problematic though its signification may be. But if my analysis is correct, both these proposals emerge not from any precise understanding of the Aboriginal information management tradition, but on a liberal, humanist, 'fair go' or equal rights argument. Attractive as they seem, these ideas may backfire. In my project report, I argued the curious probability that a national television service with no Aboriginal content would be less culturecidal for Aborigines than badly conceived and produced Aboriginal programs. These latter could be truly destructive.

I mean to have identified in my studies and my analysis here some of the particular characteristics of the clash between oral and mass media that is capable of subverting the oral tradition, and thus of destroying it. But unlike Carpenter, I am convinced that the reason orality comes out the loser is not due to any inherent vulnerability, but in the political and institutional forms which conspire to privilege modern mass media and their messages when these traditions collide. Thus, an 'oral' film or video may be possible, if the circumstances in which they are engaged can become more equitable. I sought to accomplish something like this in my own work, and have pointed to other work by Australian film-makers with similar goals. This required our own disappearance as signifier, a painful and unfamiliar abnegation for media people. There is very little that we will be able to take credit for in this enterprise. Oddly, contemporary Aboriginal politics encourage certain Aborigines, identified by the government, to position themselves much more conspicuously than the system traditionally encouraged, identifying their newly, bureaucratically constituted selves as signifiers, to engage in a massive opportunity for self-inscription that these new media provides. It is this oddity that I want to examine – and suggest a solution to – in my conclusion.

To me, the more worrying part of Carpenter's prediction involves the creation of false histories. Now it may be, if Baudrillard and others are correct, that this is the irresistible pressure of the twentieth century, and that all histories are being rewritten to satisfy the demands of the simulacra. Whether or not this is so, we may yet ask: 'Who gets to write these new histories, and to whose advantage?'

Aborigines and Aboriginality have always been subject to appropriation by European Australians, so that we consider the production of Aboriginal images for mass consumption as a right, if not a responsibility, of a nation consumed with the manufacture of its own mythology. None of this should prove to be novel considerations for Australian film scholars, engaged as we are in a self-conscious exploration of the received postmodernist debate and its application to the national situation. In that discourse we learn of the power of inscription, the disappearance of the signified, as it collapses into the signifier. What may be new is who Australia now regards as having the rights to make this appropriation. By identifying a class of people as Aborigines and providing some of these the right to authorise programs about others of these, we may risk inhibiting not only unique indigenous expressions; we risk employing media's vast transmission range to usurp local autonomy and attack the base of traditional life.

To the extent that exotic media producers dominate the discourse on Aboriginality for the public, they will write the new Aboriginal history. To the extent that Aboriginal 'experts' (politically or academically authorised) do so, they write that history. The competition seems mostly between these two non-local classes, and what has proved remarkable is the State's interest in all this; the Government's recommendations in the Task Force Report on Aboriginal Communications mostly concern models of collaboration between these more powerfully situated elites. The conditions and possibilities for remote or traditional local communities to enter the process, to image themselves, are denied by being ignored. We are engaged in an inscription process here truly capable of murdering the subject.

I think Stephen Muecke[12] is right when he claims that we have excluded Aborigines from this discourse in another sense, preferring to position them as modern subjects, or even pre-modern objects. The dominant filmic and documentary conventions (not to mention the ethics) applied to imaging Aborigines are rarely more recent than the 1950s; we engage a vulgar and ill-considered realism in the treatment of Aborigines. But do the few specialist readers we now position politically (both professional students of Aborigines and professional Aborigines themselves) to evaluate any text offer any improved insights? In the polemics that emerge here, these students and Aborigines seem to ask, as do remote people, whether an image is 'truthful'. But unlike truth in Dreaming Law, this truth is based on public relations law: is the text sympathetic to an image certain Aborigines think useful to project when based on essentially public relations notions of the persuasive function of film and TV? Attempts to challenge this notion from within film practice are being increasingly marginalised, so that works by the Cantrills and MacDougalls, for example, are not to be considered suitable candidates for Bicentennial funding. I wonder if Albee Mengles is? Certainly, CAAMA is being forced to consider the extent to which its funding commits it to public relations objectives of the government as opposed to its earlier objective of Aboriginal media for Aboriginal people.

The means by which 'Aboriginal Content', as an identified and authorised category of television and film, risks the destruction of traditional Aboriginal society, ultimately can be identified as racist. This is because it requires an act of false identification, or ascription, of Aborigines (consistent with the more general Australian conception of race) as an equivalent class whose culture is written in their blood. The point, precisely, is that culture is not written in blood, only genetics is. Culture is extra-somatic, and it is inscribed in the communication process itself. By attempting to resolve the dilemma new communications pose for traditional culture, we err terribly by offering a false cultural identification of Aboriginality. The essence of Aboriginality is localism: land-based systems working against hierarchy and authoritarianism.

Any requirement for Aboriginal content is by necessity so vague that the issue becomes not the identifying marks of the text, but the political one of just who is to designate these texts. As I conceive political privilege to be constituted in the Aboriginal bureaucracy, the contents likely to be identified are those that:

1. employ Aborigines as media subjects, perhaps as producers in certain 'approved' forms;

2. provide an opportunity for powerful Aboriginal bureaucrats to become more powerful;

3. result in a certain distribution of media production resources, probably in the direction of those already best situated to deliver products of a quality and style suited to the tastes and demands of Europeans, and

4. rewrite Aboriginal history while inscribing particular signatures as authors of this new/old Aboriginality.

None of these results begin to address the charge of media as an agent of culturecide. Indeed, they are all subject to that charge. Our newly constructed, media-simulated Aboriginality, delivered as content by AUSSAT to the remote communities, can succeed at subverting their traditions in a way that no other invasion has. It is not in the dumping of European content to these locations, then, but in the transmission of a powerful competing Aboriginal image, appropriated from the bush, purchased at the expense of local media, and filtered through the grid of a manufactured history, that culturecide could readily be accomplished.

The other way to think about all this, I propose, is simply as a particularly compelling case for localism, to be achieved through community access media projects. What other opportunity exists to avoid the divisioning of Aboriginal peoples in the authorisation and evaluation of media and communications systems in the reprehensible terms of degrees of Aboriginality?

If we take 'community' rather than 'aboriginality' to be the subject, and make 'local' the qualifier, only then do we avoid the traps of racism and paternalism in our rhetoric and practice. We also avoid empowering certain people to make decisions for others along racist lines, forcing competitors for these resources to charge each other with inclusion or exclusion from the community on the basis of some perverse and vulgar Social Darwinism. 'Community' would seem to be the correct term here, restoring us to a cultural discourse proper. Such a suggestion will admittedly not sit well with a Department of Aboriginal Affairs, which has recently asserted its right to control all projects involving Aborigines. What I am suggesting refers the matter back to the Department of Communications, which has shown no more taste for taking responsibility for the Aboriginal component of its clientele than it has for developing its brief for community television. But it will make more sense, and be more productive, I think, to tack Aboriginal requirements on to a general public television proposal than to tack public television on to an Aboriginal agenda. And it may be the only opportunity for remote community television to develop within an adequate structure of support, outside of the disastrous competition for authority I have discussed in the current system. This restores us to the positions posed earlier in my talk: that the Aboriginal media revolution signals a revolution in our own media, and that the only position capable of salvaging the Aboriginal subject will be its own disappearance.

Conclusion

The title of this address posed two questions regarding Aboriginal content: 'who's got it?' and 'who needs it?'. I want in conclusion to summarise the argument I have made in answer to these questions. But I begin by noting what I did not ask: Aboriginal content, what is it? Because I think I have demonstrated that this is not only *not* the important question, it isn't even answerable (or perhaps it has too many answers) in Australia today.

Clearly, the question of who's got Aboriginal content is the really tricky one, because in Australia it asks a question not only about texts, but perhaps more about subjects and their positioning. This too, I submit, is not a question which can be answered in any useful way right now. Rather, I meant to observe how this question, or one very much like it, operates pivotally in a neo-colonial Aboriginal discourse, and what substantial ideological and material resources get attached to any answer. I have taken the position, taken by some Aborigines themselves[13] that the rhetoric here is oppressive of its subject. 'Aboriginality', as a category, is entirely likely to destroy Aborigines. This more general argument, then, applies to the question of broadcasting and communications, where I believe precise examples of how this can and does happen are to be found too easily. Because culture is not your skin colour or your blood type, but a tradition communicated to you, the central place of communications in cultural maintenance or destruction makes this matter of introduced media of critical importance for Aborigines right now.

Which leads to the second question: who needs it? The answer to this seems largely to depend on political and social constructs. The satellite T V owner needs it because the Broadcasting Tribunal might make its licence dependent on it. The A B C might need it because the D A A has indicated that it will divert resources to the Corporation for it. But the curious fact could prove to be that remote Aborigines themselves don't need it – not just in the quantitative terms of C A A M A, whose Imparja licence may contain less of 'it' than any of its competing European controlled remote satellite licencees. Look also to the case of Yuendumu television.

Warlpiri Media Association programs only become 'Aboriginal Content' when they are exported from Yuendumu, and perhaps only when they are expropriated from Aboriginal Australia. In the context of their transmission at Yuendumu, they are simply local media. I am proposing that such content only becomes 'Aboriginal' when it becomes 'their' media. 'Our own' media never really qualifies. This distinction, at the heart of the larger public and community television effort, seems to have been missed entirely in the debate about Aborigines and their media needs. Nowhere is this collapsing of distinctions between 'us' and 'them' so dramatic as in Jupurrula's walk from on-camera compere to the camera operator's position and back again. There is, at Yuendumu Television, this collapsed distinction between object and subject, producer and talent, 'us' and 'them'. Any notions of Aboriginality are subsumed, even destroyed, by this more fundamental set of concerns.

I suppose I do also mean 'who needs it?' in the cheekier and more vernacular, dismissive sense. An Aboriginal content category simply doesn't serve those Aborigines we're supposed to be so concerned about: the people in remote communities who will be watching imported television for the first time. What we need is an adequate program for local community television. This, I submit, will serve Aboriginal interests better, and everybody else's as well.

I wish to thank the Australian Institute of Aboriginal Studies and the Torres Strait.

Notes

1 E. Sapir, *Language* (New York: Harcourt Brace, 1921).

2 B. Whorf in J. Carroll (ed.), *Language, Thought and Reality* (Cambridge, Mass.: MIT Press, 1956).

3 Marshall McLuhan, *Understanding Media* (London: Routledge & Kegan Paul, 1964).

4 S. Worth and J. Adair, *Through Navajo Eyes* (Bloomington: Indiana University Press, 1972).

5 Eric Michaels, *The Aboriginal Invention of Television 1982–6* (Canberra: AIAS, 1986).

6 Commonwealth of Australia, *Aboriginal and Torres Strait Islanders Heritage (Interim Protection) Act* (Canberra: Commonwealth Government Printer, 1984).

7 J. Ruby, 'Ethnography as Trompe l'Oeil: Film and Anthropology', in J. Ruby (ed.), *A Crack in the Mirror* (Philadelphia: University of Pennsylvania Press, 1982).

8 A. Pike, 'An ethnographic film conference', *Cantrill's Filmnotes* vol. 29 no. 3 (1979).

9 M. Mead and R. Metraux, *The Study of Culture at a Distance* (Chicago: University of Chicago Press, 1953).

10 Eric Michaels, 'Constraints on Knowledge in an Economy of Oral Information', *Current Anthropology* (October 1985).

11 Edmund Carpenter, *Oh, What A Blow That Phantom Gave Me* (New York: Holt, Rinehart & Winston, 1973).

12 K. Benterrak, S. Muecke and P. Roe, *Reading the Country* (Fremantle: Fremantle Arts Centre Press, 1984).

13 M. Langton, 'Urbanising Aborigines: The Social Scientist's Great Deception', Social Alternatives, 2/2 (1981), pp. 16–22.

two

POLITICS

ECONOMICS

AND

ADVERTISING

1
Broadcasting Politics: Communications and Consumption

KEVIN ROBINS AND FRANK WEBSTER

From *Screen* vol. 27 nos. 3–4 (May–August 1986)

Nothing recedes into the past more quickly than do some Future of Broadcasting speculations. But here Kevin Robins and Frank Webster provide a perspective on the mid-80s struggles over British broadcasting which has dated remarkably little. As the 1990s commence, the British public service broadcasting tradition still finds itself faced with competition from Competition, and still suffers from being in some respects all too traditional. Yet the battle for the truly public broadcasting which Robins and Webster desire has by no means simply been lost. This is because none of the established or new players in the broadcasting arena can operate outside a complex, historically-determined climate of public opinion, state regulation and market-economic 'realism'. (The last of these, indeed, has something to say about the costs of entry into this particular market which the more utopian versions of Thatcherism have not always taken fully into account.)

One of the most valuable aspects of the article is its preparedness to do justice to the positive aspects of both the state and the market as they have shaped broadcasting history. It is easy to find the features of 'actually existing broadcasting' so objectionable that a critical media theory gets developed of a simply adversarial sort. Especially in critically-oriented media education, and not without good reason, it has been felt that students need above all to be *warned* about the state's interference and paternalism, and the market's tendency to peddle patronising, debilitating fare. Robins and Webster suggest that critical media theory had better be careful not to dismiss either pole of the state/private dichotomy too cavalierly. Perhaps each is necessary to 'keep the other honest' – even if the current level of honesty is not all it could be. And neither state nor market shows the slightest sign of withering away.

M.A./J.O.T.

The time is out of joint. Out of the so-called 'communications revolution' of the 1980s strange and anomalous political alliances have been spawned. Of paramount importance and influence, for the moment at least, is that powerful lobby which coheres around its condemnation of the B B C – and, indeed, the whole achievement of public service broadcasting in Britain – as paternalistic, elitist and even authoritarian. Dismissing the B B C as unresponsive to audience needs and tastes, as politically compromised, critics on the left and right of the political spectrum look, optimistically and enthusiastically, to the possibilities of 'electronic publishing' through the new media (cable, video, satellite, videotex). For many radical media workers and sociologists, as for neo-liberal celebrants of market forces (Adam Smith Institute, Institute of Economic Affairs), the future belongs to unregulated competition and market forces; the stuffy, bureaucratic ethos of the B B C is considered inimical to a vital, free and plural media culture. For both interest groupings the problem is 'statism' and 'collectivism' and the solution and way forward is entrepreneurship.

Ranged against this position is another unholy, yet less influential, alliance. It represents a point of view that is now commonly dismissed as residually and anachronistically ideological. This is a perspective that aligns, on the one hand, high Tories who 'do not believe in giving the people what they want' and who are 'sufficiently Reithian' to 'wish to see our broadcasting standards maintained'[1], and, on the other, more radical protagonists of cultural traditions who argue that 'one of the best internal achievements of this country in this century has been the invention and development of the idea of broadcasting in the public service'.[2] The common factor is an Arnoldian conception of cultural values, and a strong faith in the B B C as a bastion against (American) commercial and market degradation of cultural standards.

Between these alternative positions there is no meaningful choice. The way forward to a democratic media and cultural policy for the 1990s is not at all clear. It is unfortunate and regrettable, then, that debate has become polarised around these alternatives of commerce and entrepreneurship, on the one hand, and cultural paternalism and Reithian traditions on the other. Either commercial freedom and consumer sovereignty (the way of the future?) or a patrician and bureaucratic public service (nostalgia for the past?). Is this a real choice? If we are critical of the Reithian ethos of the B B C, can we only look to alternatives of Rupert Murdoch and Ted Turner?

We are anxious here to avoid being trapped in this confining binary opposition. In our view, the issue has become too narrowly focused on media institutions and policies, and it is our intention, in this article, to broaden the debate by exploring some of the wider social and historical contexts within which the 'communications revolution' is taking place. We have chosen, particularly, to analyse the development and exploitation of television and post-television technologies within the historical development of consumer capitalism. From this perspective we are sceptical about those (thoroughly ahistorical) arguments which treat commercial broadcasting as a simple, unqualified liberation from the patrician traditions of the B B C. We find it difficult to accept 'actually existing' corporate interests as 'socially responsive and accountable', responsive and even progressive social forces.[3] This leads us to a position of qualified support for the B B C and public service broadcasting. This should not be misinterpreted as a conservative defence of cultural traditions. Our argument is that the values and achievements of public service broadcasting provide a better basis for the democratisation of mass media than do commercial interests. The objective of the current debate over the future of the BBC, we argue, should be to make the media accountable and responsive to social, not commercial, needs and priorities.

State, Market and Culture

At the heart of current debates on the future of the media is the relation of cultural forms to the state, on the one hand, and corporate and economic interests, on the other. For the purposes of our present argument, this issue can be translated into an exploration of the mechanics of social and political control: state and market, it can be argued, have operated as distinct and alternative forces for the incorporation and assimilation of those popular demands, which always exist as potentially destablising and contestatory threats to the social order. It was the achievement of Keynesian social democracy, we suggest, to articulate and co-ordinate these two forms of social control. State management of housing, welfare, health and social security went hand in glove with mass consumption, consumerism and commodification of needs in the so-called 'affluent society'. What we are now experiencing, of course, is the (legitimation) crisis of this Keynesian historic compromise.

We can make our argument more concrete by outlining, albeit in rather telegrammatic form, the specific relation of culture/leisure to state and market. During the nineteenth century, under conditions of capitalist accumulation, working-class leisure and popular cultural forms came increasingly to be seen as disruptive and anarchic; working-class culture was treated as a social problem. A rational social and industrial order was considered to be threatened by the boisterous, gregarious, undisciplined and autonomous nature of popular pursuits: 'the corruptions of leisure threatened to undo the painstakingly fashioned bonds of a new work discipline in the labour force'.[4] One response to this problem was expressed through the initiatives of evangelical, municipal and philanthropic reformers. These various interventions – all moral, didactic and paternalist in their emphasis – sought to institute 'collective moral vigilance'. Sabbatarianism, temperance, public parks, mechanics' institutes, public libraries, all aimed to promote 'rational recreation' and a sense of order, propriety, decorum and social discipline. There was a strong belief, apparent in the writings of Matthew Arnold, in the need to shape culture as a socially cohesive force; the intention of moral reformers was to promote, through liberal cultural values, a sense of 'social citizenship'.[5]

The philanthropic basis of this reform movement provided, however, an uncertain and precarious basis for the rationalisation of culture and leisure activities. During the early twentieth century it was surpassed and subsumed by state paternalism and moral leadership on an extensive and concerted scale. Fundamental in this context were Reith's elaboration of public service broadcasting, and also Grierson's philosophy of documentary cinema, which, according to Graham Murdock, 'in its concept of responsibility, its stress on the communicator's educational role and its insistence on impartiality . . . comes very close to the ethos of public service broadcasting which Reith was then forging within the other great bastion of State sponsored communication, the B B C'.[6] Both maintain and develop a strongly Arnoldian conception of the importance of cultural values for maintaining social consensus and stability. The continuity with ideas of moral reform and social citizenship is apparent in Grierson's idea of documentary's mission to associate 'private effort with a sense of public purpose'; to give the individual 'a living conception of the community which he has the privilege to serve'; to promote 'a sense of active citizenship'; and to give 'a leadership of the imagination'. For Grierson, 'the State is the machinery by which the best interests of the people are secured'; it is the state's responsibility to ensure 'that measure of social control which social justice and the complexity of the modern world demand, and on which there can be no substantial argument as between political parties'.[7]

The same moral, consensual and propagandist emphasis is apparent in the Reithian conception of public service broadcasting. This phenomenon (philosophy and institution), regarded by one commentator as 'an invention in the sphere of social science no less remarkable than the invention of radio transmission in the sphere of natural science',[8] emerged, in the 1920s, out of a Conservative/Labour alliance that was united in its condemnation of the hucksterish and tawdry U S commercial media, and its allegiance to the moral and educative cultural traditions of British society. This latter allegiance was particularly important to the strain of British Conservatism that held to an 'aristocratic' ideal of social organisation. It has often been remarked that this variant of Conservative philosophy is distinguished by its stress on 'community', on 'one nation', in which inequalities are manifest but legitimated by the 'responsibilities' of the upper class. The essence of this ethos is that the privileged do not abuse their position by acting out of self-interest, but that they 'give' voluntarily in the spirit of *noblesse oblige*, for the common good.[9] But if the idea of 'public service' appealed to this Conservative point of view, it was also consonant with a Labour philosophy that was assuming strongly corporatist and paternalist dimensions in its opposition to private capital and *laissez-faire*. This Fabian perspective, too, approved the idea of a broadcasting corporation that would be morally serious, judicious and educative. Both Conservative and Labour positions must, in this respect, be seen within that English cultural outlook – found in both Matthew Arnold and William Morris – which opposed the ravages of industrial capitalism and insisted that culture must be distanced from commerce and dedicated to the tasks of discriminating, evaluating, informing and educating.

What is important is that the public service conception that evolved from these various intellectual and political traditions became the basis of the public sphere in Britain through to the 1970s. This social democratic (Keynesian) public space existed pre-eminently through the media of radio and television; it was the B B C that created the shared public space of citizenship. The space that was established, however, was in reality a pseudo-public sphere. Participation was vicarious and remote, with the citizen as spectator consuming images of the political process. Radio, and then television, represented – in both senses of that word – the political interests of social groups. Acting as the brokers and traffickers of public opinion, these broadcasting media established their own (mediated) community of para-social interaction. It was a process through which audiences were apparently unified around a spurious collective and national identity, while, in reality, they experienced an increasingly fragmented, privatised and serialised social existence.

If private, and then state, philanthropy and paternalism have functioned as a form of cultural control, then another powerful disciplinary force has been the market. It is this phenomenon that we examine in the main part of our article, so we shall only briefly contextualise our argument here. The commercialisation of popular culture began early in the nineteenth century, alongside philanthropy and moral reform, as an alternative mechanism for the ordering and rationalisation of working-class leisure.[10] With the development of the new electrical technologies that underpinned the culture and leisure industries of the early twentieth century, this process achieved a new momentum. Absolutely crucial here was the development of radio (and subsequently television), which transformed the revolution in mass entertainment from being 'a revolution outside the home', to 'a revolution from within'.[11] The real culmination and apotheosis of this tendency comes, however, in the period after the Second World War. In this Keynesian phase of capital accumulation, economic growth is centred upon the exploitation of wage good markets: leisure and entertainment goods proliferate along with other consumer durables (refrigerators, washing machines, cars, etc.). This is a period of generalised consumer culture, a period in which the system of needs becomes subordinate to the system of objects.[12] The very principle of democracy becomes associated here with market freedom and diversity, and with consumer sovereignty and equality.

Mass consumption becomes a crucial mechanism of social and cultural control, and working-class 'free' time becomes subordinated to the 'leisure discipline' of consumerism. As Stuart Ewen has argued, the success of consumerism comes from its ability to link the market place 'to utopian ideals, to political and social freedom, to material well-being, and to the realization of fantasy'.[13] And fundamental, of course, to this apparatus for mediating social and cultural needs is television. One crucial function of the mass media has been, 'through the production and distribution of imagery, [to] have reconciled widespread vernacular demands for a better life with the general priorities of corporate capitalism'.[14] And television, particularly, has become the privileged means through which consumer capitalism enters our homes and our minds. As Peter Conrad writes:

Television has lent itself so patiently to the uses of consumerism because the set itself is a trophy of consumerism . . . as well as a theatre for the cavorting of consumer durables on the game shows or in the ads. Watching television, we're dually customers, of the medium (as spectators) and of the goods it's displaying (as potential customers). The screen is a shop window, the box a warehouse.[15]

Consumer Capitalism and
Mass Communications

The twentieth century has seen the extensive and intensive rationalisation of social relations, and in this process the mass media have played an indispensable role. This process has occurred as a function of the logic of corporate capital and the market principles through which it operates; it has expressed the values, priorities and the power of capitalist commercial interests. We want now to explore the historical process through which television and other mass media have become implicated in this logic of rationalisation.

Our starting point is the development of manufacturing in the late nineteenth century beyond a point in which affairs could be organised adequately by personal supervision of the workforce. It is well known that F. W. Taylor's enunciation of Scientific Management was an effort to improve ways of controlling the process of production. Crucial to Taylorism was the principle that management should make its primary task the precise monitoring of work required to produce a given article that it might be rigorously planned so as to be achievable with least cost and maximum efficiency. There are numerous variations of Taylorism as a practical strategy (time and motion, psychological appeal, etc.), but all management since Taylor has adhered to his axial principles that surveillance and planning are the key requisites of work organisation.

These principles entailed that information (its collection, analysis and exploitation) should become crucial for modern management, an emphasis that was always motivated by the desire to gain ever more effective control over labour in the factory. Taylorism, in short, indicates the commencement of a process (that has never ceased) which marked the first genuine 'information revolution' brought about by expanding industrial enterprises in search of better organisation of production processes.[16]

Henry Ford, developing his pioneering automobile plant, complemented Taylor by placing knowledge of production in the machinery of his assembly line. Mechanisation, the characteristic feature of modern industrial production, should be viewed as the fruition of planning operations which have observed and even anticipated the labour process, 'cognised' the skills necessary to effect production, and incorporated these wherever possible into technologies. What became known as Fordism expresses 'technical control'[17] of production, making it still more predictable, routine and planned. It continues to this day and has extended from the shopfloor into white collar and clerical work.

Taylor and Ford made information the prerequisite of effective planning and thereby of control of production within the plant, but other pressures meant that this search for control, and a vaunted role for information, would extend beyond these bounds. Not least was the pressure of corporations to integrate their production and distribution activities as they grew in size and scale of operation. A. D. Chandler describes how this gave rise to control within and without the factory by the 'visible hand' of what he calls 'managerial capitalism', the job of which is to co-ordinate and cohere manufacture and distribution. 'Managerial capitalism' brought about an end to the arbitrariness of the market in many spheres of corporate activity, replacing the unpredictability and inexactitude of procedure that accompanied reliance on the free market with proper planning of the best means for harmonising factory, warehouse and transportation.

In tandem with the coming of 'managerial capitalism' there developed what has been called the 'incorporation of America',[18] the shaping of more and more spheres of life by corporate capitalism and the intrusion of market principles into social relationships, paving the way for the spread of consumerism, particularly in urban areas, at the expense of self-reliance, so that shop and store, rather than family and neighbours, became the source of everyday needs, and the ability to pay became the arbiter of their fulfilment.

As Scientific Management was introduced into factories, and while companies founded special management teams to integrate manufacture and distribution, the impulse to control beyond the work force and corporation through to the customer became more pressing. It was inevitable that Taylorist principles of calculation would extend to the crucial area of marketing and selling. Thus Herbert Casson, an early devotee, could argue that 'What has worked so well in the acquisition of knowledge and in the production of commodities may work just as well in the distribution of those commodities.'[19] Moreover, there was the additional factor that mass production required 'efficient' mass consumption since efficiency and continuity of production could not be assured if consumption was left entirely to customer whim. For these reasons, by the second decade of the century, procedures were being developed to rationalise selling. The steady movement of clothing, cigarettes, processed foods, soaps and the like required the creation of ways of reaching customers, 'cognising' their needs and wants, and responding by persuasion and even redesigning products to make them more or newly attractive.[20]

In a word, modern *marketing*[21] began to be established – a concept that nominates and embraces the three activities of production, distribution and sales. Axiomatic to this principle was the systematic processing and dissemination of information wherever corporate imperatives so determined, in order that maximum control could be achieved. The need and imperative to gather, aggregate and accumulate information about the consumer led to the rise of market research (for demographic details, class distribution and characteristics, etc.) and the accumulation of detailed sales records and analyses. It was also, of course, vital to convey information to the consumer and this gave rise most obviously and pre-eminently to advertising, though it was also evident in packaging, trade-in deals, credit schemes and various other means of more effectively persuading the public to spend.

We are by no means claiming that these attempts at organising and orchestrating the consumer have been entirely successful – people can be fickle and recalcitrant at the point of sale furthest away from corporate pressure – but these activities undertaken in pursuit of corporate interests have, we would argue, been fundamental constraints on twentieth century social and cultural life.

The development of broadcasting, and particularly television, has shaped, and been shaped by, these developments. It has, for example, been at the heart of that phenomenon of 'mobile privatisation' which Raymond Williams sees as characteristic of the way of life under consumer capitalism.[22] But perhaps the most fundamental contribution of broadcasting to mass consumption and the consumer ethos has been its proven ability as an advertising medium, its incomparable achievement in delivering advertising into the homes of potential customers. From the outset, astute marketers were aware that broadcasting was a fine way, second only to having a salesman physically present, of business 'entering the homes of the nation through doors and windows, no matter how tightly barred, and delivering its message audibly through the loudspeaker wherever placed'.[24]

Much followed from capital's recognition that 'television is undoubtedly the greatest selling medium ever devised'.[24] There were obviously clear implications for the nature and range of programming, given that the major sources of television revenues were corporate enterprises and their advertising agencies.[25] Perhaps still more important, though clearly connected, was the fact that television's development as an agency for marketing the products and promoting the image and values of corporate capitalism led to an acute concern about who was receiving television programmes and which programme reached the largest audiences. In other words, the coming of television was accompanied by the rise of the *ratings*, which in turn came to exercise a dominant influence on the context of television.

Donald Hurwitz has situated the rise of audience research in the context of the overall development of U S capitalism. His thesis is that from the outset in the U S A 'broadcast institutions . . . became devices for organizing mass markets',[26] and that integral to this use of radio and television to boost corporate influence was accurate information about audiences. Hurwitz documents the rapid growth of increasingly sophisticated measures of audience activity (reliable survey methods, overnight ratings, computer analyses, prime-time categorisations, audimeter sets, etc.), reminding us of the importance of detailed information for business planning. He also outlines the interconnected history of broadcast and social science research (here the biography of Frank Stanton, doctoral student and co-author with the doyen of quantitative sociology Paul Lazarsfeld, who also went on to become president of C B S, is illuminating). Strikingly, while considering the career of A. C. Neilson, Hurwitz observes that Neilson cast his market research company 'in the role of the Frederick Winslow Taylor of retailing and communications. Time-and-motion study was applied to the movement of products across grocers' shelves, and to the movement of viewers across broadcast advertisers' programs.'[27]

This concern to watch, examine and monitor audiences is indicative of the impulse felt by corporate capital to harvest information so as to better manage its affairs. But the key role television played as an agency of marketing went beyond this to bear on the information it would disseminate. Most obviously, this took the form of advertising slots themselves, but the emphasis on ratings had a profound effect on the content of programmes. Bolstered by the authority and the democratic facade of accurate ratings ('the figures speak for themselves', 'the consumer is sovereign', 'we must give them what they want'), U S television from the early days transmitted a relatively narrow range composed largely of fiction and light entertainment,[28] resisting any argument that audiences might have other needs or programme-makers other responsibilities.

If we have shown that the search to better operational control meant that corporate capital had an important influence on the early development of television, we must emphasise also that the search has continued to this day: in corporate advertising, advocacy advertising, sponsorship, public relations and the like.[29] Significantly, it has led to ready exploitation of the newest technologies for marketing and commercial purposes. Now, with the greater range and versatility of video, cable and satellite television, advertising and audience monitoring are rendered still more sophisticated. According to the J. Walter Thompson Company, cable television offers 'new or improved advertising opportunities':[30] for example, test marketing, direct response advertising, placing of advertising within specialist channels, home shopping services, sponsorship, 'informercials'. What the new media allow is more advertising and more specific and targeted advertising to particular groups. And they also offer closer than ever surveillance and monitoring of the audience. Thus A G B, Britain's biggest market researcher, 'is already envisaging the day when the street interview, even telephone questioning, will be a thing of the past. Through its Cable and Viewdata company, it has a national sample of 550 homes, which it quizzes through special viewdata sets. Apart from instant judgment on commercials, it can stretch into other media fields, like the respondents' magazine readership'.[31] The same company's *Peoplemeter* has just been introduced into the United States as a means of more precisely surveying television viewing (meters can show when a set is switched on, *Peoplemeter* aims to discover whether viewers are actually watching).[32] Seen in this light it is difficult not to think of the idea of public service broadcasting as an anomaly and an anachronism insofar as it appears to constrict the commercial strategies of corporate capitalism.

While corporate capital seeks to appropriate the new communications technologies to gain access to customers and consumers, it also has other uses for them. It is common knowledge that the advanced capitalist economies are dominated by (mainly U S) transnational corporations. These corporations have expanded prodigiously to operate on a world scale, and this expansion has created a need for information and communications facilities to co-ordinate both inter- and intra-corporate transactions.[33] But it is not just the new communications that have been annexed by these corporate interests; television itself is also turned to new uses.

As transnational corporations have developed, they have used television for a number of purposes: as a means of stimulating sales, to advertise themselves as socially desirable or, at least, as socially innocuous, and to project consumption as a way of life.[34] And 'actually existing' television has invariably acted as an ally and support in the values it projects. Thus, a leading advertising agency could suggest that:

The worldwide proliferation of the Marlboro brand would not have been possible without T V and motion picture education about the virile rugged character of the American West ... At the same time, T V programmes like *Dallas* ... have crossed many national boundaries to achieve world awareness for their plots, characters, etc.[35]

Today, Saatchi and Saatchi, one of the top half-dozen world agencies, contends that the international scale of capitalism calls for 'pan-regional and world marketing ... at the heart of business strategy' (combined with ever more carefully targeted – narrowcast – advertising via cable and video). This inevitably has major consequences for television, and the new technologies that enhance it, and, in this light, it is not surprising to learn that Saatchi and Saatchi is a leading opponent of continuance of the BBC's public service traditions, and a proponent of full-scale commercialisation of the British media.

And, because transnational capitalism necessarily conceives and conducts its affairs across national frontiers, it can exercise its influence in more forceful and effective ways than the direct lobbying of a given state. Thus, it is the case that, while the BBC may be able to campaign, with some success, to retain its mode of finance and its programme guidelines, the exploitation by foreign and transnational interests of direct broadcast satellite television threatens to render a public service broadcasting system on a national scale obsolete and anachronistic. Across Europe a wave of developments, headed by Rupert Murdoch's Sky Channel, is bringing about 'Television Without Frontiers'.[36] Once established, these advertising, subscription and/or sponsor supported systems, which have an especial appeal for transnational marketing campaigns, may eat into audiences for indigenous services and make it difficult to defend broadcast systems paid for by a licence fee when only watched by a minority of viewers. In the longer term the future of any domestic public service broadcasting system would seem to depend more on the *Realpolitik* of multinational corporate interests, than on national legislation and policy decisions.

State, Market and the 'Communications Revolution'

We want now to turn to communications and broadcasting policy as it has developed over recent months (in the context of the 'communications revolution'). The first point that we would make here is that this issue cannot be seriously addressed without a historical analysis of broadcasting's role in advanced capitalist societies. Within this article we have concentrated on the part played by broadcasting in the rationalisation and organisation of cultural life, and on its elaboration as a mechanism of legitimation. Radio and television have, we suggest, played a crucial control function over the past sixty years or so. And this function has assumed two quite distinct and separate forms. On the one hand, broadcasting media have played an indispensable and privileged role in the commercial colonisation of leisure; in the process of marketing and the circulation of commodities; and in the growth of consumerism as an ideology and way of life. On the other, they have evolved out of paternalist and philanthropic traditions to 'serve' as a moral and educative social force, and as the basis of a social-democratic public sphere and consensual politics. Obviously the establishment of one or another (or a combination) of these forms in advanced capitalist societies has depended on specific national contexts. Thus, the political, cultural and economic climate of Britain nurtured, for a long time, a particular configuration of dominant public service tradition and subsidiary commercial system (strongly informed by public service ideals).

If one emphasis of this article is on the importance of historical analysis, then its other central argument is that the major issue is not simply and narrowly a question of broadcasting policy, but a matter of much broader processes and transformations. Here we have to take on board the significance of the new information and

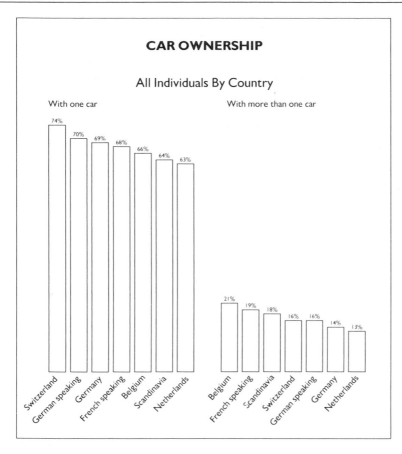

Car ownership in Western Europe: data supplied to advertisers by Sky Channel.

communications technologies, and, particularly, the context within which they are being developed and exploited. This, of course, is the crisis that has been affecting the advanced Western economies since the mid-seventies. This crisis, we must emphasise, has several dimensions. It is obviously, at one level, an economic crisis, and in this context the new technologies are the basis for a new cycle of accumulation and a new international division of labour. But it is also a crisis of legitimation, of political and cultural hegemony; it is a crisis of those social relations that have, in the post-war period, ensured (relatively) stable conditions for capital accumulation. And, at this level too, the new communications technologies play an important role.

In the British context, this crisis of hegemony is that of paternalist and statist 'moral leadership'. Those on the political Right are not alone in arguing that 'State ownership, State monopolies, State regulation and State planning, through the centralisation of economic power, inevitably lead to economic failure. . . . The fruits of centralised economic planning are corruption, poverty and servility.'[37] This concerted attack on the legitimating agencies of social democracy – the nationalised industries, the National Health Service, the state education system – also has its sights set on the tradition of public service broadcasting. There is a strong feeling that the B B C, in its present form at least, has outlived its usefulness (and even, as in the *Real Lives* debacle, becomes a positive nuisance). The Corporation, it is felt, no longer serves as a cohesive political force and a mechanism of social control. Real processes that have brought about social and political fragmentation have undermined the ideal (and ideology) of 'speaking to the nation'. The paternalist traditions of public service broadcasting, it is argued, have become sclerosed, bureaucratic and anachronistic. And, in the context of the exploitation of the new communications technologies by multinational capital, the B B C's comparatively agnostic attitude to the market and commercial forces seems to make it a positive liability.

What the new, lean and hungry, unregulated and deregulated communications seem to offer, and symbolise – in contrast to the lumbering dinosaur of public service broadcasting – is economic growth, technological progress and social advance. And the economic growth and market freedom stimulated by this neoliberal approach to the 'communications revolution' also provides the new basis of political authority and legitimation. As media consumers, we are offered a new regime of freedom, diversity and choice. 'In the new information era,' we are told, 'the way forward lies through competition and diversity, not through monopoly or centralised controls.' 'If a thousands flowers are allowed to bloom', then we can look forward to unlimited channels of information and entertainment,[38] 'opening up the sum of human knowledge and human experience to everyone'.[39] Traditional *laissez-faire* principles promise to secure a utopia of peace, harmony and democracy through universal communication and access to unlimited knowledge/information.

It is, of course, an impressive political and ideological achievement to have discredited public service ideas as bureaucratic and paternalist, and to have established – or rather, re-established – market principles as the vital force of democratic life. This represents the culmination of a process that has a long history, an expression of the extension and intensification of consumer capitalism (as way of life and ideology). The new politics of communication suggests, in fact, a recognition of the superiority of consumerism, as against philanthropic and paternalist traditions, as a form of control and legitimation.

The potential of the new communications for deepening the hold of consumer capitalism is striking. The combined delivery systems of cable, video and direct broadcast satellite could offer, in quantity at least, a far greater range and choice of programming, if only by exploiting the ready-made archives of largely U S television and cinema. And it could also open up new possibilities for time shifting and more flexible viewing. It has been argued that 'competition between multifarious channel operators ... will promote efficiency and a deep concern for the wishes of the customer', and that choice 'is the dominant feature of cable that will stimulate efficiency and progress'[40] (although counter-arguments about the monopoly tendencies already evident in U S cable are also pervasive).

Certainly new, unregulated media industries will give an enormous boost to the advertising industry. Television advertisers are particularly sensitive to the rising costs of the past few years, and they are now arguing strongly that the pressures they face necessitate competition in advertising markets. Hence their campaign to introduce advertising to the B B C. 'The availability of commercial airtime on the B B C, particularly of course on television, would provide business in the U K with a tremendous additional asset, and the capability to further develop their business and invest in the future.'[41] But their ambitions are greater than just this. Central to advertising strategies in the 'information age' is the internationalisation and globalisation of consumer and advertising markets.[42] Currently the E E C and the Council of Europe are interpreting Article 10 of the European Human Rights Convention to suggest that 'commercial speech . . . and freedom of expression are so intimately connected as being incapable of being dissociated'.[43] It is argued that Article 10, 'though perhaps primarily designed to protect expression of political, philosophical, scientific or religious ideas, covers communication of opinions, ideas or information which do not relate, directly or indirectly, to such matters'; the right to freedom of expression extends to 'commercial speech', on the basis that 'in western economies the free flow of such information is vital to the ability of consumers to make informed decisions about the various products and services available to them'.[44] Law is mobilised to constitute freedom – the freedom of consumer capitalism – as the right to transmit advertisements across national frontiers, and as the right to consume such multinational messages and images.

A massive, if longer-term, impetus to consumer capitalism comes also from the capacity of the new technologies to exploit functions and services beyond those of the traditional mass media. An integrated cable network, it is clear, can provide a whole array of new services: data and information services (e.g., Prestel); electronic banking; remote purchasing; home management services (fire and security alarms); health and education services; market research, and so on. It has been suggested that 'all the usual services of a marketplace can be offered within a large information network'. Such a network offers 'a place where suppliers of network services can show and market their wares, much like the village or town market, except that the purchasers can choose when to sample the wares and are not huckstered'. Paradoxically, as ever more functions of social life are brought under exchange relations, these are endowed with the (rural, egalitarian) attributes of the village market.

At the heart of the 'communications revolution', it seems to us, is this consolidation and reinvigoration of consumer capitalism. It is this climate that has recently provoked one prominent and embattled broadcaster to complain that the media have become 'too preoccupied with "value for money", with commercial concerns, with "cost-effectiveness", with the exploitation of what we produce – to the extent that we have damned nearly lost sight of what we are *supposed* to be about'.[45] The terms of reference of the Peacock Committee, which restrict broadcasting policy to accountancy and financial considerations, 'value for money', uncritically endorse the logic and rationality of commercial and market forces.

Such an approach appeals to the individual as consumer and represses his or her identity as a citizen. Thus, what is appealing about cable television is that 'pay-cable is in essence a private relationship between a subscriber and a cable operator. It is therefore not imbued with the public interest concerns which have given rise to the principles of public accountability, objectivity and balance that now govern broadcasting.'[46] However, we do not want to deny that commercialism has had certain liberating effects on British national-popular culture. As Stuart Hall argues, it has 'made a considerable contribution to the resistance to the more statist features of welfare-state socialism . . . [to] the loss of deference of an older and more paternalist kind, which, in its modern form, was a strong feature of welfarism'.[47] And we are not unaware of the part played by the public service broadcasting ethos in forging this paternalist and corporatist form of social regulation. But where, some twenty years ago, Perry Anderson could justifiably rail against 'rank, deference and tradition', against 'feudal consciousness', 'universal dilettantism', upper-class 'amateurism' and 'patrician political style',[48] it seems to us that this corporatist ruling-class style now represents a less important political reality. More influential than 'aristocratic' traditions of philanthropy and paternalism, is a monetarist ideology which reduces life to equations of profit and loss.

What must be avoided at all costs is a simple choice between actually existing public service and commercial organisations. Justifiable, and necessary, criticisms of public service broadcasting should not propel those in search of a democratic system of communications into the arms of multinational media corporations. When the public sphere is invaded by commercialisation, as Habermas makes clear, the difference between commodity circulation and social intercourse is erased.[49] It seems to us important to justify and defend a public forum above and beyond commodity and exchange relations. Statist and paternalist traditions are indeed in crisis, but there still remains, as Stuart Hall argues, a need for a conception of the public: 'The idea of "public space" signifies a construction of space *not* bounded by the rights of private property, a space for activities in common, the holding of space in trust as a social good.'[50] Something of this ideal, we believe, could be distilled and rescued from the public service tradition of broadcasting.

Notes

1 Julian Critchley (M P for Aldershot), *Hansard*, 2 December 1982, col. 445.

2 Richard Hoggart, 'Must We Be Casualties in the TV Explosion?', *Guardian*, 1 September 1982.

3 See Ian Connell, 'Commercial Broadcasting and the British Left', *Screen* vol. 24 no. 6 (November–December 1983), pp. 70–80.

4 Peter Bailey, *Leisure and Class in Victorian England* (London: Routledge & Kegan Paul, 1978), p. 170.

5 See Helen E. Meller, *Leisure and the Changing City 1870–1914* (London: Routledge & Kegan Paul, 1976).

6 Graham Murdock, 'Dilemmas of Radical Culture: Forms of Expression and Relations of Production', in Francis Barker *et al.* (eds.), *1936: The Sociology of Literature* vol. 2 (Colchester: University of Essex, 1979), p. 34.

7 Forsyth Hardy (ed.), *Grierson on Documentary* rev. ed. (London: Faber and Faber, 1966), pp. 110, 139, 137.

8 William A. Robson, 'The B B C as an Institution', *Political Quarterly* vol. 6 no. 4 (1935), p. 473.

9 See Martin Wiener, *English Culture and the Decline of the Industrial Spirit 1850–1980* (Cambridge: Cambridge University Press, 1981).

10 See Hugh Cunningham, *Leisure and the Industrial Revolution* (London: Croom Helm, 1980).

11 Asa Briggs, *Mass Entertainment: The Origins of a Modern Industry*, 29th Joseph Fisher Lecture in Commerce (Adelaide: Griffin Press, 1960), p. 30.

12 See Jean Baudrillard, *La Société de consommation* (Paris: Gallimard, 1978).

13 Stuart Ewen, *Captains of Consciousness: Advertising and the Social Roots of the Consumer Culture* (New York: McGraw-Hill, 1982).

14 Stuart and Elizabeth Ewen, *Channels of Desire: Mass Images and the Shaping of American Consciousness* (New York: McGraw-Hill, 1982).

15 Peter Conrad, *Television: The Medium and its Manners* (London: Routledge & Kegan Paul, 1982), pp. 121-2.

16 On Taylorism see Stephen Hill, *Competition and Control at Work* (London: Heinemann, 1981).

17 See Richard Edwardes, *Contested Terrain: The Transformations of the Workplace in the Twentieth Century* (London: Heinemann, 1979), chap. 7.

18 Alfred D. Chandler, *The Visible Hand: The Mangerial Revolution in American Business* (Cambridge, MA.: Harvard University Press, 1977); Alan Trachtenberg, *The Incorporation of America: Culture and Society in the Gilded Age* (New York: Hill and Wang, 1982), especially chaps. 3-4.

19 Herbert N. Casson, *Ads and Sales: A Study of Advertising and Selling from the Standpoint of the New Principles of Scientific Management* (Chicago: A. C. McClurg and Co., 1911), p. 7.

20 See Daniel Pope, *The Making of Modern Advertising* (New York: Basic Books, 1982).

21 See the interesting discussion in Michael Schudson, *Advertising, the Uneasy Persuasion: Its Dubious Impact on American Society* (New York: Basic Books, 1984).

22 Raymond Williams, *Television: Technology and Cultural Form* (London: Fontana, 1974), chap. 1.

23 Frank A. Arnold, *Broadcast Advertising: The Fourth Dimension, Television Edition* (New York: Wiley and Sons, 1933), pp. 41-2.

24 Martin Meyer, *Madison Avenue USA: The Inside Story of American Advertising* (London: Bodley Head, 1958), p. 198.

25 See Erik Barnouw, *The Sponsor: Notes on a Modern Potentate* (New York: Oxford University Press, 1978).

26 Donald L. Hurwitz, 'Broadcast "Ratings": The Rise and Development of Commercial Audience Research and Measurement in American Broadcasting' (PhD thesis, University of Illinois at Champaign-Urbana; Ann Arbor, MI.: University Microfilms International, 1983), p. 12.

27 Ibid., p. 204.

28 See Erik Barnouw, *The Golden Web: A History of Broadcasting in the United States* vol. II 1933-53 (New York: Oxford University Press, 1968); *The Image Empire: A History of Broadcasting in the United States* vol. III from 1953 (New York: Oxford University Press, 1970).

29 See Kevin Robbins and Frank Webster, 'The Revolution of the Fixed Wheel: Television and Social Taylorism', in Phillip Drummond and Richard Paterson (eds.), *Television in Transition* (London: British Film Institute, 1985).

30 Toby Syfret, *Cable and Advertising in the Eighties* (London: J. Walter Thompson Co., 1983), p. 30.

31 Anthony Thorncroft, 'Dawn of the Instant Reaction', *Financial Times*, 28 March 1985.

32 Jaclyn Fierman, 'Television Ratings', *Fortune*, 1 April 1985, p. 53.

33 See Dan Schiller, *Telematics and Government* (Norwood, N. J.: Ablex, 1982).

34 Herbert Schiller, *Mass Communications and American Empire* (New York: A. M. Kelley, 1970).

35 Saatchi and Saatchi Compton Worldwide, *Review of Operations*, 8 December 1983, p. 19.

36 EEC, *Television Without Frontiers*, Green Paper, 1984. See also Charles Dawson, 'TV Revolution: Why Admen Cannot Afford To Be Silent', *Campaign*, 22 November 1985, pp. 50-53.

37 Norman Tebbit, 'Old Values That Will Bolster a New Freedom', *Guardian*, 15 November 1985.

38 Andrew Neil, 'The Cable Revolution: Britain on the Brink', in Andrew Neil (ed.), *The Cable Revolution: Britain on the Brink of the Information Society* (Crawley: Visionhire Cable, 1982), pp. 22, 25.

39 Kenneth Baker, 'Towards an Information Society', speech to the British Association for the Advancement of Science, Liverpool University, 7 September 1982.

40 Gareth Locksley, 'Cable as Choice', *Telecommunications Policy* vol. 7 no. 2 (June 1983), p. 99.

41 IPA Media Policy Group, *Funding the BBC* (London: Institute of Practitioners in Advertising, November 1984), para. 2:3:6. Cf. *Funding the BBC from Advertising* (London: D'Arcy Macmanus and Masius, September 1984).

42 See Steve Winram (Saatchi and Saatchi), 'The Opportunity for World Brands', *International Journal of Advertising* vol. 3 no. 1 (1984); Stella Shamoon, 'Why Global Advertising Is "It"'', *Observer*, 23 September 1984.

43 Fritz W. Hondius, 'Freedom of Commercial Speech in Europe', *Transnational Data Report* vol. 8 no. 6 (September 1985), p. 325.

44 Anthony Lester and David Pannick, *Advertising and Freedom of Expression in Europe* (Marketing Commission of the International Chamber of Commerce, 1984); cf. George Wedell, 'Television without Frontiers?', *Government and Opposition* vol. 20 no. 1 (Winter 1985).

45 Alan Protheroe, 'The Broadcaster's Greatest Hazard Is Fear', *Index on Censorship* vol. 5 no. 1 (January 1986), p. 16.

46 Cento G. Veljanovski and William D. Bishop, *Choice By Cable*, Hobart Paper no. 96 (London: Institute of Economic Affairs, 1983), p. 107.

47 Stuart Hall, 'The Culture Gap', *Marxism Today*, January 1984, p. 19.

48 Perry Anderson, 'Origins of the Present Crisis', *New Left Review* 23 (January–February 1964).

49 Jürgen Habermas, *Strukturwandel der Offentlichteit* (Darmstadt: Luchterhard, 1962), p. 217.

50 Stuart Hall, 'The State: Socialism's Old Caretaker', *Marxism Today*, November 1984, p. 28.

Individualism Versus Collectivism

JANET STAIGER

From *Screen* vol. 24 nos. 4–5, July–October 1983

From a largely economic perspective, Janet Staiger here offers an account of Hollywood's development which significantly differs from conventional accounts. These have generally suggested that over the decades production methods in Hollywood can be characterised as following a shift from the mass production methods of the major studios to the more artisanal approach of a small independent company. (Such a shift could also be used to explain how, in the case of British television, the power of the independent sector has risen, helped by the creation of Channel 4 and the new 25% independent production quotas imposed by the government on both the BBC and the ITV companies.) However, having focused on this period of Hollywood's transition from the vertically integrated studio structure to an 'independent' system, Staiger, in a carefully documented account, advances three revisionist arguments.

Firstly, she indicates that the development of cinema production in Hollywood was not marked by a shift from collectivism to individualism because commercial independent production had always been a strong element within the industry. Secondly, she argues that independence should not, in any case, be defined in terms of *production* but in terms of *distribution*. The reason for this is that independent production houses functioned structurally in ways identical to the major studios – therefore the key factor was the lack of direct economic attachment to a distribution organisation. Thirdly, she points out that the major theatre-owning companies simultaneously required a regular output of mass produced movies to fill their schedules and therefore were prepared to conduct business with a wide range of producers.

Overall, Staiger demonstrates how, while various economic and legal changes did in fact affect the number of films produced (i.e. reduced the total number but increased the quasi-independent projects produced), nevertheless the major companies still managed to maintain their position and power. The intriguing question for British readers is: will British television experience prove similar?

M.A./J.O.T.

When historians speak of the structure of the United States film industry after World War II, they describe it as a period of the ending of mass production of films and the diffusion of independent production. Following the detailed and influential study by Michael Conant of the 1948 Paramount case,[1] scholars generally assume that the decree allowed independent film-making to flourish and eventually to dominate the industrial structure. I would propose, however, that the 1948 consent decree was only one factor, and merely a reinforcing one, in a general transition away from a regular output and mass production of films to fewer releases and higher-priced product.

From the late 1920s, studios sought to avoid stereotypical product by changing the method of top management of the mass production of films and by giving some workers greater control over special projects. This was symptomatic of an *ideology* that greater control of a film by specialists and talented individuals would produce more variety (of a certain kind) in the films. In the early 1940s, *economic* incentives enhanced the changeover to independent production. These incentives included the elimination by a 1940 consent decree of blind selling and block booking, certain effects of World War II, and an apparent tax advantage. After the war, the movement intensified because of income losses, the divorcement decree, and new distribution strategies. Furthermore, although we might term the new industrial structure 'independent', as it was eventually organised, it retained much of the earlier (studio) mode of production: work was still highly divided and in a structural hierarchy and financing was still determined by the same factors (e.g., a particular narrative form, stars, a proven director, and a good distribution contract). Although there has been a transformation in the industrial structure and mode of production, it is important to note what has been retained from the earlier systems.

The definition of US commercial independent production has not been based on its organisation of the mode of production: in fact, an independent firm could use any of several systems of production. Firms such as David O Selznick's, Samuel Goldwyn's, and Charles Chaplin's, as well as lesser known independents, had work structures much like the major studios: a producer or director topped a hierarchy of labourers. These subordinate workers were positioned within a divided labour structure.[2] Instead, an independent production firm has been defined as a company with was not owned by, or did not own, a distribution organisation.

Commercial independent production has always been part of the industrial structure in the United States. In fact, the producers which distributed through United Artists in the 1930s had an excellent record of box office successes. Furthermore, during that period, some major studios such as Paramount, RKO, and Columbia invited independent deals. In the late 1930s, Universal added such arrangements, and in early 1940 Warner Brothers did too, setting up one with Frank Capra and Robert Riskin to make *Meet John Doe*. Even tacitly, all the studios supported some independent work. MGM distributed (on quite profitable terms) Selznick's *Gone with the Wind* (1939). United Artists' producers organised one project (*So Ends the Night*, 1941) in which they bought the story from MGM, borrowed an MGM-contract cinematographer, and rented space from Universal.[3]

In the early 1930s, the management organisation in the major studios changed.

Rather than one central producer supervising 30 to 50 films per year, a group of associated producers each specialised in particular types of films and managed only six to eight films. The proponents of the change argued that the new management system would improve the quality of the product. The industry believed that certain workers concentrating on fewer and special films produced greater economic returns than the mass production of the firm's entire product.[4] This attitude – itself an ideological position about artistic reaction – continued through the 1930s. In 1939, William de Mille wrote: 'Today two conflicting theories of picture-making are struggling to determine which one shall control the future system of production; they are individualism and collectivism.' Others agreed. In the House of Representatives hearings of 1940, Capra and Leo McCarey claimed that they and others had increased freedom in decision-making. George Stevens, representing the Screen Directors Guild, attributed this trend to the firms' wanting pictures with 'the most box office'.[5]

If 'individualism' was viewed as potentially a more profitable system, what held the industry in check from an outright changeover to it? The affiliated majors (those that were fully integrated, owning theatre chains) were still tied to a release-schedule to supply their own houses. For them, a regular output and mass production were necessary. Columbia and Universal, although without the burden of self-generated demand, had weaker product. These companies had found their place in the market by supplying cheaply produced 'B' films, more efficiently made in a mass production set-up. As a result, none of these industry leaders saw a profit advantage in abandoning mass production.

Early Economic Incentives for
Independent Production

A major incentive to move away from mass production developed indirectly out of a 1940 consent decree in the federal government's anti-trust suits against the majors. The state had been involved in the industry from film's beginning: censorship, taxes, regulation of exhibition sites, labour acts and rulings, suits to investigate and prevent pools and monopolies. By the mid-1930s, public pressure groups for federal censorship of films had allied with independent theatre exhibitors to fight blind selling and block booking. The pressure groups argued that these trade practices forced independent exhibitors to show undesirable films. In a typical instance, the Senate Committee report on bill S 3012 (1936) recommending its passage claimed that one of the bill's purposes was to 'establish community freedom in the selection of motion-picture films'. Among other proposals, these bills included provisions to require the release of a 'complete and true synopsis of each picture' prior to exhibitor leasing and to prohibit films booked in groups. The majors successfully fought off each of these bills, although votes in Congress indicated strong sentiment to move in that direction; the 1940 Senate vote went in favour of the latest bill.[6]

Two years earlier, the antitrust division of the Department of Justice filed charges against the majors. While the entire history of such suits is important to the structure of the industry, here we are interested primarily in the effect of that suit.

After a two-day opening session in June 1940, the trial recessed while the partici-pants wrote a consent decree for the affiliated majors. The agreed-upon decree eliminated blind selling by requiring trade shows of the films and prevented block booking in groups larger than five films. The decree was to remain in effect until 1943 or until June 1942 if the 'little three' (Columbia, Universal, and United Artists) did not sign it.[7]

According to the *Motion Picture Herald*, the early effect of the new trade practices was to place more value on talent and spectacle, with each company loading up every film to try to make all blocks-of-five attractive.[8] This made economic sense. If motion pictures were now to be sold in groups of five rather than a large block of 30 or more, filling more films with A or Super-A production values became more necessary for competitive reasons. Differentiation – always a primary element in the economic system – intensified. Stars, directors, and stories became even more important ingredients in the product while selling by brand name decreased in value since the entire output of a firm was no longer a marketing point. This placed top talent in even more demand, allowing them greater bargaining power for contracts that included higher salaries and more desirable working conditions – and, in some instances, more production independence.

In addition, the average cost-per-film already seemed to be the best predictor of the box office success of a firm's product: concentrating on fewer, higher-priced films rather than spreading costs across a larger number of motion pictures augured greater profits. This was particularly pertinent once exhibitors could pick and choose their favourite blocks-of-five. Moreover, with implicit collusion between the affiliated companies, these integrated firms could fill each other's theatre chains with the top product, skimming off the cream (and some of the milk) of the earnings.

Even when the 'little three' did not sign the decree in 1942, ending its validity, the firms did not uniformly return to the prior practices. Perhaps the firms anticipated further attacks from government, pressure groups and exhibitors; perhaps they also realised that limiting output had economic advantages. Para-mount, R K O, and Twentieth Century-Fox stayed with blocks of five, M G M went up to ten films per block, Columbia and Universal (with the weakest product) went back to the full-season block, while Warners (like United Artists) used unit sales. Thus, the move to fewer, higher-cost films was encouraged.[9]

Another incentive to move away from mass production developed out of the effects of World War II. During the war, theatres experienced increased attend-ance, with many people having more disposable income and fewer things on which to spend it. Not only did admissions rise, but 'top budget' films commanded longer runs while Bs played out more quickly.[10] *American Cinematographer* noted in June 1943 that the next production season portended fewer films, higher budgets, and longer shooting times because all films were making money: '. . . productions given the extra time and money which make them more than just ordinarily adequate ones can command sufficient additional playing time in the theatres so that a compara-tively few genuine "A's" can earn a larger total profit than the conventional program of a few "A's" and a larger number of cheaper "B's".'[11] Monogram announced that month a 'new policy of fewer and higher-budgeted films', including an A starring Jackie Cooper with Sam Levene.[12]

In early 1945 another effect of the war forced the industry into fewer releases. War demands produced a shortage of raw film stock, and distributors were required to limit the number of exhibition prints. Although the major studios had a backlog of negatives, fewer films were released until positive film stock was more available.

That the overall number of films released by the majors declined during and after the war years is evident from U S government statistics.[13] The following is a Congressional count of features released in the 1937–55 period by Columbia, M G M, Paramount, R K O, Twentieth Century-Fox, United Artists, Universal, and Warner Bros:

1937	408	1944	262	1950	263
1938	362	1945	270	1951	320
1939	388	1946	252	1952	278
1940	363	1947	249	1953	301
1941	379	1948	248	1954	225
1942	358	1949	234	1955	215
1943	289				

Into this gap between the current and former product-supply levels stepped independents.

In 1943, as the first wave of wartime consumption patterns became apparent, signs of a resurgence of financing for independent projects developed. The *Motion Picture Herald* explained: 'The nation's box office performance of the past two years, resulting from the public's increased income and greater ability to spend money on entertainment and amusement outlets has made it possible to obtain financial support. As one producer put it, "Not since the golden days of the 20s has film money on Wall Street been so free".'[14] Cagney Productions signed a five-year agreement with United Artists to deliver up to fifteen films, with at least five starring James Cagney. Hal Wallis and Joseph Hazen left Warner Brothers, formed Hal Wallis Productions, and contracted with Paramount to deliver two films a year for five years. Paramount bought partnership in the firm.[15]

By early 1945, other workers were leaving studio-contract employment to participate in partnerships or profit-sharing. Frank Borzage completed a deal with Republic in which he would 'join that studio as a producer-director with his own unit. Borzage will have all authority over selection of stories and casts and purchases of his own vehicles, as well as a financial interest in them'. Sam Jaffe and Lloyd Bacon, who had already independently produced *The Sullivans* (1944) for Twentieth Century-Fox release, formed a firm to make *Glittering Hill* – distribution was undetermined. Walter Wanger and Fritz Lang organised new World Properties and planned their first film *Scarlet Street* (1945); Universal was to release. With two others, Lewis Milestone started Superior Pictures in order to buy *A Walk in the Sun* (1945) which he had produced and directed for Samuel Bronston's Comstock Productions.[16]

At the conclusion of the war, talents who left the major studios for independent projects included Constance Bennett, Benedict Bogeaus, Frank Capra, Gary Cooper, Lester Cowan, Bing Crosby, Joan Fontaine, John Garfield, Paulette Goddard, Bob Hope, Hedy Lamarr, Fred MacMurray, Pat O'Brien, Ginger Rogers, George Stevens, Hunt Stromberg, John Wayne, and Sam Wood. Producers fostered 'de-centralisation of studio control' and gave 'semi-independent status' to some workers – at Paramount to Cecil B. De Mille, Wallis, Bill Pine and Bill Thomas; at Warner Brothers to Bette Davis and Errol Flynn; at RKO to Dudley Nichols and Louis McCarey; at Universal to Mervyn Le Roy and Mark Hellinger.[17]

Already a number of methods of financing and distributing independent work were in operation. Some firms held long-term contracts; others found distribution upon completion of the film. Some firms were financed by banks or private investors; others were supported either partially or wholly by the major companies. As noted, with every film likely to be a success and with financing readily available, moving into independent production tempted many workers.

An additional incentive to move to independent production was a peculiar tax situation of which some firms started taking advantage. During the war, income taxes increased for higher-salaried workers, but capital gains taxes lagged in comparison: 'Under the present United States system [1947] personal incomes are taxable up to 90 per cent on every dollar. But those who forego stipulated salaries for profit-participation in individual corporation ventures can list their assets as capital gains, which are taxable only up to 25 per cent.'[18]

The next move is particularly significant: the one-film deal. One analyst pointed out why that type of independent company seemed very advantageous for a while. Investors would set up a corporation for a one-film venture, purchase stock, make the film, and then sell the stock to underwriters or distributors. Only capital gains taxes were paid and the earnings were immediately available for further speculation. In August 1946, the Bureau of Internal Revenue clamped down on this, demanding payments based on ordinary tax rates retroactive to July 1943. Samuel Goldwyn was informed that five of his 'single picture corporations' were subject to this ruling, and United Artists announced that all 35 of its films released since July 1943 had been financed this way. The Society of Independent Motion Picture Producers (S I M P P), a trade association formed by independents in January 1942, reported however that 'not many' independents would be affected. While taking advantage of the tax disparity, most independents had incorporated with the intention of taking only some profits out for personal use and retaining most earnings in the firm to continue production.[19]

Thus, by the end of the war, several economic incentives (the 1940 consent decree, the effects of the war, and tax laws) were moving the industry from mass production to fewer, higher-priced, longer-running films, and independent productions released through the majors increased. In addition, the concept of 'individualism' supported this. Although still a minor practice, independent deals spread. At the end of 1946 as the country returned to peacetime, every major firm except M G M had some independent projects as part of its regular production schedule.[20]

Later Incentives to Continue the Trend
The unique situation of World War II, particularly increased attendance, raw film shortages, and tax laws, requires that we consider the post-war context. Once war conditions ceased, why not return to mass production? What happened after the war, however, intensified the movement toward fewer, selectively-produced films.

Significantly income losses provided a powerful incentive to continue. Descriptions and explanations of the losses are plentiful. On the domestic scene, attendance declined. In Spring 1947, box office figures indicated a resumption of more normal consumption patterns as higher costs of living developed. Although 'outstanding films' still drew customers, the average film was not doing well. Universal chairman of the board Cheever Cowdin announced his firm had turned entirely to A product and warned that all costs would have to be watched. On the foreign scene, European countries moved to restrict exportation of earnings. On 8 August 1947, the US ceased exporting films to Britain in response to Britain's 75 per cent *ad valorem* tax. Five weeks later, statistics indicated that over the last year as a result of both income problems, studio employment of workers had decreased 30 per cent. The number of films shooting likewise declined.[21]

The response by the companies to these losses was typical. The firms reduced short-term costs (costumes, sets, story purchases) and fixed liabilities – particularly term contracts with labourers. Between June 1945 and August 1948 the number of writers on term contracts fell from 189 to 87; contracts for members of the Screen Actors Guild declined from 742 in February 1947 to 463 in February 1948; the number of employed skilled and unskilled workers also moved from a peak of 22,100 in 1946 to 13,400 in 1949.[22]

Unions and guilds recognised the threat to their members. The Screen Actors Guild, the International Alliance of Theatrical Stage Employees, and others constructed a 'separate category' for independent producers with a picture budget of less than 100,000 dollars. Salary scales and the required minimum number of workers on a crew were reduced.[23]

By early 1948, location shooting was also being touted as a method for solving these various problems, and this location shooting continued to reduce the formerly central role of the Hollywood studios. *Close-Up*, a Marathon Production for Eagle-Lion release, was made entirely in New York City, including all laboratory work, at '25 per cent' of what it would cost in Hollywood. As its producers admitted, however, this was possible only because the film was part of the new tendency towards 'realism'. At the end of 1949, New York City alone could boast of 35 films made partially or totally in the town over the last two years.[24]

Location shooting was also promoted as a means to unfreeze revenues in European countries. The deals arranged continued to reinforce one-time only financial agreements. The majors' trade association, the Motion Picture Association of America, announced that 'American producers may liquidate dollars now blocked in at least six foreign countries by producing in or sending pictures on location to Italy, France, Holland, Norway, Sweden and Australia.'[25] When Britain and the United States came to terms over the *ad valorem* tax in March 1948, the agreement restricted the number of American craftsmen who could work on US productions in Britain. France's 1948 agreement also stipulated that while American firms could invest up to 50 per cent of the cost of a French-produced film, the technical staff had to be French. Despite that set-back, and with the lure of potentially cheaper labour as well as an answer to their 'quest for realism' and spectacle, firms started shooting parts of their schedules abroad. In mid-1949, M G M announced seven of its next season's films would have foreign sites in eight countries. Other firms planned locations ranging from Britain, Germany, Italy, and France to the more exotic locales of Tahiti, India, Africa, and Borneo.[26]

If a post-war return to normal consumption patterns and foreign income losses affected the industry by 1948, by 1950 other domestic factors also led to continued losses: population shifts, changing recreational habits, regional unemployment, and particularly competition with television. After 1950, television's effects became more apparent as the number of sets and broadcast stations rose. A 1950 federal government survey indicated that families with television reduced their movie-theatre attendance by 72 per cent and their children's visits were down 46 per cent. A Congressional Committee reported in 1956 that 'during the first 4 years of television's growth [1948–1952] in those areas where television reception was good, 23 per cent of the theatres closed compared to only 9 per cent of the theatres closing in those areas where television was not available'. By 1953, film companies were considering specific technological strategies to outdo television – 3-D, widescreen processes, and stereophonic sound.[27]

As income losses continued, the advantage of working in separate deals, one at a time, was clear. As a year-end summary in 1948 indicated: 'Producers, more and more, are willing to hire talent as needed and are prepared, if necessary, to pay more rather than maintain expensive stock companies with those inevitable periods of idleness, the cost of which must be spread over the remainder of their annual programs.'[28] Not only did the studios eliminate fixed salaries (one of the highest portions of the budget) but the companies' risk was reduced. Either they set up the 'package' themselves or they arranged a deal with an independent firm. Both the elimination of fixed costs and the reduction of their risk were attractive incentives to support a project-by-project system of operation.

Furthermore, another incentive, divorcement of exhibition from production and distribution, eased any pressures to return to mass production. No longer concerned with a regular supply to part of its own firm, a company could concentrate on fewer, specialised projects. Divorcement had been rumoured since 1943. In August 1944, the Department of Justice, unsatisfied with the results of the 1940 consent decree, requested a modification. Asking the district court for divorcement of the exhibition sector from the production-distribution sectors, the Department re-opened the antitrust suit. As the case neared its conclusion in 1948, the trade papers reported:

There are heard, for instance, plausible-sounding whispers that the major studios are not going to throw any really big pictures into production until home office executives find out what the Supreme Court is going to decide with reference to divorcement. Local observers summon support for the report by pointing out that all of the major studios have gone more or less extensively into the practice of setting up deals with independent producers. This is readily interpreted as indicating a decision by the majors to place themselves in a position of preparedness to give up production entirely, if that becomes advisable, and convert their studios to the status of rental lots.[29]

Although the majors eventually separated the production studios from the theatre chains rather than abandoning production outright, the particular conjuncture of events again added to the overall impetus of the industrial shift.

Smaller firms such as Monogram and Universal had already moved into A production when As started do so much better than Bs at the box office. With divorcement looming, other minor companies turned in that direction, often through independent deals. Republic released *Spectre of the Rose* (1946, produced by Ben Hecht), *Moonrise* (1948, Frank Borzage), *Macbeth* (1948, Orson Welles), *Sands of Iwo Jima* (1949, Allan Dwan), *The Red Pony* (1949, Lewis Milestone), *Secret Beyond the Door* (1949, Diana Productions), and *Rio Grande* (1950, John Ford).[30]

A final incentive to move away from mass production also occurred in these post-war years. New distribution strategies played to the highly differentiated film, one which might seek only part of the audience as its clientele. Forerunners of this were David O. Selznick's *Duel in the Sun* (1946) and R K O's release *The Best Years of Our Lives* (1946, Goldwyn). *Duel in the Sun* used the tactic of mass openings across the United States (saturation booking) while both firms had 'advanced admissions' – roadshowing at higher admission prices. Encouraged by the results, majors announced their intention to show selected films at advanced prices. Not only were special 'packages' encouraged in this way, but small independents supplied the second- and third-run theatres, now being neglected by the major distributors.[31]

In addition to aiming films primarily at first-run audiences, the industry witnessed a growth in the art theatre, which also played to a particular clientele. The trade papers speculated in 1947 that the 'art film' surge was due to lack of access to foreign films during the war and to 'the French-culture-conscious "intelligentsia"' as well as the 'G.I.'s whom the war had brought into contact with European languages and customs'.[32] With the Audience Research Institute and other such companies now supplying marketing information and audience analyses, it was much more possible to tailor a film for a select group than to aim it at a mass audience. As it became clearer that only certain age-and income-levels consistently attended certain theatres, such specialisation increased.

The move away from mass production, to fewer films, with independents providing a substantial proportion, was gradual. A system which had been so successful for four decades was not readily discarded. Various factors helped ease the shift, however. One of these was the latest expansion of support firms to provide experts and technology as needed. People who had been long-term workers for major studios struck out on their own as the companies cut down the workforce. Linwood Dunn of the famed R K O special effects group and Charles Berry of Universal formed an optical printing firm, and another company built the first new studio for independents in eighteen years. Other firms moved later into leasing equipment, arguing that rather than using capital to purchase technology, by leasing it, a firm could have the latest equipment without the long-term investment. Certainly, the support-firm supply of state-of-the-art technology, studio space, and technical experts was a long-time characteristic of the industry; firms now recognised they no longer needed a self-contained studio, particularly since they were no longer mass-producing films. Overhead costs were replaced with expenditures for rentals and short-term hiring.[33]

Another factor easing the change was a new flexibility in the industry: not only was its means of production being pooled through the speciality and support firms, but the unions acted as coordinators for the supply of skilled labourers. This labour pooling eventually helped its workers make an easy transition into television. In early 1949, actors who had appeared in 'such ambitious showcases as the Ford Theater and the Philco Playhouse' included Paul Muni, Peter Lorre, Fay Emerson, Ramond Massey, Eddie Albert, Boris Karloff, and John Carradine. At the same time, *American Cinematographer* started preparing its photography experts to move into television as theatrical-exhibition film work decreased. Hal Roach Studios picked up *The Trouble with Father* series in 1951; in 1952, fifteen A S C members were shooting for television, including Lucien Andriot on *Rebound* and Karl Freund on *I Love Lucy*. By then, the cinematographers' union was 'hard pressed' to supply camera operators and assistants for all the television work, and throughout the 1950s as film employment slowed down, cinematographers found work readily available in television. With the shift to the unions as the stock pool of labour, putting together a package for either medium was comparable, and the separate media unions combined into unified ones. In 1950s, the Society of Motion Picture Engineers added 'Television' to its title; in 1954, the writers for screen, radio, and television combined into the Writers Guild of America; in 1960 the screen directors and the radio and television directors merged into the Directors Guild of America.[34]

Financing was never simple. Although during the war money had been readily available, with income losses in the late 1940s, independents felt the pinch. In 1949, banks noticeably tightened loan requirements, restimulating other financing tactics. Independent theatre-owners formed a company to finance independent projects in the A category; N. Peter Rathvon and Floyd Odlum, former R K O executives and owners, organised the Motion Picture Capital Corporation to do likewise. Companies continued to use capital gains tax advantages.[35] Finally, one of the solutions which was to become extremely common in later decades was proposed in 1949. Film financier A. Pam Blumenthal suggested that independents be financed by the major distributors. As a trade paper explained his 'formula':

... a major studio can reduce its overhead drastically by releasing substantial numbers of its contract talent to individual producers to whom it first will have supplied financing under terms requiring use of the major studio's facilities and with the product going to the major for release. Talent going to the independent company will be on their own time during pre-production periods, and producers operating on this basis will be on their own responsibility to meet the challenge of the current market.[36]

All of these financing strategies were common from the 1950s on.

The initial and later incentives to shift to an industrial structure of independent firms releasing through the majors fostered the development of a system of production in which film projects were set up on a film-by-film arrangement. By 1954, only M G M was still using the formerly-dominant studio system, but in early 1956, the trade papers reported that 'outside deals are being made even by M G M'. While in early 1950 about 25 per cent of the films in production were clearly independent productions (with other films including profit-sharing for certain staff personnel), in early 1956 the figure was about 53 per cent, and in early 1959, it was 70 per cent. Of the 21 top-grossing films in the United States and Canada in 1956, eleven were independently produced. If there was any doubt about the change, the last of the major studio production heads stepped down in 1956: Dore Schary left M G M in December 1956 and Darryl F. Zanuck relinquished his position in February of that year to go into independent production, releasing through Twentieth Century-Fox.

By this time as well, film companies had transferred their mass production techniques to television series. By January 1956, Paramount, Twentieth Century-Fox, Columbia, Warners, M G M, United Artists, Disney, Allied Artists, and Republic had interests in television. Harold Hecht and Burt Lancaster could celebrate the tenth anniversary of their independent production company in 1957.[37] Robert Wise, in looking back over his career, could date 1957 as the last time he had a multiple-film contract: 'All my films – every one since then – have been made as individual projects, even when I stayed at a particular studio for several years ... I had chosen to remain completely independent and select my own projects and work my own deals out individually on each one.'[38] By the mid-1950s, independent production had become a firm option in the Hollywood mode of production and was dominant by 1960.

In operation, the mode of production for an independent firm differed little from studio production. Middle- and lower-echelon workers were still strictly specialised (a result of unionisation and technological expertise). Only certain top management positions (producers, directors, writers, and actors) had more flexibility than in the earlier Hollywood mode of production. While industry-wide pooling of labour had occurred, work was still divided and structured in a hierarchy. Financing was based on conceptions of what would sell – now more carefully researched but still an effect of a decision to retain profit-making as the controlling goal for the suppliers of capital.[39]

It is important to understand that the shift from studio mass production to independent, specialised production has not necessarily secured a significant change in the factors which could affect the films produced, distributed and exhibited by the U S film industry. In fact, the move to independent production was not 'outside' the dominant sectors of the industry. The major studios supported an ideology of 'individualism' from the late 1920s on. Furthermore, from the early 1940s, the majors judged that concentrating on a smaller number of films per year would be more profitable. In addition, independent production reduced the risks for the majors which began to concentrate their profit-making strategies in the areas of wise investments in 'packages' and in distribution of the finished films. Finally, independent production firms in the Hollywood mainstream retained the essential characteristics of a mode of production which has been considered efficient and economical since the early teens. Thus, overall independent production had reproduced the dominant practices of Hollywood. In the conflict between individualism and collectivism, individualism may seem to have won out, but it is an individualism which retains a great number of the characteristics of its predecessor.

Notes

1 Michael Conant, *Antitrust in the Motion Picture Industry: Economic and Legal Analysis* (Berkeley: University of California Press, 1960). As an example of recent adherence to that position, see Chris Hugo, 'The Economic Background', *Movie* nos. 27–28 (Winter 1980–Spring 1981), p. 46.

2 For a detailed analysis of the Hollywood system of labour, see Janet Staiger, 'The Hollywood Mode of Production: The Construction of Divided Labour in the Film Industry' (PhD diss., University of Wisconsin-Madison, 1981).

3 'Outside Producers for Warners: 11 "Names" in New Studio Jobs', *Motion Picture Herald* (hereafter *MPH*) vol. 138 no. 6 (10 February 1940), p. 60; Albert Lewin, ' "Peccavi!" The True Confessions of a Movie Producer', *Theatre Arts*, September 1941, reprinted in Richard Koszarski (ed.), *Hollywood Directors 1941–1976* (New York: Oxford University Press, 1977), pp. 26–34.

4 Janet Staiger, 'The Hollywood Mode of Production', pp. 268–72; Janet Staiger, 'Crafting Hollywood Films: The Impact of a Concept of Film Practice on a Mode of Production' (Paper presented at the Society for Cinema Studies Conference, Los Angeles, California, 1982).

5 William C. De Mille, *Hollywood Saga* (New York: E. P. Dutton & Co., 1939), p. 310; US Interstate and Foreign Commerce Committee, House, 'Motion-Picture Films (Compulsory Block Booking and Blind Selling), hearing on S 280, 76th Cong., 3rd sess., 13 May–4 June 1940 (Washington D.C.: Government Printing Office, 1940), p. 637.

6 The vote in the Senate on S 280 (1940) was yeas 46, nays 28, not voting 22; *US Congressional Record*, 76th Cong., 1st sess. (Washington D.C.: Government Printing Office, 1939–40), pp. 9247–8. US Interstate Commerce Committee, Senate, 'To Prohibit and to Prevent Trade Practices Known as Compulsory Block Booking and Blind Selling in Leasing of Motion-Picture Films in Interstate and Foreign Commerce', report to accompany S 3012, 74th Cong., 2nd sess. (Washington D.C.: Government Printing Office, 15 June 1936), p. 1; US Interstate Commerce Committee, Senate, 'To Prohibit and Prevent Trade Practices Known as Compulsory Block Booking and Blind Selling in Leasing of Motion-Picture Films in Interstate and Foreign Commerce', report to accompany S 153, 75th Cong., 3rd sess. (Washington D.C.: Government Printing Office, 16 February 1938), p. 5.

7 Good summaries of the events surrounding *United States v. Paramount et al.* are in Ernest Borneman, 'United States versus Hollywood: The Case Study of an Antitrust Suit', in Tino Balio (ed.), *The American Film Industry* (Madison: University of Wisconsin Press, 1976), pp. 332–45; Raymond Moley, *The Hays Office* (Indianopolis: Bobbs-Merrill Company, 1945),. pp. 206–12; US Select Committee on Small Business, Senate, 'Motion-Picture Distribution Trade Practices, 1956', report, 27 July 1956 (Washington D.C.: Government Printing Office, 1956), pp. 5–6; Conant, *Antitrust*.

8 'Hollywood Places great Value on Stars in Blocks-of-5 Selling', *MPH* vol. 142 no. 9 (1 March 1941), p. 12.

9 'Mandatory Block-of-Five Sales End for 5 Majors', *MPH* vol. 148 no. 10 (5 September 1942), p. 17; 'Majors To Sell in Blocks With Decree Big "If" ', *MPH* vol. 151 no. 11 (12 June 1943), pp. 17–18.

10 *MPH* attributed the A pictures' popularity to heavier advertising and exploitation. This was

due to new trade practices, a result of the 1940 decree. 'Hollywood in Uniform', *Fortune* 25 (April 1942), pp. 92–5; 'Playdates On Top Films Increase 30 Per Cent', *MPH* vol. 151 no. 12 (19 June 1943), p. 14.

11 'Through the Editor's Finder', *American Cinematographer* (hereafter AC) vol. 24 no. 6 (June 1943), p. 213.

12 'Monogram to Offer 40 for 1943–44', *MPH* vol. 151 no. 12 (19 June 1943), p. 40.

13 US Select Committee on Small Business, 'Motion-picture Distribution Trade Practices, 1956', report, p. 38.

14 'War Booming Market for Independent Product', *MPH* vol. 153 no. 7 (13 November 1943), p. 14.

15 'Cagney, UA in Five-Year Pact', *MPH* vol. 152 no. 12 (18 September 1943), p. 44; 'Wallis Sets Five Year Paramount Production Deal', *MPH* vol. 155 no. 9 (27 May 1944), p. 36.

16 'Hal Wallis Starts Picture for Paramount Release', *MPH* vol. 158 no. 6 (10 February 1945), p. 41; 'Seven Films Are Started; 49 Now in Production', *MPH* vol. 158 no. 9 (3 March 1945), p. 33; 'Four Pictures Are Started As Strike Hampers Work', *MPH* vol. 158 no. 13 (31 March 1945), p. 45; '*They Were Expendable* Begins Rolling at MGM', *MPH* vol. 158 no. 10 (10 March 1945), p. 38.

17 Ernest Borneman, 'Rebellion in Hollywood: A Study in Motion Picture Finance', *Harper's* 193 (October 1946), pp. 337–43; Frederic Marlowe, 'The Rise of the Independents in Hollywood', *Penguin Film Review* no. 3 (August 1947), p. 72; 'Review of the Film News', *AC* vol. 26 no. 10 (October 1945), p. 33; Frank Capra, 'Breaking Hollywood's "Pattern of Sameness"', in Koszarski, *Hollywood Directors*, pp. 83–9; 'Paramount: Oscar for Profits', *Fortune* vol. 35 no. 6 (June 1947), pp. 90–5, 208–21; '42 Pictures Are Shooting: *Junior Miss* Started', *MPH* vol. 158 no. 7 (17 February 1945), p. 29; 'Talent Planning to Fight Capital Gains Tax Ruling', *MPH* vol. 164 no. 5 (3 August 1946), p. 73.

18 Marlowe, 'The Rise of the Independents in Hollywood', p. 72. Also see US Select Committee on Small Business, 'Motion-Picture Distribution Trade Practices, 1956' hearings, 84th Cong., 2nd sess., 21 March–22 May 1956 (Washington D.C.: Government Printing Office, 1956), pp. 349–50.

19 Although threatening to fight the ruling, the offending companies eventually settled with the Bureau. Borneman, 'Rebellion in Hollywood', pp. 337–43; 'No Personal Films', *MPH* vol. 164 no. 4 (27 July 1946), p. 9; 'Talent Planning to Fight Capital Gains Tax Ruling', *MPH* vol. 164 no. 5 (3 August 1946), p. 43'; 'Capital Gains Net Terms to Radio and Stage', *MPH* vol. 164 no. 6 (10 August 1946), p. 21; 'Tax Benefit Units on Coast Settle Revenue Claims', *MPH* vol. 171 no. 3 (17 April 1948), p. 14.

20 See, for instance, the lists of films starting in production in *MPH* for December 1946 and January 1947.

21 'Industry Must Readjust Price and Cost: Cowdin', *MPH* vol. 168 no. 3 (19 July 1947), p. 13; 'Pressure Forces Issues Down on Stock Market', *MPH* vol. 169 no. 13 (27 December 1947), p. 13; William R. Weaver, 'Independents Save 20%; Major Studios Stymied', *MPH* vol. 168 no. 11 (13 September 1947), pp. 13–4; 'Production Index Still Down; Metro, 20th-Fox, Warner Start "A" Films', *MPH* vol. 169 no. 13 (27 December 1947), p. 31.

22 'Editorial', *The Screen Writer* vol. 4 no. 3 (September 1948), p. 4; Anthony A. P. Dawson, 'Hollywood's Labor Troubles', *Industrial and Labor Relations Review* vol. 1 no. 4 (July 1948), p. 642; William R. Weaver, 'Studio Employment – A 12-Year Study', *MPH* vol. 174 no. 6 (5 February 1949), p. 15; 'Employment at Studios Hit 13-year Low in 1949', *MPH* vol. 178 no. 8 (25 February 1950), p. 35.

23 William R. Weaver, 'Independents Save 20%; Major Studios Stymied', *MPH* vol. 168 no. 11 (13 September 1947), pp. 13–4.

24 William R. Weaver, 'Studios Hold Gains with Six Pictures Starting', *MPH* vol. 170 no. 6 (7 February 1948), p. 25; Fred Hift, 'Those Big City Scenes Are Really Shot On The Spot', *MPH* vol. 177 no. 13 (24 December 1949), p. 25.

25 'Hollywood Is Traveling Abroad for Production', *MPH* vol. 170 no. 3 (17 January 1948), p. 13.

26 'British Pact Signed and US Ready To Deliver', *MPH* vol. 170 no. 12 (20 March 1948), p. 13; William R. Weaver, 'Impact of British-US Deal on Production Is Worrying Hollywood', *MPH* vol. 171 no. 7 (15 May 1948), p. 27; 'Report 20th-Fox Will Make 12 Top Films in Europe', *MPH* vol. 172 no. 10, (4 September 1948), p. 12; '20th-Fox To Offer 32 In Month-By-Month Schedule', *MPH* vol. 172 no. 12 (18 September 1948), p. 17; 'Shoot More Films Abroad', *MPH* vol. 176 no. 4 (23 July 1949), p. 16.

27 'Video Hurts, Survey Says', *MPH* vol. 178 no. 6 (11 February 1950), p. 22; US Select Committee on Small Business, 'Motion-picture Distribution Trade Practices, 1956', report, p. 22. This latter source is excellent on the effects of television (see pp. 29–31); the analysis includes the argument that drive-ins had a relatively low impact on four-wall exhibition (pp. 28–9).

28 Red Kann, 'Hollywood in '49', *MPH* vol. 174 no. 4 (22 January 1949), p. 18.

29 William R. Weaver, 'Production Up But Big Pictures Are Held Off', *MPH* vol. 170 no. 11 (13 March 1948), p. 35.

30 Lincoln, 'Comeback of the Movies', p. 131; Merrill Lynch, *Radio, Television, Motion Pictures*, pp. 21, 24; Charles Flynn and Todd McCarthy, *Kings of the Bs* (New York: E. P. Dutton, 1975), p. 30.

31 'Six Majors Plan 7 Films Sold At Advanced Prices', *MPH* vol. 168 no. 9 (30 August 1947), p. 23.

32 'Importers Seek Theatre Outlets', *MPH* vol. 166 no. 6 (8 February 1947), p. 50.

33 'New Special Effects Company Formed', *AC* vol. 28 no. 2 (February 1947), p. 66; 'Motion Picture Center: Hollywood's Newest Studio'; *AC* vol. 28 no. 9 (September 1947), pp. 314–5; John Forbes, 'Want to Expand? Leasing Is the Answer', *AC* vol. 41 no. 2 (February 1960), pp. 100, 116.

34 Fred Hift, 'Coast Talent Poised Over Television Pond', *MPH* vol. 174 no. 9 (26 February 1946), p. 19. See *AC* through the 1950s but particularly: Victor Milner, 'ASC Inaugurates Research on Photography for Television', *AC* vol. 30 no. 3 (March 1949), pp. 86, 100–2; John De Mos, 'The Cinematographer's Place in Television', *AC* vol. 30 no. 3 (March 1949), pp. 87, 102, 104–5; Walter Strenge, 'In the Best Professional Manner', *AC* vol. 32 no. 5 (May 1951), p. 186, 200–1; Leigh Allen, 'Television Film Production', *AC* vol. 33 no. 2 (February 1952), p. 69; Frederick Foster, 'The Big Switch Is To TV!', *AC* vol. 36 no. 1 (January 1955), pp. 27, 38–40; Arthur Miller, 'Hollywood's Cameramen at Work', *AC* vol. 38 no. 9 (September 1957), pp. 580–1. Estimates for 1955 were that ten times the work for television companies compared to theatrical exhibition was being done in Hollywood: Morris Gelman, 'The Hollywood Story', *Television Magazine* 20 (September 1963).

35 'UA to Study Financing of Producers', *MPH* vol. 174 no. 1 (1 January 1949), p. 25; Red Kann, 'Hollywood in '49', *MPH* vol. 174 no. 4 (22 January 1949), p. 18; William R. Weaver, 'Giannini Says Bank's Loans At New Peak', *MPH* vol. 175 no. 12 (18 June 1949), p. 23; Red Kann, 'Circuit Owners Form Company to Finance Product', *MPH* vol. 176 no. 1 (2 July 1949), pp. 13–4; William R. Weaver, 'Partnership Aid Helps Financing Unit Pay', *MPH* vol. 176 no. 7 (13 August 1949), p. 23; J. A. Otten, 'Tax, Credit and Labor Matters Are On Washington Agenda for 1957', *MPH* vol. 206 no. 1 (5 January 1957), p. 21.

36 William R. Weaver, 'See Problems Eased by Blumenthal Formula', *MPH* vol. 174 no. 12 (19 March 1949), p. 33.

37 Lincoln, 'Comeback of the movies', p. 130; 'Outlook for 1956', *MPH* vol. 202 no. 1 (7 January

1956), p. 8; films listed in production for January through March 1950, 1955 and 1959, *M P H*; 'Top Grossing Pictures of 1956', *M P H* vol. 206 no. 1 (5 January 1957), pp. 12–3; 'Name Adler to Zanuck Post', *M P H* vol. 202 no. 6 (11 February 1956), p. 18; Vincent Canby, 'Hollywood Pushes Into T V Production Arena', *M P H* vol. 198 no. 4 (22 January 1955), p. 13; Jay Remer, 'Hollywood Eyes T V As New Production Source', *M P H* vol. 202 no. 2 (14 January 1956), p. 12; William R. Weaver, 'Hecht-Hill-Lancaster Plan Nine Features', *M P H* vol. 206 no. 1 (5 January 1957), p. 20.

38 'Robert Wise Talks About "The New Hollywood"', *A C* vol. 57 no. 7 (July 1976), pp. 770–1.

39 Staiger, 'The Hollywood Mode of Production', pp. 319–27.

III
Towards a Workers' History of the US Film Industry

MICHAEL NIELSEN

From *The Critical Communications Review I*, edited by Vincent Mosco and Janet Wasko (Norwood, N. J.: Ablex, 1983)

What follows is the latter half of an exciting, sprawling article in which Michael Nielsen, signalling his intention 'eventually to produce a workers' history of the US film industry' (p. 48 of the full version), covers a time-span from the earliest days of the cinema to the time of writing (c. 1981). His project is committed to 'that humanist core of Marxist thought, namely the human consequences of industrial relationships' (p. 48), and we include this extract as an example of the sort of detailed historical work that largely remains to be undertaken, or made widely available, if such consequences and the resulting struggles and compromises are to be properly remembered. Nielsen begins his article trenchantly: 'The given history of the US film industry is largely a mass of nostalgic or meaningless distinctions drawn by film "buffs", corporate apologists, and academes absorbed by minutiae at the expense of material analysis of the industry per se' (p. 47). The revisionist history he provides is a valuable interim account which brings home sharply the weight of the organisational forces that effectively stifled the development of a Left trade unionism in Hollywood. And as he brings his narrative into the 80s, the legacy of that history merges with technological and commercial developments in a picture of 'New Hollywood' employment practices which are still, given North America's world media dominance, of relevance to us all.

We pick up the story – its breathlessness and ruthlessness is well conveyed by Nielsen's narrative style – as developments in the mid-1930s set up the conditions which will ultimately make the House Un-American Activities Committee's purge of the Hollywood Left possible. The IA is the International Alliance of Theatrical and Stage Employees; founded as a National union in 1893, and becoming International as it added Canada to its area of recruitment in 1903, it had since 1934 been controlled by 'the Browne-Bioff axis of corruption'. George E. Browne, before being elected union President, was business manager of IA Local No. 2 in Hollywood; he became an associate of Willie Bioff, 'what one might call a freelance hoodlum' (p. 64) who had been part of the Capone organisation. Frank Nitti, Capone's successor, sent in his 'boys' to make sure that Browne was elected President. Browne and Bioff were able to deliver a useful degree of union 'realism' to Nicholas Schenck of Loews, Inc. (parent corporation of M G M and owner of a major chain of cinemas). Now read on. . . .

M.A./J.O.T.

Worker Revolt Stage One

The Painters Union had left the Studio Basic Agreement in 1932 over dissatisfaction with the grievance procedure provided by the Agreement. The Painters felt that the procedure was too roundabout and that it weakened local autonomy. When the Painters left the Agreement, they took with them the majority of make-up artists, a group claimed by the I A. With C I O help, the Painters Local 644 formed a loose-kit organization of studio locals including plasterers, stationary engineers, plumbers, molders, cooks, scenic artists, boilermakers, laborers, make-up artists, set designers, hair stylists, and the painters themselves. The new group was called the Federated Motion Picture Crafts (F M P C). The F M P C had some Communist ties, as did many progressive labor groups in the 1930s. The leader of the F M P C, Jeff Kibre, was alternately reputed to be a Communist agent sent to destroy peaceful labor relations in Hollywood or a progressive labor leader attempting to restore local autonomy and democracy to the obviously dictatorial and corrupt Hollywood labor scene.[1] Kibre's background and affiliations are points off the center of the F M P C - I A struggle, however, because his leadership was soon supplanted by a rank-and-file painter, Herb Sorrell, business agent of Painters Local 644, the motion picture studios local.

In April, 1937, the Supreme Court upheld the constitutionality of the National Labor Relations Act of 1935, or as it is more commonly known, the Wagner Act. This set the stage for a united campaign by studio locals not covered by the Studio Basic Agreement to obtain producer recognition as guaranteed under the terms of the Wagner Act. The Agreement favored the international unions already party to the Agreement by holding that, in effect, the international unions could assert jurisdictional claims as they saw fit and that locals not party to the Agreement could not obtain recognition if their jurisdictions overlapped with any claimed by the international. Prior to the upholding of the Wagner Act, the choices for the film workers were slight indeed – either be disenfranchised or become a part of the Browne-Bioff axis of corruption.

When the I A was readmitted to the Agreement in 1936, it obtained for its members a 10 per cent wage increase. The F M P C locals struck on 30 April 1937 to obtain this raise granted to I A members and, more significantly, to obtain producer recognition. The just-formed Screen Actor's Guild (S A G) promised to join the F M P C strike, but it was diverted by an offer from Bioff. In return for I A support of S A G in its bid for producer recognition, S A G refused to support the F M P C strike, leaving the workers high and dry. In a further strategic move, Bioff and Browne created a new IA laborer's local and obtained a wage of 82½¢ an hour from the friendly producers. Since the FMPC laborers had gone on strike to increase their rate from 60¢ to 75¢ per hour, many laborers defected to the new IA local. In short order, make-up artists and hair stylists fell prey to the same strategy, and the FMPC strike was broken, as was the organization itself. However, the Painters eventually obtained a 15 per cent increase, a closed shop, and the distinction of becoming the first local to receive producer recognition.

Meanwhile, within the IA itself, a group called the 'IA Progressives' began to make itself heard. The Progressives called for an investigation of Bioff, instigated by the disclosure that Joseph Schenck (brother of Nicholas) had made a $100,000 'loan' to Bioff shortly after the crushing of the FMPC strike. (This was the first public disclosure of any wrongdoing on the part of Bioff in his negotiator role.) Bioff bought California Assembly Speaker William J. Jones for $5,000 to quash the investigation. Subsequently, the Assembly conducted a quick 48-hour investigation of Brown and Bioff (without subpoenaing either man) and gave the union a 'clean bill of health'.[2]

However, the Assembly investigation became the subject of a grand jury investigation in the following year. The revelations noted previously forced Nitti to withdraw Bioff from Hollywood until 'the heat was off'. The IA Progressives seemed to have won a substantial victory when the IA Executive Board returned local autonomy to the Hollywood locals under emergency conditions and lifted the 2 per cent assessment levied by Browne and Bioff. However, the Board shortly thereafter split up the strongest of the Progressive locals, Local 37, into five smaller and ineffective locals.

In response, the Progressives joined with Sorrell's Painters Local 644 in forming the short-lived United Studio Technicians Guild (USTG). The strategy of this new alternative group was to use the mechanism of the National Labor Relations Board (NLRB) representation election to defeat the IA. The CIO's grant of a charter to the USTG in 1939 had the unfortunate effect of turning the CIO's rival, the AFL, against the USTG. Also, the CIO's ties with the Communist party gave the IA red-baiting ammunition, on which the IA did not fail to capitalize. Just one month before the NLRB election was to be held, the IA signed a five-year pact with the producers, loudly reporting that a 20 per cent wage increase would soon be negotiated. The IA won the election by a two-to-one margin, and six days later accepted a 10 per cent wage increase rather than the promised 20 per cent. A few months later, the producers asked the IA to relinquish even the 10 per cent raise, citing lost revenues from the war-shrunk foreign market for films. By this time, Bioff had returned to Hollywood and, perhaps as a show of reform (or perhaps merely as a Nitti ploy), he held on to the 10 per cent increase. Bioff's good will, however, did not extend to the leaders of the USTG, many of whom were IA members and studio workers. Bioff blacklisted these people, and several were permanently denied employment in the studios.[3]

Meanwhile, George Browne was again re-elected to the IA Presidency in 1938. At the convention, Sidney Kent, President of Twentieth Century-Fox, praised Browne's efforts in promoting 'less interruption in employment, less hard feelings, less recrimination and ... more good will than any industry I know of in this country'.[4] Browne responded:

The appearance of President Kent, I do believe, shows indication of a new era in the relationship between the employer and the employee ... I think it is going to do great things for us and the country in general. ... As we sow, so shall we reap.[5]

Subsequent investigations revealed that Kent accompanied Nicholas Schenck to the hotel suite of Browne and Bioff in 1936 to make the first instalment of the I A payoff.[6] As we sow. ...

In the midst of Bioff's fights against dissident factions, he attempted to bring the screen actors under I A control through the I A affiliate, American Federation of Actors. S A G President Robert Montgomery retaliated by hiring two ex- F B I agents to conduct a private investigation of Bioff. The private report was then forwarded to journalist Westbrook Pegler who subsequently wrote an article calling attention to Bioff's unserved six-month pandering sentence in Chicago. The I A fought Bioff's extradition (with legal fees paid by members' dues) but to no avail. Bioff was returned to Chicago and began serving his sentence in the beginning of 1940. Immediately upon release in September of that same year, Bioff was back on the I A payroll in Hollywood, but not for long. Joseph Schenck, under indictment for income tax evasion, bargained for a reduced sentence in return for revealing the true nature of the producer's deals with Browne and Bioff. Neither the testimony of Schenck nor the silence of Browne and Bioff had revealed the link to Nitti, although federal investigators were pursuing this connection. Browne and Bioff were found guilty of extortion and sentenced to terms of eight and ten years respectively. Shortly after their imprisonments, the two men became aware that Nitti was interested in permanently silencing anyone who might eventually testify about the syndicate's involvement in the motion picture industry and the I A. In return for grants of immunity from further prosecution and reduced sentences, Browne and Bioff revealed the full story of the Browne and Bioff era of I A corruption, linking Nitti and his associates with the names of prominent industry executives. Nitti and several of his associates were indicted by a grand jury. Nitti escaped prosecution in the classic manner by committing suicide on the day the indictments were returned. Browne, after serving his time, went underground and has not been heard from since. Bioff also attempted to go underground but was killed by a bomb planted in his pickup truck in Phoenix, Arizona in 1955.

Succeeding Browne in 1942 as I A President was Richard Walsh, vice-president under Browne. At the 1942 convention, the I A leadership purged itself of association with Bioff, and indicated that it had no knowledge of wrongdoing within the I A during the Browne-Bioff era: 'William Bioff is not now and never has been a member of this Alliance.'[7] Technically, this was a true statement. Bioff was never a member but rather an employee, hired by Browne as international representative. Of course, the mere fact that Bioff was the *de facto* leader of the union for six years seems to have escaped the I A Executive Board's attention. The Board contended that confidence in Browne was rooted in a 'clever conspiracy' on his and Bioff's parts, although delegates to the convention in 1934 and 1936 probably could have used other adjectives to describe Nitti's conventioneering techniques. The 1942 Board stated also that Browne's record, as he presented it to the Board, was most impressive:

In view of such a record, it is not surprising that the delegates to the convention in Louisville in 1940 would vote unanimously to support Browne. It is true that at that time rumors were being circulated alleging certain illegal conduct on the part of Bioff and intimating that perhaps Browne was involved. However as the sources of these rumors were known to be hostile to the labor movement as a whole, no recognition was given to them either by the delegates or the officers of the I A.[8]

This statement is a major rewrite of I A history. Could the I A Progressive be fairly labeled as 'hostile to the labor movement as a whole'? Could the Executive Board (essentially the same in 1936 as in 1942) be totally unaware of the deals struck in New York hotel suites between the producers and Bioff? Who on the Board was responsible for overseeing the disbursement of the special assessment funds that disappeared into syndicate hands? How could such a negligent or unintelligent group of men be expected to manage the affairs of the union that dominated the livelihood of so many film workers? Such questions were swept under the wheels of the union machine, as it rolled along toward the second and final stage of its complete destruction of any vestiges of union democracy in the motion picture industry.

As for the management, all but Joseph Schenck were given free passes by the government in regard to their 'creative management' campaigns of the 1930s, even though government hearings revealed that the major producers had saved some $14 million by 'submitting' to Bioff and Browne. Despite his prominent role in this conspiracy to defraud workers of their bargaining rights and fair wages, Nicholas Schenck would never be called to testify in any hearings regarding the Browne-Bioff deals. In this period, Schenck was pulling down some $345,000 per year in salary and incentive payments. The average steadily employed film worker was earning about $1,900 yearly before taxes and those good old union dues.[9]

The Conference of Studio Unions

The loss of the N L R B decision in 1939 did not deter Sorrell from his militant campaign against the I A. In 1940, Painters Local 644 granted a charter to the motion picture cartoonists laboring under the iron hand of Walt Disney's open shop. In 1941, the cartoonists won a nine-week strike against Disney and obtained recognition from M G M and Warners in the process without having to strike those two firms. During the Disney strike, the cartoonists were joined by the Painters, machinists (I A M), office employees, and film technicians locals, all of whom were granted closed shop status at the end of the strike. Out of this success, the locals formed the Conference of Studio Unions (C S U) with the Painters' business agent Sorrell as its first and last leader. In later U S Congressional hearings, Disney would testify that Sorrell 'used the [War] Labor Board to suit his purpose,' as if the union shop was a Communist plot.[10]

The C S U continued to expand its ranks in 1942 as publicists, story analysts, office employees, and set decorators were all issued charters by Painters Local 644.

Soon the studio locals of the IBEW and Carpenters had joined the CSU, significantly increasing the CSU's total membership. The CSU was not a union itself but rather a group of locals united to preserve member locals' autonomy and to form joint strategy to improve worker welfare. Locals were encouraged to negotiate their own contracts with the producers. Unorganized groups were granted charters from Local 644 regardless of their skill classification.

In his *Report on Blacklisting*, John Cogley summed up the various expectations that were part of the formation of the CSU:

A number of groups had a stake in the CSU. The AFL craft unions saw it as a rival to their ancient rival, the IA. The Communists saw it as a base for party operations in Hollywood. The studios saw it as an IA rival which could sap IA strength. And Herb Sorrell, its fiery leader, may have seen it as a vehicle for his own ambitions.[11]

On the other hand, a writer more sympathetic with the plight of the workers has written that the CSU was 'a symbol of hope in Hollywood, of democratic and honest trade unionism'.[12] The account of the rise and fall of the CSU as presented below is an attempt to blend both of these perspectives on the CSU, taking into account the institutional and personal levels of activity involved in the story. However, it should be remembered that the workers' stories have yet to be told. The journalistic account can provide only a framework for truth, which itself must arise from the workers' own perspectives.

The conflict between the IA and the CSU actually originated prior to the formation of the latter. As already noted, Herb Sorrell was its main spokesman, and the most numerically significant locals within the CSU (IBEW and Carpenters) were traditional rivals of the IA from its very inception. The CSU was organized largely to unseat the IA because that union, despite the fall of Browne and Bioff, was still a dictatorial union that controlled the workers with either an iron hand or through total negligence. The IA Executive Board was only slightly changed from the same Board that rubber stamped the criminal activities of Bioff and Browne. IA locals were still deprived of direct input into wage negotiations. And, although the new IA leader Richard Walsh could not be charged with fraud or criminal conspiracy, subsequent events would substantiate the tacit worker belief that the IA was a sweetheart union.

The first volleys fired in this new jurisdictional and ideological conflict were over which union would represent some 77 studio set decorators. In the early days of the NLRB, the set decorators formed the Society of Motion Picture Interior Decorators and signed a five-year contract with the producers. In 1939, the IA attempted to expand the jurisdiction of its local 44 to include the set decorators, but the producers declined to recognize this claim, noting that they already had a contract with the set decorators. At renewal time in 1942, the IA again attempted to assert jurisdiction and was again denied. Fearing possible absorption by the dictatorial IA, the set decorators chose to accept representation as one of the chartered spin-off locals of Painters Local 644 and subsequently joined the CSU in 1943. The producers refused to recognize this new local until it had been certified by the NLRB. The issue was clouded somewhat by the fact that a small percentage of the set decorators also held I A property workers cards. (Set decorator was the next step up for the property workers, who occasionally had to 'step down' in the changing schedule of demand for various skills needed for certain kinds of productions.) The producers stalled negotiations with the set decorators past the expiration date of their contract and, after seven months of stalling, repeated their demand that the group must get N L R B certification before the producers would negotiate. This demand was issued long after the producers had tacitly acknowledged the rightful claim of the Painters charter by dealing with the set decorators under this new charter for some seven months or more. An N L R B election was blocked by the I A because of the property workers' cards issue.

The set decorators local retaliated by calling a strike, but the federal wartime policies obliged the War Labor Board to head off the strike as quickly as possible. The arbitrator decided in favor of the Painters charter, but the producers continued to stall. Finally, on 12 March 1945, after fifteen months of frustration, the Painters struck and gained the support of all but four of the C S U locals. In light of subsequent accusations of Communist domination of the C S U, it was interesting that the four locals returning to work were, by their actions, adhering to the current Communist Party line of no strikes during wartime.[13] Sorrell's strike call was roundly criticized in several C P newspaper articles and pamphlets.

By the time of the strike, the C S U's locals represented some 10,000 workers in comparison to the I A's total of 16,000 studio workers.[14]

Thus, a dispute originally involving 77 workers had finally snowballed into mass proportions. C S U members were kept out of work for eight or nine months while I A scabs took their jobs. In an N L R B ruling, the regional director found that the producers had not bargained in good faith with the set decorators, and the Group was finally given recognition as a Painters union affiliate. During the strike, C S U workers lost more than wages. The largest picket lines at Warners were attacked by 'scabs, thugs, tear gas, fire hoses, and the studio's private police and fire departments'.[15] A more recent description of the events states that the attack was undertaken by 'a vigilante squad of one thousand I A T S E thugs, led by I A officials and equipped with chains, rubber hoses, blackjacks, and metal cables . . .'[16]

The strike did not officially end until A F L intervention in late October. The A F L Executive Council called for: (1) an immediate end to the strike; (2) local inter-union negotiations for thirty days on jurisdictional questions; (3) a return of all strikers to their former jobs; and (4) final disposition of all disputes left unsettled after the thirty-day period to be determined by a three-man committee drawn from the A F L Executive Council.[17]

This intervention proved to be only a band-aid on the spreading cancer of labor disruption and management collusion with the I A. Many C S U workers refused to work with the I A scabs. No significant disputes were settled in the thirty-day period, and the A F L three-man committee issued a jurisdictional ruling on 'set erection' that was so ambiguous that over 300 Carpenters were unintentionally displaced from their usual jobs. The Carpenters did not immediately strike, but called instead for a clarification from the A F L. On 16 August 1946, the A F L committee issued its clarification on the matter, stating that the committee had not intended by its findings to change traditional jurisdictional boundaries and that set erection belonged to the Carpenters. On this same day or shortly thereafter, the producers and the IA's Hollywood representative Roy Brewer began a series of secret meetings to establish a plan to destroy the CSU. The minutes of these meetings were entered into the Congressional Record in the following year. They were supplied by none other than Pat Casey, the producer's labor representative for twenty-five years. The plan was for the IA to refuse to relinquish the set erection jobs while the producers would continue to give IA members the work. Then the CSU carpenters and painters were called upon to work on the 'hot sets', which, of course, brought about another lengthy and bloody strike.

Roy Brewer had come to Hollywood on the very day of the outbreak of the first CSU strike in 1945. His red-baiting in that dispute was directed not only at the CSU but at the talent guilds as well, in which progressive members were attempting to throw support behind the more democratic CSU. Brewer issued a letter to left-leaning and liberal film personalities asking them to repudiate the CSU or face particularized projectionist strikes against their films. The actors voted overwhelmingly to cross the CSU picket lines, led by none other than dashing Ronald Reagan. The writers split into leftist and conservative factions that would eventually bring about the most serious cases of Hollywood blacklisting of leftist intellectuals.[18] In the heyday of the blacklisting era, Roy Brewer would become the 'man-to-see' to clear oneself of charges of being a Communist sympathizer. But for now, his energy was focused on ridding the IA of all opposition.

The refusal of the Painters and Carpenters to work on hot sets was followed by the usual strike-breaking tactics including IA scabs, beatings, fire hoses, and the like. Scabs were transported through the picket lines by Teamsters, despite the fact that the rank and file Teamsters themselves had voted against crossing the picket lines. Their business agent manoeuvered the drivers into crossing the lines through a series of threats and replacements of 'troublemakers'. He was shortly thereafter given a job as an industrial relations director for National Theaters, a firm headed by none other than Joseph Schenk.[19]

In such activities, one begins to see a pattern of unions developing into mere extensions of the studios' personnel departments, paradoxically funded by workers' union dues. And, as if this humiliating manipulation was not bad enough, the workers were turned against one another. They became their own worst enemies:

Many of the antagonisms behind the strikes had their origins in the fact that members of different intersectional unions worked side by side on the set or in the shop, so that their members were aware of any violation of their jurisdictional prerogatives.[20]

Thus, accounts of 'IATSE thugs' written from leftist intellectual perspectives should be taken with a grain of salt. While there is no sense in condoning hooligan violence perpetrated by one group of workers against another, there is also no sense in lumping together all members of a particular union without regard to the real human motives behind the violent actions.

Brewer and the IA, in collusion with the producers, managed to eventually stall settlement of the 1946 dispute for so long that the final NLRB election was not held until 1949. By this time, the C S U was a mere skeletal organization, since most of its members had been forced either to join the scab I A locals or to leave the industry altogether. The I A won the 1949 N L R B election by a landslide and has continued to dominate Hollywood labor ever since.

This centralization of power had numerous structural and personal repercussions that still reverberate within the studio labor force. The decentralization and democracy of the C S U period has been replaced by top-down labor relations. Contracts are negotiated by I A international representatives who are far removed from the experience of the labor involved. These representatives earn much more than the workers they represent and, from a practical sociological perspective, have more in common with management than workers. In jurisdictional disputes, the I A has much more power over its locals than the A F L had over its affiliates. From one perspective, this ability of the I A to internally handle jurisdictional disputes has meant a much more efficient handling of such problems. On the other hand, union members remark that the official I A 'family' (its leadership handed down in dynastic fashion) never forgives locals who make trouble. Such locals face difficulties going into negotiations. International representatives might trade away their wages or working conditions for a more favored local. Favored status is determined by toeing the 'family' line under all circumstances, particularly at the biennial I A conventions.

The defeat of the C S U also meant the erosion of the base for all progressives within the motion picture industry. Englund and Ceplair quote one anonymous leftist still active in Hollywood labor:

It was a devastating loss for everything progressive, autonomous or liberal in the Hollywood labor movement. Hundreds were blacklisted; their homes and lives were shattered; some committed suicide.[21]

The talent guilds were purged of progressives, and the overall chilling effect on the involvement in leftist politics would persist in force throughout the fifties. The defeat of the C S U opened the door for the vicious second round of H U A C hearings on the motion picture industry started in 1951. Roy Brewer, the I A's Hollywood representative, would ride high through all these hearings as the friendliest of the 'friendly' witnesses. He used the 1947 hearings to smear Sorrell in the national press and thus undercut the C S U position. Following these hearings, Brewer became a self-appointed sanitizer of ex-progressives who could confess their sins and obtain economic redemption. In effect, he became the hatchet man for the studio executives while simultaneously purporting to represent the interests of labor as the I A Hollywood representative. It is not surprising that Brewer, after failing to unseat incumbent I A president Richard Walsh at the 1954 convention, immediately moved into an executive position with Allied Artists, one of the smaller motion picture producers.

At certain times in Brewer's story, it is difficult to tell if he was using anti-Communism to further I A strength or if he was using I A strength to fight the red menace. While his red-bashing of Herb Sorrell certainly undercut the C S U's position, his subsequent campaign against the film *Salt of the Earth* in the 1950s seemed more ideological in its purpose. The film was produced by Herbert Biberman and Paul Jarrico (both blacklisted) and was in fact the most pro-union film ever made in the United States. It was a strong endictment of the Taft-Hartley amendment in addition to being a rather advanced polemic on racism and sexism. The film was made in spite of the film industry's united efforts, spearheaded by Brewer, to block its production. At one point in post-production editing and laboratory work, Biberman was forced to rename the film to get a lab to work on it, since all lab work was controlled by the IA.

The men and women in the laboratory were most curious about the film as they saw bits and pieces of it. What was it? It seemed a pro-union film! Who had made it? And how come? . . .

The sense that the film was pro-union inspired the men and the women in the lab to give it the most preferred treatment.[22]

Subsequently, a projectionist who worked in the lab inadvertently 'spilled the beans' to an IA official who immediately threatened the lab owner with a walkout of his staff unless the owner agreed to stop working on the film. The workers, of course, found themselves inevitably in the powerless middle of the struggle. Later in the same book, Biberman related how IA projectionists were obviously coerced by union leaders to refuse to project the film. In Chicago, one projectionist who assured Biberman that he could stand up to the union, promised to run the film because:

He was too old, he said, to turn his back upon the old established principles of working people and become party to a racketeering operation parading as trade unionism.[23]

At show time, the projectionist had disappeared. When Biberman caught sight of the man on the following day in front of the Chicago projectionists local's office, he tried to find out what had happened. The projectionist explained to Biberman:

They locked me in that office last night. . . . You been in Hollywood. You know these people. You know what they're like.

Mr Jallas, business agent of the Chicago local, was simply carrying out Brewer's orders and, in fact, had never seen the film. Biberman had recourse via Taft Hartley, but he refused to take action for obvious ideological reasons. A union official had managed to stop workers from promoting pro-union ideals and principles. Whether Biberman's intentions were noble or subversive, after reading his account of the struggle to make the film *Salt of the Earth*, one is left with a chilling impression of the dictatorial nature of the IA leaders. One is also struck again by the extreme distance between the leaders and the led. And finally, one is left with a sympathetic feeling for the workers themselves whose skills had become so specialized that they could find work only with one of the oligopolistic firms. These workers can either follow orders or leave the industry altogether. The oligopolistic unionism of the IA left little room for individuals to manoeuvre.

New Technologies, Old Problems

In 1948, Paramount became the first of the major producing firms to sign a consent decree to divorce itself from its theater chain. The other major firms soon followed suit and, over the next nine years, sold their theaters. They also modified some of their unfair trade practices in the area of distribution. Along with this restructuring, television began to impact seriously on theater attendance. In the period 1947–1956, profits for the major producers fell from an industry total of $121 million to $32 million, attendance was halved, and studio employment was reduced from 24,000 to 10,000. Employment in domestic production was also cut by runaway production, a problem originating in the complex web of the historic U S domination of overseas film markets. England, for example, in retaliation to U S domination, first established quota systems and then initiated financial incentive plans to encourage U S companies to film in England. In recent years, blockbuster films such as *Superman*, *Star Wars*, and *Raiders of the Lost Ark* – despite their 'American' aura – were actually filmed in British studios. As with so many other industries, the motion picture industry is becoming a transnational enterprise, both in production and distribution. Labor unions, whose control does not extend beyond the U S and Canada, are hard put to cope with runaway production.

By the mid-1960s, television had become a dual market for the motion picture producers. Feature films had become a regular part of prime time viewing, and many television series were being produced by subsidiaries of the motion picture firms.

By the early 1960s, Hollywood dominated prime time programs. Nearly three-fourths of its work force owed its employment directly or indirectly to T V film activity . . .[P]roduction centered mainly in six factory complexes: Universal, Desilu, M G M, Screen Gems, General Service Studios, and C B S's Studio Center.[24]

Television's development and employment patterns caused several reversals in I A members' fortunes. Live television production of entertainment programs required crews of trained stagehands, property workers, grips, gaffers, and other personnel. The three major networks hired I A workers to fill many of these jobs. The I A envisioned a gold mine in the television industry, whose voracious appetite for daily live programming seemed to offer endless employment for many I A workers. Production was initially spread out in three major centers: New York, Chicago, and Los Angeles. Unfortunately for Chicago's I A members, N B C shortly abandoned Chicago production in favor of the coasts. Employment at the Chicago N B C studios fell from two-hundred to less than fifty in one year.

With the advent of videotape in the late 1950s, the possibility of replacing 'live' shows cut back employment severely, particularly weekend overtime. T V studios could now normalize production schedules – that is, operate largely on a nine-to-five, Monday-through-Friday basis. Videotape and video camera operation eventually fell to the jurisdiction of a new rival of the I A, the National Association of Broadcast Employees and Technicians (N A B E T). Throughout the 1960s, as videotape technology improved, N A B E T became a serious contender for the control of television production personnel. At the local stations, the min-cam gradually replaced sound film for news and commercials. At the networks, although filmed entertainment continued to be dominant, the success of Norman Lear's *All in the Family* initiated an obvious upsurge in videotape production.

The census data on the changes in employment patterns and unemployment figures for the motion picture industry are unfortunately aggregated with other entertainment industries. Such figures make it difficult to tell recent history. Rather, the story must be told in more descriptive fashion.

In the theaters, employment has steadily declined since 1975, owing to several factors. The multiplex theater, in which a single building houses several small theaters, has meant a savings in concession and ticket personnel. Along with the development of the multiplex, most theaters have adopted the platter system of projection, in which an entire film is spliced together rather than run in 'change-over' fashion. Also, the Xenon lamp has simplified the task of throwing a good image. These technological advances have meant that a single projectionist can handle four or more theaters simultaneously. They also have meant that many theaters have begun to lock out union projectionists at contract renewal time, simply by demanding terms that the management knows will be unacceptable to the projectionists. In 1981, I A President Walter Diehl reported that as many as 60 per cent of all U S theaters were non-union. In Los Angeles in 1977, a business agent of projectionists Local 150 was convicted of paying juveniles to stinkbomb and firebomb non-union theaters.[25] But, in general, the locals have begrudgingly accepted this erosion of union strength in the booths. While some platter booths are still manned by union projectionists, the prospects of either a continuous loop system or the slightly more far-fetched possibility of theatrical video projection augers a gradual and total passing of the projectionists' task in the 1980s.[26] The I A may be able to intervene and protect the remaining jobs, but the current trend indicates that this will not happen. In this regard, it is interesting to note that the I A, like many other unions that are hardpressed by technological changes, has begun to diversify its base of support by organizing casino workers in Atlantic City, New Jersey, and employees of Disneyworld near Orlando, Florida.[27]

For the production workers, the future is clouded by radical technological changes involving the use of videotape. Recent rumblings in the trade press have hinted at the future outlines of the motion picture industry. New technologies under development by the major firms and their subsidiaries include digital sound systems, digital storage of filmed images, and satellite transmission to theaters.[28] But the most unsettling area of development is that of high-definition television (H D T V). By doubling the number of television scan lines, a video image can be created that is reputed to match the resolution of 35-mm motion picture film.[29] Production on videotape via H D T V would provide a more versatile first-generation copy that could be easily converted to film, videocassette, videodisc, or even stored on the equivalent of motion picture microfiche. Videotape production is more efficient than film in its ability to provide instant playback of shots, electronic editing, and the ability to do location shooting linked to a central recording facility via microwave transmission or even satellites.[30] The decision may ultimately be forced upon the producers either through market trends, such as the direct sale of product to pay television by bypass theaters altogether, or through the economies offered by videotape itself.[31]

For the IA and NABET, videotape is a crucial issue. NABET has resisted merger with the IA (despite moves toward such a merger in the talent guilds SAG and AFTRA – the television talent guild), probably because of the IA's notorious dictatorial control of its studio locals. However, in 1981, NABET President Edward Lynch indicated that he was interested in such a merger. However he expressed reservations:

There would have to be an entirely new approach to organizational structure with a procedure established in advance as to how to adopt such a structure.[32]

NABET seems to be concerned that the IA's traditional domination of the studios may be the deciding factor in the upcoming videotape controversy. Motion picture director Robert Aldrich recently suggested an alternate course for the development of videotape:

It's going to be a jurisdictional war. . . . Those guys who have been working on tape (NABET) make a third or a quarter of what the (IATSE) technicians working on film make. They've been sitting out in the tules watching technicians working on a film making a comparative fortune. But soon, they're going to say, 'Wait a minute, you wouldn't let us in the cameramen's local or the sound local or the cutting (editing) local, so fine, you sit out here – we're going to make movies on tape.' . . . All the unions that deal exclusively with tape are going to move in and push these unions out that deal with film.[33]

At this stage of development, there is no telling how this issue will be resolved. The IA has initiated a Videotape Training Programme 'to upgrade the talents of those individuals currently employed in specific technical crafts', beginning in the areas of stagecraft, technical, and post-production.[34]

In more general terms, the film production workers have won substantial wage increases in recent years, as shown in Table 3.1. Table 3.2 indicates that the total number of workers engaged in motion picture production and distribution in the US has also substantially increased in recent years. Apparently, the major firms are currently interested in stockpiling films for possible distribution via pay cable or video software. In this new market, theatrical distribution is increasingly becoming of secondary importance in the overall marketing strategy. Theatrical distribution is becoming more like a 'market test' than the bread and butter of the motion picture industry. Table 3.3. shows that, as employment in production and distribution has steadily increased since 1975, employment in theaters has decreased slightly. It should also be noted that employment figures for both production/distribution and theaters continue to follow seasonal patterns of casualization. Differences for high and low months in production/distribution average about 12,000 per year.

Conclusions

According to Daniel Bertaux, the critical perspective that 'might be satisfied with unraveling exploitation and capital accumulation'

Table 3.1
Non-supervisory Worker Average Hourly Earnings

1972	1974	1976	1978
$5.64	5.83	6.70	9.84

Table 3.2
Non-supervisory Employees Engaged in Production & Distribution (in thousands)

1972	1974	1976	1978
53.1	56.1	59.8	71.4

Table 3.3
Motion Picture Theater Employment (in thousands)

1972	1974	1976	1978
126.7	129.3	128.5	127.6

Source: U S Department of Labor, Bureau of Labor Statistics, Bulletin 1312–11, *Employment and Earnings, 1909–1978*, pp. 808–809, Washington, D C, 1979.

fails to come to terms with 'what such a relation of production does to men's and women's lives'.[35] Union enrollment statistics can hardly begin to explain the difference between an I A progressive and an I A thug. How were workers manipulated into such ideologically polarized camps? Why have workers tolerated the supposed dictatorial I A leadership for so long? What is the true nature of creativity in motion pictures – the kind of creativity that the critics miss but that the cost-conscious producer loves? Rather than conclusions, the author finds himself asking more and more questions. The bones of the true history of the U S motion picture industry have been unearthed, but it is up to the workers to flesh out the beast with their own life stories. The bottom-up story must be told.

Notes

1 Jeff Kibre was subsequently purged by C I O leaders from his office in the Fishermen's Union for his Communist affiliations.

2 J. Hutchinson, *The Imperfect Union* (New York: Dutton, 1970), pp. 133–4.

3 M. Ross, *Stars and Strikes* (New York: Columbia University Press, 1941), pp. 200–1.

4 Hutchinson, p. 133.

5 Ibid.

6 Hutchinson, p. 132.

7 Hutchinson, p. 137.

8 Ibid.

9 Tino Balio (ed.), *The American Film Industry* (Madison: University of Wisconsin Press, 1976), p. 280.

10 *New York Times*, 25 October 1947.

11 John Cogley, *Report on Blacklisting 1. Movies* (New York: Fund for the Republic, 1956), p. 60.

12 G. H. Dunne, *Hollywood Labor Dispute* (Los Angeles: Conference Publishing, 1950), p. 24.

13 Cogley, p. 61; S. Englund and L. Ceplair, *The Inquisition in Hollywood* (New York: Anchor Press/Doubleday, 1980), p. 218.

14 Ibid.

15 Dunne, op. cit.

16 Englund and Ceplair, p. 220.

17 Cogley, p. 65.

18 The screenwriter's story is told in Englund and Ceplair, op. cit.

19 Dunne, p. 37.

20 H. Lovell and T. Carter, *Collective Bargaining in the Motion Picture Industry, a Struggle for Stability* (Berkeley: University of California Press, 1955), p. 25.

21 Englund and Ceplair, p. 224.

22 Herbert Biberman, *Salt of the Earth* (Boston: Beacon Press, 1965), pp. 149–50.

23 Biberman, p. 189.

24 Balio, p. 322.

25 *Variety*, 9 January 1977, p. 4.

26 *Film Journal*, 21 September 1981, p. 26.

27 This same pattern of jurisdictional diversification has recently occurred in two other communications unions, the Communication Workers of America (the phone companies' employees) and the international Typographical Union.

28 *Variety*, 14 October 1981, p. 5.

29 R. G. Caldwell, 'Electric cinematography: H D T V', *Filmmakers Monthly* (October 1981), pp. 31–3.

30 In a recent interview, Francis Ford Coppola has suggested that the on-location satellite scenario may be just around the corner. See J. Wells, 'Francis Ford Coppola; part II', *Film Journal* (21 September 1981), pp. 8–10.

31 At the time of writing, Fox and H B O were in the process of striking a deal for films to be produced for direct release on pay cable. See W. Tusher, 'Films-made-for-toll no menace?', *Variety*, 19 August 1981, p. 4.

32 *I A T S E Official Bulletin*, Autumn 1981, p. 14.

33 D. Robb, 'Spectre of labor unrest looms in videotape future: Aldrich', *Hollywood Reporter*, 23 October 1981, pp. 1–13.

34 *I A T S E Official Bulletin*, Autumn 1981, p. 7.

35 Daniel Bertaux, *Biography and Society* (Beverly Hills: Sage, 1981), pp. 171–2.

IV
Advertising and the Manufacture of Difference

BILL BONNEY AND HELEN WILSON

From *Australia's Commercial Media* (Melbourne: Macmillan, 1983)

n the sections on advertising in *Australia's Commercial Media* (1983), Bill Bonney and Helen Wilson make good use of the analytic framework that emerged in the 1970s as central to critical media studies' approach to advertising. The extract that follows is typical in its deployment of a semiological approach based on the distinction between denotation and connotation in the advertising message. But it begins with an exceptionally lucid exposition of the Positioning Metaphor which has regularly framed semiological discussion and served to connect it with issues of power and control.

M.A./J.O.T.

The notion of the 'positioning' of products and subjects is essentially a spatial concept, having to do with location in physical space. It is extended metaphorically, however, in relation to both products and subjects, to include social/cultural, as well as physical, space. We begin by discussing the positioning of subjects in physical space, relating it to the notion of the construction of subjectivity, and then turn to this concept in its extended metaphorical sense.

The perceived unity and continuity of space (and time) is basic to our consciousness of ourselves as unified and coherent subjects. Knowing who we are at any time depends in large part on knowing where we are and where we have been. Any person's sense of self-identity is immediately rendered problematic by loss of memory and unfamiliar surroundings, or by hallucinatory or dream experiences which obscure spatial relations between perceived objects and one's own position in relation to them. Though subjects of experience are not themselves *objects* in physical space, we are each able, in normal circumstances, to locate ourselves, as unified subjects, in specific positions in relation to perceived objects, and our ability to do so depends on being able to see objects as occupying definite positions in a single space.

This is also a condition of being able to read photographs and paintings spatially. But in this case the unifying space is *constructed*, the elements in the picture being read as occupying positions in a three-dimensional space, not merely the two-dimensional space of the picture's surface. The construction of this space – seeing it as if one were in the picture as in the real world – is facilitated, in the case of still images, primarily by perspective. In the case of film and television, reading constructed space is a more complex achievement, as indeed it is in radio listening. But in each case what is brought to bear by readers is their common experience of objects in a unitary and continuous physical space. As we shall see, reading the social/cultural space in advertisements likewise draws upon common experience of the social/cultural world. That experience, as we have argued, however, is not a neutral given, but is mediated by dominant practices and conceptualisations. In consequence, the reading of advertisements not only draws upon dominant ideologies, but in doing so reproduces them. That does not mean, however, that advertisements are always wholly conservative in their conceptualisation of reality, for contradictions in social/cultural reality are sometimes in the commercial interests of advertisers.

The connection between the spatial reading of images and common experience of objects in physical space is evident if we contrast conventional perspective painting with cubist paintings which incorporate several spaces at once. Unlike objects in a conventional perspective painting, a face in a cubist painting, drawn as if viewed from several angles at once, does not easily admit of being read as a coherent object in a single space. And, while conventional perspective painting assigns to the viewer a definite position in the constructed space of the painting, cubist paintings do not. In the one case the viewer is invited to occupy a particular imaginary position from which to see the objects in the painting as a *spectator*; in the other no such position is proffered, and the onus of understanding, interpretation or reading is thrown onto the viewer. What this does, among other things – and this is a large part of the political importance of this sort of art – is to confront the viewer with the fact that subjective unity is not simply given, but constructed. Conventional painting, on the other hand, offering viewers safe, unchallenged spectator positions, simply reproduces the dominant, ideological representation of subjectivity as given and autonomous. Once the difference is extended beyond the construction or non-construction of *physical* viewer positions to social/cultural positions, the difference in political/ideological thrust is, of course, even more pronounced.[1]

A clear illustration of the construction of physical space in a picture, and the positioning of the viewer in it, is provided by the magazine advertisement for 'Sterling' cigarettes in *photo 1*. The advertisement constructs a single, continuous physical space. The boat, for example, is in a definite position in relation to the bridge and the trees. It is also clear where the hands and the cigarettes are in relation to the boat. What is more important, it is clear where the audience/subject is. If a woman, she is in the boat on the left side; if a man, he is in the right side of the boat. These positions are fixed partly by the boat itself, with only the prow visible. But they are even more firmly determined by the hands – *our* hands – which we see in front of us. The picture constructs two unified, coherent and definite positions for

photo 1

viewers to occupy according to their sex. These positions are ready-made, locating viewers in the boat and hence in the action, not inviting them merely to watch. However, as we have said, viewers' recognition of the positions constructed for them and hence their occupation of those positions, depends crucially on their ability to read the picture, an ability which draws on their everyday experience of space.

The spatial reading of cultural artefacts is, on the whole, more of a feat in the case of the moving images of film and television than it is with still images. What we see on the cinema or television screen is a series of distinct shots. A shot is a continuous take by the one camera. The camera may remain stationary for the whole of the shot, as in the case of a news-reader reading the introduction to a news item, or it may pan, track, or zoom in or out. The end of a shot and the transition to a new shot may occur in various ways. The first shot may, for example, dissolve into the next, the first may fade slowly and then give way to the second, or there may be an abrupt cut, and so on. What distinguishes the first shot from the second, using traditional studio television technology, is the switch from one camera to another, or, in the case of film, from one take by the camera to a new take using the camera in a different position. Now, at least in the case of orthodox narratives, the audience *reads* such sequences of discrete shots as making up a unified and coherent whole, and this reading of the object – the film or television program – as unified and coherent is a condition of the audience recognising and occupying determinate positions in the constructed space of the text.

To illustrate this point, consider first the viewing of a studio interview on television. There may be two people in the studio and two cameras, one on each person. As the interview proceeds, the director, determining which camera input to broadcast, cuts from one person to the other. What the viewing audience sees is a sequence of images, first of the interviewer, then of the interviewee, and so on. These images, however, are not read simply as one face after another on the screen. They are read as the faces of two people occupying the same space and in close proximity to each other. This unified space may have been constructed for the viewer by an opening medium shot showing the two participants sitting on opposite sides of a table, or it may be left entirely to the viewer to construct the space on the basis of experience in watching interviews on television. But, however it is achieved, the construction of the unified space is a condition of the viewer being able, in imagination, to occupy appropriate spatial positions in relation to the two speakers. In this particular case, the viewer will occupy in imagination, not one but two positions, shifting with each cut from looking with the interviewer at the interviewee to looking with the interviewee at the interviewer. Viewers, in reading the visual text, construct in imagination a unified space, locate the two speakers in it and themselves occupy imaginary positions in it. Being able to do this is a condition of being able to make sense of the visual part of the presentation. The verbal part, of course, by virtue of being an on-going discussion not a random collection of remarks, contributes to the viewer's unified spatial reading of the program.

The construction of a unified and coherent constructed space is also important in the reading of narrative films, television drama and televised sport. Understanding the progress of the action involves, among other things, being able to locate elements of it in relation to each other and to the imaginary positions of the viewer. This involves being able to put the discrete parts, the discrete shots, together to form a complex unity, an achievement aided but, in general, not wholly determined by the on-going narrative of the verbal text. Viewers of televised sport may be positioned as (stationary or moving) spectators or as participants. A condition of this positioning, and changing the position, of the audience without loss of intelligibility is the construction of a single space in which the game is viewed as taking place. The simplest form of televised sport is that in which there is only one camera. In that case, the audience is placed in a fixed spectator position and the space in which the game takes place is shown as the camera pans and zooms. More complex, and demanding more work on the part of the audience, is the situation where there are several cameras in different spectator positions and in some participator positions (for example, in the mouth of the goal or next to the driver of a racing car). In such cases, intelligibility of the telecast demands more knowledge, on the part of the audience, of the sport being televised than in the simple one camera case.

There are, in principle, no fixed limits to the complexity of telecasting beyond which intelligibility would be lost. For the ability to construct a coherent space out of the series of discrete shots depends on the audience's level of understanding of the activity being televised. The on-going game plays a crucial part in the construction of unity and coherence. It is this which enables viewers to be moved in imagination from one spectator position to another without loss of intelligibility. More difficult for the viewer to incorporate into a unified space would be unpredictable or erratic movements from one, not easily identifiable, position to another. Similar difficulties would arise in the televising of football if there were cutting from one side of the field to the other as the game proceeded, since successive shots would show the same team kicking first from left to right on the screen and then from right to left. But there is no reason in principle why such successive shots could not be incorporated into a unified and coherent space, provided that in each shot the imaginary position of the viewer in relation to the action is identifiable. Given sufficient knowledge of the game, and an adequate understanding of the technology and the conventions and codes of camera work, together with the ongoing narrative of the commentary, an audience could find such a telecast intelligible and even easy to read.

We have dwelt at some length on the connections between the construction of unified space out of sequences of shots, the spatial positioning of the viewing subject and the reading of texts, because two of the concepts which are important in the analysis of advertising texts – positioning the product and positioning the audience – are both spatial metaphors. Several points emerge which can carry over from physical space to social/cultural space. First, positioning is always positioning within a *system*. Objects are not positioned simply in space; they are positioned in *relation* to other objects in space. Secondly, the space in visual artefacts is not simply given but is constructed and read on the basis of viewer's experience of space and being located in it. The extent to which the visual and verbal text does the work of constructing its space, or demands that of the viewer, varies from text to text. Similarly, texts vary in this respect in the extent to which reading them spatially depends on knowledge outside the text. Thirdly, the intelligibility of texts depends not on their assigning the viewer to a fixed position in their constructed space, but on the identifiability of the various positions, if there are several or many, constructed for the viewer. Much of the discussion in the rest of this chapter is concerned with the extension of these three points to the social/cultural spaces constructed in selected advertising texts. But the transition from the physical to the social/cultural can first be illustrated by referring again to cubist painting.

We said that such paintings reject the conventional practice of constructing a unified space in the painting and an identifiable spatial position for the viewer, thereby placing the onus of reading wholly on the viewer. This represented a revolutionary break with conventional painting, and a rejection of conventional ways of consuming art. However, given that Picasso though a revolutionary painter became an astonishing commercial success, his works, including his cubist paintings, came to acquire a meaning constructed neither by the painter nor by viewers as such, but by the international market for *objets d'art*. Though cubist paintings do not admit of being read as constructing a physical space with a comfortable place for the viewer, they have come to be read in terms of the positions they occupy in the market. Like bars of gold and bank notes, they have acquired *exchange values*, enabling them to be read not as problematic paintings confronting viewers with the constructedness of their subjectivity, but as an international currency. Their problematic and revolutionary place as paintings has thus given way to their unproblematic place in another system, the system of exchange. Thus relocated, they are now intelligible to viewers with no interest in their original point but a knowledge of the international art market. As a consequence, they can now be seen as constructing viewer positions, not indeed spatial positions, but positions involving social relations such as owner, bidder, buyer, seller, and so on. This transformation is a powerful illustration of the point made earlier, that reading texts cannot be separated from the contexts of production, distribution and consumption. It is also a testimony to the remarkable capacity of capitalism to nullify opposition by embracing and co-opting it.

Positioning within systems other than, or in addition to, spatial relations – metaphorical positioning – can now be illustrated by referring again to *photo 1*. Besides male and female spatial positions, the advertisement also constructs a particular kind of *personal* relationship between the two subjects, as signified by the glasses, the champagne and the verbal text. They are not, for example, strangers, enemies, business partners; they are a couple, an 'us', as evidenced by the woman's remark 'Let's just . . .'. Precisely what sort of a couple isn't specified, except that their relationship is, or is becoming, sexual. Its sexual nature is signified by the phallic prow of the boat heading towards the dark cavern beneath the illuminated bridge and the phallic proffered cigarette about to be grasped between the woman's thumb and forefinger. The two subjects are positioned as lovers enjoying the pleasure of each other's company in idyllic circumstances, and the point of the advertisement is to seek to transfer that recognisable pleasure to the cigarettes. It is addressed to audiences of both sexes who can be assumed to recognise the pleasure depicted, and invites them to attach that pleasure, in imagination, to 'Sterling'. The product is thus positioned with champagne as having a central place in a certain kind of sexual ritual.

It is also positioned, like champagne, as 'upper-class',[2] though as something to which others may aspire, at least on special occasions. The class of the two subjects is signified by the hands, which show no signs of having done manual work, and by the obviously aristocratic, English surroundings. Englishness and its association with 'quality' is also built into the name, 'Sterling'. In addition, by virtue of the greenery and the phrase 'mild menthol', the product is positioned as smooth and healthy, and its mildness is signified by the phrase 'glide through the greenery'. The advertisement thus addresses those who not only recognise the pleasure of a certain kind of sexual ritual and aspire to the leisured lifestyle of the aristocracy, but who also value good health. It is noteworthy, also, that the only voices to speak are the voices of the two subjects, as signified by the quotation marks. In occupying the two subject positions, in being drawn into the advertisement, we, the audience, address ourselves. The implication is that we don't need to be told what to do – to glide through the greenery and smoke 'Sterling'. Doing so is as natural as the water and the trees.

In the extension of the term 'position' metaphorically beyond its literal meaning of location in physical space, one of the central elements in its meaning, crucial in textual analysis, is retained. Positioning, whether in physical, social or cultural space, means locating a thing by distinguishing it from, and relating it to, other things within the same system of relations. It means placing it along the various appropriate *dimensions*. To position subjects or products as 'upper-class' is to say where they are located in the system of social relations. To position the two subjects as lovers is to locate the relationship between them within the range of human relationships – friends, enemies, employer/employee, strangers. acquaintances, and so on. To position them as placing a value on good health is to place their attitude to health at a determinate point in the range which extends from total disregard to chronic anxiety. We now need to consider how, in the reading of a text, such positionings are produced.

Signification

A verbal text might simply say of someone that they are upper-class. In that case the positioning is determined by the literal meaning of the words used, which depends in turn on the position of those words in the language. Alternatively, it might hint, suggest, or imply that someone is upper-class by, for example, describing their hands, clothes, tastes or lifestyle. In this case, the positioning of the person depends not only on the literal meaning of the words used, but also on the reader's knowledge of social structure and the kinds of hands, lifestyle, and so on, that go with being 'upper-class'. It draws on the reader's knowledge not only of the relevant linguistic system but also of relevant aspects of the social/cultural system. In the advertisement just discussed, the verbal text is minimal. The positioning of the product and the subjects is achieved almost entirely by visual elements – the prow of the boat, the cavern under the bridge, the green of the water and the trees, the hands, the champagne. This is possible because these visual items, no less than words in a language, are *signifiers*, bearers of signification, meaning. What they signify on a particular occasion is determined partly by their juxtaposition with other visual and verbal signifiers in the text, and partly by their position in relation to other signifiers in the system to which they belong.

This last point about position in a system of signifiers can be illustrated by considering the bottle of champagne in the advertisement. Champagne carries a range of significations: wealth, leisure, celebration, aristocracy. In this advertisement, it signifies wealth, leisure and aristocracy rather than celebration because the aristocratic hands and the leisurely atmosphere suggest that 'gliding through the greenery' is what the subjects do naturally and not as an act of celebration. Now consider the effect of substituting beer, or sweet sherry, or claret or 'Coca-Cola' for the champagne. Only the claret has any prospect of being congruent with the other signifiers in the advertisement, because the other possible substitutions carry significations –working-class, vulgarity, and frivolous youth – which are at variance with the hands and the idyllic environment. Even the claret fits uneasily into the cool atmosphere created by the other signifiers. Only another kind of white wine could be substituted, but any wine other than champagne would reduce the force of the signification of leisured wealth. Champagne carries the signification it does by virtue of its position in relation to, and in contrast with, other signifiers in the same range, the category of drinks, or, more narrowly conceived, the category of alcoholic drinks.

The point can be illustrated further by noting that the bottle of champagne is unopened. This contrasts with an empty bottle of champagne, a half-empty bottle, and so on. The effect of substituting an empty bottle would be to signify that the height of the pleasure has passed, and a half-empty bottle would signify that it is in full swing. The bottle in the advertisement is unopened in order to signify that the high point is yet to come, just as the full packet of cigarettes shows that the smoking pleasure is yet to be enjoyed. Substitution of empty beer cans, an empty sweet sherry or an empty gin bottle would obviously introduce a signification very different from that which the advertisement seeks to attach to 'Sterling'.

Substitutions for other signifying elements in the advertisement also illustrate the point that signification depends on the signifier's place in a system of signifiers belonging to the same category. Take colour, for example. The dominant green of the water and the trees signifies both naturalness and peace, the peace, quiet and naturalness of a gentle stream and an ancient bridge. It also signifies Spring with pleasures to come, as opposed to Autumn with the cold of the Winter to look forward to. The temperature signified is warm without being too hot. Substitution of blue would signify coldness and freshness and would conflict with signification of peace and naturalness. Red would signify heat; too hot for the peaceful and *mild* pleasure the advertisement seeks to construct as the 'image' of Sterling. Similarly, substitution of a dam or, worse still, a waterfall for the bridge would remove the signification of tranquility and pleasurable expectation. Other possible substitutions, all of which would carry different significance from the elements they replace are: feet for the hands, rapids for the still water, a motor boat for the punt, gum trees for the deciduous English trees, black hands for the white, gnarled hands for the soft, and so on. All of these are possible signifiers, but for obvious reasons are not utilised in this case.

Turning now to the matter of the juxtaposition of the signifying elements in the advertisement, it is evident that the social space, like the physical space constructed by this advertisement, is unified and simple. The hands, as we have said, show no sign of having done manual work, and this accords with the leisurely, relaxed aristocratic surroundings. In the advertisement there are no tensions or contradictions, physically or socially, and it is for that reason that it positions 'Sterling' *unambiguously* as a 'quality' cigarette. This positioning depends not only on what signifiers are in the advertisement but also on how they are juxtaposed. For example, if the champagne bottle were not in the boat but on another boat passing by, it would not signify pleasure for the two subjects. If the bridge were not directly in front of the prow of the boat, part of the sexual significance of the picture would be lost. If the two subjects were not in the boat but sitting on the bank watching it go by, the signification of imminent pleasure would be lost or reduced. And if the hands in the foreground were not pointing towards each other but were placed so as to separate the two subjects, the signification of a particular relationship between them would be lost. In general, then, it is necessary in the analysis of advertisements to take account both of the signifying elements and their juxtaposition. The meaning of the advertisement may be varied either by replacing one or more of the signifying elements by another element from the same range or by rearranging the elements in the picture. In much of the literature on textual analysis, the first of these two parameters of possible variation is called the *paradigmatic* dimension and the second the *syntagmatic* dimension. Signifying elements are said to belong to a paradigm (or paradigms) consisting of the elements which could be substituted for them and with which they are contrasted, and the structures into which they may be slotted are called syntagms.

Since the cultural context in which they are produced and consumed is fluid and contradictory, advertisements are often themselves internally contradictory, unlike *photo 1*. We consider examples of this later. Many advertisements are also less precise in the positioning of subjects than *photo 1*. This is illustrated by another 'Sterling' advertisement, shown in *photo 2*.

There are, in fact, in the 'Sterling' campaign a number of different advertisements, all utilising the idea of the subject's hands in the foreground. In *photo 2* there is nothing but the hands, the green, the cigarettes and the verbal text. It is, therefore, a more open advertisement than *photo 1*, since it is not tied specifically to leisure and relaxation. What is striking about *photo 2* is the fact that both hands are female. As in *photo 1*, they show no sign of manual labour, though they could be the hands of, for example, a model or possibly someone in an administrative or executive position, as suggested by the watch which contrasts with the bangle in *photo 1*. So, there is no suggestion of leisure. But what is especially noteworthy about this advertisement is the fact that the two hands can be read as belonging to the same woman. The advertisement can be read either as constructing two female subject positions, or as constructing only one. In the latter case, the verbal text is the subject speaking to herself, a fact which further illustrates the inadequacy of sender-

"Why not try a mild menthol for a change?" "What a Sterling idea."

STERLING 25s
by BENSON and HEDGES

STERLING
Mild Menthol

photo 2

message-receiver model criticised in Chapter 1. In this advertisement, then, the constructed subject position is less circumscribed than in *photo 1* because the social space constructed by the advertisement is less defined.

Advertisements construct more or less definite positions – spatial, social and cultural – for audiences to occupy. The construction of subject *positions* in particular advertisements is not the same as the construction of *subjects*, since the latter is the result of a whole complex of experiences and practices. But it is part of this elaborate process. Advertisements assume and address already formed subjects and construct positions for them to occupy. But these already formed subjects are not fully and finally formed. The process of subject formation is an on-going one and subjects are always in the process of being constructed. Moreover, since social and cultural space is not unambiguously unified and coherent, but complex, fluid and to varying degrees contradictory, subjects are formed as *complex* and often *contradictory* unities.

Generally speaking, the location of subjects of experience in physical space is determinate and unambiguous, though there are, of course, well known perceptual illusions which produce indeterminacy. By contrast, a subject's position in social/cultural space is not guided by anything as clear-cut as physical perspective, and there are conflicting ideologies which produce different constructions of social/cultural space and, in consequence, ambiguous or contradictory subjects. If the unity and coherence of subjects is not the unity and coherence of autonomous objects, but a product of the perceived unity and coherence of experience, then subjectivity embodies the contradictions as well as the unity and coherence of the social/cultural world. Further, the social/cultural world is not simply and transparently given but mediated through ideologies. Advertising is one set of practices, among others, which contributes to the production of particular conceptualisations of the world and our place(s) in it. Like other social and cultural practices, therefore, it contributes to the production of subjects. It does not merely address already formed subjects and seek acceptance of its 'messages'. It actively contributes to their formation. At the same time, advertisers do not have unformed subjects to work on; they have to take account of what has already gone into the subjects they address and position. Thus, Malcolm Spry, managing directory of Monahan Dayman Adams is reported as saying after that agency had been awarded the Westpac account, that 'if the advertising is too radical it challenges people's belief systems. We have to work within their prejudices about banks'.[3]

The phrase 'belief system', however, is misleading since it suggests a degree of coherence which may not exist. It plays down the extent to which subjects embody contradictions. In Chapter 1 we noted the existence of two opposed ideologies, individualism and solidarity, both of which are active and whose reconciliation is always tenuous. Both currents are present in the consciousness of the subjects which advertisements address, and it is not difficult to distinguish between advertisements which construct these two different kinds of subject position. There is, for example, a genre of television and magazine advertisements addressed to men which construct a highly individualist, self-reliant, out-doors subject. The genre includes not only the 'Marlboro man' and the 'Solo man', but also the range of

Toohey's beer commercials featuring competitively successful sportsmen. By contrast, corporate commercials for oil companies operating in Australia focus on the company and its employees working 'for Australia', as in the B P 'Quiet Achiever' campaign or in the representation of Esso as 'Securing Australia's future'. The position these commercials construct for subjects is that of being part of a team working for a common cause. In both cases, individualist and collectivist, the advertisements address aspects of already formed, complex and potentially contradictory subjects.

[. . .]

Connotations and Culture

We have discussed the signifying power of various non-linguistic elements in advertisements. But there is a distinction, which we have not yet drawn, between literal or direct signification, on the one hand, and implied or indirect signification, on the other. This is what is often referred to as the distinction between *denotation* and *connotation*. It applies both to linguistic and non-linguistic signifiers. In advertisements, it is usually the connotation rather than the denotation of a signifying element that is important. The distinction and connection between denotation and connotation can be illustrated by examining the advertisements in *photos 3–6*.

In *photo 3*, the crucial signifying element is the serpent. But the picture is to be read not simply as a woman holding a bottle of perfume with a serpent round her neck. The point of the serpent is to signify temptation, which it does by virtue of its place in the story of the Fall in *Genesis*. Thus it is the connotation of that element, not its denotation, which is of prime importance. However, the denotation is not irrelevant. Indeed, it is a condition of the connotation. For if the coloured shape round the woman's neck were not read first as a serpent, it could not also be read as signifying temptation. The standard way of expressing this in the literature on textual analysis is to say that the signifier plus its signif*ied* – the signifying element together with its literal meaning – is a *sign*, and it is signs which carry connotations.

In the case of *photo 4*, the sign 'gold' connotes quality and value. The thrust of the advertisement is not that 'Nescafé' has the literal properties of gold but rather that it has those properties which gold connotes. As with *photo 3*, the advertisement seeks to transfer the properties signified connotatively by the dominant sign in the picture to the commodity being promoted. The same is true of *photo 5*, where the French masterpiece is the dominant sign whose connoted properties – value, uniqueness – the advertisement seeks to transfer to the promoted commodity. In *photo 6*, there is also an attempt to transfer the properties conveyed by a sign to a commodity. But it does so in a different way from the advertisements just discussed. In the case of *photo 6*, the crucial sign, Paris, is not itself present, except for its name in the verbal text. In the visual text, Paris is represented by the reflected image of the Eiffel Tower. The Eiffel Tower, because it is unique and generally known to be in Paris, stands in for Paris in this advertisement. It is not necessary to include a picture of the whole, or even a large part of Paris; the Eiffel Tower is enough. It is a *metonym*, an abbreviation, for Paris. This metonymic introduction of Paris into the

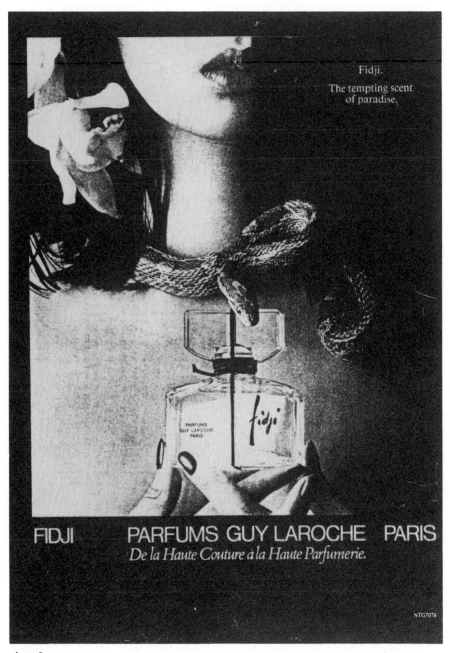

Fidji.
The tempting scent
of paradise.

FIDJI   PARFUMS GUY LAROCHE   PARIS
De la Haute Couture à la Haute Parfumerie.

NTG7076

photo 3

photo 4

photo 5

photo 6

picture brings with it all the connotations of Paris – elegance, high culture, innovation and taste – and these are transferred to the liqueur by virtue of the juxtaposition of the relevant items.

There is another thing to notice about this last advertisement. The verbal text is not a full sentence but only an 'if'-clause, which requires a 'then' -clause to complete it. The appropriate 'then'-clause – 'then it would be Grand Marnier' – is what the viewer is invited to supply. It thus has something in common with *photo 1* and *2*, since the subject is drawn into the text by virtue of supplying (part of) the verbal text. Note also that some of the liqueur has been poured into a glass ready for the subject, thus further defining the subject position by constructing a place at the table. The same is true of the 'Chatelle' advertisement (*photo 5*), which also includes the Eiffel Tower in the background, though the signifying element to which the verbal text refers is the Renoir painting.

The distinction between denotation and connotation opens up and accounts for a distinction between the *manifest* content of a text and its *latent* content.[4] At one level, *photo 3* could be read simply as depicting a young woman with a snake round her neck. This is its manifest content. But at another level, it is read in terms of temptation, and this is its latent content. Similarly the sexual content of *photo 1*, associated with the prow of the boat and the bridge, is latent content. In Chapter 5, we referred to a N S W Health Commission television commercial which the Broadcasting Tribunal rejected on the grounds that it could cause offence. The commercial showed a heterosexual couple enjoying eating fruit, and including a shot of the woman eating a banana. In reading this as representing oral sex, the Tribunal was making a tacit appeal to the manifest content/latent content distinction. However, in giving its reasons for decision, it made no reference to any theory of signification with which to justify such a distinction. Instead, it adopted the empiricist stance of concerning itself with the supposed effects of the commercial, though it did not do what such a stance would imply, namely produce the results of a survey. Any regulatory body which seeks to regulate content, including latent content, is obliged to exercise discretion since it is impossible to legislate explicitly about the way texts are to be read. The informed exercise of such discretion would require analysis of texts with reference to an explicit theory of signification. Failing that, regulatory bodies can only resort to surveys. In the Health Commission case, however, the Tribunal did neither.

In *photos 3–6*, the subjects are constructed as persons of good taste who value quality. In *photo 5*, a contrast is drawn between the masterpiece 'you can't afford' (the Renoir) and the one you can (the 'Chatelle'). The implication is that though the one is accessible only to the very rich, the other is available to 'you', the middle-class person who, though not rich, has the good taste of the upper class. We shall return to the implication of democratisation through mass production and consumption later. In *photo 4*, where 'gold says it all', the distinction is recognised in the verbal text between instant coffee and percolated coffee, but the thrust of the advertisement is to counter the implication of inferiority. Though 'Nescafé Gold' is an instant coffee, it has a 'rich, pure, percolated taste'. Like percolated coffee, the advertisement implies, it has the qualities of pure gold.

Notes

1 For a detailed and penetrating discussion of the ideological force of traditional painting and its relation to advertising, see John Berger, *Ways of Seeing* (Harmondsworth: Penguin, 1972). See also Rosie Parker and Griselda Pollock, *Old Mistresses – Women, Art and Ideology* (London: Routledge & Kegan Paul, 1981).

2 We use the vague term 'upper-class' here, rather than ruling class or bourgeoisie, to indicate that the ad does not address its audiences strictly in class terms. The desirability of the lifestyle represented in the ad has also, in the interests of maximising potential consumers, to be represented as attainable by all those addressed, not just the bourgeoisie.

3 *b & t*, 27 April 1982.

4 For a detailed discussion of this distinction, denotation and connotation, signs and signification and the notion of reading, see J. Fiske and J. Hartley, *Reading Television* (London: Methuen, 1978).

V

The Valorisation of Consciousness: The Political Economy of Symbolism

SUT JHALLY (WITH BILL LEVANT)

From *The Codes of Advertising: Fetishism and the Political Economy of Meaning in the Consumer Society* (London: Frances Pinter, 1987)

I t has been felt by many that Positioning Theory can be excessively deterministic in arguing from the text of an ad to necessary effects. A different sort of critique of advertising's grip on its readers and viewers is offered by Sut Jhally in *The Codes of Advertising* (1987). Why think in terms of an optical metaphor when the actual, concrete activity of consuming ads can be seen as Work, and the Marxist tradition of understanding labour under capitalism then be applied to it? Our extract from Jhally gives the nub of this position, and suggests how it can be used to illuminate the history of (particularly North American) commercial television.

M.A./J.O.T.

Watching as Working: Viewing and Wage Labour

[...] I have [...] used the familiar concepts of Marxian economic theory to analyse the valorisation of time by the networks. It was not a coincidental choice because central to the whole paradigm of Marxian economics is the notion that it is human *labour* that is the basis of the productivity of societies. It is not capital or technology that produces value in capitalist society, it is labour. Similarly, in the analysis of broadcasting economics, it is audience *watching* that is vital to the whole process. Without the activity of the working class, capitalism would grind to a halt. Without the activity of the audience broadcasting, too, would collapse in its present form. In a very real sense we can see that there are many similarities between industrial labour and watching activity. In fact watching is a form of labour. I wish to argue in this section that in fact when the audience watches commercial television it is working for the media, producing both value and surplus-value. This is not meant as an analogy. Indeed, watching is an extension of factory labour, not a metaphor. Let us compare the basic concepts that explain the productivity of the working day in the factory and those that explain the productivity of the viewing day within broadcasting.

In Marx's analysis of the working day, the productivity of capitalism is based upon the purchase of one key commodity – labour power. This is the only element in the means of production that produces more value than it takes to reproduce itself. Like all commodities, it has a value, a cost – the cost of its production (or reproduction). The cost of labour power (the capacity to labour) is the cost of the socially determined level of the means of subsistence: that is, what it costs to ensure that the labourer can live and be fit for work the next day. The amount of labour time that it takes to produce value equivalent to this minimum cost is labelled by Marx socially necessary labour (necessary to reproduce labour power). Socially necessary labour time produces value equivalent, then, to wages. The remaining labour time is labelled surplus labour time and it is on this time that the profitability of capital rests. This is where surplus value is generated. In the non-work part of the

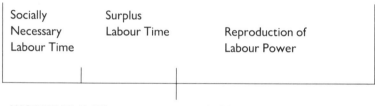

| Socially Necessary Labour Time | Surplus Labour Time | Reproduction of Labour Power |

WORKING DAY   **NON-WORK TIME**

day workers spend wages (on shelter, food, children, and so on) that will ensure that they will be fit and healthy enough to go to work. During non-work time they *reproduce* their labour power. If they did not (if they did not eat, for example) then they would not be able to sell their labour power to capitalists because they would not be healthy enough to work. During the necessary labour time they make commodities that produce value equivalent to their wage. The remainder of the time they work for capital.

Notice how similar this model is to the previous analysis of the valorisation of viewing time. The production of audience time is like any other industrial production process. The capitalist (the network) owns the means of production (communication) which makes possible the production of commodities and which gives the capitalist (network) *ownership* of that produce.[1] Also employed is the *value-creating* element of the means of production – human labour power. Just as workers sell labour power to capitalists, so audiences sell *watching power* to media owners; and just as the use-value of labour power is labour, so the use-value of watching-power is watching, the capacity to watch. In addition, as the value of labour power is fixed at the socially determined level of the means of subsistence (thus assuring that labour power will be reproduced) so the value of watching power is the cost of its reproduction – the cost of programming, which ensures that viewers will watch and be in a position to watch extra (the time of advertising). In this formulation it is only the time of *advertising* that comprises the 'working day' for the audience. The programming, the value of watching power, is the *wage* of the audience, the variable capital of the communications industry. It is also time for the reproduction of watching power, the time of *consumption*, the time of non-work. As the working day is split into two so the work part of the viewing day, advertising time, is split between socially necessary watching time and surplus watching time.

Labour and watching share many other characteristics in addition to this formal analysis. Historically, they have evolved in similar ways. For instance, the early history of industrial capitalism is tied up with attempts by capital to extend the time of the working day, to manipulate the necessary-surplus ratio by extending in an absolute sense the time of work (the extraction of absolute surplus value). Within the development of the commercial media system, this phase is represented by broadcasting from the late 1920s to the early 1960s. In the first years of commercial broadcasting (extending into the 1930s) broadcasters struggled to persuade advertisers to sponsor shows. After Paley's dramatic shift in giving away all unsponsored programming[2] the networks could no longer generate revenue from selling messages but only from selling audience-time: the more shows that were sponsored, the more audiences that could be sold to advertisers. This was an extension in time that people watched or listened for capital. It also has to be remembered that until the introduction of spot-selling in the 1960s, programmes were advertising agency creations with the sponsor's name and product appearing everywhere – not only in advertisements.[3]

However, Marx realised that this absolute extension of the working day cannot go on indefinitely. Working-class resistance through unions and collective bargaining limited the length of the working day. In such a situation, capital has to increase the *intensity* of labour. The concept of relative surplus value initially meant the cheapening of consumer goods that reproduce labour power so that the amount of necessary time would be decreased. In the era of monopoly capitalism two other major factors contribute to the extraction of *relative* surplus value – the reorganisation of the workplace and introduction of technologically efficient instruments of production.[4] [. . .]

In a very important text, published in English for the first time in 1976, Marx talks about the transition from absolute to relative surplus value in a more concrete and detailed manner. In 'Results of the Immediate Process of Production'[5] a distinction is made between the *formal* and the *real* subsumption of labour. Marx here is writing about the expansion of capitalism and the relations that prevail between capitalism and other modes of production. Thus, as capitalist relations of production expand, they come into contact with other types of relations of production – for example, feudal relations in agriculture. The two different sets of relations cannot ignore each other for they have become interdependent. However, in the first instance capitalism does not effect a change in these other relations. It merely 'tacks on' these relations to its own operations. Marx writes that 'capital subsumes the labour process as it finds it, that is to say, it takes over an *existing labour process*, developed by different and more archaic modes of production'. Thus while capital subsumes it, it does not establish specifically capitalist relations of production in that sphere. It does not need to. The old relations are used in ways that benefit capital without being organised under its relations of production. Marx argues that the formal subsumption of labour is based upon increasing the length of the working day: that is, on absolute surplus value.

In broadcasting, the formal subsumption of watching activity is linked to the period when advertisers had direct control of programming (when they wrote and produced it). Broadcasting did not develop initially as an advertising medium. Its first purpose was to aid in the selling of radio sets. It was only later that time on the airwaves began to be sold by AT&T to bring in additional revenue. Even when advertising became prominent in the late 1920s and 1930s networks did little more than lease facilities and sell airtime to advertisers who had total control of broadcasting. In this way we can see how capital (advertisers) took over 'more archaic' modes of watching for their own ends. Advertisers were interested primarily in the activities of the audience as they related to the consumption of their products. Watching here was tacked on to specifically capitalist relations of production without being organised in the same manner.

However, Marx writes, the two different relations of production cannot exist side by side indefinitely. Indeed capitalism constantly works to make the other mode of production 'wither away' and to introduce capitalist relations of production into that previously independent (from capitalist relations) domain. This is labelled the *real* subsumption of labour. At this stage (which corresponds with the extraction of relative surplus value) 'the entire real form of production is altered and a *specifically capitalist form of production* comes into being (at the technological level too)'.[6]

The old 'archaic' forms of production disappear to be replaced with capitalist relations of production. The old realm is no longer directly subordinate to other domains but itself becomes a proper capitalist enterprise. It is interested primarily in its own productivity rather than being a peripheral (yet vital) activity to something else.

In broadcasting the shift from the formal to the real subsumption of watching takes place in the late 1950s. It was then that the networks started to move against advertisers' total control of programming by introducing the concept of 'magazine programming', whereby the network would control the programming and sell spots within it to different advertisers. It was proving inefficient (for the network) to have the audience watch exclusively for one advertiser for thirty to sixty minutes. The media could generate more revenue for themselves if they could *reorganise* the time of watching by rationalising their programme schedule. The move to spot-selling was an attempt to increase the ratio of necessary to surplus watching time. More value could be generated by networks producing programming that would attract audiences that could be sold to several advertisers than by selling watching time to one advertiser. There was a limit to how much one advertiser could pay for a thirty- or sixty-minute programme. If the networks could control the programming and the advertising time within it, then they could generate more revenue (by selling spots) from multiple advertisers, all of whom individually paid less. Initially advertisers resisted this rationalisation and the subsumption of their individual interests under the general interests of media capital. In the end, however, rising programme costs, legal objections to advertisers' control, and old-fashioned scandals drove the networks to move towards full control of their schedules.[7] This resulted in the double reorganisation of the watching population and the watching process under specifically capitalist relations of production.

There is, in addition to these, another dimension along which watching-labour shares characteristics with labour in the economy in general – both are viewed as *unpleasant* by the people who have to perform either activity. The history of working-class resistance to the process of wage labour and various sociological studies illustrate that for many people in modern society, work is not an enjoyable activity. People, on the whole, work not because they like their jobs but because they have to, to get what they really need – wages to spend in consumption. Work has become a means to an end rather than an end in itself. Labour is a form of *alienated* activity. Similarly, consider the attitudes of the watching audience to the time of advertising. Despite the fact that huge amounts of money (much more than on programming) are spent on producing attractive commercials, people do all they can to avoid them. They leave the room, they talk with other people, or they simply switch channels in the hope that they can find another programme to watch, rather than more advertisements. (Switching between the major networks is rather unproductive on this score as they all tend to have their commercial breaks at the same time.) Indeed a 1984 report by the J. Walter Thompson advertising company estimated that by 1989 only 55 to 60 per cent of television audiences will remain tuned in during the commercial break. Commercial viewing levels are decreasing. The remote channel changer is a major factor in this 'zapping' of commercials. In addition to this, American data indicate that almost 30 per cent of viewers simply leave the room or get into alternative technologies during the commercial breaks.[8] The spread of video cassette recorders (V C Rs) is also a major threat to the viewing levels of commercials. When programmes are recorded to be watched at a later time, one can simply skip over the commercials by fast-forwarding through them. The owners of the means of communication are faced here with a curious problem – the audience could watch programmes (get paid) without doing the work (watching) that produces value and surplus-value.

All these findings have not been lost on the advertising or the television industry and there has been an increasing recognition in recent years that the traditional concept of a 'ratings point' may no longer be valid. Ratings measure programme watching rather than commercial watching. Indeed it seems that there is much disparity between the two and advertisers are starting to voice their discontent at having to pay for viewers who may not be watching their advertisements at all. This has led the ratings companies to experiment with new measures of the audience. The most intriguing development has been the experiment with 'people meters'. This involves a device on the T V that has a separate button for each individual member of the household that is participating in the measuring of watching. Individuals would 'punch in' when they start watching and 'punch out' when they cease watching. In this way advertisers and broadcasters will have a more precise measure of the level of commercial viewing. It seems there could be no clearer indication of the similarities between watching and labour. Just as workers in a factory punch in and punch out, so viewers too will be evaluated along similar lines. It is constructive to note that no one would be worried if people were 'zapping' the *programmes* and watching advertisements in greater numbers. The industry would be undisturbed. But when the new technologies of cable and v c Rs threaten the viewing patterns of commercial time then the very foundations of the broadcasting industry begin to shake in anticipation of the consequences.

Notes

1 See Sut Jhally, 'Probing the Blindspot: The Audience Commodity', *Canadian Journal of Political and Social Theory* vol. 6 nos. 1–2 (1982).

2 Paley's strategy was to give affiliate stations *unsponsored* programmes free, in return for access in the affiliates' schedules for any *sponsored* programmes at c b s' chosen time. This meant that without further laborious negotiation c b s could guarantee an advertiser coast-to-coast audiences, while affiliates moved over to c b s at the prospect of getting 'free' product.

3 See L. Bergreen, *Look Now, Pay Later* (New York: Mentor, 1980).

4 H. Braverman, *Labor and Monopoly Capital* (New York: Monthly Review Press, 1974).

5 Karl Marx, *Capital* vol. 1, trans. Ben Brewster (Harmondsworth: Penguin, 1976), pp. 943–1085.

6 Marx, op. cit., p. 1024.

7 Erik Barnouw, *The Sponsor: Notes on a Modern Potentate* (New York: Oxford University Press, 1978).

8 B. Fiber, 'Tuning Out Ads, a Growing Trend', *Globe and Mail*, 31 October 1984.

VI
Editorial

JULES GODDARD
From *International Journal of Advertising* vol. 4 no. 4 (1985)

In both of the preceding texts, the point of studying advertising is clearly to understand how its consumers are dominated by it. But *are* they? As the eighties draw to a close, the 'victim' picture increasingly seemed to need, at the very least, some complementing by accounts which allowed readers and viewers to experience advertising as less than wholly binding upon them. (When did *you* last see an ad and act upon it?) And, like it or not, the late eighties also found media studies confronted with the resurgence, in intellectual as well as political terms, of ideas based on an appreciation of the positive aspects of the Market. (And if the name 'Thatcher' comes to mind, so will the name 'Gorbachev'.)

The following text by Jules Goddard, which appeared in 1985 as an editorial in the *International Journal of Advertising*, captures the feel of the shift towards applying Market principles to the understanding of what ads really are there for. In some ways, his move is formally similar to Jhally's: take advertising out of the common-sense frame we usually see it in and apply to it the considerations we would bring to other aspects of life under capitalism. But here the move refocuses on the text, seen now as a commodity in its own right rather than as merely instrumental in selling other products – and celebrated as such.

M.A./J.O.T.

Advertising is a commodity. Advertisements are supplied only because the market demands them. The value that consumers place on advertisements is roughly equal to their cost (generally between 1 and 2 per cent of GNP). A *marketing* approach to advertising asks: 'What is it that consumers are buying when they buy advertisements?' and 'Which particular human needs are more economically met by advertising than by any other economic goods?' In some markets, advertising is more highly valued than in others. What characterizes these markets? What sets them apart as heavy demanders of advertising? The orthodox view is that people are buying economies of large-scale production. This is a piece of sophistry. They may *sometimes* be buying a lower price. But, more often than not, they are buying a product, where the product is the meaning of the advertising.

The meaning of an advertisement is the use to which consumers put it. To understand how people make use of advertising is the first step in knowing how best to market the product that advertising embodies. Presumably, advertisements are used in many, many ways. And this is something that merits more research. But, as a first guess, we might want to say that, when people buy *advertising*, they are buying the self-assurance of the manufacturer ('it must be good to merit advertising') and the market share of the brand ('it must sell well to afford advertising'); and when people buy an *advertisement* they are returning a compliment (the creative ad is the ad which makes the consumer creative) and applauding a performance (all creativity demands criticism). Advertisements, then, are products on an equal footing with the things made in factories, and advertising agencies are their manufacturers. This releases them from the misleading notion that they are communicators. They are only communicators in the sense that any manufacturer's product carries significance to a market.

The best advertisements draw attention to themselves as advertisements. Indeed, only by doing so can they be charged with meaning and emotion. We feel emotion when our expectations are not fulfilled; we lend the emotion meaning in trying to interpret it. In both cases, we need to locate an advertisement in a tradition of advertising for it to be potent. Blue, in itself, is almost meaningless; blue-rather-than-green, however, begins to acquire significance. In short, advertisements would be better if they emulated works of art (where meaning derives from their handling of the rules of the game) rather than editorials (where meaning derives from the presentation of an argument). This is because consumers perceive advertisements in aesthetic space and do not make use of ads as though they were salesmen. After a time, as Kant suggested, promises become empty if they are continuously broken.

What are the implications of this marketing view of advertising?

Advertising plans should be different
– concentrating on positioning the *advertisements*, not the product. The product may even be a red herring.
– built around responses to the advertisements as products in their own right.

Advertising research should be different
– concentrating on *intensity* of response rather than *content* of response, relating this to the optimal levels in the collative variables (novelty, ambiguity, surprisingness, change, blurredness, etc.).
– locating meaning and emotion in the gap between people's expectations and preconceptions on the one hand (the 'background') and the reality of the advertisements on the other (the 'foreground').

Advertisements themselves should be different
– with writers and art directors released from the need to change the market's perception of the factory product and working instead to satisfy the aesthetic and novelty-seeking needs of the market.

– with campaigns designed in such a way that each ad in the series sets up expectations that its successor can feed off.

Advertising controls should be different
– focusing on the sales and consumption of the ads rather than the sales and consumption of the factory product.
– accepting the possibility that the product may be detracting from the sales of the advertisements.

Agency–client relationships should be different
– founded on the premise that both sides are *fellow-manufacturers*, each trying to live up to the market quality of the other's product.
– recognizing that in some markets the factory product, and in others the advertising product, will yield a higher return.

VII
Advertising's Rationality

JOHN O. THOMPSON

As a conclusion to the advertising sequence, here is a small dialogue in which John Thompson imagines a speaker who has been influenced by the late-eighties mood outlining (to a not-very-sceptical questioner) an account of advertising in which the reader or viewer is taken to be a fully rational, empowered agent. (Bonney and Wilson's spectator is moved away from rationality by the ad; Jhally's is left generally powerless by capitalism.) The speaker draws upon Rational Choice Theory (perhaps he has been reading the selection of readings on the subject, *Rational Choice*, edited in 1986 by Jon Elster (Oxford: Blackwell), who as it happens has been much concerned elsewhere to bring this tradition to bear on classical Marxist theory) for his model of the spectator, while taking Goddard's point about what might make ads successful commodities in their own right. The effect is to present the advertisement as analytically divisible into two components: a Rational Core and a Decorative Periphery. Each contributes to the successful ad's 'reader-friendliness'; and it may be a virtue of A's approach, that it brings out how readers *could*, without sacrificing human dignity, actually find ads friendly. (Because, of course, we do.)

M.A./J.O.T.

Q: What would constitute a rational approach to deciding whether or not to buy something?

A: You need to set the advantages of spending money on a product against those of reserving the money for later use; you need to compare one version of the product with competing versions.

Q: What, then, do you need if you are to make a rational consumer choice?

A: You need Resources (cash, credit) sufficient to participate in the potential transaction; Information of several sorts; and a Subjectivity capable of retaining, broadly consistently over time, a basic rank-ordering of your pleasures. That is, you need to be able to sustain *stable preferences*; otherwise one day's decisions will look terrible from tomorrow's new perspective.

Q: Advertisers obviously aren't in the business of providing the consumer with extra resources (though they may provide information about the credit possibilities on offer). Are they in the information business or in the preference-moulding business?

A: Probably both; but a Rational Choice model for advertising will stress information over preference-moulding. If advertising really created False Needs, those needs would have to supplant existing needs or be grafted onto them. It seems sensible in many cases to think in terms of grafting: so a 'need' for convenience foods is a modification of existing, more basic preferences as to Food, Kitchen-Labour and Time rather than appearing as a wholly new need. But anyway, while it may be argued that *capitalism* creates False Needs, it is hard to think of products of which we'd want to say that *advertising itself* provides the chief reason anyone would have for wanting them.

Of course, the aggregate effects of a Culture of the Advertisement might plausibly be argued to contribute to broad tendencies as to what it is culturally legitimate to prefer. Purchasable things may be ranked higher than they otherwise would be. (Note, incidentally, that the *rational* case against such a ranking lies not in some anti-selfishness ethic but in worries about short-termism: ecological considerations, it is argued, make some consumption patterns eventually unsustainable, especially if we think globally.) However, we have very little hard evidence suggesting that people's interest in non-consumption values is being eroded under capitalism. Models of unselfish behaviour still abound and are widely promulgated. One can live utterly in terms of a Service Ethic and still have decisions to make about what to wear, what to eat, how to furnish the front room and so forth, and it's these decisions that advertisers aim to influence.

Q: Back then to Information. Let's say that I possess a stable enough character that, though I may not 'know what I want' in terms I could make verbally explicit, I behave from month to month and indeed from year to year in a generally consistent way as a consumer (thus enabling economists to speak of my *revealed* preferences – revealed by my behaviour). I'm presumably doing this, as a Rational Agent, on the basis of information about the goods and services on offer. Do I therefore use advertisements first and foremost as sources of such information?

A: You would be ill-advised to do so in a completely straightforward way. The reason will be obvious to you as a Rational Agent: the advertising message is by definition *not disinterested*. It is in the advertiser's interest to lead you to conclude 'I want that'. The information the advertisement provides will be tailored to that end.

Q: Would it be rational for me simply to disregard advertising messages, then?

A: No. This would amount to treating them as *lies*. Such a move haunts advertising as the consumer reaction that would most devastate it. Not surprisingly, the industry itself is keen to self-regulate, and to be seen to do so – to establish 'rules of the game' so that the hallmark of the lie, the False Statement, gets excluded from the advertising repertoire. You can (and will) expect the advertising message to concentrate on the positive, persuasive fact, or to forsake the domain of fact altogether; but both these strategies leave ads as information-bearing messages.

Q: I can see how an ad could be information-bearing by expressing a truth even if it isn't anything like the Whole Truth. But if no factual claims are made, what information can be conveyed?

A: The fact that the advertiser is in a position to advertise at all testifies to a certain level of corporate strength. You might, other things being equal, feel this to be reassuring, at least about the minimum quality-level to be expected from the product.

Q: Nevertheless, given the partial nature of the advertising message, and indeed the constraint of brevity which most advertising formats impose, is it not irrational for the consumer to use ads as sources of information?

A: At this point we need to think about the fact that information itself is a costly commodity. Sometimes you pay money to obtain it, as when you buy a book or pay for a telephone call. Sometimes your expenditure is chiefly a matter of time, as when you budget an hour to consult a consumer-advice magazine in your Free Public Library.

A reproach that used to be levelled against economists was that they assumed that their Rational Economic Agent was in possession of complete information about the outcomes that would result from the choices on offer – clearly an unrealistic assumption in real life. But once it is grasped that the costs of acquiring information – and especially the costs of acquiring *further* information – are themselves part of the Agent's calculations, then matters become clearer. It is to Herbert Simon that we owe the distinction between *maximizing* behaviour, which assumes a perfect-information setting, and *satisficing* behaviour, as he terms it. In the latter case, we make a decision on the basis of 'good-enough-for-the-purpose' information, where the cost of gaining further information wouldn't be justified by any proportionate benefit to our decision-making. Different consumer decisions call for different amounts of information. It may be that minimal information conveyed by an advertisement may still be as much as it would be reasonable for a consumer to seek, at least through that route. And whatever you get from the ad has the advantage of being experienced as 'free': you haven't (given the separation of ads from the textual material they interrupt, which is supposed to be your main focus of interest) spent time or money *specifically* to encounter the ad.

Q: Faced with some ads, I find it difficult to see them as bearing anything that could be called information. What's going on here?

A: I think we need to distinguish in ads between a *rational core* and a *decorative periphery*. The rational core is the ad's persuasive/informative appeal to your calculation as a rational agent; the decorative periphery is there to give you pleasure.

The point to grasp is that it can be rational for the rational core to dwindle almost to nothing in some circumstances.

For this to happen, two conditions need to be met.

1. The decision to be made should be one to which verbal argument is largely irrelevant. Take the choice of a perfume, for example. Our vocabulary for describing smells is so limited that a verbal statement about the advantages of a particular scent is virtually useless. The rational consumer chooses at the point of purchase, by comparing smells. So the rational core of a perfume ad can only really consist of a sort of nudge: 'Remember, when you *are* comparing perfumes, you might want to give X a try'. The situation would be very different if you were about to purchase a computer; and computer ads duly exhibit a much larger rational core.

2. The rational justification of the decorative periphery is that which must justify any decorative phenomenon: the ad must become a 'good' in its own right, however minor. It must please us, whether by amusing us, by being visually attractive or striking, or by presenting us with an occasion for fantasy. This is Goddard's point, quoted above: 'Advertisements . . . are products on an equal footing with the things made in factories'.

Q: In cases where the rational core of an ad is vanishingly small, why bother with it as fundamental to advertising analysis?

A: The core/periphery distinction is useful as ammunition against one of the moves students typically make when invited to interpret ads, a move which almost never convinces me. Imagine a perfume ad picturing a beautiful woman sitting opposite a handsome man, both well-dressed, outside a Paris café (Eiffel Tower in background). Students regularly write: 'The connotations of this ad are meant to suggest that if you use X perfume you will get to travel to Paris, meet attractive men, be able to afford expensive clothes . . .'. The problem with this is that clearly anyone who *did* believe any such thing as a result of exposure to the advertising message would be gullible to the point of madness, as eccentric as those often-posited, rarely-met individuals who believe in the reality of soap-opera fictions. Students themselves never own up to any such belief, and it is not likely that advertising's power can be based on any *mass* delusional system of this sort.

What goes wrong here is that operations that belong to the decorative periphery of the advertisement are brought into its rational core, where there really is a pattern of argument of the 'if-then' variety: 'If you buy X, then Y will follow'. This mode of argument certainly is invoked by advertisers when it is appropriate. If an automobile manufacturer has a better rust-proofing system than its rivals, it may well explicitly state in its ads that *if* you were to buy Car X, *then* you will have fewer rust problems than if you had bought any other car. But, in the absence of an explicit argument of this sort, we would be unwise to leap to the conclusion that the consumer of an ad is being 'hiddenly persuaded' by a covert (and remarkably unconvincing when made overt) argument via connotation. The good looks, the good times and the Eiffel Tower can be seen as images meant to please us rather than to persuade us, once the minimal-but-sufficient rational content of the 'nudge' is recognised.

Q: Does this mean that an ideological critique of advertising ought to be abandoned?

A: No. The decorative periphery is up for criticism even after it is recognised for what it is. You can object to it, not as misleading, but as seeking to please via images of perfection and pleasure which themselves are oppressive. However, if these images are peripheral rather than core, the puzzle about why so many people can be exposed to advertising without turning into monsters or fools recedes somewhat.

Q: Could Jhally's approach to advertising be reconciled with a Rational Choice approach?

A: Jhally seems to be describing with historical accuracy a stage of advertising in which the genre misunderstood itself and was disliked accordingly. The ads he describes are tedious, like assembly-line work. Such ads are precisely those which you make the coffee during or fast-forward through. The rational core may or may not be there, but the decorative periphery hasn't been worked up enough to turn the ad into an object of pleasure in its own right. It is part of the very logic he unfolds that advertisers, in the face of new technologies which allow ads to be avoided when not wanted, should have to move in the direction indicated by Goddard, whereby ads become 'art'.

VIII
Gandhiana and Gandhiology

ASHISH RAJADHYAKSHA

From *Framework* no. 22–23 (Autumn 1983)

One of the most theoretically influential pieces of film criticism published in the early 70s was a collective text by the editors of *Cahiers du Cinéma* about John Ford's *Young Mr Lincoln*. Among the many issues explored in this text, two areas relate to Ashish Rajadhyaksha's account of Richard Attenborough's film *Gandhi*. The first is the attempt to analyse the film in 'conjunctural' terms, to try and understand how an apparently 'historical' film functions in the current ideological and political battles of India. The second concerns the audience and argues that the reason the historical veracity of the film is not important is because the film suppresses history in favour of myth – one of the most enduring popular genres in the cinema.

Rajadhyaksha argues that in conjunctural terms the functional value of the film is to re-inforce 'nationalism' at a time of increasing belligerence from regionalist forces (the Sikh struggles are only one of the better publicised such uprisings).

Secondly he contends that it is not the historical inaccuracy of the film which is a problem but rather its dehistoricisation of Gandhi's life. This lack of historical information provides a problem – or a structured absence – for the audience to which Rajadhyaksha offers an intriguing explanation for the film's success: 'It is the sensuous impact of the portrayal that forces the audience to bridge for themselves the deficiencies of the fiction'. Rajadhyaksha is also concerned that his article should not be read as a 'review' of the film which would thereby legitimise and validate it. This problem of the privileging of the 'exemplary text' continually confronts the critic who, in the very process of questioning the text, becomes in a very real sense its promoter.

M.A./J.O.T.

I am appalled by the violence in the world today . . . and I am going to do something about it. I am going to show that there is something else for youth besides street gangs and switch blades . . . I am going to tell the story of Baden-Powell and the Boy Scouts. Imagine! The final Jamboree, when the old man

is almost eighty, with a hundred thousand youngsters of every
race and colour gathered around him in peace and happiness
... It will be my last film, and my greatest.

Cecil B. DeMille

It had to happen. The usual epithet given to such projects is 'epic'; a notion that has
clearly grown over the years from its original early Hollywood context to being a
vehicle for portraying the grand proportions of the values and mythologies of any
ruling class that may wish to purchase it from its professional manufacturers. It has
drawn its myths from the Bible and from the great Wars, from big business and
nuclear disaster. It has taken shape in response to the demands of a new political and
technological age, an age that sees more than ever the need to underline a highly
questionable value-system with the width of the 'epic' canvas.

The 'epic' – or the mass-spectacular – in the classical Hollywood tradition, is
the indicator of the superstructural dimensions of the commodity. At its simplest
this is the money spent on the film, the vastness of the sets and the size of the crowd
scenes. At more complex levels, however, as with DeMille, it relates also to another
kind of extravagance in the myths that are mobilised, the overpowering emotions
that it indulges. By its very weight it is an indicator of the system that produces and
markets it.

It had to happen that the tradition that thrived on imperialist grandeur would
one day also sense equally 'epic' possibilities in movements that have countered just
such grandeur. If there is anything new about *Gandhi*, it is only in the sense that it
gives an old search, generated by the voraciousness of the mass-spectacular, a new
twist. The Raj films are already upon us, and as the Indian government gets the
hang of the form, Naxalbari, Mrs Gandhi's 1971 election victory and the growth of
Sanjayism are all subjects that await an inspired film-maker to sense in them their
'epic' possibilities.

At the time of writing, *Gandhi* is entering its 11th week in six theatres in
Bombay. It has been granted tax-exemption by the Maharashtra government, and a
directive has been issued from the Prime Minister's desk to all State Governments
that they grant a similar exemption. Every screening in the city has seats block-
reserved for primary-school children who see the film as part of their history lesson,
and they are not the only ones who are being shown the film as history come alive.
Practically the whole of Bombay's upper-middle class is awash in a wave of nostalgia
for the leader of its nationalist movement.

It is clear that, in a way, there has been a certain merging of interests – between
Attenborough's financial backers who must have first seen commercial possibilities
in an 'authorised' biography of Gandhi, and the Indian ruling-classes, who have
received their main myth polished and renovated for their own ideological use. But
what makes the form so remarkably suitable for such a project? This becomes a vital
question in the present Indian context where all indications are that a shaky Indian
bourgeoisie, badly in need of a retelling of its glorious nationalist past, is quite
clearly resorting to professional renovators of myths who would undoubtedly use
techniques akin to advertising to refurbish its sagging image. Maybe reasons can be

found in the very conventions of the 'epic' that permit a superficial resemblance with history, while detaching the fiction of the film from the exigencies of historical analysis, and which – once they have won the freedom to do so – permit further interpretations of that history.

The first thing the 'spectacular' usually does, once it has got a saleable commodity worked out, is to indicate its crucial role in larger social processes of change. A publicity brochure for *Close Encounters of the Third Kind* says that 'There can be little doubt that Steven Spielberg's blockbuster . . . will have a positive effect on the status of current U F O research. Over the last three decades the scientists and other professionals, willing to go out on a limb and suggest that the subject needed to be investigated properly, were far and few between.'[1] The myth says, for reality to be taken seriously, it must be told convincingly.

In *Gandhi* the myth is created when the film *subordinates* the historical character and events to which it refers to its internal design. It begins by making an appeal for a subjective assessment: an initial title says that no film can ever hope to capture all the details about a man's life (which is obviously true) and that it is therefore more important to get to the 'heart of the man' (which does not follow at all). But nowhere is the subjectivity of the interpretation acknowledged. The effect throughout is that this is history *as it happened*. In creating within the spectator a vicarious thrill of witnessing historical events as they happen, the film neatly transfers emphasis from the events themselves to the characters that took part in them. This is how your heroes of that time looked, says the film, this is how they dressed, how they spoke to each other, these are their mannerisms and gestures. The film generates an interest in the individual – or rather, the Individual – and the events are little more than dramatic props with which to highlight their greatness. A major component of the myth is the creation of the 'epic' individual who can interpret in the context of the bourgeois identity the 'epic' nature of the events in which he participates.

From the very first shot – a fiery, red morning, by the Sabarmati – the film compresses certain impressions about the past, certain premises that provide the context for the spectator. The most 'spectacular' of the scenes, the funeral march, also occurs at the beginning: we are being readied to witness the saga. This process of providing the scale, the 'epic' dimension, at the start of the film, is a vital aspect of the conventions of this form. The rapidity with which Gandhi rises to his full stature – (Scene 1, Gandhi thrown out of a train; scene 2, he recognises injustice for the first time; scene 3 establishes the South African Congress; scene 4, General Smuts is worried already; scene 5, notices in the paper; scene 6, he meets C.F. Andrews, compresses his philosophy into a short statement during the walk; scene 7, Smuts says to Walker 'He's the shrewdest man you're likely ever to meet'; scene 8, establishment of his ashram) – is possible only because the history is known, the audience acquainted beforehand with what is to follow. It will also be obvious that this prior knowledge need not be extra-filmic, for the initial scenes themselves provide it.

But since the spectator is to participate in the events as they unfold, a certain feigned indecisiveness is also called for.[2] And so we have little dramatic encounters, like the one of Gandhi with the white youths on the pavement, and the suspense generated by these is what substitutes for the actual, agonizing decisions Gandhi himself must have made at various points in his life.

For the problem here is not to build a myth, but to negotiate its realisation and even more to rid it of its historical roots in order to liberate its universal and historical meaning.[3]

This process of *liberating* the myth comes, in *Gandhi*, with the fictional encounters that build up the episodic narrative. Every action that takes the film forward has to be placed dramatically, and, consequently, has to find its cause in a dramatic episode that precedes it. So Gandhi virtually seems to have discovered his role in life *because* he was thrown out of the train (it is amazing how many people seeing the film actually discuss what would have happened to us all if he had *not* been thrown out of the train); Chauri Chaura occurs *because* some policemen act beyond their brief; the Partition riots occur *because* one man throws a stone. It is, ultimately, this simple behavioural cause-effect logic that transfers interest from historical analysis to historical detail, for physical likeness somehow seems so much more important than quibbling about what *actually* happened.

And it is, in the final analysis, this factor – the ability of such a form of analytic-dramatic cinema to *deny* the historical – that must be seen as the main reason for its success in finding roots in any culture whatsoever and the source of its unique ability to sell anything, from soap to revolution. The primary thrust is to depoliticise, to make the man into a being somehow beyond the events, to trivialise the immediate circumstances before the enduring, universal 'message'. Once the *individual* is established, and finds identity with every man in the audience, the entire *epic* superstructure may be elaborated upon it. That relationship then grows so over-whelming, so fascistic really, that the material conditions which established the character are easily pushed into the background. And so all signs of actual signifying *work* are glossed over, the anxiety of choice reduced to the pseudo-knowledge of history.

Having created the artificial image, the tradition immediately reinforces it with all the 'spectacular' accoutrements at its disposal. The first major close-up comes when Gandhi addresses the non-white audience in the theatre; the camera moves even closer when Gandhi and Ba face each other after she has refused to clean her toilet, paradoxically at just the time when Ba says to him: 'You're human, you're only human'. Then we have Gandhi's peaceful march, which is charged down by mounted South African police. As the horses bear down upon the peaceful demon-strators, the soundtrack is magnified, close-ups of thundering horsehooves give the impression that thousands of horses are charging, with low-angle shots of the animals about to crush the puny man before them. Passive repulsion thus itself gets elevated to an 'epic' counterpoint, a worthy successor to the tremendous elevating shots of the man speaking to his audience in the previous scene.

As the unequal battle proceeds, the 'castration'[4] of Gandhi from his historico-political milieu is completed. The superstar arrives one day upon the earth, speaks the myth, leads a sub-continent to freedom, and, more importantly, preaches a doctrine of world peace. However, there is an immediate return to the historical and the political on a different level. The 'castration' is not just a denial of historical context; it is the creation of an arbitrary context which the character then justifies through the 'spectacular' in him. A public figure, representing in his own life-story an extremely significant era in a nation's history, is in this film not shown as representing that history, *save by virtue of some inner powers he is said to possess*. But in denying the one context, Attenborough has not accepted the responsibility of subjectively looking at the figure in another – nowhere is the *public* Gandhi transcended, and in fact all the appendages of the form have reinforced what is mainly the public figure.

It is the sensuous impact of the portrayal that forces the audience to bridge for themselves the deficiencies of the fiction. Furthermore, the reinforced public image now reinforces in turn a whole host of prejudicial notions about its time, which intervene in the ideological battles fought today. It is really these battles which we should be careful to recognise.

In the first sequence of the main story, we are introduced to the young Gandhi when he, presumably reading the Bible, asks a black porter the apparently irrelevant question: 'Tell me, do you ever think about hell?' In the next scene, with Khan, Gandhi is given the line: 'It is very unchristian; we are all children of God'. In that scene we are also introduced to 'Mr Baker', who, as the sympathetic common Englishman, is a recurring figure in the film. Next sentence: 'We come from an ancient civilisation'. In sequence five, with Andrews, there is another reference to Christ and Gandhi describes his philosophy as 'turning the other cheek'. Why on earth should Gandhi's philosophy be described so emphatically in Christian terms? The answer is obvious, really: within the broadly conservative tradition that lends itself most easily to the value system of the mass-spectacular, Biblical references naturally present themselves as the carriers of such a 'humanist' ideology; DeMille's work is an obvious example. Having established the Christian context, the film turns to 'India' – that 'ancient civilisation'. Gokhale virtually hands over the crown to the young prince and tells Gandhi not to listen to 'those people' but to see 'India' instead. The next shots present slow pans across the Indian countryside to the accompaniment of Ravi Shankar's strains on the sitar, but with a Western tabla percussion. Two more scenes and we are in the middle of Champaran, because 'the people seem to want me here': the arrival of the messiah whose very presence is enough to galvanise the nation to revolt. This is the 'castration' of Gandhi, his definitive separation from Indian history as he becomes cast into a Western mold. But who recognises this avatar? Not the generally grim-faced Indians around Gandhi, although Gokhale sees in him a 'successor' and Nehru comes to him for spiritual advice. Neither do the masses because they are never shown to be anything but faceless. The Indian leaders are more concerned with the question of power, while the British bureaucracy (barring the glamorous Mountbatten) is concerned only because Gandhi appears to be a shrewder antagonist than the others. It is the 'Mr Bakers' of the film, the 'common' British folk like Kallenbach, Andrews and Mirabehn – and as Mirabehn says to Gandhi about the people 'back home': 'They understand – they really do' – who carry the legacy forward. And ultimately the two journalists in the film, Walker and Margaret Bourke-White, are the historians who make the world aware by recording for posterity the phenomenon they are witnessing. These figures are the ones offered for identification, they are the site from where the narration is organised, standing in for the director's point of view and programming that of the viewer.

The pattern is thus clear. Within the dramatic cause-and-effect style of story-telling, one action 'naturally' leads to another: the riots occur because one man throws a stone. That is the absurd implication of a refusal to view events as part of a historical process. The use of dramatic cause-and-effect chains is also a common tactic, for instance, in government investigations of riots where causes are sought by analysing the immediate events as 'perceived' and transmitted by the privileged witness, the on-the-spot chronicler and, later, he who revives the chronicler's account. These are the people to whom the true significance of these historical processes is to be credited: Walker, Bourke-White and ... Attenborough. And if it is they, not the Indians, who recognise Gandhi's greatness, they can do so only in their own context, i.e. Gandhi has become transformed into a Christian messiah. This process has been described by the editors of *Cahiers du Cinéma*:

A double operation of addition and subtraction at the end of which the historical axis, having been abolished and mythified, returns cleansed of all impurities and thus recuperable to the service of not just Morality but of the morality reasserted by capitalist ideology. Morality not only rejects politics and surpasses history, it also rewrites them.[5]

The 'epic' of this tradition then does not distort history, it rewrites history. It rewrites in the context of the present for it cannot succeed unless it becomes relevant to contemporary ideological positions. Equally, however, it seeks to disown that present, by preaching from a pulpit placed in timelessness. In preaching, it moralises, placing itself above the political. The rewriting, which leaves significant parts unsaid, gets away with all this because it places the version above the fact, while of course feeding upon the fact. The distilling machine for history is thus complete.

In this, since both the beginning and the end are detached from their material context (the beginning by creating the heroic character, the end by curtailing the logical conclusion of creating such a character) it is possible to indulge the masses with mass-spectaculars that are in a sense drawn from themselves. It is a process more nefarious than commodity production itself, for here the masses are made to feed upon themselves, upon their own history.

The usefulness of such a procedure for any ruling class is blatant. In India today, with the growth of regionalist reaction threatening the nationalist bourgeoisie with increasing belligerence, more than ever before does the latter need a resurgence of nationalist values. For a long time now, the All-India commercial cinema in Hindi has been effective in keeping regionalist sentiments down. (It is interesting to see how in the South it is the regional cinema that is in the forefront of separatist movements, and how N.T. Rama Rao and M.G. Ramachandran have used this.) But there has never been the expertise required to raise nationalism above its naive populist forms in mass media, and to peddle it in the name of 'art'. It is here that *Gandhi* has made what could be the first formal breakthrough. Of course, one wouldn't want to attribute any of this to the film-makers as a conscious intention. But at the same time, it is no accident, surely, that it is exactly that tribe of ideological high priests which enters into such 'contracts' with third world ruling classes, 'purchasing' a major nationalist myth and 'reselling' it back to them in a renovated form. See for instance the manner in which Sir Richard has legitimised his authority to intervene in that history, founding his claim on personal acquaintance with its principals (he dedicated the film to Nehru, Mountbatten and Motilal Kothari) or that one instance when, denied the right to shoot in the Rashtrapati Bhavan by the then president, he is said to have stated that the first Indian President, Dr Rajendra Prasad, had personally invited him to shoot in the Bhavan, and the statement went conspicuously unchallenged. All this is a clear indication of the understanding between Sir Richard and the Indian government. Far from a Griffith, a Ford or a Welles, it is difficult to imagine even a Huston or a Lean stooping so low.

One can already see the trend developing in India. Govind Nihilani's latest film, *Vijeta*, has been produced by the Indian Air Force as part of its golden jubilee celebrations, and it is all about an Indian youth discovering the national cause. The film has been given tax exemption in New Delhi. Shyam Benegal is making a film for the Soviet government on Nehru and with the perverse cynicism of an advertising man, he is also making a film on Nehru for an American producer – a 'socialist' and a 'capitalist' Nehru by the same film-maker! One can only conclude with the hope that the very mediocrity that has led to such uses of cinema will itself betray the intentions of its sponsors. As happened during the Emergency five years ago, too much mediocre propaganda can also boomerang on those supposedly benefiting from it.

I would like to express my gratitude to Parag Amladi, who was closely associated with the writings of this article and who supplied the references from *Cahiers du Cinéma*.

Notes

1 Official Collectors Edition, *Close Encounters of the Third Kind*, p. 28.
2 Much of the next argument is based on *Cahiers du Cinéma*'s reading of John Ford's *Young Mr Lincoln*, translated in *Screen Reader 1* (London: SEFT, 1979). This reference p. 123.
3 *Young Mr Lincoln*, p. 127.
4 *Young Mr Lincoln*, p. 126.
5 *Young Mr Lincoln*, p. 127.

IX
The Problem of 'Authenticity' in the German Wartime Newsreels[1]

KARL STAMM

From *Hitler's Fall: The Newsreel Witness*, edited by K.R.M. Short and Stephen Dolezel (London: Croom Helm, 1988)

Notions of the 'real' or the 'authentic' have been put under close, often hostile scrutiny in writings on film and television over the last two decades. But they are not going to go away! What seems endlessly required is vigilance. The common-sense doctrines about realism aren't nonsense, but they are richly contradictory from a conceptual point of view. Often they are involved in blissful ignorance of the technical and historical factors determining the production of images under particular conditions. So Media Studies writing and teaching will need to criticise and supplement them constantly. But perhaps that point has by now been generally grasped – at least as a *general* point. It may be time to concentrate on more detailed treatments of particular 'realism' problems, past and present.

Karl Stamm's remarks about the puzzles involved in dealing with Nazi newsreel material are fascinating in this regard. Stamm is Curator of the Köln Museums, and brings an archivist's eye to material which we may be at first prone to 'demonize', given the horrors of the Hitler years. It comes as a salutary shock to be led coolly through these particular authenticity dilemmas and to find them not so different from those that always arise in the documentary mode. Especially valuable is the step-by-step way in which Stamm breaks down the newsreel text (images and sounds), reminds us of the conditions under which filming and editing took place, and distinguishes what is really misleading in the texts from 'inauthenticities' that arise because any film (or television) representation of the real must involve selection and construction.

It is salutary as well to be reminded that this terrible regime, *too*, operated in terms of the 'truthful presentation', the 'faithful description', the avoidance of the obviously contrived, just as we do ourselves.

M.A./J.O.T.

Motto: 'Pictures can't lie!'[2]

The question of the 'authenticity' of the German wartime newsreels is somewhat confused: on the one hand the veracity and documentary character of the newsreels was always emphasized during the period of the 'Third Reich' itself,[3] but on the other hand since the end of the war the same newsreels have been considered as a deception used by Propaganda Minister Goebbels. There have even been specific accusations that, for example, pictures of the Russian campaign were filmed on the Oberwiesenfeld in Munich.[4]

As the source of material necessary to discuss this question is extremely diffuse, it is perhaps useful, before going into details, to ask what exactly the term 'authenticity' means in this context, for whom and for what purposes particular film material was authentic and whether authenticity itself cannot have different forms.

A categorical formulation may be made at the outset: propaganda films are authentic as propaganda rather than in terms of the facts by which the propaganda is disseminated – in the same way that advertising films are authentic as publicity rather than in terms of the actual features of the products being advertised. Unfortunately this analogy cannot be taken any further because, in contrast to the fictive and illusionary nature of advertising films, however well it is disguised, newsreels deal with reality documented in other media – photography, radio, military reports, special reports by the Armed Forces High Command (O K W), not to mention eyewitnesses. In view of this it would seem appropriate to compare these different types of sources, as Peter Bucher did, most interestingly in my opinion, for the Ufa-Tonwoche (451/1939).[5]

In a totalitarian state where the information media are extensively co-ordinated there is, however, a limit to such a media comparison. For this reason it is important in the case of the newsreels, consisting as they do of separate components such as image and sound (noise, music, commentary), to determine whether all these components are equally authentic from the point of view of the event shown or 'depicted', or whether they can be classified by degrees. This method of approach is not uncontroversial. In terms of philosophical or scientific methodology, it can be argued that a film document must be either authentic or not authentic.[6] By the same token, however, the term 'authenticity' has already established itself in the context of discussion of the information and/or propaganda content of the German war newsreels in such a way that it would seem more practical to retain this term as it is, rather than to continue discussing terminology which might not be generally known or understood, particularly as the problems arising out of an investigation of the war newsreels tend to be of an interdisciplinary nature and are by no means restricted to the scientific sphere. As a proviso, however, it should be added that the term 'authentic' in this sense is used as a general expression meaning factually correct as opposed to 'falsified', 'manipulated' or 'simulated' ('posed'). The term can only be modified by examining the individual elements of the wartime newsreels in greater detail. It would be preferable, however, to proceed chronologically, i.e. in the sequence in which the newsreels originated.[7]

The *image* is a very authentic element of the newsreel, at least potentially. The large network of cameramen in the propaganda companies and the great technical and personnel involvement[8] meant that, for most of the war at least, exemplary material filmed on the spot in the various 'theatres of war' was at all events available. The short reports sent in most cases by the film-reporters to accompany the shipments generally permitted very precise identification and classification of the material received.[9] A high degree of authenticity may be attributed to this material, often filmed under hazardous circumstances, as typified by the uncut colour material of Hans Bastanier from the summer of 1942, filmed near Kharkov in the Ukraine.[10]

In this context it is worth noting the following extracts from instructions to film-reporters issued in September 1943:

1. Always remember that through your personal effort millions can participate in world events and that in your work you must give this and coming generations a *truthful* and vivid presentation of the gigantic struggle for Germany's greatness. . . .

4. *Avoid posed battle pictures* as they do not look genuine and endanger the reputation of the film reporter . . .

10. Send in a detailed report with the film material (date, exact location, *faithful* description of course of events).[11]

All kinds of qualifications have also to be made, however, with regard to the picture:

1. Pictures were sometimes 'touched up', i.e. adapted a little to the prevailing photo and film aesthetics through the artificial addition of 'scenery', such as the inclusion of branches in the picture to make it more 'graphic'. From our point of view, however, this hardly affects the question of authenticity, particularly as it is highly unlikely, for example, that palm trees will have been included in footage from East Prussia.

2. It was not usually possible to take pictures during the actual battles and for this reason it was generally the preparations for battle or the situation following it that was filmed (although in comparison to the newsreel material from the First World War the footage was often very vivid and close to the action, and not only with film shot from cameras fixed into aeroplanes, etc). As this was considered to be a shortcoming, many films were shot and later edited in such a way that they appeared to have been filmed in actual battle situations.

From the vast array of possible subjects the U-boat stories are selected here. These usually had a fixed 'iconography': life on board, emotive images (sunsets, etc.), then alarm, hatch down, dive, torpedoes away, surface, etc. The attack in a real alarm situation could not be filmed in the necessary visual quality and was thus simulated, as if there had been an actual alarm – not to mention the fact that U-boat attacks frequently took place at dawn and could not be filmed because of the poor light.

When processing U-boat material in the newsreel company other aids were often used: film supposedly shot through a periscope was often simulated with the aid of superimposed masks (with cross hairs and scales) and one editor specialising in U-boat stories admits having ready a few rolls of film with convoys (from earlier films) which could be included at appropriate points.

An extreme example of a U-boat story of this type is provided in the 5th sequence from DW 753/8/1945 which was probably fabricated completely at the cutting desk.[12]

Makers of the newsreels did not regard these 'as if' representations as falsifications, arguing rather that this type of action could have taken place except that under real conditions it would not have been possible to film adequately, if at all. The desire (or compulsion?) to show this type of film to the public provided the justification for the specific style.

Another variation of the 'as if' category is provided by certain newsreel reports in which minor military engagements were more or less staged, e.g. with the numerous shock troop engagements during the Russian campaign.

3. There were also cases in which specific situations were filmed deliberately in a specific manner for use as film evidence of completely different situations. In one instance, described by an eyewitness cameraman, reporters filmed shots of passing merchant vessels in the Baltic with the most powerful wide-angle lens available. These shots gave the impression that the ships were just visible on the horizon and were included in corresponding U-boat films to depict enemy convoys (or at least commissioned with this purpose in mind).

4. There were also cases of obvious manipulation of external film material in the war newsreels (known examples include speeded-up shots during the Western campaign intended to suggest the impetuous and hectic behaviour of politicians in 'so-called democracies'). These should be distinguished from falsifications such as the use of American newsreel material from 1937 at the start of DW 754/9/1945 to illustrate a contemporary situation. [13]

It is, however, significant that, as far as the author is aware, this type of manipulation and faking in film took place not at the shooting but rather at the editing stage.

5. In this context mention must be made of *non-existent material*, i.e. that which, because of military censorship, [14] although relevant from the point of view of authenticity, was eliminated and stored in the archives from the very beginning. Involved here in particular were new weapons and means of transport, etc., details of which were to be kept from the enemy. [15]

Apart from the official censorship one can also talk, at least retrospectively, of 'unofficial' censorship in the form of self-censoring in a way which the film-reporters of the time might not have been completely aware of: although they were basically at liberty to film what they considered of importance, there was some consensus between the newsreel company and the cameramen as to what ought to be filmed and what not (because it would not have been included in the newsreel in any case, such as pictures of dead German soldiers). It is not, however, easy to determine the date and extent of this consensus.

To give a concrete example: during the battle for the Crimea a reporter shot film, at great personal risk, of Soviet positions directly after a German flame-thrower attack – until he was informed from Berlin that he had filmed sufficient material of this nature, (either because the pictures were too gruesome or because the avoidance of international discussion of the use of flame-throwers was sought).

The *sound* in German war newsreels was seldom authentic because very little film was shot with an original soundtrack, as was the case, for example, with the 'Führer's speeches' where a lead camera with combined sound recording was used while other silent cameras supplied the cut-ins. The other sounds were dubbed on later, although great importance was attached to their correctness. Following complaints by the military censors, an extensive archive of the noises of all types of weapons had been established so that the silent films could be dubbed in an analogous (although not strictly authentic on-the-spot) manner.

The *music* which played such an important part in the inspirational quality and hence the propaganda effect of the newsreels is not of significance in considering the authenticity of what was shown, because it was applied later and usually without real connection with the theatre. (Along with the commentary, however, it is a very good indication of how the material was meant to be interpreted).

During the entire war the *commentary* gave the newsreels the meaning desired by the Ministry of Propaganda and the army propaganda. It is only authentic in terms of the material shown when it gives objective explanations of the images, based on the reports by the cameramen (which front, which type of weapons, etc.), although such comments were limited. Its achievement was in the way it impressed the watcher through pathos or specific intonation, and not in the way it conveyed authentic information.

Apart from this brief *cross-sectional* analysis which examines, albeit summarily and generally, the authenticity of the individual elements, it is also interesting to look at the same problem from the point of view of *longitudinal-section* analysis. If the newsreels are looked at chronologically it can be seen that the truth content of the commentaries gradually collapses: during periods of military success there was little need for falsification (except for racist comments and verbal descriptions of the enemy which were written into the text by the Ministry of Propaganda), whereas at times of military stagnation or defeat and retreat the pictures were unscrupulously falsified with speeches enjoining to hold on for the final victory. The same applies to the music: the victory music is comparatively appropriate for the initial military successes, whereas towards the end of the war even film of retreat (particularly from Russia) was dubbed, at the instigation of the Ministry of Propaganda, with 'advance music'.

Oddly enough, the opposite is true of the images: the less material available and the more it was necessary to use relatively fewer shots more extensively, the greater the authenticity conveyed and the more the watcher has the feeling of 'being there', as now, instead of large montages of heterogeneous material, more intensive and coherent film reports of militarily meaningless retreats were produced. As the single fighter comes to the fore, he loses his anonymity as 'the German soldier', as portrayed at the start of the war. Furthermore, the film became more realistic and verifiable and in greater contrast, at least from our point of view today, with the music and commentary –thus contributing in no small measure to the 'perverse honesty'[16] of the 1945 newsreels which, as a medium, failed as the military operation collapsed, being designed from the eagle symbol onwards as victory newsreel.

Returning, after these brief comments, to considering for whom and what purpose the newsreels were and are (more or less) authentic, in other words what the term 'authenticity' actually means, we should perhaps ask ourselves the following questions:

Do we really want to know whether tank A, number B, fired the shot seen in the newsreel at time C on date D in location E, whether it belonged to company F, operating to strategic plan G? Apart from the question of whether the military history reports are structured finely enough to be able to make something of such detailed information (if we had it), we are more concerned today with deciding whether we can have any idea whatsoever of how the advance on and retreat from the Russian front, for example, actually took place.

Again, is it really so important to know whether the celebrations on Hitler's return to Berlin in the final sequences of D W 514/29/1940 come from an original sound recording or from a preserved celebration recording on Hitler's return after the Munich Pact or after the entry into Sudetenland?[17] Didn't the people in the street cheer wildly, sometimes hysterically, on all these occasions? Would a new and original sound recording in some way improve the state of our knowledge today (or that of the cinema-goers of the time) – not to mention the fact that, because of technology available at the time, the sound recordings in any case were only partially authentic, and were adapted by means of a sound controller – or falsified – when being synchronised with the pictures? Is it not more important that a sequence such as this is capable of fictionally recreating 50 years later the situation and mood of the time? There was no necessity, from a propaganda point of view, to falsify the overall impression – on the contrary. In addition, the film-makers would surely have been aware that many people had seen the event with their own eyes and would have reacted negatively to any falsification – a further criterion for the authenticity of the newsreels, whose true and documentary character was not questioned at the time.

Authenticity cannot have been a matter of details: even when the length of the newsreels was tripled, the events of the week could only be summarised briefly because of the number of different theatres of war (not to mention domestic events), and for this reason topographically heterogeneous film material had to be combined and provided with a relatively general commentary.[18] The intention was to convey a 'picture of the whole', while the public at the time wanted to '*see*' how it was' and 'be there'. Given the established newsreel format and the amount of material received it was completely feasible to present a new show every week – and it is here that these newsreels are of value to us today as a pictorial chronicle of the Second World War whose 'picture', then as now, was and is characterised by the newsreels.[19]

Because of its propaganda nature, however, this pictorial chronicle must be regarded critically, which normally means that we should penetrate through the secondary and obscuring propaganda effect of the soundtrack to the primary and potentially authentic pictures or, in other words, read the pictures 'against the grain'. To do this it is necessary firstly to confront these pictures with other material, such as the war diaries of the Armed Forces High Command and the results of post-war historical research – a further example of media variety, albeit with diachronic material. Secondly, efforts must be made to increase our knowledge of how the newsreels were made in general, and the way in which specific commissions were dealt with (in the form of case studies) so as to obtain further criteria by which to judge the extent to which the film material is authentic.

This, in turn, presupposes that the evidence (including oral history) is safeguarded, that documentary and photographic material in the hands of former members of the propaganda companies and employees of the Deutsche Wochenschau GmbH is saved from destruction, and that the existing and complete newsreel footage is researched intensively from an 'iconographic' angle, in other words that the 'topoi' – specific film language platitudes and the specific propaganda (which are almost inseparably linked) – are listed and evaluated.[20] Art historians would talk of a distinction between type, motif and (period and individual) style.

This might sound like a complicated process and prompt the question as to whether such efforts can be justified. In response it may be said that the opportunity of separating pictures of the past from the propaganda is worth taking, both to 'redeem the physical reality' as Siegfried Kracauer has put it and, in particular, with regard to future generations, who would otherwise be completely at a loss if we were unable to develop criteria and to make plausible standards by which the authenticity of the existing audio-visual material can be measured.

To avoid any misconceptions it should be stated that it is not the intention, as part of some 'change of heart', to state now that the newsreels of the Second World War are authentic, any more than the Nazi newspaper reporting in the *Völkischer Beobachter* can be called objective historical writing. The aim is rather to make proper scientific use of the material, including oral reports, in a discriminating manner made possible by the distance in time now separating us from the events, and to pass on the findings to a wider and, as has been shown, inquisitive audience (a feat which will require even more effort). This has to be done before it is too late – and, given the age of the eyewitnesses still living, the time is running out. The authentic experiences in their former activities are an essential prerequisite for judging the authenticity of the German war newsreels.

Notes

1 This is a revised version of a paper delivered at the 11th IAMHIST Congress '1945 – From War to Peace' at the Institute for Scientific Film, Göttingen, 21–24 August 1985. This paper has benefited from the critical comments of Hermann Kalkofen, Göttingen, and Ernst Opgenoorth, Bonn. I would like to thank all former employees of the Deutsche Wochenschau, whose information was instrumental in the preparation of this paper. My thanks also to Stephen Dolezel, Hans Barkhausen and Heinrich Bodensieck for reading the manuscript and offering suggestions for improving it. The author is responsible, however, for all possible errors.

2 This is the unanimous feeling of former film-reporters of the Second World War, as expressed at a conference at the Munich College of Television and Film at the Academy for Political Education in Tutzing (17–21 March 1980) (*Zweimal Deutschland seit 1945 im Film und Fernsehen. I: Von der Kino-Wochenschau zum aktuellen Fernsehen* – the corresponding publication is by Karl Friedrich Reimers, Monika Lerch-Stumpf and Rüdiger Steinmetz, published in the series '*Kommunikation Audiovisuell – Beiträge aus der Hochschule für Fernsehen und Film*

München', vol. 3, Ölschläger-Verlag, Munich, 1983). In this paper an attempt is made to describe conditions by which this slogan can be measured.

3 See collection of quotations by the author in his article *'Das "Erlebnis" des Krieges in der Deutschen Wochenschau'* in *Die Dekoration der Gewalt: Kunst und Medien im Faschismus*, published by Hinz/Mittig/Schäche/Schönberger (Giessen: 1979), pp. 116–18.

4 According to Jost van Rennings, *'Die Gefilmte Zeitung'*, Phil. diss., Munich 1956 (typed copy). Unfortunately no source is mentioned for this quotation. In such cases insufficient attention is often paid today to the army film department (*Heeresfilmstelle*) which in its films frequently used captured weapons such as Anglo-Saxon or Soviet tanks.

5 Peter Bucher, 'Hitler's 50. *Geburtstag. Zur Quellenvielfalt im Bundesarchiv'*, in *Aus der Arbeit des Bundesarchivs*, published by Heinz Boberach and Hans Booms (Papers of the Federal Archive 25) (Boppard am Rhein: 1977), pp. 423–46.

6 Herman Kalkofen argued in the discussion following the Göttingen paper that the term 'authenticity' should not be falsified and that 'semi-authentic' would be better termed 'veridical' (a term from perceptual psychology).

7 See Stamm, *'Das "Erlebnis" des Krieges in der Deutschen Wochenschau'* (see note 3), pp. 118–19. In the discussion following the Göttingen paper Ernst Opgenoorth expressed his misgivings with regard to a 'genetic' classification of the term authenticity and opined that the final audio-visual version of the newsreel should be regarded as a unit which is either authentic in terms of itself, or not, although he was well aware that pragmatically there are grey or black areas of authenticity.

The distinction used by Opgenoorth between 'specific' and 'unspecific' film (e.g. the barrel of a gun to represent a threat, irrespective of which type of weapon it is, as in this context it is unspecific) is claimed by the author to be a particularly fortunate choice of terms which he would like to make use of when classifying (film) shots. The question remains, however, of the grey area between 'specific' and 'authentic' footage, dependent on the definition in a particular case.

8 See most recently Hans Barkhausen, *Filmpropaganda für Deutschland im Ersten und Zweiten Weltkrieg* (Hildesheim/Zürich/New York: 1982), pp. 205–43.

9 Copies of such reports have survived in some cases, e.g. those of Navy film-reporter Horst Grund in the Federal Archive in Koblenz.

10 The film material is in the Federal Archive, Koblenz. There is an interesting television film about these pictures and Hans Bastanier himself made by Dieter Zimmer (broadcast on Z D F on 23 June 1981).

11 *'12 Gebote für den Filmberichter'* with dateline 'Berlin, September 1943', without sender (probably OKW/WFSt/WPr(F) = Armed Forces High Command, Armed Forces Operational Staff, Army Propaganda (Film Department), as is the case with comparable documents), hectographed copy in the possession of Horst Grund at the Federal Archive, Koblenz. Author's italics.

12 See the IWF publication by the author to accompany DW 753/8/1945 (G152), Göttingen 1979, pp. 20–1 and 36.

13 See the IWF publication to accompany DW 754/9/1945 (G153) by Martin Friedel, Göttingen 1979, p. 34.

14 See Barkhausen, *Filmpropaganda*, pp. 222–3 (see note 8) and Stamm, IWF edition G152, 1979, p. 8, note 17 (see note 12).

15 A good estimate of the extent of military censorship is obtained by looking at random at the 'black list' kept by the Federal Archive in Koblenz, which makes reference to the footage taken by the Navy film-reporter Horst Grund between June 1941 and December 1943 and can be compared with the copies of his short reports on these films (see note 9).

16 Ulrich Kurowski, *Lexikon Film* (Munich: 1976), p. 196.

17 The author has information of corresponding remarks by former employees of the Deutsche Wochenschau.

18 Here the newsreel is distinguished as a type from scientific film documentaries, for example, in which experiments are filmed simultaneously at a single location and are therefore authentic in another sense.

19 Despite a series of newsreels ('Messter-Woche' and 'Eiko-Woche') available, the picture of the First World War is more influenced by early sound films such as *All Quiet on the Western Front* and *Western Front 1918*. As far as the Second World War is concerned, however, feature films (such as Karl Ritter's *Stukas*) played and continue to play an insignificant role.

20 Presumably the model for this is not so much Hans Magnus Enzensberger's 'Scherbenwelt. Die Anatomie einer Wochenschau' in *Einzelheiten I, Bewusstseins-Industrie*, edition suhrkamp 63, 8th edition (Frankfurt on Main: 1973), pp. 106–33 as Helmut Regel's '*Zur Topographie des NS-Films*', *Filmkritik* vol. 10 no. 1, 1966, pp. 5–18.

X
Visions of Instability: US Television's Law and Order News of El Salvador

ROBIN ANDERSEN
From *Media, Culture and Society* vol. 10 no. 2 (April 1988)

O ver the last thirty years there has developed a large body of analytic work which examines the Media's coverage of various wars and violent conflicts – Vietnam, Northern Ireland, Nicaragua, the Falklands/ Malvinas, to list the more obvious. In an early but highly influential article Johan Galtung and Mari Ruge listed and systematised a substantial series of factors they found to be criteria of newsworthiness in the selection of foreign news.*

Robin Andersen continues in that tradition by examining the way in which U S T V network journalists attempted to construct a coherent account of what appeared to be a highly confusing and contradictory situation taking place in El Salvador. Contrary to the claims of the U S government, the overthrow of the brutal dictatorship of General Carlos Humberto Romero in 1979 by a group of supposedly progressive young military officers did not lead to peace and democracy. Instead, popular opposition and brutal repression by the authorities continued and the U S journalists had to report the situation within 'a framework of understanding and interpretation that editors would accept and that the North American public would recognise'.

Drawing upon a wealth of empirical evidence, Robin Andersen concentrates on one area of criteria in the presentation of news stories about El Salvador. He thereby provides a useful demonstration of how the continued use of what the British media analyst Justin Wren-Lewis termed the 'law and order' frame to interpret political developments, enables journalists to construct and maintain the 'event' orientation (as opposed to the 'process' orientation) of traditional Western media news 'stories'.

M.A./J.O.T.

---

* 'The structure of foreign news: The presentation of the Congo, Cuba and Cyprus crises in four foreign newspapers', originally published in *Journal of Peace Research* no. 1 (1965); now more widely available in a shortened version as Johan Galtung and Mari Ruge, 'Structuring and selecting news', in Stanley Cohen and Jock Young (eds.), *The Manufacture of News – Social Problems, Deviance and the Mass Media* (revised edition, London: Constable, Beverly Hills: Sage, 1981).

> 'Very wild' is how a Western diplomat describes the situation
> in San Salvador tonight. Government troops there sur-
> rounded an estimated 20,000 rebelling leftists . . .
>
> CBS Evening News, 23 January 1980

From a foreign Latin American country violent civil disorder explodes on the television screen. Fast moving footage of people running in the streets; some being wounded – soldiers, tanks and crossfire – with audio actuality of screams and gunshots. These were the images that characterized the television news coverage of El Salvador at the end of 1979 and into 1980. At this time El Salvador was still unknown. The small Central American country had not yet become a major concern to the architects of US foreign policy. The anchorman had to explain that 'tiny' El Salvador was part of Central America, and that San Salvador was the capital city. 'Tiny' foreign countries do not usually become the focus of news stories unless there is a coup or an earthquake.[1] El Salvador had just had a coup.

Official statements being disseminated from the US government and the new ruling junta went like this. Young progressive military officers had ousted Romero, a right-wing general and the perpetrator of brutal repression, who had ruled the country with an iron fist. A corrupt system of social and economic injustice had developed over decades, and was maintained by police and military accustomed to the use of force. All this was to stop. Right-wing oligarchs, who up to that point had kept the wealth of the country to themselves, were to relinquish a small fraction of their privilege. From this more equitable arrangement, a middle class would emerge, creating a corresponding politically moderate centre. A fledgling, lawful democracy would replace revolution. The 'left' would be appeased with reforms, and 'extremists' would be controlled. The excesses of the military would stop, but most importantly, the status quo would be preserved; US interests would be safe.

If this scenario had actually been carried out, if reforms had been implemented, repression controlled, and economic disparities reconciled, there would have been little to report from the tiny country. To news editors, the normal functioning of Third World countries is not considered valuable news fare.[2] Reports continued because, instead of easing conflict, the coup and subsequent events propelled ever greater turmoil. Reports continued because something was happening in El Salvador that legitimate sources of information and power had not explained, and could not manage to control. People in large numbers were demonstrating in the streets and getting shot, also in large numbers. The new government said they were under attack by extremists, and had to react.

The political dynamic in El Salvador following the coup was wrought with conflict, and not easy to grasp at first journalistic glance. Popular expectations to create a new government responsive to the needs of the majority were high. The junta promised reforms, but they were slow to materialize. A popular revolutionary struggle continued and entered a phase of actions which included strikes, mass mobilizations and occupations. These actions were being carried out by the largest growing unified opposition in the history of El Salvador. It threatened the very foundations of the status quo and United States hegemony.

This large and popular opposition continued to be attacked by the 'reform-minded' junta and paramilitary organizations that, in spite of official declarations to the contrary, remained intact. Moderate civilians on the junta were helpless to stop the military, which continued to open fire on demonstrations and violently attack striking workers. The actions of the new government made it clear that it did not represent majority interests. Decades of social and economic injustice, perpetuated by a rich minority, continued to be maintained by security forces and paramilitary death squads.

Journalists were confronted with the contradictions between the situation they saw and the information they were given by the government. They were told that reforms were being carried out, that the death squads had been dismantled, and that abuses by security forces were being curtailed. But massive demonstrations with continuing demands were the order of the day, and human rights reports revealed that the new government's response was increasingly more violent, even more violent in fact than under the previous dictatorship of General Romero.[3]

The foreign press corps was unprepared. Television correspondents, particularly, are not chosen on the basis of their knowledge of the region they are sent to cover. Nor did they have the first-hand experience which would have given them at least some background knowledge of El Salvador, because it had only just become the story. For many it was their first time in Central America; many did not speak Spanish. Nonetheless, they had to make a story out of it. It had to make sense for US television. It had to fit within a framework of understanding and interpretation that editors would accept and that the North American public would recognize. It had to fit, and be fit for, television.

Given these historical circumstances, the presentation on US network television of events in El Salvador, for the period immediately following the coup of 15 October 1979, will be the topic of this article.

The Law and Order Frame

The freelance network news crew, based in Mexico City to cover Central America, called themselves the 'budget bang-bang crew'.[4] They were sent to El Salvador when demonstrations were planned, and/or when they were informed that some type of violence would occur. They were well aware that the main news value of El Salvador coverage at that time was entertainment violence.[5] They sought after and hoped to capture exciting and disturbing visuals of the social conflict spilling into the streets of San Salvador. 'Action' coverage of social disruption, such as demonstrations under attack, was the most likely to be aired, and stories that did not include violence of some sort were not considered newsworthy.[6] With the media spotlight trained on violent conflict, stories focused on and were organized around the action footage taken of social disorder. Concentration on conflict and violence largely prescribed the treatment and interpretation foreign correspondents would find appropriate for news coverage of El Salvador during this period.

With very little background on the region, and without strong foreign policy concerns publicly articulated by the US State Department, journalists relied on a more or less standard media frame, one which would accommodate the requirements for exciting, dramatic visual footage. This frame, which we will call the law and order frame, has been described and analysed by British media observers who have noted its frequent use by the BBC in reporting crime and urban riots.[7] The guiding focus of the frame is to represent civil actions and demonstrations as social chaos which pose problems for the continuation of law and social order. Wren-Lewis describes the frame as rigid and narrowly focused:

The representation of outbreaks of violent public disorder on television is fused with conventions governing what can and cannot be seen or said. The most prominent of these, solidified over many years, is what might be called the 'law and order' frame, informed by a discourse of a dangerously pre-emptive and frequently mythical character.[8]

Not surprisingly, the most important structural element of the law and order frame is violence. News stories sent out of El Salvador during this period contained violent conflict with few exceptions, and can be recognized as standardized law and order news reporting. Conflict usually begins the news report, either in the anchorman's introduction, or at the beginning of the story itself. As Wren-Lewis states, this is characteristic of the law and order frame: 'The focal point of the law and order frame is the moment of conflict itself, the moment signalling the beginning of a headline news story.[9] A few examples of opening lines from news stories about El Salvador during this period are instructive:

In other foreign news today, the military junta in El Salvador is but three days old, but has already fought off one leftist attempt to overthrow it . . .

ABC, 17 October 1979

In the Central American country of El Salvador the leftist fight against the new military junta there intensified . . .

ABC, 4 November 1979

In El Salvador more turmoil, leftist demonstrators in the capital city of San Salvador attacked the American embassy . . .

NBC, 30 October 1979

As we can see from these reports, the conflict in El Salvador is portrayed as having been initiated by leftists, and/or demonstrators. Other stories use labels, such as guerrillas, extremists, students, or some variation thereof. The leftists are always attacking, fighting, or rebelling against the newly established government. The effect of this repetition is the impression that the legitimate government is continually under a state of siege, a state which threatens the fundamental social order.

The disruption of social order is a recurring theme of news stories. Herbert Gans has noted that 'The frequent appearance of disorder stories suggests that order is an important value in the news . . .'[10] The popularity of social disruption as a dominant news theme is not coincidental, particularly for television news. Opening with attack and disruption is the beginning of a good story. Dramatic conflict, especially since it can be depicted visually, is exciting, and gains the attention of the viewer. That attention is held as the viewer becomes engaged in the unfolding crisis situation which will be resolved, in one way or another, within the story. A crisis is made to order for a television news report of the developing world, because little or no background knowledge is needed for an exciting and ostensibly coherent story.

After the dramatic crisis situation has been introduced, the law and order story unfolds. A problem has been presented; leftist violence is threatening the social order. As the story continues, a solution is sought for the restoration of that order. The disruption of social normality has posed a problem of order for *those in power*. It calls on those in legitimate positions of authority to react. It is they who must develop strategies for the restoration of order, and solve the problem of social disruption. As Wren-Lewis states, when the problem has been defined as one of law and order, it is '. . . a problematic whose solution necessitates the strengthening of the agents of law and order to overcome those agencies who come into conflict with it'.[11]

In the news stories of El Salvador, the agents of law and order are the army and the security forces directed by the new junta. It is they who react to leftist violence, and after a battle, restore order. The 'leftists', who have been said to cause the problem, are thereby set in dramatic conflict with those who restore order, as these stories illustrate:

> . . . The army also wants the leftists to put down their weapons, but despite that call for peace, a leftist group early this morning took over a neighborhood in San Salvador the capital. The national guard *had to be brought in* to get them out . . . [emphasis added]
>
> A B C, 16 October 1979

> El Salvador's new government today made its first get-tough *reply* to protesting leftists . . . [emphasis added]
>
> C B S, 28 October 1979

The 'strengthening of the agents of law and order' is always presented as defensive, reactive, and necessary. They 'had to be' called in, and they had to 'get tough'. In acting out this drama between leftists and security forces, the scales are always tilted in favour of those in positions of state-sanctioned power. As Wren-Lewis points out, their social positions are strictly pre-defined within the law and order frame: 'The policeman signifies within the sacred realm of "the law" – the policeman represents the law and therefore is the law – while the demonstrator/rioter is entrenched within the realm of the arrested or arrestable'.[12]

These significations and categories are much more extreme when applied to a country such as El Salvador where the status quo is maintained by force. When the law and order frame is used to cover El Salvador, the leftist demonstrator/rioter is not only within the realm of the arrestable, but within that of the killable, as this C B S story shows: '. . . But so far leftist uprisings have failed, seventeen people were killed in San Marcos when the army quashed a guerrilla takeover of that city . . .' (C B S, 18 October 1979).

The information that seventeen people were killed follows the phrase, 'but so far leftist uprisings have failed'. The sequence establishes that the leftists initiated violence which threatened order, but the army maintained control. In this context, the fact that people were killed is portrayed merely as a consequence of the army's obligation to restore order. The added use of the word 'quashed' makes it also seem to have been somehow gentle, as if brute force were not really exerted, even though quite a few people died. Within the law and order context, putting down uprisings is something the army is supposed to do, a positive act. The consequence of the frame, then, is to make the killing of leftists, and even 'innocent' people, a palatable event; a necessary, if lamentable, outcome of maintaining order.

As the Salvador stories of law and order continue, after giving the body count and other related details, the story is 'wrapped up as neatly as possible'.[13] The restoration of order, or at least a temporary calm, closes the narrative, as do these ending lines: '. . . Late reports say students have now begun to leave the University campus and that the city is quiet . . .' (A B C, 23 January 1980) or, as with this story, in which an action taken by the government promises order in the near future: '. . . The new junta has suspended constitutional rights until the crisis is under control . . .' (A B C, 16 October 1979).

Many times the restoration of order is only temporary, and there is the threat of violence to come. In situations such as these, it is not at all easy for the correspondent to 'wrap it up'. Different visual images are used to signify calm, or at least pseudo-normality: an empty city street; people who look relieved-that-it's-all-over; casual images of dogs, women, and children.[14] One story ends with a funeral, the finality of burying the dead signifying calm, if only for the time being. Other stories end with speculation as to whether the junta will be able to survive the onslaughts, effecting closure by featuring those that maintain social order, and pointing to at least temporary normality. A threatened disruption in the future signifies order at present, and serves the added function of setting the stage for future stories: '. . . Everyone expects more killing. The four month old government may not be able to survive either . . .' (A B C, 23 January 1980).

Video News as Action Drama:
No Contexts, No Information

The story is wrapped up tight with its crisis (leftist violence)/resolution (army restoration of order). The narrative introduced a crisis, pitted characters against one another, was filled in with how many shots were fired, what part of town it was in, and how many people died. The drama of leftists battling with security forces was fast-paced and exciting, and therefore entertaining. Closure was effected when calm returned and the forces of law and order were once again in control, if only temporarily.

Because the El Salvador story was just that, a story, it remained entertaining, while not being informative. Questions such as why demonstrations and so-called attacks took place at all were never asked (let alone answered). When the law and order frame is used, there is a profound lack of information, information which could offer some sort of explanation as to the causes of situations and events which lead to violence. Explanations and motivations for social actions are lost when reports revolve around the axis of restoring and maintaining order. Within the law and order frame, it is through the use of the story line that this information gap goes largely undetected.

The action-centred narrative severely truncates news reporting, because motivations and explanations simply will not fit within its parameters. Once the simple narrative of crisis/resolution is set up, only aspects of events relating to that central theme are included in the report. Reasons for 'attacks', demonstrations and occupations are simply not part of the story, and these actions do indeed appear to be totally without logical design, much less political purpose. Leftists' actions suddenly appear out of a mysterious void – as if from nowhere. This explanatory lack is fundamental to law and order news stories because, as Bazalgette and Paterson have also noted, they make use of 'a particular kind of narrative in which the disruption is *unmotivated*' (emphasis added).[15]

With the 'leftists'' motivations and social causal explanations suspended, the incident or event is effectively depoliticized. It is removed from the social historical context. Only with these types of explanations could the viewer understand the social unrest, and therefore the human motivations, which explode on their television screens. As one observer notes, news stories present a fragmented and mystifying picture of the world. 'In place of seeing a coherent world with clear historical trends, the public sees a world driven into chaos by seemingly arbitrary and mysterious forces.'[16]

Once action is ripped out of the social milieu, the resulting void is filled with a familiar tautological and mythical explanation, that leftists cause violent social disruption simply because they are extremists *by nature*. This tautology which exists within the law and order frame has also been pointed out by Wren-Lewis '. . . notions of causality are tautological in the mythic sense – a criminal is criminal is criminal'.[17] The presentation of leftists as extremist by nature is also a venal justification which serves to mollify the viewer's emotional response to reports of their deaths.

The lack of explanation for social unrest and the resulting tautology are both consequences of focusing on violence and crisis *per se*, out of context, as the primary issues and only social problems. As Wren-Lewis has noted:

For other explanations and solutions to come into play, the site of the problem needs to shift. The dramatic opening headlines and violent film sequences need to be recognised as significations of something beyond and outside them, a world of *conditions which precipitated* such startling significations [emphasis added].[18]

Conditions precipitating such startling events in El Salvador were/are decades of economic disparity and unjust political and social institutions. Structures which existed under the corrupt and brutal dictatorship of General Romero. Structures which remained intact even after the new junta came to power. Structures which were/are maintained by force through the military might of the army, security forces, and paramilitary organizations. Because the law and order frame constructs a story around violence and order, these broader social conditions and their significance are disregarded.

If the focal point of news coverage were shifted from violence to problems of political, social, economic and repressive realities (which ultimately lead to violence), a whole different set of solutions and outcomes responding to issues of social causality would necessarily come into play within news reports. (But it would not make such a good 'story'.) If the focus were turned around, logic would dictate at least questioning, on the part of the correspondent, whether attempts were being made to resolve existing social inequities within the country. The resulting solutions would look to actions such as improvements in working and living conditions. This set of social-causal resolutions would consist of, for example, agreeing to fair wages and safe working conditions, allowing for better housing and nutrition, providing public services, such as potable water, electric power and sanitation, just to list a very few. It would mean, in essence, pointing out the necessity for economic reform (which was the alleged objective for the 15 October coup). Above all, it would mean solving the problem of military abuses. The repressive role of the military – of ensuring the continued existence of an unsupportable system – would become apparent. Security forces would fall well within the realm of problems, instead of being looked to for solutions, as is done with the standard emphasis on order.

This restructuring and re-emphasis would help the viewer understand the real problems and social realities which exist within the country, and this better informed coverage would also point to a very different set of interpretations and outcomes than those offered by the law and order frame. Instead of looking to the military to maintain the status quo, the new problems presented would demand dramatic changes of the status quo. It would become all too obvious that only through fundamental social change could these entrenched social disparities be corrected. We are left with the irony that social change (or at least some improvements) was precisely what 'leftists' and 'demonstrators' were asking for; what security forces were preventing; and what the law and order frame omitted from discussion.

The characteristics of law and order news satisfied the media requirements for coverage of El Salvador during that period – violence, narrative format, entertainment value, all with an emphasis on stability and social order. But as we shall see in the following pages, frames 'made to fit' for television may satisfy media requirements, but do not necessarily depict reality with any degree of veracity. To demonstrate this, we will now compare the depiction of El Salvador on television news with independent documentation of the country at that time.

The Moderate Face of Military Repression

> We see now that this political project was, from the very beginning, a maneuver against the people. But we do not regret having participated in this government, having put all our efforts and skills toward a different outcome. But now that everything is clear, we should regret for the rest of our lives any further collaboration.

Salvador Samayoa and Enrique Alvarez Cordova. Letter of resignation from the first junta, 29 December 1979.[19]

The coup of 15 October reportedly brought to power a moderate government willing to make structural changes within Salvadoran society. The main premise of the law and order frame, and what it based its legitimacy on, was the assertion that the junta was moderate and committed to making reforms, and that these reforms were being carried out. Brutality in the person of Romero had been overthrown, and a just society was in the making. This is what gave the security forces the right to 'get tough' against those who refused to operate within the legitimate political arena – who used violence instead. The assertion that the junta was moderate legitimized the status quo, and the maintenance of order.

However, the junta never lived up to this characterization, even though news coverage never failed to make the claim. In fact, the most important 'clash' taking place in El Salvador during this period, though it was never reported on television, was the struggle for power going on within the junta itself. It was true that 'reform-minded' officers were among those who led the coup. They did promise to begin the process that would abolish injustice, and they asked civilians to join them in the task of restructuring Salvadoran society. Armstrong and Shenk have rightly characterized these civilians as 'men of impeccable democratic credentials'.[20] In the beginning then, the junta was a coalition of military and civilian progressives willing to work for change. It also included, however, military conservatives such as José Guillermo Garcia and Jaime Abdule Gutierrez who led the right-wing faction of the military. Adolfo Majano, leader of the progressive military, together with civilian leaders such as Guillermo Ungo and Roman Mayorga on the Junta, and Enrique Alvarez Cordova and Salvador Samayoa as cabinet ministers, would struggle to gain executive control over security forces for the three months that followed the coup, a battle they would lose against the right-wing influences of Gutierrez and Garcia.

From the beginning television news reports characterized the junta as centrist and moderate:

... The State Department in Washington said the leadership appeared centrist and moderate ...

NBC, 16 October 1979

The State Department said today the new military government in El Salvador appears to be moderate and its first statements are encouraging ...

ABC, 16 October 1979

On 18 October 1979, CBS reported the appointment of civilians to the new government:

... Three civilians considered sympathizers of the moderate opposition party were appointed to serve on the junta ...

This CBS report goes on to describe the 'moderate' credentials of Roman Mayorga, a former university president, and a man educated at MIT. This is the last we are to hear of the structure and nature of the junta. From this time on it is labelled 'reform-minded', 'moderate', 'centrist', or 'civilian/military'. Although the moderate label solidified, the centrist junta did not.

The political power struggles taking place within the new government during this period were to make an historic difference, but television viewers would not be privy to this information. Almost immediately the progressive officers and civilians found it impossible to control the actions of the right-wing elements within the military. The human rights report confirms that the civilians on the junta found it impossible to control continuing abuses:

The Majano-led wing soon found its influence over the army was limited or in the case of the National Guard and the Treasury Police, virtually non-existent. Members of the latter two branches of the Security Forces also belonged to various paramilitary groups that played an ever-more-violent role in the last months of 1979.[21]

Because neither Majano nor the civilians were able to stop the actions of security forces or paramilitary organizations, the civilian members of the junta resigned in protest, after three months of internal struggles. On 29 December, Salvador Samayoa, then Minister of Education, and Enrique Alvarez Cordova, Minister of Agriculture, along with three other ministers, resigned. Then on 3 January 1980, Guillermo Ungo and Roman Mayorga resigned along with virtually the entire cabinet and all high-ranking officials. In the words of Armstrong and Shenk 'The center had collapsed'.[22] This interpretation is corroborated in the report on human rights which states that: 'With the fall of the "First Junta" the centrist alternative was effectively closed, and the conservatives were back in unquestioned control'.[23]

None of the networks reported any of these events, nor the final resignation of the junta members.[24] Even CBS, which had reported at length on the appointment of Roman Mayorga, failed to report his resignation, or any of the others. For television news viewers, these political developments never happened. Television news coverage omitted every reference to this all-important political power struggle that could have accounted for the abuses that continued, and would eventually determine the political course the country was to follow. The civilians' lack of control, and even their resignations, had no effect on the way in which the news characterized the junta; it continued to be labelled moderate. A report aired on NBC, 1 January 1980, never mentioned that any of these struggles were taking place: '... The leftists oppose the moderate junta which took power here last October ...', even after the resignations: '... The Carter Administration is considering proposals to send military advisors to help bolster the moderate government now in power ...' (NBC, 19 February 1980), and even when it would seem to be a contradiction in terms: '... The ruling moderate junta clamped a news blackout on radio stations ...' (CBS, 23 January 1980).

As has been pointed out, the final blow to the centrist position of the first junta came at the beginning of 1980. But it must be remembered that the junta was never in control of the security forces. The army never acted in a moderate way. The civilians finally resigned because they realized that they were the democratic face which shielded the military from criticism. The media bought this front assiduously. In spite of continuing demands for reform, and contrary to what TV news reported, repression actually increased after the coup, as the human rights report documents: 'Popular pressure for reform, including an end to repression, intensified, but the level of repression actually increased.'[25]

Hiding behind the moderate label so often repeated, the established military toyed with the progressives, giving lip service to moderation, but acting as they had always done: 'Security Forces acted with the same brutality as those under Romero. ... Within a week, the government was held responsible for more than 100 killings of demonstrators and striking workers ...'.[26]

These facts fly in the face of the dominant interpretations and categories that the media used to represent the situation in El Salvador at the time. According to T V news, the junta was 'moderate' and violent attacks were initiated by 'leftists'. But independent sources describe a very different situation, one of continued, and even escalating, military abuses against a large sector of the population. Media assertions would not have been so easily accepted, had either journalists or the American public known anything at all about the history of El Salvador.

The Historical Void

Television news functions in the here and now. Today's news has currency; yesterday's news is old news with little or no significance. Television increasingly seeks the most dramatic, the most dynamic stories, as it is felt that analysis, history and context will not hold the audience through to the next commercial break. The result is an audience with little or no background information, which fails to understand that situations and events are the products of political, social and economic structures *which have evolved over time*.

A familiar argument is that those who are genuinely concerned with understanding their world will find other more detailed sources that offer both background and context for understanding. But the underlying messages and impressions left by news stories (in addition to 'facts' reported) offer their own interpretation and understanding of events. We are given a more or less coherent package, at least on the ideological level. The Salvador stories make sense; a new 'reform-minded' junta had come to power hoping to improve conditions in that tiny country, but their efforts were constantly thwarted by extremists and violent radicals who caused 'instability'. Stability, no matter how unjust, is always preferred to 'chaos', chaos being the term used to characterize wars of national liberation. It is an old familiar 'Third World' story. It is recognized, the situation is understood; more information would be redundant. History would simply confuse the issues.

The history of El Salvador would certainly confuse the issues of the law and order frame. According to law and order interpretations, it was simple; the coup clearly succeeded in transforming the country from a dictatorship to a 'fledgling democracy' overnight. Even a cursory look at the history of El Salvador would have uncovered the patent absurdity of those assertions. It would also have provided the context through which the internal power struggles within the new junta could have been reported. But this is all far too complex, time-consuming, and boring for television.

The historic wedding between those who hold the economic power and wealth in El Salvador and the military is a bond not easily torn asunder. One *New York Times* journalist took the time to find out that this fundamental relationship is what has kept that system functioning for over fifty years. As Raymond Bonner writes:

Most Latin American countries have been controlled by economic elites during the past couple of hundred years. But nowhere, with the possible exception of Guatemala, has their grip been as tight and long-reigning as in El Salvador. The Salvadoran wealthy survived, and grew richer, because they had formed an alliance with an ally far more powerful and reliable than the United States: the military. For fifty years, while the wealthy made money, the colonels and generals kept the peasants and workers in line.[27]

This history clearly illustrates that a progressive *coup d'état* would not meet with immediate success, simply by the disposing of one petty dictator. The wealthy elite and their right-wing cohorts within the military would not so easily relinquish fifty years of power and privilege. Entrenched economic and military practices are not so easily restructured, even though simplicity is a requirement for TV news. These historic details and analyses are beyond the scope of television.

[. . .]

'Pictures in our Heads' Lead to Interventions in Our World

> . . . the only feeling that anyone can have about an event he does not experience is the feeling aroused by his mental image of that event.
>
> Walter Lippmann[28]

Media images of chaos and instability in El Salvador are pernicious because they are fragmented and inaccurate, and facilitate standard interpretations. But this entire media configuration also has an effect on *realpolitik*. Feelings aroused by television images have an effect on the real world. They are acted upon; or worse, they preclude action. They promote hegemonic policies and forestall alternative courses of action. In sum, media images shape our world.

All of our worst Hobbesian fears of disorder and instability in the Third World are confirmed through law and order news; and it is happening in our own back yard via our collective living-room. The fragmentation of bits and pieces leaves the viewer in a state of confusion, but he/she hopes and believes that those in power, who direct foreign policy, have more information and know what they are doing.

The logical directions for a foreign policy based on law and order assumptions are obvious: the continued bolstering of the 'moderate' government and the quest for strategies to eliminate the 'radical' opposition. This is done through constant increases in military aid, because legitimate governments do not negotiate with 'violent radicals'. The role played by the media in forming public opinion produces a complacent public and stifles opposing opinions which call for alternative policy directives.

Quite literally, if the American public were made acutely aware of what went on in Central America behind the veil of the media images and discourse the implementation of foreign policy would be disrupted.

Conclusion

The purpose of this study has been to articulate one of the ways in which news messages, produced under conditions of relative autonomy, supported hegemonic assumptions of the developing world. Facts and interpretations which seriously question the legitimacy of the status quo are omitted from the media discourse. The framing of news under the constraints of hegemonic ideology is a much neater way of constructing the preferred interpretations of events than censorship. It is a process which makes the media all the more credible and influential. It allows the purveyors of the dominant culture to hold tightly to their claim of independence and objective disinterest.

As the networks, jealously guarding rating points, move closer to the genres of fiction, the more highly subject to hegemonic pressures they become. The use of highly denuded and etiolated narrative formulas facilitates ideological formulations. We have tried to show how telling exciting stories prevents the presentation of social and historical context through which the viewer might better understand foreign events. The real world, constituted through the movement of social forces and historical imperatives, is reduced to fragments; broken into bits and pieces. Fragmented glimpses, ripped out of context, are unintelligible – a baffling morass of 'random violence'. These selected bits are, however, reconstituted within an ideological totality. A familiar view of the world; one which does make sense. A world of assumptions and beliefs which pervade the production of media frames, and industrial culture in general. A world in which all questions are answered, motivations understood and common sense reinforced.

It has been argued that an essential understanding of foreign events will not be gained through the routinized application of a 'natural' language of given categories and prescribed themes, assembled into extraordinarily denuded narrative forms. Understanding of what can be considered 'truth', or at least something which more closely resembles reality, is usually found by looking beyond surface appearances and into essential functions, be they political motivations, historical facts, or social exigencies. Scouting the boundaries of surface appearances usually involves the use of more complex narrative structures, not the fragmented elements characteristic of television news stories.

The specific task of seriously examining news coverage of El Salvador during this period should not be slighted. Though not important by virtue of sheer quantity, it was the funnel through which all subsequent coverage flowed. It established the main interpretive categories to be used, and from that period to the time of this writing, news coverage continues to be affected.

A few examples: strategies such as the mystification of violence were continued and reached levels of absurdity in news coverage during the Carter presidency. In this way, the incredible loss of human life at the hands of the death-squads and security forces went unblamed. The moderate label affixed to the government has held tight through numerous reshufflings, even in the face of one of the most brutal periods of selective repression in modern memory. And finally, the belittling of the mass opposition movement, executed under law and order news, allowed subsequent coverage to discount the importance of the internal political dynamics of the country and subsume all political discourse under the external constraints of the East/West conflict; the interpretive framework which has characterized coverage during the Reagan years. Because television is a system of internal references, the constellation of law and order has itself become, for television, the history of El Salvador. It is always important to confront these myths with the literal history.

Notes

1 This well-recognized criticism of news coverage is also the title of a book by journalist Mort Rosenblum, *Coups and Earthquakes* (New York: Harper & Row, 1979).

2 There are numerous anthologies and articles which discuss the problem of the emphasis on disaster and disruption in news coverage of the developing world. See William C. Adams (ed.), *Television Coverage of International Affairs* (New Jersey: Ablex, 1982), and Jim Richstad and Michael Anderson, *Crisis in International News* (New York: Columbia University Press, 1981). For a long-term quantitative study of network news coverage of the developing world, see James F. Larson, *Television's Window on the World: International Affairs Coverage of the US Networks* (New Jersey: Ablex, 1984).

3 Americas Watch Committee and the American Civil Liberties Union, *Report on Human Rights in El Salvador* (New York: Random House, 1982).

4 This terminology was used during the time the author did field research with a freelance network news crew on assignment in El Salvador at the beginning of 1980.

5 There are numerous articles and books which discuss the topic of TV news as entertainment. See David L. Altheide, *Creating Reality: How TV Distorts Events* (Beverly Hills: Sage, 1976); Neil Postman, *Amusing Ourselves to Death* (New York: Elisabeth Siften Books, Viking, 1984); Elayne Rapping, *The Looking Glass World of Nonfiction Television* (Boston: South End Press, 1987). The news crew the author worked with would often acknowledge they were looking for exciting footage.

6 The TV news crew the author worked with in El Salvador at the beginning of 1980 often worried that if they did not get some dramatic 'bang-bang' their stories most likely would not be aired. One of their stories (aired February 1980) had file footage of a dead body edited on to it because they were not able to film any violence that week.

7 See Justin Wren-Lewis, 'The Story of a Riot: The Television Coverage of Civil Unrest in 1981', *Screen Education* no. 40 (Autumn/Winter 1981–2), pp. 15–33; also Cary Bazalgette and Richard Paterson, 'Real Entertainment: The Iranian Embassy Siege', *Screen Education* no. 37 (Winter 1980–1), pp. 55–67.

8 Wren-Lewis, p. 15.

9 Ibid.

10 Herbert Gans, *Deciding What's News* (New York: Pantheon, 1979), p. 57.

11 Wren-Lewis, p. 16.

12 Ibid.

13 Todd Gitlin, *The Whole World Is Watching* (Berkeley: University of California Press, 1980), briefly discusses a television news format which uses a story line. He states that the correspondent 'wraps it up', providing an ending to the story.

14 For a discussion of images of dogs, women and children as signifiers of normality, see Bazalgette and Paterson, p. 66.

15 Bazalgette and Paterson, p. 63.

16 W. Lance Bennett, *News: The Politics of Illusion* (New York: Longman, 1983), p. 24.

17 Wren-Lewis, p. 16.

18 Ibid.

19 Robert Armstrong and Janet Shenk, *El Salvador: The Face of Revolution* (Boston: South End Press, 1982), p. 130.

20 Armstrong and Shenk, p. 122.

21 Americas Watch Committee, p. xxxiii.

22 Armstrong and Shenk, p. 130.

23 Americas Watch Committee, p. xxiv.

24 Even though the collapse of the first junta did not make headline news in the United States, the resignation letter of Ungo and Samayoa was carried on the front page of *Le Monde*.

25 Americas Watch Committee, p. xxxiii.

26 This quote is recorded in both Americas Watch Committee, p. xl and Armstrong and Shenk, p. 120–1. It was originally documented by Amnesty International Report, *Report on El Salvador* (London: AL Publications, 1980).

27 Raymond Bonner, *Weakness and Deceit* (New York: Times Books, 1984).

28 Walter Lippmann, *Public Opinion* (New York: Free Press, 1922).

three

PLEASURES

AND

EXPECTATIONS

I
The Classic TV Detective Genre

MICHAEL WESTLAKE
From *Framework* no. 13 (Autumn 1980)

The pleasures offered by media texts depend not only on the sheer familiarity of generic content, the way in which we feel at home with repeated variations on a theme, but on the internal logic governing the material being repeated. In this article Michael Westlake suggests that as the detective genre moves from the cinema to TV, a subtle but significant reorganisation of the genre's logic takes place. A decade later, the patterns which Westlake isolates still seem to underlie the vast majority of TV law-and-order narratives, just as the genre itself continues to be central to television's notions of what constitutes a satisfying Moral Tale.

M.A./J.O.T.

The Classic Genre

The detective, from the beginning, has sought to do one or other or both of two things: the unmasking of the criminal, the capture of the criminal.

The former is possible through the destruction of the intimacy of the pre-capitalist world where everyone knew everyone else's business – this is the condition of the masking; and through the use of the rational deductive empirical methods of science by which it is known that things are not what they seem to be and that what they are can be ascertained by the application of the method – this is the condition of the unmasking. The detective is a scientist, committed to finding out the truth, what really goes on. So just as much as the rise of capitalism is needed to provide the conditions of anonymity through which the criminal can survive, so too it provides the methodology by which he can be unmasked. The detective is a modern man, as is the criminal. Both are free individuals, moving at will through the non-hierarchical legal space of bourgeois society, engaged in a struggle that apparently involves none but themselves. Their independence is, of course, an illusion: each is bound to the other by the Law that divides them, and the existence of which, in turn, depends upon the existence of the State. And the State is fictionalised as the necessity required to protect men from themselves. So is the public born, that fiction whose safety is guaranteed by the detective acting ultimately in the name of Law; that same reading film-going public whose sympathy lies with the criminal while it condemns the crime.

At the moment of capture, too, the same four elements will converge: the detective who has tracked down the criminal, the State in its repressive aspect ready with the handcuffs, the public, mute witness to what is going on in its midst.

Of the various relationships among the elements of the structure, that between the criminal and the detective is pivotal. Without it the rest of the structure would collapse. The detective and the criminal engage across the differentiating mark of the Law: that which keeps them distinct, prevents their curious symmetry from collapsing into identity. Yet the Law is a barrier that can be crossed. In the pursuit of the criminal, the detective must know him, be as him, though not, finally, identical with him. And the criminal, in his flight, must preserve the mask of respectability, must appear to be on the right side of the Law. In his thought, he constructs and acts upon the image of abiding by the Law – until such time as he is unmasked and has to use his resources of action to remain free.

The detective, too, does in thought what the criminal does in reality. He must 'reconstruct' the crime. He must 'get to know the criminal mind'. In this respect the detective is analogous to the censor, whether film or Freudian. To function, the censor must see the film, read the book, know the inadmissible thought in order to deem it unsuitable for public or conscious consumption. As such, he is set apart, is given a peculiar status at once within and beyond the Law. His special rights and duties – my emphasis is now upon the detective – makes him something of an outlaw himself, a bit touched (by what he has seen or thought), given over to moods or marginal behaviour. Such strangeness may be underlined by foreignness, or physical disability (one thinks of Oedipus), or social ex-centricity. He cannot be the same as one of us, the public. But – and this an important but – his entry into the realm of the repressed cannot entirely win him over to the other side, for if it did he would in fact be indistinguishable from the criminal. To resist the temptations which his practice offers him – we know, were he the criminal, that he would get away with it, for who would there be to outwit or catch him? – he must, like the censor, be made of stern stuff. He can resist the lure of what is beyond the law, the various offers made, not for fear of being caught – for he wouldn't be – but because within himself he embodies the Law. His own conscience is the guarantor of his immunity. In this respect, too, he is different from us, the public, who need the law to protect us from ourselves.

The detective, then, is the bearer of the Law who can pass beyond the frontier of law without breaking it. Symbolically, the detective cannot fail to bring to mind the figure of the good father who respects the Law, having acknowledged the castrating power of his own father. The criminal, on the other hand, having the power but not the knowledge of how not to use it, is what the detective would have been had he not made his sacrifice – Moriarty, the master criminal, Holmes' alter ego. The detective must continually track down his own repressed in order that it will not return and destroy the uneasy peace.

Just as the detective is bound to the criminal, so too is the criminal fixated on the detective, as authority, against whom, in some sense, all his criminal acts are directed, his whole project orientated. He is the child monster grown up having refused the token castration that would have socialised him. He can never escape the detective, in fact or in fiction, for his very identity is based upon the Law that gives him his name. In the end, we know – for that too is part of the fiction – he will get his comeuppance, will be forced to pay his accumulated symbolic debt.

The other terms of the generic structure emerge as subordinate to the dominant relation of detective/criminal.

The State has a determining position – it is the origin of the law around which detective and criminal pivot – that nonetheless cannot in general be acknowledged, and hence it crops up in odd and indeterminate guises which vary according to whether the detective is within or outside it. When the eye is private, the State, as the police, may be presented as incompetent (and in need of the intelligence of a Holmes), corrupt (and liable to hamstring a Marlowe), deferential (to Lord Peter Wimsey), etc.; when the eye is public the State is represented as faceless or nameless authority (one thinks of M in James Bond).

The public is the residual category, defined through its supposed demand for the State to protect it from itself. As public, as mass, it is liable to produce from within its midst that which will threaten its security; the State is the contractual necessity which will guarantee it continued freedom to be what it chooses. Such legalistic fictions are woven into the texture of the fiction which the thus-constituted public consumes (reads, watches) in the satisfaction of its desire to both break and uphold the law. The public wavers before the twin images set up before it, the image of the lawbreaker, the image of the upholder of the law; and as a complement, it rebukes the other terms of the quartet, that which it is supposed to be and suspects it is not and that which is set up against it as a universal necessity, and whose representatives it knows, depending upon its class-rooted ideological disposition, as amiable servants or unamiable masters. The detective fiction enacts the imaginary separation of 'publicity' into that which hides and that which seeks, into that which flees and that which makes the capture. The public dissolves in its failure to identify with the constitutional myth of its own being public. The struggle of detective and criminal, each of whom emerges from the would-be homogenous public, symbolises the irruption of class into the unity invoked by bourgeois ideology.

The TV Genre

The structure outlined above represents an abstraction which may never find itself fully represented in any one instance of the genre. Particular instances will deviate through the suppression of particular elements within the structure or shifts along axes of possible variance. A number of such suppressions and shifts are discussed in what follows.

The analysis is limited to the genre as a whole, and would benefit from individual analyses of particular examples of the genre. A further point is that the term 'TV genre' is taken to refer to the characteristic products since the genre achieved dominance – thus my remarks may not be applicable to early shows like

Highway Patrol and *Dixon of Dock Green*, which have more in common with the classic genre.

Four distinct features, then, are the nodal points of the discussion: (a) the detective is a cop, (b) his/her primary aim is capture rather than unmasking, (c) the figure of the criminal is largely suppressed, (d) violence is emphasised.

(a) The police detective necessarily has a different relation to the State from the private eye, since he/she is a part of it, but beyond this necessity are a number of contingent aspects characteristic of the T V genre. On the one hand the State figures as 'the courts', which need to be convinced of the guilt of the criminal – something both detective and viewer knows as a fact. Guilt is established beyond all reasonable doubt (one of the consequences of realism) before the criminal is ever brought to court, only the guilty are charged, innocence before proven guilt is a legalistic fiction, and verdicts of not-guilty mean only that the guilty party has got away with it. Thus the judiciary is represented as an obstacle in the way of justice; and the police as bearers of judicial truth. The prosecution is always in the right, and the defence consists of fools or rogues.

The State also figures as 'the politicians'. Again, the implications are that 'City Hall' or 'councillor Jones' are obstructing the course of justice in their well-meaning (sometimes) attempts to preserve the judicial notions of liberal democracy. Either the politicians are the dupes of the criminals, or they themselves are marginally criminal (this distrust is more pronounced in U S products). The upshot of all this is that the logic of the relation of police to State is that the police would be better off without the State; that is to say, the State which would suit the police best, and by implication the public, is the police state.

Next, by virtue of his/her insertion into the State, the T V detective has less need of reliance on his/her own conscience. Instead of the private eye who carries the moral law entirely within himself, the T V cop has a boss. The law is carried within the organisation, within the police, not within the individual. One consequence of this is that individual cops may be shown to be corruptible (though not the stars) without threatening the incorruptibility of the force as a whole. Another aspect of the detective as cop arises in respect to the police station, the site of the organisation of which he/she is a part. In general the atmosphere is one of support and solidarity (in striking contrast to the representation of the world outside). The cop can count on the support of his/her buddies. Such generalised representation of *gemeinschaft* is of particular importance when it comes to considering the possible forms of identification offered to the viewer. The detective at once offers an identity that is secure, competent and 'individual', and that can rely upon the support, trust, affection of his/her colleagues. Individuality plus community, in fact. (Examples of one without the other would be the private eye – individuality, no community – and the soldier – community, not much individuality.) Exactly why the appeal of this combination should be so strong currently is not clear. More obvious is the contemporary relevance of other forms of reassurance. To show the police as 'human', rational, non-sadistic, protective of the innocent, and so on, without doubt satisfies a desire that this might be the case when rumours to the contrary are increasingly rife.

(b) The T V detective fiction is centred around the theme of capture rather than unmasking. There is no doubt, generally speaking, about the identity of the criminal either in the mind of the viewer or that of the cop (though it may take the latter some little time to reach the conclusion that's been forced on the viewer by what's shown on the screen). The task of the cop, then, is to catch the criminal; or catch him out, that is, using the rules of the bourgeois game, to be in a position to provide the evidence to make the charge stick. Again, there is the implication that the task of catching the criminal would be that much easier were it not for the necessity of having to come up with the evidence to convince a court of his guilt.

The methods used reflect the task. Instead of the methodology of the scientist finding the reality behind the appearance, there are the purely technical problems of constructing or finding the evidence and catching the criminal. The individual scientific discoverer becomes the technician with the resources of the organisation to back him up. The production of the effects of knowledge replaces the production of knowledge itself.

(c) The figure of the criminal is largely suppressed. Instead of the antagonist, almost but not quite equal to the detective of the classic genre, T V series offer a collection of malcontents, misfits, psychopaths, neurotics and juveniles. Holmes' Moriarty and Bulldog Drummond's Carl Peterson have given way to Kojak's junkie and Barlow's tearaway. The criminal is no longer the rational if evil man who has chosen crime for gain or pleasure; he is the irrational victim of circumstances beyond his control. This inequality is compounded by the regular appearance of cop heroes, contrasted with the one-off and into oblivion of the criminal. The criminal is defeated, not in the end as in the classic genre, but from the very beginning.

A double process would appear to be going on here. On the one hand there is the recuperation of the notion that people are determined by circumstances, though without the concomitant notion that this discovery obviates the point of retribution – the State still exacts revenge even though it is implied that the criminals have been chosen by a way of life rather than the other way round. On the other hand there is a process of denial that there could be any advantage to crime, since no one who was fully sane could be anything other than a law-abiding citizen. The putative identity between the detective and the criminal of the classic genre has largely disappeared. The detective now includes ethnic, 'hip' or counter-cultural values enabling him/ her to enter the criminal mind: Kojak is Greek, the Anglo-Saxon enclosure of 'Hutch' contains the elemental (and East European) openness of 'Star-Sky'. But the reciprocal finding of detective and criminal, one in the other, has been replaced by recuperation: identity gives way to incorporation from the side of the State.

(d) T V serials are preoccupied with certain topical crimes of violence: mugging, drugs, extortion, robbery with violence, G B H, and, above all, murder. Other violent crimes are relatively ignored: rape, infanticide, wife-beating. The explicit and extensive violence on the part of both criminals and police contrasts with the classic genre in which the struggle takes place in the realm of thought for the most part, even when the original crime may have been of a violent nature. The classic genre sublimates the violence that is necessarily attendant upon repression. The rules of the bourgeois game are not called into question. The criminal knows when 'it's a fair cop' and allows himself to be meekly taken into custody. Any violence that does occur is generally clean and decisive; and the violence of the State is usually non-explicit and is anyway known as force.

Several comments are appropriate here. Firstly, the release of the violence of the repressed (in the T V genre), of the criminal, calls into being the violence of the repressor to cope with it. There is a sense in which the lowering of self-repression on the part of the criminal – much less of a criminal superego, in fact – requires a surplus of violence to keep the anti-social repressed precisely repressed. It is not difficult to trace a recent historical expression of this theme in the relative lowering of repression, both in the political and psychoanalytic sense, in the sixties, followed by, in politics at least, an increase in the seventies.

Secondly, the violence of the criminal threatens the public – both in the fiction, and as viewer – in a way which the more discriminate violence of the classic genre rarely did. The violence of the cop provides imaginary satisfaction of the desire to wreak vengeance; and the threat legitimates the counter-violence employed by the State. The imaginary resolution of real fears (for urban violence has been increasing) at the same time increases those fears in that it requires the return of the imaginary threat. Hence a return to the screen for further reassurance.

Thirdly, the arbitrary and random nature of criminal violence in the T V genre increases the sense of threat. Anyone may be attacked anywhere, anytime, it would seem; hence the demand for pre-emptive violence on the part of the State. The satisfaction of this demand has yet to be carried out in the T V detective genre, quasi-fascist strands notwithstanding.

To sum up, then: the classic genre can be defined around four elements (detective/criminal/the State/the public) in which the criminal-detective relationship is pivotal. The innovations of the recent T V genre can be marked off against this outline: the detective is a cop whose aim is capture rather than unmasking, the figure of the criminal is suppressed and violence is foregrounded.

▋▋
Melodrama, Serial Form and Television Today

JANE FEUER
From *Screen* vol. 25 no. 1 (January–February 1984)

Melodrama, as a popular cultural form, has become increasingly recognised as an important critical concept for Film and T V Studies through the 1980s. As Jane Feuer indicates, this work was largely British-initiated in the 1970s. In its earliest manifestations this criticism focused on the way style transcended and ruptured narrative flow – thus were the U s films of Douglas Sirk *et al.* read by critics around *Screen*, as contesting and exposing the dominant ideology embodied in the conventions of melodrama.

Feuer both critiques this position and also briefly outlines work which developed and 'sophisticated' it. Out of the recognition that melodrama both problematises questions of audience (in particular the notion of single readings) and requires a notion of *excess* in film criticism, Jane Feuer seeks to assess the critical value of such concepts when applied to the world's most successful television programmes of the 1980s – the North American produced prime time series such as *Dallas* and *Dynasty*.

The Hollywood melodramas of the 1950s are here considered to share certain features with these 1980s T V serials but it is their points of divergence and difference which Feuer finds to be most critically productive. Thus she provides a useful schematic outline of some of these key differences and their implications, for example narrative closure versus non-closure; the attainment of marital happiness versus marriage as the site of bourgeois dis-harmony. Finally, using the socially-conscious situation comedy of the 1970s (a genre unique to the U s) as a point of comparison, Feuer argues that T V melodrama, while not textually offering a political critique of the family in 'late capitalism', nevertheless offers a series of particularly open texts which explore cultural contradictions thereby making available a wide range of critical responses and audience positions.

M.A./J.O.T.

'The indulgence of strong emotionalism; moral polarization and schematization; extreme states of being, situations, action; overt villainy, persecution of the good, and final reward of virtue; inflated and extravagant expression; dark plottings, suspense, breathtaking peripety' . . . What Peter Brooks calls the 'everyday conno- tations' of the term 'melodrama'[1] describes almost perfectly the current form-in- dominance on American network television: the continuing serial or 'soap opera'. Although only a few years ago there seemed to be no equivalent on prime-time television[2] to the film melodramas of the 1950s recently rescued from obscurity by film theorists, we now find the domestic melodrama encroaching upon the domain of the sitcom and the cop show. At the same time, daytime soap operas are expanding, having risen to an astonishing peak of popularity.[3] Indeed awareness of their own significance seems to have reached the producers of daytime dramas. In a 1982 broadcast of the immensely popular daytime soap *All My Children*, a young woman character, Silver Kane, begged her sister's lover to get her a part on a soap, explaining what an honour that would be – they even teach them in college, she tells him, as a form of 'folk drama'.

For the purposes of this article, I am choosing to stress the similarities between daytime soaps and the prime-time continuing melodramatic serials such as *Dallas*, *Dynasty*, *Falcon Crest*, *Knots Landing*, *Flamingo Road* and the short-lived *Bare Essence*. I do this because I feel they have overriding similarities in terms of the theories I will discuss. Daytime and prime-time serials share a narrative form consisting of multiple plot lines and a continuing narrative (no closure). Both concentrate on the domestic sphere, although the prime-time serials also encompass the world of business and power (designed to appeal to the greater number of males in the evening viewing audience).

However, there are significant differences between the two forms, some of which will come out in my discussion. In *The Soap Opera*, Muriel Cantor and Suzanne Pingree do not consider the prime-time programmes or other related programmes (e.g. limited serials such as the British *Forsyte Saga* or U S mini-series) to fit their definition of soap opera.[4] They believe the primary difference is one of 'content'. Prime-time serials, they state, have a less conservative morality, deal with power and big business, and contain more action. They believe the most significant difference is that daytime soap operas are manifestations of women's culture, and prime-time serials are not. Although these are significant points, much of what I will argue in this paper transcends the distinction between the two forms. I would also argue that due to the influence of prime-time serials, many daytime soaps have added amoral wealthy families and faster action. Moreover, by excluding so many distant relatives of the daytime soap (including the serial cop show *Hill Street Blues* and the serial medical show *St Elsewhere*), Cantor and Pingree are unable to stress the pervasive influence of serial form and multiple plot structure upon *all* of American television. I will use the term 'television melodrama' to encompass both and to exclude other program types which take the form of episodic series as opposed to continuing serials.

Fortunately, we need not start from scratch in studying the new form of the prime-time melodramatic serial. Melodrama has flourished before, and we can benefit from the body of ideas surrounding Hollywood melodramas of the 1950s. I would like to begin by surveying and offering a critique of that theory, and then go on to consider its possible applications to the prime-time continuing serials *Dallas* and *Dynasty*.

Initially, critical interest in the films of Sirk bore little relationship to interest in the still-despised genre in which he most often worked. Quite the contrary: interest in Sirk stemmed from an extreme formalist tendency in *auteur* criticism, an attempt to bypass the narrative level in order to capture pure expressivity through *mise en scène*. *Mise en scène* critics were drawn to Sirk (as to other melodramatists such as Minnelli and Ophuls) for the way in which his style seemed to transcend the narrative level. In a much more sophisticated way, interest in style seemingly for its own sake dominated expositions of Sirk's films in several articles in the 1972 Edinburgh booklet on Sirk,[5] extending positions taken in the Summer 1971 issue of *Screen*.[6] One of these essays, Paul Willemen's 'Distanciation and Douglas Sirk', links the early interest in Sirk as a stylist to a new interest in a level of style which precludes audience identification in the usual sense.[7] Because this 'Brechtian' position haunts Sirk criticism from this point on, it is worth summarising in some detail.

Willemen explains Sirk's style as an 'intensification' of generic practices, not as irony *per se*. Since he had to appeal to a mass audience, Sirk drew on Expressionist and Brechtian theatrical experience 'not to break the rules ... but to intensify them'. According to Willemen, this was accomplished through the magnification of emotionality, use of pathos, choreography and music, and through aspects of *mise en scène* such as 'mirror-ridden walls'. Such intensification puts a distance, though not necessarily one perceived by the audience, between 'the film and its narrative pretext'. Even if not perceived by the mass audience, Willemen argues, distanciation 'may still exist within the film itself'. According to this view, a discrepancy exists between the audience Sirk is aiming at and the audience he knows will come to his films. The 'formalist' critics had also conceptualised a rupture between the narrative/dramatic and the filmic codes in Sirk. Willemen's hypothesis gives us an explanation for this rupture.

Following Willemen's logic, one must conceptualise a Sirk film as two films in one. The 'primary' text, the one which the mass audience will read and which consists of the narrative level, is melodrama, pure and simple. Whereas the secondary text springs from the distance 'intensification' opens up between Sirk's formal level and his narrative/dramatic generic level. For melodrama itself, according to this line of reasoning, lies fully within the 'dominant ideology'. Stylisation, Willemen argues, 'can also be used to parody the stylistic procedures which traditionally convey an extremely smug, self-righteous and *petit bourgeois* world view paramount in the American melodrama'.[8] Willemen proceeds to place Sirk's work in the category of films which – according to the well-known classification system of post-'68 *Cahiers* – turns out to be ambiguous in terms of the dominant ideology even though, at first glance, they may seem to rest fully within such an ideology.

This is the theoretical justification for Willemen's interest in Sirk and the way in which formalist readings of Sirk's films may be linked to a new interest in film as ideology. To put it in terms of the 'two texts', the primary Sirk text is fully within the dominant ideology because the narrative/dramatic level consists of pure melo-drama, indistinguishable from any run-of-the-mill Hollywood melodrama (indeed two of Sirk's most lauded films were remakes). It is the secondary text, which, through authorial intervention at the level of *mise en scène* is subversive of this dominant ideology. However, in actual practice, distinguishing between the two texts can be difficult.[9] If it is true that only an *auteur* such as Sirk is capable of bringing stylistic pressure to bear upon the purely ideological melodramatic ma-terial and thus causing it to 'rupture' and reveal its own textual gaps in terms of the dominant ideology, then only an elite audience, indeed one already committed to subversive ideas, would be able to read the secondary text. Such a position does not explicate the spectator position melodrama allows for its intended audience.

Out of this impasse emerged a number of theoretical articles which, while retaining notions of distanciation and rupture, nevertheless shifted the emphasis from a specifically authorial and intentional subversive practice to the idea that melodrama *qua* melodrama contained the potential for exposing contradictions in the dominant ideology and for readings 'against the grain'. These new feminist and psychoanalytical readings open up the possibility of application to the distinctly non-authorial texts of American network television.

A close relationship between melodrama as a form and the ideology of capital-ism had already been stressed in Thomas Elsaesser's influential 1973 article 'Tales of Sound and Fury: Observations on the Family Melodrama'. Elsaesser traces the roots of the 1950s family melodrama to the eighteenth and nineteenth century sentimental novel in order to show that the form has always been embedded in a social context:

an element of interiorisation and personalisation of what are primarily ideological conflicts, together with the metaphorical interpretation of class-conflict as sexual exploitation and rape, is important in all subsequent forms of melodrama.[10]

Elsaesser argues that melodrama functions as either subversive or escapist relative to the given historical and social context. It is also relative to where the emphasis lies – upon the ideological conflicts or upon the happy ending.[11] Several other critics took up this emphasis on the exposure of contradictions, although they disagree as to whether the form is ultimately subversive or not. Geoffrey Nowell-Smith gave the debate a psychoanalytical slant, arguing that the audience knew the happy endings in melodramas were often impossible: 'a happy end which takes the form of an acceptance of castration is achieved only at the cost of repression'.[12] According to Nowell-Smith's view,

the importance of melodrama lies precisely in its ideological failure. Because it cannot accommo-date its problems either in a real present or an ideal future, but lays them open in their contradictori-ness, it opens a space which most Hollywood films have studiously closed off.[13]

Yet, other critics questioned the nature of the 'space' thus opened. In a feminist reading of Sirk, Laura Mulvey suggested that melodrama as a form opens up contradictions in bourgeois ideology in the domestic sphere. However, she sees the purpose of opening ideological contradictions as providing a 'safety valve' rather than as progressive. Mulvey believes this view of melodrama places it 'in the context of wider problems'.[14] One of these wider problems would be the relationship between melodrama as a form and the capitalist social formation. According to Chuck Kleinhans, the raw material of any melodrama consists in exposing contradictions of capitalism in the personal sphere. Kleinhans believes that the main contradiction melodrama explores is the expectation that the family should fulfil all needs society can't fill. His conclusion is that melodramas offer artistic presentations of genuine problems but locate these problems in the family, the place where they can't be solved. He sees melodrama as serving an important function for women in capitalist society, but sees its form as ultimately self-defeating.[15]

A few currents run consistently through the shifting theoretical viewpoints just delineated. Melodrama seemed amenable to a variety of theoretical approaches because melodramas seemed to encourage different levels of reading to a greater extent than did other 'classical narrative' films. Traditionally male-oriented genres such as the western or the gangster film did not problematise the reader in the same way as melodrama. Thus few articles appeared on 'The Western and the Male Spectator'. If one assumes, as early studies of male genres did, a non-problematic and universalised male subject, then westerns and gangster films can be studied by means of the textually-based structuralism in vogue during the late 1960s and early 1970s. Melodrama, in problematising questions of spectatorship and gender, demands reader-response based modes of analysis such as psychoanalysis.

Central to all the theoretical positions I have just enumerated is the concept of melodrama as creating an *excess*, whether that excess be defined as a split between the level of narrative and that of *mise en scène* or as a form of 'hysteria', the visually articulated return of the ideologically repressed. Despite the changing theoretical stances, all see the excess not merely as aesthetic but as *ideological*, opening up a textual space which may be read against the seemingly hegemonic surface. The key text for the theorisation of visual excess has tended to be Sirk's *Written on the Wind* with its intricately layered (and thus visually ruptured) mirror shots, phallic symbolism and 'hysterical' montage. More than any other film this oil dynasty saga seems to provide a prototype for *Dallas* and *Dynasty*. More than any other Sirk film *Written on the Wind* seems to occupy the same representational field as today's prime-time serial melodramas. Unlike Sirk's other melodramas and also unlike daytime soap operas, *Written on the Wind*, *Dallas* and *Dynasty* focus on the capitalist ruling elite rather than the bourgeois family. The address is not so uniformly from one bourgeois to another as it is in other forms of melodrama.[16] (Although of course the representation of the upper classes is intended to be *read* by a bourgeois audience.) Despite the similarity of representational field, today's prime-time melodrama does not take the same visual and narrative form as *Written on the Wind*. Unlike the texts upon which much of the theory of film melodrama has been constructed, *Dallas*, *Dynasty* and their imitators appear to lack visual excess as it has been described in the fifties family melodrama.[17] Moreover, they lack another element crucial to theories of textual deficiencies which run counter to the dominant ideology – that is to say, they lack closure.

Is there a potential for reading *Dallas* and *Dynasty* in terms of excesses and contradictions? Are these programmes the conventional domestic melodramas of their time which now seek an *auteur* to subvert them? Or do they already contain the potential for subversive readings? In the analysis that follows I will focus on some of the conventions employed in episodes from the 1981–82 seasons of *Dallas* and *Dynasty*. (The dates used throughout are for US seasons, rather than British transmissions.) My argument will be that excess needs to be defined not in terms of the norms for films of the fifties but rather in terms of those for television of the seventies.

Seen in terms of their own medium, the seemingly simple *mise en scène* and editing style of the prime-time serials takes on a new signification. Although *mise en scène* in *Dallas* and *Dynasty* does not take on the hysterical dimensions of a Sirk or Fassbinder film it does seem at the very least *opulent* compared to other prime-time programmes and certainly compared to the daytime soaps. Budgetary considerations alone show the emphasis placed on *mise en scène*. According to one source, 'Dynasty costs approximately one million dollars an hour because of the show's cavernous and opulent sets, not to mention the dazzling fashions worn by cast members.'[18] While there is nothing inherently subversive about such splendour, it does serve to take the family dynasty serials outside the normal upper-middle class milieu of most film and television melodrama. The very rich portrayed in these narratives exceed the norms of their audience both economically and morally; luxurious *mise en scène* objectifies such excess. But in order to fulfil the theory that excess leads to a counter-current in the text, some authorial voice would need to use the visual excess against the narrative level. This does not appear to happen. Although the programmes appear to be aware of their own splendid tackiness, they do not appear to set out explicitly to subvert any generic codes, as did the comic parody *Soap* or the ambiguously conventional version of daytime soaps *Mary Hartman, Mary Hartman*.

For *Dallas* and *Dynasty*, *mise en scène* would appear to function for the most part expressively, as in the so-called conventional film melodramas. For example, an unusually complex 'layered' composition in *Dynasty* featured Alexis Carrington in the foreground of the frame arranging flowers in her ex-husband's drawing room as Krystle, the current Mrs Carrington and Alexis' arch-rival, enters to the rear of the frame carrying an identical flower arrangement. The flowers externalise the emotions of the characters without in any way splitting the perception of the viewer. Another episode of *Dynasty* featured a classically Oedipal composition as Fallon, the father-fixated daughter, and her father Blake Carrington kiss over her baby's crib as Fallon's husband enters into the centre of the composition. To be sure, character relationships of an 'hysterical' nature are expressed, but the *mise en scène* represents this hysteria rather than being itself hysterical and thus calling into question that which is represented.

Excess in prime-time serials cannot easily centre upon *mise en scène*, for television's limited visual scale places its representational emphasis elsewhere. Acting, editing, musical underscoring and the use of the zoom lens frequently conspire to create scenes of high (melo)drama, even more so when these televisual conventions are overdetermined by heavily psychoanalytical representations. If, as

David Thorburn has written, all television acting is operatic, then prime-time soap opera acting must be positively Wagnerian.[19] In fact it is the acting conventions of soap opera which are most often ridiculed for their excess, their seeming to transgress the norms for a 'realistic' television acting style. Compared to Peter Brooks' description of melodramatic acting in the nineteenth-century French theatre with its eye-rolling and teeth-gnashing, acting on TV serials approaches minimalism; nevertheless it appears excessive in comparison to the more naturalistic mode currently employed in other forms of television and in the cinema, just as the overblown 'bad acting' in Sirk's films did for its time.[20] Yet both forms of melodramatic acting are in keeping with related conventions for distilling and intensifying emotion.

On *Dallas* and *Dynasty*, as on daytime soaps, the majority of scenes consist of intense emotional confrontations between individuals closely related either by blood or by marriage. Most scenes are filmed in medium close-up to give full reign to emotionality without obscuring the decor. The hyper-intensity of each confrontation is accentuated by a use of underscoring not found in any other TV genre, and by conventions of exchanged glances, shot duration and the zoom lens. Although television does not often avail itself of the elaborate moving camera and mirror shots Sirk employed in the fifties (and Fassbinder in the seventies) to Brechtian effect, these televisual codes appear to serve many of the same functions in terms of exceeding the norms of their medium.

Following and exaggerating a convention of daytime soaps, *Dallas* and *Dynasty* typically hold a shot on the screen for at least a 'beat' after the dialogue has ended, usually in combination with shot-reverse shot cuts between the actors' locked gazes. This conventional manner of closing a scene (usually accompanied by a dramatic burst of music) leaves a residue of emotional intensity just prior to a scene change or commercial break. It serves as a form of punctuation, signifying momentary closure, but it also carries meaning within the scene, a meaning connected to the intense interpersonal involvements each scene depicts. Another intensifying technique adapted from daytime drama is the use of zooms-in of varying speeds and durations, with the fast zoom-in to freeze frame being the most dramatic, as when it is used on a close-up of JR at the finale of most episodes of *Dallas*. For coding moments of 'peak' hysteria, *Dallas* and *Dynasty* will employ repeated zooms-in to close-ups of all actors in a scene. Reserved for moments of climactic intensity, this technique was used to create the end-of season cliffhanger for the 1981–82 season of *Dynasty*. In this case the climax was both narrative and sexual, with the zooms used on the injured Blake Carrington intercut with scenes of Alexis Carrington making love to Blake's enemy Cecil Colby. *Dallas* employed a similar device in a scene where JR finally accepts his father's death and we zoom repeatedly to a portrait of Jock on the wall at Southfork.

But it would be misleading to discuss clotural conventions as excessive without considering their relationship to the narrative/dramatic structure. For, as we have seen, moments of melodramatic excess relate to the serial structure of these dramas and occur as a form of temporary closure within and between episodes and even entire seasons. It is serial form, even more than visual conventions, which most distinguishes the contemporary television melodrama from its cinematic predecessors. And it is over the issue of serial form that arguments similar to the Brechtian and feminist positions on Sirk have been proposed in recent theories of daytime serials.

A concept of closure is crucial to an argument that the 'happy endings' in Sirk's films fail to contain their narrative excess, allowing contradictions in the text to remain exposed. According to several articles on this subject, the contradictions seemingly burst through the weakly knit textual seams, rendering closure ineffective. In this view a successful closure of the narrative would be seen as ideologically complicit with a 'smug, *petit bourgeois*' view of the world. However the Sirk melodramas question that world view by leaving contradictions unresolved.[21] But what becomes of this argument when the representational field of melodrama takes the form of a serial drama that has no real beginning or end but only (as one critic describes it) 'an indefinitely expandable middle'?[22] Since serials offer only temporary resolutions, it could be argued that the teleological metaphysics of classical narrative structure have been subverted.[23] The moral universe of the prime-time serials is one in which the good can never ultimately receive their just rewards, yet evil can never wholly triumph. Any ultimate resolution – for good or for ill – goes against the only moral imperative of the continuing serial form: the plot must go on. A moment of resolution in a serial drama is experienced in a very different way from the closure of a classical narrative film. Compare, for example, the ending of *Written on the Wind* to the re-marriage of JR and Sue Ellen Ewing in the 1982–83 plotline of *Dallas*. When, at the end of the Sirk film, Rock Hudson and Lauren Bacall drive off together, the meaning is ambiguous because too much has been exposed to allow us to believe they will live simply and happily ever after. However, any speculation about the 'afterlife' of the characters that a viewer might indulge in is just that, speculation. When on the other hand, Sue Ellen approaches the altar and JR, we feel a sense of impending doom (accentuated by having Cliff Barnes rise up in protest as a cliffhanger) that we *know* will be fulfilled in future plotlines.

Marriage – with its consequent integration into the social order – is never viewed as a symbol of narrative closure as it is in so many comic forms. Indeed to be happily married in a serial is to be on the periphery of the narrative. There are moments of equilibrium and even joy on TV serials, but in general we know that every happy marriage is eventually headed for divorce and that the very existence of the continuing serial rests upon the premise that 'all my children' cannot be happy at once.[24] Thus the fate of various couples depends not upon any fixed and eternal character traits, e.g. good/evil, happy/sad, but rather upon a curious fulcrum principle in relationship to other couples in the current plotline. Characters who represent the societal 'good' of happy monogamy with a desire to procreate are just as miserable as the fornicators. During the 1982–83 season, the two marriages that seemed above the vagaries of intrigue – those of Pam and Bobby Ewing, and Blake and Krystle Carrington – were torn asunder by obviously contrived plot devices. Even the implicit moral goodness of a character such as Pamela was called into question. In the plutocracies of *Dallas* and *Dynasty*, as in the more bourgeois worlds of daytime soaps, happy marriage does not make for interesting plot complications.

From this it might be argued that prime-time family dynasty serials in particular offer a criticism of the institution of bourgeois marriage, since marital happiness is never shown as a final state. Wedded bliss is desirable but also unobtainable. Moreover, that cornerstone of bourgeois morality – marriage for love – also appears to be demystified. Both *Dallas* and *Dynasty* deal with the economics of multinational corporations but they do so in terms of the familial conflicts which control the destinies of these companies. This is typical of the domestic melodrama's oft-noted tendency to portray all ideological conflicts in terms of the family. However, *Dallas* and *Dynasty* also depict the family in economic terms, thus apparently demystifying the middle-class notion of marriage based upon romantic love (e.g. JR's remarrying of Sue Ellen in order to regain control of his son and heir; the Byzantine interweavings of the Colby and Carrington empires in *Dynasty*). In one episode of *Dynasty*, Blake Carrington buys his wife, Krystle, a new Rolls Royce, telling her that he is giving her the Rolls because she is giving him a child. This would seem to reduce their love to a financial contract, thus exposing its material basis. Yet in a sense these characters are beyond bourgeois morality because they represent the ruling class. One critic has offered the interpretation that the transgressions of the *nouveau riche* decadents of prime-time ultimately serve to reinforce bourgeois norms:

Dallas, *Dynasty* and *Falcon Crest* give us the satisfaction of feeling superior to them: We can look down on their skewed values and perverted family lives from the high ground of middle-class respectability. When Angela Channing (*Falcon Crest*) coolly threatens to disinherit her grandson if he won't wed a woman he despises (the marriage would tighten her hold on the valley's wine industry), our own superior respect for love and marriage is confirmed. The prime-time soaps also confirm the suspicion that great wealth and power are predicated on sin, and, even more satisfying, don't buy happiness anyway.[25]

How can the same programmes yield up such diametrically opposed readings? According to two recent feminist studies, serial form and multiple plot structure appear to give T V melodrama a greater potential for multiple and aberrant readings than do other forms of popular narrative.[26] Since no action is irreversible, every ideological position may be countered by its opposite. Thus the family dynasty sagas may be read either as critical of the dominant ideology of capitalism or as belonging to it, depending upon the position from which the reader comes at it.

Of course most U S television programmes are structured to appeal to a broad mass audience and to avoid offending any segment of that audience. The 'openness' of T V texts does not in and of itself represent a salutory or progressive stance. Nevertheless, I would argue that the continuing melodramatic serial seems to offer an especially active role for the spectator, even in comparison to the previous decade's form-in-dominance, the socially-conscious situation comedy of the early-mid-'70s.[27] The popular press bemoaned the transition from these 'quality' sitcoms to 'mindless' comedies and 'escapist' serials later in the decade. The popular sitcoms of the 1970s – for example, Norman Lear's *All in the Family* and *Maude*, and M T M Enterprises' *The Mary Tyler Moore Show* and *Rhoda* – were engaged with their times, often to the point of encompassing overtly political themes with a progressive bent. *Dallas* and *Dynasty* seem by contrast to be conservative Republican programmes. The article by Michael Pollan goes on to argue that prime-time soaps duplicate the imagery of Reaganism and reinforce its ideology.

... both imply that the American dream of self-made success is alive and might be made well by releasing the frontier instincts of the wealthy from the twin shackles of taxes and regulation.[28]

Although the sitcoms contained overtly liberal 'messages', their strong drive toward narrative closure tended to mask contradictions and force a false sense of social integration by the end of each episode. For example, the problems raised by *All in the Family* had to have easy solutions within the family so that a new 'topical' issue could be introduced in the next episode. TV critic Michael J. Arlen has described this phenomenon very well in his essay, 'The Media Dramas of Norman Lear':

Modern, psychiatrically inspired or induced ambivalence may, indeed, be the key dramatic principle behind this new genre of popular entertainment. A step is taken, and then a step back. A gesture is made and then withdrawn – blurred into distracting laughter, or somehow forgotten. This seems especially true in the area of topicality . . .[29]

(It is no accident, I believe, that Norman Lear's subsequent (1976) venture into social satire took the form of the continuing serial *Mary Hartman, Mary Hartman*; nor that both *Mary Hartman* and *Soap* (1977) blended situation comedy with elements of melodrama.)

Prime-time melodramas by contrast can never *resolve* contradictions by containing them within the family, since the family is the very site of economic struggle and moral corruption. In these serials, the corruption of the very rich much more often stands exposed and remains exposed. If, for example, Blake Carrington reconciles with his homosexual son, it does not represent an easy resolution to or liberal blurring of the challenge Stephen's gayness poses to the disposal of the Carrington fortune. The temporary reconciliation merely portends yet another breach between father and son which does in fact ensue when Stephen takes his son and moves in with his male lover.

To put it schematically, the 1970s sitcoms dealt with liberal 'messages' within a narrative form (the episodic series sitcom) limited by its own conservatism. The prime-time serials reverse this, bearing what appears to be a right-wing ideology by means of a potentially progressive narrative form. This is not to imply that narrative forms *in themselves* structure the ideologies of an era. Quite the contrary. It would seem that the multiplication of social contradictions in the 1980s could not be expressed within the boundaries of the situation comedy. Narrative forms *do* have expressive limitations, and, in the case at hand, one can correlate a shift in the dominant narrative form of American network television with a shift in sensibilities outside the text. This is not to say, as many have argued, that the new serials represent a turning away from social concerns. The emergence of the melodramatic serial in the 1980s represents a *radical* response to and expression of cultural contradictions. Whether that response is interpreted to the Right or to the Left is not a question the texts themselves can answer.

Notes

1   Peter Brooks, *The Melodramatic Imagination* (New Haven: Yale University Press, 1976), pp. 11–12.

2   American national network television is divided into two major time periods, each of which has its own corporate division and advertising policies, as well as specific programme types. Daytime lasts from about 10 am until 4 pm. Its main fare consists of soap operas, quiz programmes and talk shows. Prime-time, so called because it is the 'prime' viewing period with the largest audiences and highest advertising rates, lasts from 8–11 pm. Most prime-time programmes have traditionally been episodic series, with the major genres being the situation comedy and action-adventure drama. *Dallas* started a trend toward continuing serial dramas in prime-time.

3   U S daytime serials are broadcast in the late morning and early afternoon on all three networks, five days a week, 52 weeks a year. Each day about 25 million viewers, 80% of whom are women, watch them (*World Almanac*, 1982). In 1982 there were 13 daytime soap operas on the air, most of an hour's duration.

4   Muriel Cantor and Suzanne Pingree, *The Soap Opera* (Beverly Hills: Sage, 1983).

5   Laura Mulvey and Jon Halliday (eds.), *Douglas Sirk* (Edinburgh Film Festival, 1972).

6   The formalist positions taken by David Grosz and Fred Camper are summarised in Jean-Loup Bourget, 'Sirk and the Critics', *Bright Lights* no. 2 (Winter 1977–8), pp. 6–11.

7   Paul Willemen, 'Distanciation and Douglas Sirk', *Screen* vol. 12 no. 2 (Summer 1971), pp. 63–7. Reprinted in Mulvey and Halliday, op. cit.

8   Willemen, *Douglas Sirk*, p. 28.

9   Especially since none of the authors I discuss offers as a 'control' group a detailed comparison to other 1950s melodramas similar to those of Sirk, Ray and Minnelli, e.g. *Hilda Crane* (directed by Philip Dunne, 1956) or *Peyton Place* (directed by Mark Robson, 1957).

10 Thomas Elsaesser, 'Tales of Sound and Fury: Observations on the Family Melodrama', *Monogram* no. 4 (1973), p. 3.

11 Elsaesser, p. 4.

12 Geoffrey Nowell-Smith, 'Minnelli and Melodrama', *Screen* vol. 18 no. 2 (Summer 1977), p. 117.

13 Nowell-Smith, p. 118.

14 Laura Mulvey, 'Douglas Sirk and Melodrama', *Movie* no. 25 (Winter 1977–8), p. 53.

15 Chuck Kleinhans, 'Notes on Melodrama and the Family Under Capitalism', *Film Reader* no. 3 (1978), pp. 40–8.

16 As noted by Nowell-Smith, op. cit.

17 I am indebted to the Melodrama Seminar at the 1981 British Film Institute Summer School for this point, and especially to Charlotte Brunsdon for the idea that 'melodrama' consists of an 'ideological problematic' *and* a 'mode of address', so that it may manifest itself in different forms in different historical periods.

18 *Soap Opera Digest* no. 7 (7 December 1982), p. 141.

19 David Thorburn, 'Television Melodrama', in Horace Newcomb (ed.), *Television: The Critical View*, 3rd ed. (New York: Oxford University Press, 1982), p. 536.

20 Peter Brooks, p. 47.

21 See, for example, Christopher Orr, 'Closure and Containment: Marylee Hadley in *Written on the Wind*', *Wide Angle* vol. 4 no. 2 (1980), pp. 28–35.

22 Dennis Porter, 'Soap Time: Thoughts on a Commodity Art Form', *College English* 38 (1977), p. 783.

23 This issue is addressed in Tania Modleski, 'The Search for Tomorrow in Today's Soap Operas', *Film Quarterly* vol. 33 no. 1 (1979), pp. 17–18.

24 See Tania Modleski, *Loving With a Vengeance: Mass Produced Fantasies for Women* (Hamden, Conn.: The Shoe String Press, 1982), p. 90.

25 Michael Pollan, 'The Season of the Reagan Rich', *Channels of Communication* 2 (November/December 1982), pp. 14–15.

26 Modleski, *Loving With a Vengeance*, and Ellen Seiter, 'Eco's T V Guide – the Soaps', *Tabloid* 5 (Winter 1982), pp. 35–43.

27 This is not to imply a quantitative conception of dominance. Rather, I'm referring to a hegemonic form, one which appears to be at the centre of a decade's ideology.

28 Pollan, p. 86.

29 Michael J. Arlen, 'The Media Dreams of Norman Lear', *The View from Highway 1* (New York: Farrar, Straus & Giroux, 1974), p. 59.

III

How A B C Capitalised on Cultural Logic
The 'Moonlighting' Story

PHILIP HAYWARD

From *Mediamatic* vol. 2 no. 4 (June 1988)

Postmodernism became the major theoretical cultural argument of the 1980s. Originating in France – in relation to the politico-philosophic tradition of Situationism – it was the English translations of some of the work of J. F. Lyotard and Jean Baudrillard, and the publication of a now celebrated essay by the American critic Fredric Jameson,* which led to major debates taking place in anglophone conferences and publications throughout the rest of the decade.

Postmodernism has proved a notoriously slippery term to define. It has been applied to all the areas of cultural production, and accounts can range from postmodernism as a stylistic form through to it being a stage of socio-economic organisation. Jameson himself proposes postmodernism as a homology between a stylistic superstructure and its economic base.

In this entertaining and suggestive article Philip Hayward applies certain postmodernist characteristics – such as the deconstruction and reorganisation of aesthetic categories of cinema – to an analysis of the highly innovative and successful U S television series *Moonlighting*. In the process he offers an interesting institutional account of how such a stylistically imaginative programme came to be made for the highly formulaic system that constitutes network prime-time T V in the States, intriguingly suggests that it is possible for producers to exploit the media literacy of the audience, and indicates just how it was possible for a series to adopt non-naturalist styles within mainstream popular television.

Postmodernism thus allows Hayward to celebrate what he terms the 'popular culture *bricolage*' of the pleasures offered in the 'experimentation, innovation and surprise' of *Moonlighting*.

M.A./J.O.T.

---

* 'Postmodernism, or the Cultural Logic of Late Capitalism', in *New Left Review* no. 146 (July/ August 1984).

By virtue of developing a series of bold formal precedents within mainstream television drama, the American romantic cop show *Moonlighting* has become one of the most significantly innovative examples of popular television to be produced over the last twenty years. While it is too soon to tell how its example will affect subsequent television drama production, its multiple violations of the established tenets of naturalism (within a successful and whole-heartedly populist format) look likely, at the very least, to have set a precedent for the development of further non-naturalist styles of drama within mainstream programming.

Following on the heels of the self consciously *quality* commercial programming style pioneered by the M T M company with series such as *Lou Grant* and *Hill Street Blues* (and subsequently developed by the producers of series such as *Cagney and Lacey* and *L A Law*), *Moonlighting* has succeeded in going further than simply proving that popular television drama can be made with intelligence and style. By drawing on audiences' familiarity with such contemporary forms as the fractured narrative and collage styles of pop videos and television adverts, *Moonlighting* has gone against the standard rhetoric of television bosses the (Western) world over and proved that that supposedly inert and conservative mass *the T V audience* can take (and even warm to) elements of anti-naturalism in mainstream drama.

To Delight

The series' innovatory significance derives from both its regular inclusion of markedly anti-naturalist sequences and the purpose for which they are deployed. Instead of featuring as neo-Brechtian *Verfremdungen* (alienation effects) in the manner of radical theatre and Counter-Cinema, they are employed as *Besonderheiten* (*features or treats*) intended to delight their audiences rather than estrange them.

This use of formal devices usually exclusively employed by the avant garde places the show not only distinctly outside of the vanguard of experimental media practice (as would be expected of popular T V drama), but also *at odds* with it. Despite superficial similarities, the series cannot be said to embrace any traditions of avant garde practice but rather offers a threat to them. In adopting many of the formal devices of the (once) *avant garde*, the show has actually both justified the literal meaning of that term (by leading the cultural mainstream into anti-naturalist territory) and showed that the original ground rules of the cultural conflict have changed beyond recognition. Instead of dreams of radical, analytically deconstructive television the media mutation of the late Eighties has followed hot on the prophecy of theory and witnessed an eclectic pillaging of once esoteric formal devices, pressing them into forms of popular cultural *bricolage* glacially unconcerned with niceties of radical schools or purist debates.

Moonlighting's strength, originality and challenge to aspects of avant garde (and/or *alternative*) media practice is in its subtle inter-textualities and formal devices being produced for a popular T V audience, *within* its own paradigms and with none of the cares of the avant garde and no allegiance to any movement or practice beyond that of populism.

Despite their undisputed achievements, the work of individual television mavericks such as Wim Schippers and Jaap Drupsteen or recent Video Art packages such as *Time Code* and *Ghosts in the Machine* have stayed resolutely marginal to popular broadcast television. Similarly, acclaimed anti-naturalist television drama productions such as John Mackenzie and John McGrath's *The Cheviot, the Stag and The Black Black Oil* or Jean-Christophe Averty's *Ubu Roi* have remained remarkable *causes celèbres* for their singularity (rather than example). *Moonlighting* is therefore both significantly different and paradoxical, having achieved its quiet coup from a resolutely mainstream position. In order to understand the nature of this paradox and the origins and success of the series itself it is necessary to understand the specific background of the American television industry from which it emerged. The structure of the American television system differs from that of most Western European systems due to its minimal regulation. In direct contrast to the sort of systems prevailing in countries such as Britain and the Netherlands, American television has a group of commercial networks directly competing against each other with very similar styles of programming. This leads to a highly formulaic approach which has channels often scheduling similar shows against each other at the same times – networks will for example have a cop show scheduled against a rival network's cop show, a sitcom scheduled against a sitcom, a games show against a games show, etc. A B C's *Moonlighting* springs from just such a scheduling battle.

During the Seventies A B C (overall America's third most popular network) managed to get top national ratings on Tuesday nights across America with a programme mix that included shows like *Happy Days* and *Hart to Hart*, but lost out in the early Eighties when a succession of new programmes flopped and N B C took their place with a Tuesday night mix that included *The A-Team* and *Remington Steele*. In 1985 in another bid to try to recapture the Tuesday night audience they introduced a new show called *Moonlighting* for a short six-week run as a direct competitor to *Remington Steele* (based around a similar male/female detective duo). While it didn't beat *Remington Steele* in the ratings, it did take a bite out of its audience. Encouraged by this A B C made a further series and moved it back an hour to compete with the key prime-time N B C show, the action-adventure *Riptide*, calculating that *Riptide* had a largely male audience and could beaten with a show with a mixed gender appeal. The calculations proved correct: *Moonlighting* won the ratings battle and re-established A B C as *the* Tuesday night network.[1]

It not only achieved best overall viewing figures, analysis also showed that it attracted a large proportion of the high-income bracket 25–50 year old audience (a section of the television audience particularly attractive to advertisers); and proved so popular that it acted as an *anchor* for the rest of the channel over the evening (pulling viewers to A B C). But this success was not without its pressures – the particular sort of audience that the show appealed to was notoriously fickle, not having the strong programme allegiances of other age and class groups. So in order to maintain an audience for the show it had to keep introducing new tricks and surprises into the basic format. The area it successfully identified and exploited was the media literacy of its viewers, the conversance of its audience with the conventions of both established television genres and contemporary and vintage Hollywood cinema. Drawing on this the series self-consciously played with these conventions in a way that its (largely college-educated audience) would both recognise as witty and clever and recognise as being premised on their own conversance. In clear contradiction to perceptions of American television and its *production line* basis as innately conservative, the series prioritised experimentation, innovation and, above all, surprise as key elements of its appeal; clearly locating the series' aesthetic within what Fredric Jameson saw as the fundamental characteristic of cultural production under Late Capitalism, where

... aesthetic production today has become integrated into commodity production generally: the frantic economic urgency of producing fresh waves of ever more novel-seeming goods ...

At ever greater rates of turnover, now assigns an increasingly essential structural function and position to aesthetic innovation and experimentation.[2]

Due to the importance of *Moonlighting* for the network and the emphasis on experiment and surprise (unusual elements in successful popular programming), A B C allowed the show's creative team (headed by producer/writer Glenn Caron) a substantially greater degree of creative licence than that normally allowed for series production. The basic production agreements were exceptional in themselves (allowing them nine days to shoot a fifty-minute episode rather than the standard seven days) but the show was additionally granted the almost unheard of licence of being allowed to go significantly over-budget (and over-schedule) on individual episodes if they were felt to *artistically* merit it. In addition, its creative team were given carte blanche to experiment with themes, styles, design, etc. no matter how odd or offbeat any of their approaches might appear.

As a result the *Moonlighting* series established a series of highly distinctive formal trademarks (such as the combination of quick-fire verbal repartee and fast cross-cutting which became a virtual *leitmotiv* of the series), developed a wide variety of foregrounded violations of naturalist conventions (of the sort usually only used within the avant garde or Art Cinema) and exploited the budgetary flexibility which allowed for occasional lavish big budget episodes (if offset by corresponding low budget ones). This allowed the series a notable variability which during the peak of its third and fourth series encompassed an unpredictable variety of episodes which ranged from *relatively* conventional attempts at issue drama such as *Every Father's Daughter A Virgin* through to such stylistically experimental episodes as those discussed below.

Though subjective preferences as to personal favourites obviously differ, three individual episodes exemplify the combination of sophisticated intertextuality, formal innovation and sheer audacious style that the series managed to produce at its peak: the highly crafted *mode retro* of *The Dream Sequence Always Rings Twice*, the sublimely eclectic *Atomic Shakespeare* and the self referential *bricolage* of *The Straight Poop*.

The Dream Sequence Always Rings Twice

Of all the episodes in the series to date, *The Dream Sequence Always Rings Twice* is the most studiedly elaborate in terms of both its construction of visual style and conscious reference to a single specific aspect of media practice. Built around two sustained monochrome dream sequences and framed by a slender plot line, the episode is both a successful and noticeably lavish piece of popular television and a finely honed example of that *mode retro* practice characterised by Jameson as distinctly Postmodern.[3] While none of the episode's formal devices are either significantly contemporary or particularly innovative in themselves (dream sequences being staple elements of cinema since the early days, use of monochrome/colour switches to indicate transitions between dual diegeses being previously used in films such as Powell and Pressburger's *A Matter of Life and Death*; and pseudo period-piece costume episodes being used in a variety of popular television shows from *Star Trek* to *Bewitched*), they are notable for being used as a framework to construct two particularly pronounced *mode retro* sequences which go beyond any *representative* approach to an actual past and instead concern themselves with *conveying* pastness *by the glossy qualities of the image, and* 1930s-ness *or* 1950s-ness *by the attributes of fashion*.[4]

Indeed so perfectly do the sequences exemplify the tendency identified by Jameson that they seem almost a programmatic application of theory to practice.

The original idea for the programme was substantially less ambitious than the final version. After making an episode which used the distinctive lighting and colour styles of *Hammer horror films* for a scenario based around a funeral parlour; the production team decided to make an episode which recreated the feel of classic 1940s Hollywood cinema. The initial idea was to shoot an episode which featured two black and white 'dream sequence' inserts, with these being shot in colour and processed into black and white at the laboratories, but director of photography Gerald Finnerman proposed a more ambitious approach. Finnerman successfully argued for the sequences to be both shot on monochrome film stock *and* filmed in different styles based on the contrasting 'house styles' of M G M and Warner Brothers during the 1940s. Since this required each dream sequence to be shot with different lighting set-ups and required additional work to get visual effects not usually attempted in standard television colour production, the episode proved significantly more expensive than usual. The additional outlay on shooting and the construction of the *Flamingo Club* set necessitated a budget which eventually rose to $2 million. As a result A B C decided to capitalise on their expenditure by promoting the episode as a one-off special (prestige) production and even hired Orson Welles to record a celebrity prologue. The publicity campaign and effectiveness of the black and white sequences secured high viewing figures for the episode and critical response was similarly positive, getting Finnerman's cinematography nominated for an *Emmy* (the American television equivalent of an *Oscar*), ensuring still further publicity for the series.[5]

The programme itself is by any standards (filmic or televisual) a highly crafted and inventive piece of work; both playing self reflexively on *Noir* conventions (particularly in the voice-over sequences) and also creating distinctly different visual styles for the two dream sequences (Maddie's Dream lit and shot in the bright glittery M G M style typified by *A Streetcar Named Desire* and David's Dream modelled on the low key gritty Warner Brothers style typified by *Casablanca*). But what marks the episode and its dream sequences out from such meticulous hommages as Robert Benton's Hitchcockian *Still of the Night* is their sense of supplementary excess, their emphasis on being a *simulacra* in the sense meant by Baudrillard, *a more perfect copy*. It is this aspect which locates *The Dream Sequence* ... within *mode retro* rather than simply *period recreation*. The sequences do not attempt to either recreate or even evoke a specific past style but rather work in a manner akin to that of Madonna's appropriation of Marilyn Monroe imagery for her *True Blue* album cover design and title track video – overtly signalling themselves as selectively intensified stylisations.

This excessive *amplified* stylisation is perhaps most perfectly crystallised by Shepherd's performance in *Maddie's Dream*, where her on-stage rendition of *Now Get Out* attempts to condense key motifs from Rita Hayworth's sexually charged performance in the title role of Charles Vidor's 1946 film *Gilda*. While Shepherd does not attempt the mock-striptease sequence from the original, her stage act both features her wearing a dress modelled on the legendary black strapless outfit worn by Hayworth for her film performance of *Put the Blame on Mame* (but significantly exposing far more of Shepherd's cleavage than the original did of Hayworth's – playing on the selective intensification of memory on the part of its audience); and recreates Hayworth's celebrated introduction into *Gilda*'s narrative, where she bursts into the picture frame throwing back her head in an erotic cascade of hair.

Atomic Shakespeare

If the hyper-stylised *mode retro* of the *The Dream Sequence Always Rings Twice* episode typifies one distinctive aspect of Postmodernism, the vertiginously eclectic narrative of *Atomic Shakespeare* represents another. Based loosely around Shakespeare's *Taming Of The Shrew*, *Atomic Shakespeare* deviates markedly from all the other episodes of series made to date by having a script written in iambic pentameters, being performed as a period piece in a set designated *Medieval Padua* and having such incidental sequences as a mock Chinese martial arts fight and a rousing version of *True Love* sung by Willis to a bride trussed in bondage at the altar. Aside from its evident delight in disorientating its audience by framing its highly unexpected diegesis with only the briefest of (and least explanatory) introductory sequences; its heady comic rush exhibits a pronounced irreverence and playfulness in its cultural reference which both parallels and transcends the practice of that contemporary school of architecture which incorporates motifs drawn from the suburban vernacular into even the most serious of its civic commissions (an approach first advocated by Robert Venturi in his manifesto *Learning from Las Vegas*).

But while *The Dream Sequence* ... episode is significant for its precise realisation of a tendency identified by Jameson, *Atomic Shakespeare* is significant for its deviation from his analysis, its textual style and approach emphasising the further development of cultural tendencies which have taken play since Jameson first formulated his study in 1983. Whereas Jameson's seminal work charted the broad stylistic shifts evident in a range of cultural production during the Seventies and early Eighties (asserting them as evidence of the emergence of a new cultural episteme complementary to the development of late multinational capitalism),

Moonlighting's *Atomic Shakespeare* episode is chiefly significant for being more a product of an *existing* rather than *emergent* culture. It represents an area of media production which has recognised, utilised and assimilated bricolage (defined by Jameson as a textual style which *proceeds by differentiation rather than unification*)[6] and moved on to a distinctive style of its own.[7]

Instead of simply pastiching its principal referent (*The Taming of the Shrew*) via *bricolage*, *Atomic Shakespeare* incorporates aspects of it in a more integrated fashion, wrenching it from its traditional cultural context, commodifying it as (popular) entertainment, fragmenting it and using it as a framework for a profusion of other styles and emphases. This approach effectively samples its referent in a manner more closely akin to that sampling technique used in recent popular dance records (such as MARRS' *Pump Up the Volume* and Bomb the Bass's *Beat This*) than conventional bricolage. Eschewing both parody and pastiche the episode affects a straight-forward modification of its referent which utilises the surface of Shakespeare's linguistic style (its iambic pentameters), its traditional period visualisation (in costumes, sets, etc.), its gender sparring and broad characterisation (a parallel to the series' own) as a loose (*ready-made*) referent whose more complex structures and meanings are not drawn upon to significantly reinforce its own meaning. There is for instance nothing about the episode and its relation to its Shakespearean referent which attempts a radical cultural statement in the manner of Marcel Duchamp's drawing of a moustache on *The Mona Lisa* for L.H.O.O.Q. nor a pastiche in the blankly parodic sense indicated by Jameson.

It is perhaps the novel (and thereby elusive) nature of its referential or interpretative mode which marks its contemporaneity (and which makes it resistant to conventional critical analysis – operating outside the paradigms of both 'High' and popular culture rather than simply blurring them). The ambiguous nature of its mode of address to its referent text was for instance tellingly reflected in the semantic confusion evident in a review of the episode which appeared in the *Shakespeare on Film* Newsletter (a publication concerned with monitoring the transition between the august literary-theatrical tradition and the profane media of contemporary film and television). Rather surprisingly, the review is somewhat disconcertingly positive, both praising the programme for its wit (in the traditional as well as contemporary sense) and noting its successful interpretation of the key character interaction of its referent.

But while the positivity of the review is in itself evidence of a surprisingly open-minded critical approach, it is the combination of this with the reviewer's fumbling attempts to classify its referential mode which most precisely indicates its unusual address; reviewer Jack Oruch tacitly acknowledging the irrecognisable tone and stance of the *Atomic Shakespeare* episode by labelling it as both a *radically altered adaptation* and a *parody*, praising aspects such as characterisation and general production, and only referring to features such as horses bedecked with B M W ornaments and sunglasses as *anachronistic and farcical* details, commenting overall that the episode: *freely departs from Shakespeare's text, honouring it only with parody*.[8]

The slippage in use of *adaptation* and *parody* (where neither seems actually to signify the concept the reviewer is seeking to articulate) ably indicates both the novel nature of the mode of textual interpretation and the difficulties involved in considering distinct contemporary modes and forms within the framework of conventional critical paradigms.

The Straight Poop

Despite the various degrees of complementarity and divergence between Jameson's analysis and the two episodes discussed above, it is perhaps *The Straight Poop* episode which best exemplifies just how far *Moonlighting* has managed to deviate from the standard format of naturalist television drama whilst retaining its audience.

Unlike other episodes in the series, *The Straight Poop* primarily re-works material from earlier episodes rather than developing a new one. Like *The Dream Sequence* . . . and *Atomic Shakespeare* it uses a skeletal naturalist framework in order to contain and contextualise its non-naturalist elements and (in this case) its non-linear narrative sequences. Its specific framework is a (fictional) investigative News report looking into the reasons behind the non-arrival of a new episode of the show. Using real-life T V reporter Rona Barrett, this strand of the programme imitates a location News recording (complete with shakey camera work, re-focusing on subjects during shooting, etc.) to investigate the reasons for the dispute between the Maddie Hayes and David Addison characters which has led to the halt in production.

Anderson questions the two protagonists about their grievances in two separate sequences which edit together incidents and action from previous episodes. But while the rapidity and rhythmic qualities of some of these montages (such as the door slamming, simultaneous conversation and screaming sequences) are so pronounced that they resemble the *Scratch* styles of video-makers such as George Barber, the episode draws on the conventions of forms such as the Pop Video, the on-air (and cinematic) preview *trailer* and the fragmented nature of American T V itself (with its frequent interruptions of narrative flow through commercial breaks) rather than any experimental schools of work. Its highly fragmented style and token over-arching syntagmatic is not then an example of any attempt at programmatic postmodernism, but rather a result of the programme's self commodification and evident delight in its own textuality (leading it to even incorporate a succession of its own *blooper* out-takes as a final sequence).

Along with this use of extended sequences of fractured non-linear narrative, the episode is also noteworthy for its complex play upon another key aspect of naturalist drama: the difference between the actor as *real-life* individual and as character in fiction and the suspension of the audience's knowledge of actors' *real identities* during the period of the fiction. The narrative of *The Straight Poop* involves a major dismantling of this on-screen/off-screen, role/actor division and employs a labyrinthine doubling to *score* its narrative *points*. In doing this, the show involves itself in a process of commodification which goes one stage beyond the classic Hollywood process of manufacturing stars and star status and effectively contrives to produce a star status for the show itself.

The construction of *star* status in the classic Hollwood system consisted of creating a glamorous identity for the star as a celebrity in addition to their on-screen roles and led to a fictionalisation of the stars in their off-screen existence (creating a triple role system – star in role – star in role as star – star as real (private) person (as much as the latter was possible)). But within the overall series logic of *Moonlighting*, however, the series effectively tries to construct off-screen roles for the David and Maddie *characters* through the representation of their on-screen characters as having a direct (though un-theorised and untenable existence) as the performing artists of their own roles.

The *The Straight Poop*'s scenario was inspired by Press publicity about the alleged (real-life) friction between Shepherd and Willis during production of the series. The episode therefore constitutes an attempt to represent this within the series; but significantly, in attempting to refer out to this off-screen publicity, had to abandon the traditional representational role and further complicate matters by a logical slippage where the David/Maddie characters were represented as responsible for the dispute which prevented filming of the show (which is of course an extra-textual function fulfilled by the 'real life' Shepherd and Willis characters). Thus David and Maddie effectively acted Willis and Shepherd acting David and Maddie as themselves (!) – this being further compounded by the appearance of the *real life* former husband of Shepherd (director Peter Bogdanovich) appearing in the narrative as a former lover of the fictional Maddie character but also referring to another ex-romance of his with a *model from Memphis* – Shepherd in her *real life* role. This *slippage* within the episode affects a clearly identifiable transgression of both conventional representation (the separation of signifier and signified) and a collapse in the surface-depth model; which both testifies to the accuity of Jameson's analysis of the advanced commodification of cultural artefacts and demonstrates how audience's perceptions and understandings have undergone a quiet and complementary shift symmetrical with that of cultural production.

Media Literacy

At the time of writing (March 1988) it looks as if the formal innovations (and pronounced budgetary flexibility) which marked the second and third series of the show have been largely dispensed with, perhaps never to return as the series continues to slip in the ratings. Shepherd's enforced absence through pregnancy was undoubtedly a serious destabilising factor, depriving the series of the key *chemistry* between the David and Maddie characters; but the producers' decision to experiment with in-series pilots for a comic format based on the Dipest Viola characters and produce a group of episodes (directed by Allan Arkush) which comprised little more than uninspired re-runs of ideas and sequences from earlier episodes, looks to have been a mistake with potentially terminal implications. There is of course no guarantee that an outbreak of anti-naturalist experimentation will sweep through either American or international television drama in *Moonlighting*'s wake (although the success of programmes such as the B B C's *The Ritz* seems to indicate its influential precedent); but the show has proved beyond any doubt that high ratings are not exclusively dependent on bankable cliches and that programme-makers can exploit the hitherto unrecognised media literacy of their audiences. At its best, in for instance the three episodes described above, the series has created not only examples of stylish drama for a tele-literate audience but also showed the potential for escaping the restrictive dogma of naturalism and opening up television drama to wider influences. This in turn offers hope that those programme-makers interested in formal innovation can escape from the marginal *ghetto slots* of T V Arts programming and move into the prime time.

Notes

1 For further accounts of A B C's scheduling and development of the show see Jack Curry, 'Can *Moonlighting* Save A B C?', *American Film*, May 1986, pp. 48–50.

2 Fredric Jameson, 'Postmodernism or the Cultural Logic of Late Capital', *New Left Review* no. 146 (July–August 1984), p. 56.

3 Ibid.

4 Jameson, p. 67.

5 For a more detailed account of Gerald Finnerman's cinematography for the series, see Bob Fisher, 'Tender Loving Care for *Moonlighting*', *American Cinematographer*, July 1986, pp. 40–6.

6 See Jameson, p. 75.

7 A shift also clearly evident in the work of British video artist George Barber, who has moved beyond the quintessentially postmodern style of Scratch Video which he pioneered, and developed a more integrated (though nonetheless eclectic and tangential) approach in the drama fictions of his more recent work such as *Taxi Driver II* and *The Venetian Ghost*.

8 Jack Oruch, 'Shakespeare for the Millions – Kiss Me, Petruchio', *Shakespeare on Film Newsletter* vol. 11 no. 2 (April 1987), p. 7.

IV

The Clinical Eye
Medical Discourses in the
'Woman's Film' of the 1940s

MARY ANN DOANE
From *The Desire to Desire: The Woman's Film of the 1940s*
(Bloomington: Indiana University Press, 1987)

Mary Ann Doane's *The Desire to Desire* (1987) typifies the strength of the strand of feminist film analysis and critique which has developed over the last fifteen years around notions of woman as screen spectacle. As a whole, the book tackles the difficult question of how the 'woman's film' of the Hollywood 1940s was even possible, given the assumptions of male spectatorship and patriarchal values within which the classical Hollywood cinema operated. In this half-chapter extract, Doane turns to a particularly striking theme within 40s melodramas constructed with a female audience in mind: that of the Doctor, whose on-screen knowing gaze deals somewhat differently with the fascinating/frightening feminine than do the other controlling male gazes of the time.

Discussion in this general area maintains a distinctly problematic relationship to psychoanalytic thinking: here, as elsewhere, Freudian and post-Freudian conceptualisations can seem both an essential starting-point, with profoundly liberating implications, and fatally committed to some particularly virulent versions of standard patriarchal themes. A fascinating aspect of Doane's writing here is how the sexism threatening the 'serious' Freudianism on which her enterprise depends can itself be seen in ludicrously magnified form within the film texts she is discussing, in the form of the Hollywood-*popularised* version of psychoanalysis. In these films, she finds, 'psychoanalysis is used very explicitly to reinforce a status quo of sexual difference'. Doane is also perfectly aware of a further irony in her argument: the way to look at these films today for the post-patriarchal spectator is itself metaphorically medical, with the text itself read as *symptom* of the phallocentric dilemma then and now.

M.A./J.O.T.

An important component of what Michel Foucault refers to as 'the fantasy link between knowledge and pain'[1] is the association, within patriarchal configurations, of femininity with the pathological. Disease and the woman have something in common – they are both socially devalued or undesirable, marginalized elements which constantly threaten to infiltrate and contaminate that which is more central, health or masculinity. There is even a sense in which the female body could be said to harbor disease within physical configurations that are enigmatic to the male. As is frequently noted, the word 'hysteria' is derived from the Greek word for 'uterus' and the 19th century defined this disease quite specifically as a disturbance of the womb – the woman's betrayal by her own reproductive organs. The patient whose discourse is read and interpreted at the origin of psychoanalysis, as the text of the unconscious, is the female hysteric. As Phyllis Chesler points out, 'Although the ethic and referent of mental health in our society is a masculine one, most psycho-analytic theoreticians have written primarily about women'.[2] It is thus as an aberration in relation to an unattainable norm that the woman becomes narratively 'interesting', the subject for a case history. A narrativization of the woman which might otherwise be fairly difficult is facilitated by the association of women with the pathological.

This tendency to 'medicalize' the woman is particularly strong in a cinematic genre often referred to as the 'woman's film' or 'woman's picture'. The 'woman's film' is a group of American films produced during the 1930s and 1940s which deal with a female protagonist and issues or problems specified as 'female' – problems revolving around domestic life, the family, the maternal, self-sacrifice, romance, etc. Often popularly known as 'weepies' or 'tear-jerkers', these films were addressed to a female spectator and, at least partially for this reason, are only now becoming the focus of a critical attention made possible through the conceptual framework of feminist theory. The genre provides a particularly rich image-repertoire of classical feminine poses – those associated with sacrifice and hence masochism, hysteria, and paranoia. Furthermore, because theories of spectatorship in the cinema have been dominated by the analysis of the male spectator,[3] the terms of address in the 'woman's film', terms which make it a somewhat aberrant form of the classical Hollywood text, open up a space for a potentially radical feminist re-writing of that theory.

One extremely significant sub-genre of the woman's film, most prominent in the 1940s when Hollywood attempted on a rather large scale to incorporate and popularize psychoanalysis as the latest medical 'technology', is a cluster of films which depict female madness, hysteria, or psychosis. These films manifest an instability in the representation of female subjectivity and situate the woman as the object of a medical discourse.[4] As the example of hysteria and the more modern conceptualization of hormones and their effects indicate, the border between physical and mental illness is often of little consequence in the medicalization of femininity. Represented as possessing a body which is *over*-present, unavoidable, in constant sympathy with the emotional and mental faculties, the woman resides just outside the boundaries of the problematic wherein Western culture operates a mind/body dualism. Hence the illnesses associated with women in the many films of the 1940s which activate a medical discourse are never restricted or localized – they always affect or are the effects of a 'character' or an essence, implicating the woman's entire being. In the majority of the films discussed here, the female character suffers from some kind of mental illness: depression, nervous breakdown, catatonia, amnesia, psychosis. Yet even in the films which focus on a physical illness or defect, such as *Dark Victory* (1939), or *A Woman's Face* (1941), where it is a question of a brain tumor and a facial scar respectively, the discovery or the treatment of the illness initiates a radical change in the very life styles of the women concerned. In *Beyond the Forest* (1949), Bette Davis ostensibly dies of peritonitis, the effect of a self-induced miscarriage, but her death is really caused by an irrepressible and feverish desire to leave her small town life behind and take the train to Chicago.

This blurring of the boundaries between the psychical and the somatic is predicated upon a shift in the status of the female body. When it is represented within mainstream classical cinema as spectacle, as the object of an erotic gaze, signification is spread out over a surface – a surface which refers only to itself and does not simultaneously conceal and reveal an interior. Such a fetishization of the surface is, of course, the very limit of the logic of this specular system, a limit which is rarely attained since it implies that there is no attribution of an interiority whatsoever and hence no 'characterization' (this extreme point is most apparent in certain Busby Berkeley musical numbers). The logical limit nevertheless exemplifies the system's major tendency and entails that the body is both signifier and signified, its meaning in effect tautological. The female body exhausts its signification entirely in its status as an object of male vision. In films of the medical discourse, on the other hand, the female body functions in a slightly different way: it is not spectacular but symptomatic, and the visible becomes fully a signifier, pointing to an invisible signified. The medical discourse films attribute to the woman both a surface and a depth, the specificity of the depth being first and foremost that it is not immediately perceptible. A technician is called for – a technician of essences, and it is the figure of the doctor who fills that role. Medicine introduces a detour in the male's relation to the female body through an eroticization of the very process of knowing the female subject. Thus, while the female body is despecularized, the doctor–patient relation is, somewhat paradoxically, eroticized.

The logic of the symptom – so essential to an understanding of the films of the 1940s which activate a medical discourse – is caught within the nexus of metaphors of visibility and invisibility. The symptom makes visible and material invisible forces to which we would otherwise have no access; it is a delegate of the unconscious. But even outside the specifically psychoanalytic postulate of the unconscious, the organization of clinical experience, as Foucault points out, demands the elaboration of a multi-levelled structure.

The structure, at once perceptual and epistemological, that commands clinical anatomy, and all medicine that derives from it, is that of *invisible visibility*. Truth, which, by right of nature, is made for the eye, is taken from her, but at once surreptitiously revealed by that which tries to evade it. Knowledge *develops* in accordance with a whole interplay of envelopes. . . .[5]

It is the task of the doctor to *see through* this series of envelopes and reveal the essential kernel of truth which attempts to escape the eye. Physiology and psychoanalysis share this system which posits a relation between different levels – a surface and a depth, visibility and invisibility. In breaking away from biology it was perhaps inevitable that Freud should do so through recourse to an illness, hysteria, in which the body is transformed into a text – enigmatic but still decipherable. In his case history of Dora (another 'woman's narrative'), Freud posits a privileged relation between hysteria and the somatic. 'Somatic compliance' is the concept Freud elaborated to designate the process whereby the body complies with the psychical demands of the illness by providing a space and a material for the inscription of its signs. He analyzes a case of a female hysteric whose contorted face can be read as a direct translation into physical terms of the verbal cliché for an insult – a 'slap in the face'. In *Studies on Hysteria*, Freud and Breuer delineate the types of symptoms which require that the body act as the expression of the illness: neuralgias and anaesthesias, contractures and paralyses, hysterical attacks, epileptoid convulsions, tics, chronic vomiting and anorexia, disturbance of vision, etc.[6]

From the nineteenth to the twentieth century, however, hysteria is subdued and the relation between mental disturbances and the space of the body is modified. In the 1940s films of the medical discourse, neuroses and even psychoses are evidenced not by contorted limbs and paralysis but by a marked lack of narcissism on the part of the sick woman. The illness of the woman is signalled by the fact that she no longer cares about her appearance. In the beginning of *Possessed* (1947), when Joan Crawford – clearly demented – walks the city streets misrecognizing every man for the one she has just killed, she is represented as quite plain, in documentary style shots, without make-up, in stark contrast to scenes in flashback of an earlier time when she was not yet ill. Still the victim of a psychosis at the end of the film, she never quite regains her 'looks'. This despecularization of the woman is present in films such as *Now Voyager* (1942) and *Johnny Belinda* (1948) as well. In both films the woman's illness is registered as an undesirable appearance. Charlotte (Bette Davis), in the beginning of *Now Voyager*, wears glasses, clumsy shoes, an unattractive dress, and is presented as being overweight, with heavy eyebrows and a harsh hairstyle. Belinda (Jane Wyman), before she meets the doctor in *Johnny Belinda*, is dirty and unkempt, her hair uncombed. In these films, as well as in *A Woman's Face*, the woman's 'cure' consists precisely in a beautification of body/face. The doctor's work is the transformation of the woman into a specular object. Nevertheless, the woman's status as specular object of desire is synonymous with her 'health' – her illness is characterized as the very lack of that status. The narratives thus trace a movement from the medical gaze to the erotic gaze in relation to the central female figure, activating a process of despecularization/respecularization.

The lack or impairment of a narcissism purportedly specific to femininity is hence symptomatic in these films. Although Rosa Moline (Bette Davis) begins in *Beyond the Forest* with a strong desire to constitute herself as spectacle, her fever at the end of the film is signified by her misapplication of make-up as she gazes into the mirror. Her lipstick exceeds the outline of her mouth and eyeliner is drawn on in a crooked line far from the boundary of the eye. Her dress askew as well, she is the figure of an impaired narcissism. The pathetic nature of her condition is emphasized by the fact that the signs of her excessive desire are inscribed upon her body in a hyperbolic manner. Because narcissism is the convergence of desire on the subject's own body, its opposite – over-investment in an object relation – is also symptomatic of a serious deficiency of narcissistic libido. In *Possessed*, Louise's (Joan Crawford) illness is depicted as over-possessiveness, as a relentless desire for a man who no longer loves her.

However, the classical film – and the medical discourse film, whatever its particularities, does belong to this category – also manifests a profound ambivalence on precisely this issue of the woman's narcissism. For its logic entails the possibility of a woman being overly narcissistic as well, a condition which inevitably signifies evil tendencies on her part (this is, in fact, the case in *Beyond the Forest*). The constant subtext accompanying the text of spectacle in the classical cinema proclaims that outward appearances do not matter, that an essential core of goodness may be veiled by a misleading, even unattractive exterior. The spectacular aspect of classical cinema, its concentration upon visual pleasure, carries within it its own denial. Hence, too great an insistence by the woman herself on her status as image for the male gaze is prohibited – it is unseemly, wrong-headed and potentially indicative of an illness associated with misplaced ambition. *Dark Mirror* (1946) links psychical disturbance to female narcissism and violence, via the shattered mirror acting as an endpoint to its long first shot and a more general emphasis upon mirrors throughout its narrative about twin sisters. In *Caught* (1949), the medicalization of Leonora (Barbara Bel Geddes) is synonymous with her despecularization. At the end of the film, the obstetrician's final diagnosis of Bel Geddes consists of a rejection of the object which at the beginning of the film epitomized the woman's desire, a mink coat ('If my diagnosis is correct, she won't want that anyway'). Because the mink coat is associated with femininity as spectacle and image – its first inscription in the film is within the pages of a fashion magazine – the doctor's diagnosis has the effect of a certain despecularization of the female body. That body is, instead, symptomatic, and demands a reading.[7]

Hence, there are two strong yet contradictory impulses within the classical cinema concerning the representation of the female body. The body is either fetishized as an object of beauty or de-emphasized as totally non-revelatory, even deceptive – this is the logic of 'appearances can be deceiving'. Yet the overwhelming force of the drive to specularize is manifested by the fact that the second impulse is not concretized through the representation of 'ugly' or even 'unattractive' women. When a woman is designated as 'plain' within the classical cinema, she is not really 'plain' in relation to any contemporary standards of attractiveness (Joan Fontaine in *Rebecca*, purportedly contrasted with the beautiful but significantly absent Rebecca, is a good example of this). Furthermore, instead of going so far as actually to depict a woman as having a face or body coded as unattractive – and unchangeably so – in order to demonstrate that it is the 'interior' which really 'counts', the classical text multiplies its figures of feminine beauty. This is particularly the case in identical twin films of the 1940s such as *Dark Mirror* and *A Stolen Life* (1946). In each film, the twin sisters look exactly alike but are essentially different. In *A Stolen Life*, the major male character refers to one twin as 'cake' and the other 'icing', comparing them on the basis of a distinction between substance and excess. But because the two women are identical in appearance, a specialist is often needed to allay the effects of this 'double-vision' on the part of the male, to penetrate the surface. In *Dark Mirror*, one of the twins has committed a murder and the other covers up for her, one is paranoid and the other relatively healthy. Because it is impossible to differentiate between the two on the basis of appearance – both are played by Olivia de Havilland – a psychiatrist is needed to *see through* the surface exterior to the interior truths of the two sisters, in other words, to perform a symptomatic reading.

In this branch of the 'woman's film', the erotic gaze becomes the medical gaze. The female body is located not so much as spectacle but as an element in the discourse of medicine, a manuscript to be read for the symptoms which betray her story, her identity. Hence the need, in these films, for the figure of the doctor as reader or interpreter, as the site of a knowledge which dominates and controls female subjectivity. A scenario of reading is provided within the films themselves, a hermeneutics of pathology which requires that the body approximate a two-levelled text. The doctor's look in the cinema, because it *penetrates*, appears to be closer to what Foucault describes as the medical glance rather than the gaze. The gaze observes an exterior, it scans a field, expanding in a horizontal rather than a vertical direction; it is 'endlessly modulated' while the glance 'goes straight to its object'.

The glance chooses a line that instantly distinguishes the essential; it therefore goes beyond what it sees; it is not misled by the immediate forms of the sensible, for it knows how to traverse them; it is essentially demystifying. ....[8]

The symptomatic reading which the doctor performs in these films by means of the instrument of the glance[9] unveils a previously invisible essence, ultimately the essence of the female character concerned. The ideology which the films promote therefore rests on a particularly extreme form of essentialism.

But the logic of the symptom might be used to read the film texts differently. Althusserian theory and strategies of interpretation derived from it assume that what is invisible, what the symptom indicates, is not an essence, as in the films, but a structure, a logic, in short, an ideological systematicity which is by definition unconscious. A symptomatic reading in this sense reveals what is excluded as the invisible of a particular discourse, what is unthought or what the discourse wishes very precisely not to think.

... the invisible is the theoretical problematic's non-vision of its non-objects, the invisible is the darkness, the blinded eye of the theoretical problematic's self-reflection when it scans its non-objects, its non-problems without seeing them, *in order not to look at them*.[10]

The non-object of the woman's film, what ceaselessly exceeds its grasp, is what would appear to be dictated by its own logic – the coherent representation of female subjectivity. Breakdowns and instability in the representation of female subjectivity are evident in all types of the woman's film, but in the films of the medical discourse they receive a special twist. For these incoherences and instabilities do not remain unseen or unrecognized by the texts; on the contrary, they are recuperated as the signs of illness or psychosis. In this way, the purported subject of the discourse, the woman, becomes its object, and her lapses or difficulties in subjectivity are organized for purposes of medical observation and study. The doctor is thus a crucial figure of constraint. Nevertheless, there are leakages which are manifested as symptoms in the body of the text as a whole.

The genre which is most frequently described as the site of this 'return of the repressed' is the melodrama. Geoffrey Nowell-Smith, for instance, explicitly compares certain strategies of the melodrama with the mechanism of what Freud designated as conversion hysteria. The text is seen as analogous to the body and 'the film itself somatises its own unaccommodated excess, which thus appears displaced or in the wrong place'.[11] The hysteria frequently attributed to the female protagonist in the woman's film often proliferates, effecting a more general 'hystericization' of the text as a body of signifiers.

Such textual hysterical symptoms are, as Althusser points out, 'failures in the rigour' of the discourse, the 'outer limits of its effort',[12] sites of the collapse or near-collapse of its own logic. In the films of medical discourse, these breaking points or ruptures cluster in several different areas; in what follows I shall concentrate on the assimilation of psychoanalysis within the Hollywood cinema, on narration and the woman's access to language and vision, and on the eroticization of the doctor–patient relation. The films I shall examine in some detail – *The Cat People* (1942), *Possessed* (1947), and *Beyond the Forest* (1949) – were not chosen on the basis of their 'typicality'. Rather, in the spirit of symptomatic reading, they are all in some ways extreme instances, limit-texts which inadvertently reveal the weaknesses or breaking points of a contradictory ideological project, that of a classical genre addressed to a female spectator.

Psychoanalysis in the Hollywood Cinema

It is not at all surprising that the medical figure in many of these films is a psychoanalyst, a psychiatrist, or a psychologist (Hollywood often makes no distinction between these three categories). For 1940–1950 is the decade of the most intense incorporation of psychoanalysis within the Hollywood system. Films like *Lady in the Dark*, *Spellbound* (1945), *The Cat People*, *Shock* (1946), *Nightmare Alley* (1947), and *The Snake Pit* (1948), exploited a growing curiosity about psychoanalysis and psychology. This incorporation is synchronous with a more general popularization of psychoanalysis in the late 30s and 40s which was at least partially stimulated by the influx of European refugee analysts, psychiatrists, and intellectuals at this time.[13] The movie industry called upon psychoanalytic authorities and experts to act as consultants for its productions and to guarantee the authenticity of its representations. Both *Dark Mirror* and *Sleep My Love* (1948) brought in psychoanalysts as technical advisors, and advertised that fact.[14]

The popularized version of psychoanalysis rejects what Freud theorized as a polymorphously perverse sexuality which is only gradually channelled in socially acceptable ways. Instead, it uses psychoanalysis to validate socially constructed modes of sexual difference which are already in place, although potentially threatened by a war-time reorganization. Hence, it is not surprising that women far outnumber men as patients in these films (in a film like *Spellbound* (1945), where precisely the opposite may appear to be the case since Ingrid Bergman is a psychoanalyst and Gregory Peck her patient, it can in fact be demonstrated that she is ultimately constituted as analysand – she suffers from a frigidity constantly associated with intellectual women in the cinema). When psychoanalysis *is* activated in relation to a male patient diagnosed as suffering from some form of neurosis or psychosis, the effects of the pathological conditions are often held in check, restricted and localized by linking the illness directly to a war trauma (e.g. in *Home of the Brave* (1949) and the documentary *Let There Be Light* (1946)). What is diagnosed in the women patients is generally some form of sexual dysfunction or resistance to their own femininity. (*Now Voyager, The Snake Pit*, and *Lady in the Dark* are examples of this tendency.) Psychoanalysis is used very explicitly to reinforce a status quo of sexual difference.

While most of these films situate the psychoanalyst as a kind of epistemological hero, the guarantor of the final emergence of truth, Hollywood is also cognizant of the potential excesses of psychoanalysis and its methods, of the other side of a science which purports to manipulate the mind. This problematic is elaborated in films like *Shock* (1946), *Sleep My Love* (1948), and *Whirlpool* (1949). *The Cat People* is by far one of the most intriguing of this group of films which investigate the unscrupulous or suspect dimension of psychoanalysis, for it elaborates and plays on two of the most important premises of the films of the medical discourse: the specification of the doctor or of the psychoanalyst as the pivotal figure linking the visible and the invisible in the construction of knowledge (about the woman); and the constitution of the female body as symptomatic and hence a vehicle of hysteria.

The Cat People, focusing on a woman's problem – what might even be termed a woman's domestic problem since it concerns the happiness of her marriage – is exemplary of the extent to which the horror film acts as intertext of the woman's film. Irena (Simone Simon) is obsessed with a legend concerning the Serbian village of her origin. This legend maintains that sexuality and/or jealousy causes the women of the village to be transformed into great cats, panthers, who take the men as their prey. According to the legend, a King John liberated the village by killing many of the cat people (Irena keeps a statue of King John on a horse, his sword raised high, impaling a cat). In America, Irena meets Oliver Reed (Kent Smith) who describes himself as a 'good old Americano' and who attempts to dispel Irena's belief in the Serbian legend. Oliver falls in love with Irena and marries her; however, because Irena fears what the legend delineates as the effects of sexuality, their relationship remains platonic. Kind and understanding at first, Oliver gradually becomes tense and dissatisfied and urges Irena to see a psychoanalyst, Dr Louis Judd. When Irena refuses to return to the psychoanalyst because he is interested in her 'mind' rather than her 'soul', Oliver begins to get more and more interested in the 'girl at the office', Alice, who is contrasted with Irena in every way. While Alice defines love as 'understanding' and 'you and me', Oliver describes his feeling for Irena as an obsessive need to watch and touch her because 'there's a warmth when she's in the room', despite the fact that he admits he does not know her at all. Irena's jealousy of Alice triggers several events which convince both Alice and Oliver that Irena can and does metamorphose into a panther. The psychoanalyst, however, a supreme rationalist, resists this hypothesis and is killed by the panther/Irena after he attempts to kiss her. Before dying, the psychoanalyst manages to stab Irena fatally with his cane/knife and she dies after letting loose the panther at a nearby zoo.

The Cat People is, on the one hand, the dramatization of a quasi-psychoanalytic scenario – the surfacing of the invisible, chaotic forces of instinct or the unconscious.[15] On the other hand, the film demonstrates the limits of psychoanalysis and rationality in general when faced with femininity. Forcing an equation whereby the unconscious = female sexuality = the irrational, the film can claim that the importance of psychoanalysis stems from the unfathomable nature of its object of study – the woman and her sexuality. The psychoanalyst's insistence upon rationalizing entails that he cannot *see* the 'invisible' of the woman precisely because it is coincident with the irrational and hence outside the range of his professional vision. In moving from an opening text constituted by a quote from the scientist, Dr Louis Judd, to an ending epitaph from a poem by John Donne, the film sustains a strict opposition between science and poetry, the rational and the irrational. This opposition is mapped onto what in 1942 was necessarily another heavily loaded opposition – that between the native and the foreign, the 'good old Americano' and the Serbian, the familiar (Alice) and the strange (Irena). *The Cat People* transforms the unconscious or the instinctual not only into an object which is, by definition, outside the grasp of psychoanalysis, but also into an object which incites its murderous impulses – it is the psychoanalyst's phallic cane/knife which kills Irena. Yet, her death demands that of the psychoanalyst; it entails the death of a science which purports to include what should remain excluded: female sexuality and all that is beyond conscious reason.

Thus, the psychoanalyst, rather than acting as a link between rationality and irrationality, between visibility and invisibility, becomes the figure of their absolute disjunction. This problematic has the effect of safeguarding visibility, rationality and the native/familiar from what is absolutely other. The film would like very much to believe that the symptom does not inhabit the norm, that visibility and invisibility, correlated with rationality and irrationality, occupy two entirely different spaces. Yet, the *mise en scène* belies the possibility of such a desire and hence the film operates on the epistemological threshold of the classical text's organization of the seen and the unseen and the dialectic which insures simultaneously their interaction and their separation. It dwells on the mixture, the composite, the effect of a transgression of barriers.

Although the image is indubitably the register of truth in the classical cinema, the place where knowledge resides,[16] there is also a kind of truth which is invisible, which cannot be imaged. The supernatural is one instance. The truth of a person is another. *The Cat People* conflates the two in the character of Irena. In the horror film in general, the unseen may appear to have a greater degree of truth value than the seen. This is why the horror film emphasizes the edge of the frame as a border and exploits the phobia attached to the truth of the unseen. But this fetishization of the frame-line as border guarantees that the invisible remains an alien external entity, excluded from a discourse which privileges the evidence of the eyes – once it is visible, the monster of the horror film can be fought and subdued. The very technology of the cinema automatically protects the realm of visibility against otherness. Yet *The Cat People* unwittingly elaborates a formal textual logic which, paradoxically, interiorizes the frame-line, constituting the division between visibility and invisibility not as a limit but as an alien internal entity. Such a strategy accomplishes what SSamuel Weber claims is characteristic of the mechanism of repression – it establishes 'a relation to exteriority at the core of all that is enclosed'.[17]

The Cat People does so by consistently elaborating a discourse on barriers, a discourse on the same and the other. Such, for instance, is the significance of the scene which dwells on the chain separating Irena from the panther in the cage at the zoo. Irena, pacing back and forth in front of the chain which in a way imprisons her, is the mirror image of the panther pacing in its cage. But the film has no difficulty in visualizing either Irena or the panther. What it cannot incorporate within the terms of its image system is the transposition of one into the other. In the famous scene in which Irena 'stalks' Alice, her transformation into a panther is represented by the movement from the sound of high heels to silence on the soundtrack. Irena's subsequent metamorphosis back into a woman is signified by the gradual conversion of tracks of paws into those of high heels.

Thus, what is most true for the film is never directly imaged – the compatibility and substitutability of feline and female. The narrative is a literalization of the idea that the female body is symptomatic and hence the vehicle of hysteria. The mechanism which Freud pinpointed as characteristic of hysteria – conversion, 'the translation of a purely psychical excitation into physical terms'[18] – is hyperbolized when the return of repressed sexuality demands the transformation of the woman's entire body into the symptom. The film depicts an extreme instance of 'somatic compliance'. And the choice of symptom is not innocent. In his article, 'On Narcissism: An Introduction', Freud compares the self-sufficiency and inaccessibility of the narcissistic woman to that of 'cats and the large beasts of prey' – as well as that of the child, the criminal, and the humorist. The cat is the signifier of a female sexuality which is self-enclosed, self-sufficient, and, above all, objectless. This sexuality, in its inaccessibility, forecloses the possibility of knowledge, thus generating a string of metaphors – cat, criminal, child, humorist.[19] *The Cat People* designates female sexuality as that excess which escapes psychoanalysis; it is that which inhabits the realm of the unknowable. On the one hand, this is a well-worn figure, particularly in another genre of the period, the *film noir*. On the other hand, not only does female sexuality escape the objectification of the medical discourse but, by means of psychoanalysis' own formulation – conversion hysteria – that femininity returns to kill the representative of psychoanalytic authority. The female body is entirely subsumed by the symptom. As the zoo-keeper points out, quoting the Bible, the panther is the figure of a failed mimesis: 'Like unto a leopard but not a leopard.' For the biblical text the panther is unnameable. Similarly, the film demonstrates that the woman, in becoming most like herself, that is, the embodiment of female sexuality, must become *other*. What we are left with is the asexual Alice, perfect and unthreatening mate for the 'good old Americano'.

Narration and Female Subjectivity

Because the implementation of psychoanalysis in the cinema is forcefully linked to a process of revelation, to an exposure of the answer to the text's hermeneutic question, it is inseparable from issues of narration and the woman's access to language and vision – issues which are intensified within the context of the 'woman's film's' attempt to foreground female subjectivity. The tendency in these films to organize narrative as a memory which is retrieved is evocative of Freud and Breuer's famous claim, *'Hysterics suffer mainly from reminiscences'*.[20] The study of hysteria and the films of the medical discourse are quite close in their revelation of a curious and dynamic interaction between the narrativization of the female patient and her inducement to narrate, to become a story-teller as a part of her cure. Breuer represents his relation to Fräulein Anna O. as that of listener but it is clear that her stories are not always spontaneous.

I used to visit her in the evening, when I knew I should find her in her hypnosis, and I then relieved her of the whole stock of imaginative products which she had accumulated since my last visit. It was essential that this should be effected completely if good results were to follow. When this was done she became perfectly calm, and next day she would be agreeable, easy to manage, industrious and even cheerful; but on the second day she would be increasingly moody, contrary and unpleasant, and this would become still more marked on the third day. When she was like this it was not always easy to get her to talk, even in her hypnosis. She aptly described this procedure, speaking seriously, as a 'talking cure', while she referred to it jokingly as 'chimney-sweeping'. She knew that after she had given utterance to her hallucinations she would lose all her obstinacy and what she described as her 'energy'; and when, after some comparatively long interval, she was in a bad temper, she would refuse to talk, and I was obliged to overcome her unwillingness by urging and pleading and using devices such as repeating a formula with which she was in the habit of introducing her stories.[21]

Later in the analysis, when Breuer was forced to separate from his patient for several weeks, he claims that 'the situation only became tolerable after I had arranged for the patient to be brought back to Vienna for a week and evening after evening made her tell me three to five stories'. Without Breuer, 'her imaginative and poetic vein was drying up'.[22]

The woman's assumption of the position of narrator is thus constituted as therapeutic, an essential component of her cure. Furthermore, there is a compulsiveness attached to this requirement – the woman must channel all of her energy into narrativity and thus exhaust the other more aggressive or 'unpleasant' tendencies she might possess. However, *Studies on Hysteria* also demonstrates, very curiously, that the woman's imagination, her story-telling capability, is not only therapeutic but disease-producing as well. For it is day-dreaming which instigates the illness in the first place – an uncontrolled and addressee-less daydreaming. Freud and Breuer, referring to the hypnoid states which are associated with hysteria, claim: 'They often, it would seem, grow out of the day-dreams which are so common even in healthy people and to which needlework and similar occupations render women especially prone'.[23] The pathological aspect of the female relation to creativity, daydreaming, and mental productions in general is also underlined by Breuer in his introduction of Anna O. to the reader. After citing the 'extremely monotonous existence in her puritanically minded family', he maintains that 'She embellished her life in a manner which probably influenced her decisively in the direction of her illness, by indulging in systematic daydreaming, which she described as her "private theater" '.[24]

The distinction between the two types of narrativity – an excessive narrativity as one of the causes of illness and a constant incitement to narrate as a therapeutic strategy – might at first appear to rest on another distinction between two different species of narrative: story as fantasy or imagination unleashed and story as history, as an accurate reflection of past events. The opposition would thus be one between fantasy and mimesis, where mimesis would be endowed with curative powers. While this explanation might prove attractive since the dangers imputed to day-dreaming reside in the fact that it is totally unanchored, unrestrained and independent of referent or reference, we know that the necessity for historical truth in fantasy was never established for Freud. *Psychical* truth was most important and in this respect it was virtually impossible for the subject to lie, for the narrative to become *too* fantastic. Rather, the distinction between the two types of narrativity has more to do with the structuring effect of the presence or absence of a narratee – the doctor. The daydream is produced by the woman for herself. It is thus not only prone to excess and non-utility – an unnecessary by-product of 'needlework and similar occupations' – but it feeds that narcissistic self-sufficiency to which women are always prey. The woman's narrative acumen is thus transformed into the symptom of illness. Her narrative cannot stand on its own, it must be interpreted. Narration by the woman is therefore therapeutic only when constrained and regulated by the purposeful ear of the listening doctor. By embedding her words in a case history, psychoanalysis can control the woman's access to language and the agency of narration. In Breuer's account, the woman, 'narrated-out', loses her energy, becomes pliable and subdued. The logic seems to be this: if the woman must assume the agency of speech, of narration, let her do so within the well-regulated context of an institutionalized dialogue – psychoanalysis, the hospital, the court of law. Psychoanalysis and the cinema alike present the woman with a very carefully constructed relation to enunciation.

That is why, in the films, the woman's narration is so often framed within an encompassing discourse. *The Locket* (1946), constructed as flashback within flash-back – only the central one the property of the woman who is the subject of all the stories – is an extreme instance of this. And if the woman hesitates, in the manner of Anna O., she is compelled to tell, to produce an account of herself. In *Possessed*, the mute Louise (Joan Crawford) is given an injection which induces a series of flashbacks constituting the cinematic narrative. In *Shock* (1946), a female victim of amnesia is also given an injection so that the doctor can discover what she knows, what she has seen.

A medical discourse thus allows this group of films to bracket the speech of the woman, her access to language, and in some instances to negate it entirely. The attribution of muteness to the woman is by no means rare in these films. In *Shock*,

Possessed, and *The Spiral Staircase* (1946), the female character loses the power of speech as the result of a psychical trauma, while in *Johnny Belinda* she is deaf/mute from birth. But in all cases language is the gift of the male character, a somewhat violent 'gift' in the case of *Shock* and *Possessed* where the woman is induced to talk through an injection, and more benign, paternalistic in *Johnny Belinda* where the doctor provides Belinda with sign language.

The phenomenon of the mute woman is, however, only an extreme instance of a more generalized strategy whereby the films manage simultaneously to grant the woman access to narration and withhold it from her. The woman's narrative reticence, her amnesia, silence, or muteness all act as justifications for the framing of her discourse within a masculine narration. Thus, Louise's flashback narration in *Possessed* is situated by the doctors/listeners as the discourse of a madwoman. What is really at issue with respect to specifically filmic narration is not control of language but control of the image. For there is a sense in which vision becomes the signifier of speech in the cinema. Within the context of a psychoanalytic dramatization in particular, the flashback structure acts as the metaphor of speech in the doctor–patient relation. The flashback is the most explicit and frequent signifier of the process of narration in a cinema which is, in general, assumed to be narrator-less in its capture and reproduction of unfolding events. The great instability of the flashback as a signifier of narration, however, is that beyond the point of its introduction, the flashback effectively erases the subject of the enunciation in the same manner as the rest of the classical text, its organization partaking of the same material of representation. The very term 'flashback' implies the immediacy of the past in the present. Flashback narration should therefore, and often does, assume the same reality-effect, the same impartiality, as the framing filmic discourse.

But when the woman's illness or madness rationalizes the limited attribution of narrational authority to her, the flashback structure can easily become destabilized, uncertain, especially if her delirium is allowed to infiltrate and contaminate the image. This is the case in *Possessed*, which at a particular moment departs radically from the logic of the classical text. In the middle of Louise's flashback account, she describes a scene in which she strikes her own stepdaughter who then falls down a long flight of stairs. This scene, in which Louise apparently kills her stepdaughter, is situated only retrospectively and traumatically as a subjectivized scenario – the image, in effect, lies. The sequence is in no way demarcated initially as a hallucination.

Possessed is structured as Louise's flashback account of her life, told to two doctors and prompted by an injection. The audience of the film is thus represented within the text: the spectator's eye becomes that of a doctor and the spectator is given, by proxy, a medical or therapeutic role. Although the narrative is presented as subjective, the spectator always knows more than the female character, is always an accomplice of the diagnosis. The scene on the stairway just described, however, is an important exception to this rule of the narrative. The revelation after the fact that the scene is hallucinatory is jolting, for it involves the image in a deviation from the truth. The viewer of the film is drawn into Louise's illness, into her hallucination. The spectator is therefore no longer diagnosing, but becomes a part of what is diagnosed, forced into sharing her illness. In this way the filmic trajectory, at least momentarily, collapses the opposition between clarity and blurring of vision. An image which purportedly carries a generalizable truth and a guarantee of knowledge is undermined by the revelation that it is the possession not only of a single character, but of a madwoman. As Foucault points out, in the classical paradigm 'madness will begin only in the act which gives the value of truth to the image' and madness is 'inside the image, confiscated by it, and incapable of escaping from it'.[25] In a limited moment *Possessed* unveils, through the representation of a distorted female subjectivity, that collective and naturalized madness – the investment in an image – which supports the cinema as an institution.

The woman's problematic relation to the image thus accompanies a delineation of her failure or lack with respect to language. And in many ways the disturbance or development into crisis of the relation between the image and truth that she causes is potentially much more dangerous, given the epistemological framework of the classical text. The woman's deficient relation to the image disrupts filmic significa-tion to such an extent that it is easier and safer to displace the representation of this deficient relation to the level of narrative content rather than to the organization of narration. Hence the films of the medical discourse often attribute to their female characters aberrations in seeing. As the field of the masculine medical gaze is expanded, the woman's vision is reduced. Although in the beginning of *Possessed*, extreme and extended point-of-view shots are attributed to Joan Crawford as she is wheeled into the hospital, she is contradictorily *represented* as having an empty gaze, seeing nothing, blinded by the huge lamps aimed at her by the doctors. In *Shock*, the woman is made ill by an image. Like Jimmy Stewart in *Rear Window*, the female protagonist in *Shock* looks out the window when she should not, and sees what she should not have seen – a husband murdering his wife. But unlike *Rear Window*, the woman goes into shock as a result of this sight, of this image which suggests itself as a microcosm of the cinema–spectator relation. The murderer turns out to be a psychiatrist who is called in to treat the catatonic woman suffering from what she has seen. All of his efforts are directed toward making her forget the image and maintaining her in a state in which she is unable to articulate her story. In *Dark Victory*, difficulties in vision, and ultimately, blindness, are not the disease itself but major – and extremely significant – symptoms of a brain tumor. At the end of the film, the major character's heroism is delineated as her ability to mime sight, to represent herself as the subject of vision.

In *Shock*, the female protagonist is dazzled by an image; in *Dark Victory*, she points out, to her doctor husband, a shining brightness which is only a signifier of her blindness; and in *Possessed* the woman, totally confused, is dispossessed of a focused gaze. The films of the medical discourse activate the classical paradigm wherein, as Foucault points out, madness is understood as dazzlement, an aber-ration of seeing: '. . . delirium and dazzlement are in a relation which constitutes the essence of madness, exactly as truth and light, in their fundamental relation, constitute classical reason'.[26] To be dazzled is not to be blinded by darkness but by too much light – too fully to possess the means of seeing, but to lack an object of sight. The doctor, on the other hand, as the figure of classical reason itself, always possesses not only a limited and hence controllable light, but an object to be illuminated – the woman. Over and over in these films, the scenario of a doctor training a light on a woman, illuminating her irrationality with his own reason, is repeated – in *Dark Victory*, *Lady in the Dark*, *The Cat People*, *Possessed*, *A Woman's Face*. In *The Snake Pit*, Dr Kik demonstrates the mechanism of psychoanalysis to his female patient with a dark room and a light switch analogy: 'If you know where the switch is, you don't even have to know how it works.' Light is the figure of rationality in these films. But light also enables the look, the male gaze, it makes the woman specularizable. The doctor's light legitimates scopophilia and is the mechanism by which the films of the medical discourse insure the compatibility of rationality and desire.

The Eroticization of the
Doctor–Patient Relation

Desire is not absent from the doctor–patient relation. On the contrary, that relation is eroticized in many of the films. In *Dark Victory*, *A Woman's Face*, *Dark Mirror*, and *Johnny Belinda*, a benevolent and paternalistic relation of doctor to patient is almost imperceptibly transformed into an amorous alliance. As Foucault stresses, the doctor and the patient form a 'couple' in complicity against disease and madness.[27] It was perhaps inevitable that this complicity should be mapped onto a heterosexual relation within a classical cinema which depends so heavily upon the couple for its narrative configurations and its sense of closure. The language of medicine and the love story become interchangeable. Sexuality or the erotic relation is thus given scientific legitimation in the figure of the doctor who acts simultaneously as a moral and social guardian.

By disturbing the structure wherein the couple is medicalized, perverting its figures, *Beyond the Forest* unveils the punitive nature of illness in the classical text and in some ways acts as a negation of the medical discourse. The charitable humanitarianism of a doctor–husband is refused by a patient–wife whose sexuality and desires cannot be contained but, instead, act as a fever which ultimately consumes her. Rosa Moline (Bette Davis) rejects the benevolence of her doctor–husband, knocks the medicine out of his hand, and acts out her illness as an exaggerated narcissism. The film activates a classical city/country opposition in which Rosa's major desire – to take the train to Chicago and leave behind what she perceives as the boredom and claustrophobia of small town life – is embodied in the soundtrack's insistent repetition of the song 'Chicago, Chicago'. Rose puts on her best clothes and walks to the station every day simply to *watch* the train departing for Chicago, simultaneously becoming a spectacle herself for the gaze of the townspeople. Her fascination with the train is a fascination with its phallic power to transport her to 'another place'.

Beyond the Forest begins with a documentary-like voice-over introducing the town, Loyalton, Wisconsin, and describing it as a factory town whose major source of income, a saw-mill, is constantly visible in the background. Noting the unrelenting image of the 'hot glow of sawdust', the voice-over refers to the saw-mill's 'flickering which burns through the eyelids at night if the shades aren't pulled down' (an 'if' of the narration which becomes a *scene* in the narrative when Rosa, unable to sleep, is forced to remind her husband to pull down the shade). Shots of the saw-mill's flame abound in the film and the fire and the heat are associated with a repressed sexuality. Rosa's problem is that she cannot maintain the repression, cannot channel her energies into the family ('You certainly go in for mass production, don't you?' Rosa tells a woman who has just had her eighth child, and Rosa refers to her own pregnancy as a 'mark of death'). She is the epitome of excessive female desire: 'Think of all the things I could have,' she tells her husband; in a shot of her studying a book of Accounts Receivable in her drive to get money, the only segment of her body in frame is a hand with painted nails. Rosa's usurpation of the position of desiring subject is also evidenced by the fact that she is specified as having a 'good eye' – she can shoot, both pool and guns. The film constructs a clearly legible metonymic chain connecting fire, heat, passion, desire, fever, and death. Rosa figuratively burns up, is consumed by a fever at the end of the film; unrepressed female sexuality leads to death.

Rosa's death-walk to the train at the end of the film is, in a sense, a parody of her earlier walks in which, dressed in her fanciest attire, she is clearly pleased to elicit a masculine whistle. But this time it is spectacle gone berserk – feminine spectacle deprived of a masculine spectator. Having knocked the medicine out of her husband's hand, thus forcing him to travel a large distance for more, Rosa dresses herself up, with the help of her maid, in order to catch the ten o'clock train to Chicago. Maddened by the fever and with an unquenchable thirst, Rosa misapplies lipstick and eye-liner, producing a grotesque image of herself, and unsteadily walks toward the train station. Just short of her desired goal, there is a cut and the camera assumes a position on the other side of the tracks. The whistle blows, the train begins to pull out and Rosa's dead body, outstretched toward the train, can be seen between sets of wheels.

In *Beyond the Forest*, the woman's desire to desire is signified by a fever, in other words, a symptom – a symptom which, as in *The Cat People*, consumes and destroys her. The symptom for the woman, as sign or inscription upon her body, gives witness to a dangerous over-closeness which precludes the possibility of desire. The mechanism of symptom-formation as it is described in relation to femininity differs markedly from that attributed to masculinity. While Freud refused to define hysteria as a disease which afflicted only women (there were male hysterics as well), he nevertheless aligned it closely with femininity, producing a binary opposition of types of neuroses: 'there is no doubt that hysteria has a strong affinity with femininity, just as obsessional neurosis has with masculinity . . .'[28] The mechanisms for effecting repression and hence symptom formation are significantly different in the two types of illnesses. In hysteria the mechanism is that of '*conversion* into somatic innervation' (somatic compliance), while obsessional neurosis makes use of the 'method of *substitution* (viz. by displacement along the lines of certain categories of associations)'.[29] In hysteria, in other words, the body is in compliance with the psyche while in obsessional neurosis the body can be bracketed or elided altogether by a displacement along a line of psychical representations. Foucault speaks of a theme common to hysteria and hypochondria: 'Diseases of the nerves are diseases of corporeal continuity. A body too close to itself, too intimate in each of its parts, an organic space which is, in a sense, strangely constricted'.[30] Because desire is constituted by the operations of substitution and displacement in relation to an object, the female hysteric, her symptoms inscribed upon her body, is denied any access to a desiring subjectivity. She can only futilely and inelegantly, like Rosa Moline in *Beyond the Forest*, desire to desire.

There are thus two major aspects of hysteria which are relevant to the woman's incorporation within a medical discourse in these films; first, hysteria is characterized by the mechanism of conversion and uses the body as the space for the inscription of its signs; and secondly, it is strongly linked to narrativity, both in relation to its cause (excessive daydreaming) and its treatment (the 'talking cure'). The narrativization of the female body is by no means specific to the genre of the 'woman's film' in the Hollywood cinema. But in this group of films the female body is narrativized differently. The muteness which is constantly attributed to the woman is in some ways paradigmatic for the genre. For it is ultimately the symptoms of the female body which 'speak', while the woman as subject of discourse is absent. The female body thus acts as a vehicle for hysterical speech. The marked ease of the metonymic slippage in these films between the woman, illness, the bed, muteness, blindness, and a medical discourse indicates yet another contradiction in the construction of a discourse which purportedly represents a female subjectivity. If the woman must be given a genre and hence a voice, the addition of a medical discourse makes it possible once again to confine female discourse to the body, to disperse her access to language across a body which now no longer finds its major function in spectacle. Yet, despecularized in its illness, that body is nevertheless interpretable, knowable, subject to a control which is no longer entirely subsumed by an erotic gaze. If interpretation is not possible, if the medical figure is incapable of relating a surface to a depth, of restoring an immediacy of vision so that the surface matches the interior, then the disease is invariably fatal.

A Pathology of Female Spectatorship

With the exception of *Dark Victory* and *Now Voyager*, the films of the medical discourse do not encourage or facilitate spectatorial identification with their diseased female protagonists. Rather, they take the form of a didactic exercise designed to produce some knowledge about the woman. If female spectatorship is constituted as an oscillation between a feminine and a masculine position,[31] the films of the medical discourse encourage the female spectator to repudiate the feminine pole and to ally herself with the one who diagnoses, the one with a medical gaze. Identification with a female character is then allowable to the extent that she and the doctor form a 'couple' as the condition of a cure. But the 'properly feminine' aspect of spectatorship is not altogether lost – it is, instead, represented *within* the films across the female body in its illness.

Female spectatorship is generally understood in its alignment with other qualities culturally ascribed to the woman – in particular, an excess of emotion, sentiment, affect, empathy. That is why 'women's films' are often referred to as 'weepies'. From this perspective, the female gaze exhibits, in contrast to male distance, a proximity to the image which is the mark of over-identification and hence, of a heightened sympathy. But the concept of sympathy is a physiological/ medical one as well, of particular interest to the female subject. The meaning of 'sympathy' in physiology and pathology is, the Oxford English Dictionary tells us, 'a relation between two bodily organs or parts (or between two persons) such that disorder, or any condition, of the one induces a corresponding condition in the other'. Sympathy connotes a process of contagion within the body, or between bodies, an instantaneous communication and affinity. In female spectatorship, it is a capitulation to the image, an over-investment in, and over-identification with, the story and its characters. Unable to negotiate the distance which is a prerequisite to desire and its displacements, the female spectator is always, in some sense, consti- tuted as a hysteric. And yet, the films of the medical discourse, precisely by encouraging the female spectator to ally herself with the one who diagnoses, attempt to de-hystericize their spectator, to 'cure' her.

By activating a therapeutic mode, the films of the medical discourse become the most fully recuperated form of the 'woman's film'. The therapy put into effect in relation to the spectator completely forecloses the possibility of a feminine position, freezing the oscillation between feminine and masculine poles which is characteris- tic of female spectatorship. The clinical eye is a most masculine eye. The female spectator, in becoming de-hystericized (distanced from the female character who suffers from the disease of femininity), must also become defeminized, must don the surgical gown. The marginal masochism which remains – linked to the pleasure of being 'under the knife' – is subsumed beneath the overwhelming need to appropriate the only gaze which can see, the medical gaze which knows and can diagnose.

Nevertheless, the connotations attached to female spectatorship – a heightened sympathy, constriction and over-closeness, the immediacy of the process of conta- gion – are not lost in these films. Rather, these mechanisms are represented within the texts as elements of the disease. This process of narrativizing female spectator- ship is parallel to the strategy discussed earlier, whereby the woman's purportedly deficient relation to the image is internalized by the texts and thematized as the blindness – actual or metaphorical – of the female protagonist. The internalization and narrativization of female spectatorship constitutes an extremely strong process of recuperation, containing the more disruptive aspects of female spectatorship by specifying them as pathological. The illness of the female character is not accidental but essential, implicating her entire being. For this reason, her body becomes the privileged site for the representation of sympathy as an over-closeness, a disorder of contagion. In other words, the sympathy usually activated in the film/spectator relation in the woman's picture is, in these films, reflected and reinscribed in the medical mapping of the woman's body *within* the text – a mapping which ultimately owes more to the nineteenth century than to the twentieth. According to Foucault,

Diseases of the nerves are essentially disorders of sympathy; they presuppose a state of general vigilance in the nervous system which makes each organ susceptible of entering into sympathy with any other. . . . The entire female body is riddled by obscure but strangely direct paths of sympathy;

it is always in an immediate complicity with itself, to the point of forming a kind of absolutely privileged site for the sympathies; from one extremity of its organic space to another, it encloses a perpetual possibility of hysteria.[32]

In hysteria, the paradigmatic female disease, the body is in sympathy with the psyche to the extent that there is no differentiation between them. Illness affects and defines her whole being. The ease with which the woman slips into the role of patient is certainly linked to the fact that the doctor exercises an automatic power and mastery in the relation, which is only a hyperbolization of the socially acceptable 'norm' of the heterosexual alliance. The doctor–patient relation is a quite specific one, however, which unrelentingly draws together power, knowledge, the body and the psyche in the context of an institution. Therein lies its force in convincing the woman that her way of looking is ill.

Notes

1 Michel Foucault, *The Birth of the Clinic: An Archaeology of Medical Perception* trans. A. M. Sheridan Smith (New York: Pantheon, 1973), p. x.

2 Phyllis Chesler, *Women and Madness* (New York: Avon Books, 1972), p. 75.

3 Christian Metz, 'The Imaginary Signifier', *Screen* vol. 16 no. 2 (1975), pp. 14–76.

4 The films discussed in this essay as contributors to this problematic include: *Dark Victory* (Edmund Goulding, 1939); *A Woman's Face* (George Cukor, 1941); *The Cat People* (Jacques Tourneur, 1942); *Now Voyager* (Irving Rapper, 1942); *Guest in the House* (John Brahm, 1944); *Lady in the Dark* (Mitchell Leisen, 1944); *Dark Mirror* (Robert Siodmak, 1946); *A Stolen Life* (Curtis Bernhardt, 1946); *The Locket* (John Brahm, 1946); *Shock* (Alfred Werker, 1946); *Possessed* (Curtis Bernhardt, 1946); *Johnny Belinda* (Jean Negulesco, 1948); *The Snake Pit* (Anatole Litvak, 1948); *Beyond the Forest* (King Vidor, 1949); *Whirlpool* (Otto Preminger, 1949).

5 Foucault, *Birth of the Clinic*, pp. 165–6.

6 S. Freud and J. Breuer, *Studies on Hysteria* trans. and ed. James Strachey (New York: Avon Books, 1966), p. 38.

7 For a more extensive analysis of the medical discourse in *Caught*, see my article '*Caught* and *Rebecca*: The Inscription of Femininity as Absence', *Enclitic* vol. 5 no. 2/vol. 6 no. 1 (Fall 1981/ Spring 1982), pp. 75–89.

8 Foucault, *Birth of the Clinic*, p. 121.

9 Future references to the look of the doctor will make use of the term 'gaze' despite Foucault's very important distinction, in this context, between the glance and the gaze. I continue to utilize 'gaze' due to its connotative relation to temporality. While the glance is rapid, punctual, momentary, gaze implies a sustained process of looking which more accurately describes the strategy of the films. For my purpose, the most significant aspect of Foucault's distinction is its correlation with the opposition surface/depth.

10 Louis Althusser and Etienne Balibar, *Reading Capital* (London: New Left Books, 1970), p. 26.

11 Geoffrey Nowell-Smith, 'Minnelli and Melodrama', *Screen* vol. 18 no. 2 (1977), pp. 113–8.

12 *Reading Capital*, p. 86.

13 I. Schneider, 'Images of the Mind: Psychiatry in the Commercial Film', *American Journal of Psychiatry* vol. 134, no. 6 (1977), p. 615.

14 See the Press Books for *Dark Mirror* (International Pictures, 1946) and *Sleep My Love* (United Artists 1948).

15 The analysis of *The Cat People* which follows owes a great deal to discussions I had with Deborah Linderman about the film in Spring 1983.

16 See Colin MacCabe, 'Realism and the Cinema: Notes on some Brechtian Theses', *Screen* vol. 15 no. 2 (1974), pp. 7–27.

17 Samuel Weber, *The Legend of Freud* (Minneapolis: University of Minnesota Press, 1982), p. 47.

18 Sigmund Freud, *Dora: An Analysis of a Case of Hysteria*, ed. Philip Rieff (New York: Collier Books, 1963), pp. 70–1.

19 Sigmund Freud, 'On Narcissism: An Introduction', in *General Psychological Theory* ed. Philip Rieff (New York: Collier Books, 1963), p. 70.

20 Freud and Breuer, *Studies on Hysteria*, p. 42.

21 *Studies on Hysteria*, pp. 64–5.

22 *Studies on Hysteria*, p. 66.

23 *Studies on Hysteria*, p. 47.

24 *Studies on Hysteria*, p. 56.

25 Michel Foucault, *Madness and Civilization* trans. Richard Howard (New York: Random House, 1965), p. 94.

26 *Madness and Civilization*, p. 108.

27 *Madness and Civilization*, p. 274.

28 Sigmund Freud, *Inhibitions, Symptoms and Anxiety* trans. Alix Strachey (New York: W. W. Norton & Company, 1959), p. 69.

29 Sigmund Freud, 'A Case of Chronic Paranoia', in James Strachey et al. (eds.), *The Standard Edition of the Complete Psychological Works* vol. iii (London: The Hogarth Press and The Institute of Psychoanalysis, 1962), p. 175.

30 *Madness and Civilization*, p. 154.

31 See Laura Mulvey, 'Afterthoughts . . . Inspired by *Duel in the Sun*', *Framework* nos. 15–17 (Summer 1981), and my article 'Film and the Masquerade: theorising the female spectator', *Screen* vol. 23 nos. 3–4 (September–October 1982), pp. 74–84.

32 *Madness and Civilization*, p. 153–4.

V
Prime Time
Deride and Conquer

MARK CRISPIN MILLER

From *Watching Television*, edited by Todd Gitlin (New York: Pantheon, 1987)

Mark Crispin Miller's devastating assessment of late-80s US television combines an acute eye for detail with an intricate broader argument. On the face of it, the sort of mainstream TV fare he is discussing – an international phenomenon, of course, both as directly exported and as copied by other national televisions – seems pluralist, anti-authoritarian, even 'progressive' in content, and wittily self-reflexive in form. Yet something is wrong.

Miller touches on a wide variety of genres, but it is in the shift from 50s to 80s versions of the family sitcom that the development he is describing is most clearly visible. That development amounts to the perfecting of programme styles so as to exclude representations of any content that would disrupt the medium's economic mission to deliver audiences to advertisers. In the early days of US television – which Miller refuses to romanticise – the way had not yet been found to integrate programmes and ads with maximal smoothness. Nor had the viewer's skepticism towards both been neutralised. Now, Miller argues, these objectives have *in a sense* been achieved, although with serious unintended side-effects, and leaving a certain overall gloom generally felt: 'TV manages to do its job even as it only yammers in the background, despised by those who keep it going. And it certainly is despised. Everybody watches it, but no one really likes it.'

The detail of Miller's argument revolves around the way in which every potential source of 'transcendence', of otherness to television's own norms, becomes either a target for derision or is silently expunged from the screen. Classical forms of paternal authority, in particular, need to be displaced if consumer culture is to be maximised. Miller shows the apparently transgressive moves made against the 'Dad' figures to be thoroughly contained: as television purifies itself by becoming increasingly a closed system representing only itself and the viewer's situation, laughing at Dads and laughing at ads both become gestures within, not against, patriarchy and the market.

M.A./J.O.T.

[. . .] There was for years a stark contrast between the naturalistic gray of T V's 'public interest' programming (the news and 'educational television') and the bright, speedy images surrounding it – a contrast that sustained, however vaguely, the recognition of a world beyond the ads and game shows. That difference is gone now that the news has been turned into a mere extension of prime time, relying on the same techniques and rhetoric that define the ads. Similarly, there was once a visible distinction, on T V, between the televisual and the cinematic, sustained by the frequent broadcast of 'old movies', each a grandiose reminder of the theater, of 'the stars', of narrative – possibilities quite alien to the process of network T V, which has since obliterated the distinction. Now *The Late Night Movie* will turn out to be a rerun of *Barney Miller*, and the first broadcast of the latest telefilm is called 'A World Premiere'.

Through such gradual exclusions, T V has almost purified itself, aspiring to a spectacle that can remind us of no prior or extrinsic vision. As a result, the full-time viewer has become more likely to accept whatever T V sells, since that selling process seems to be the only process in existence. Yet it would be wrong to argue that T V treats its audience like a mass of wide-eyed bumpkins, approaching them as easy marks; for such a claim would underestimate the subtlety of T V's self-promotion. T V does not solicit our rapt absorption or hearty agreement, but – like the ads that subsidize it – actually flatters us for the very boredom and distrust which it inspires in us. T V solicits each viewer's allegiance by reflecting back his/her own automatic skepticism toward T V. Thus, T V protects itself from criticism or rejection by incorporating our very animus against the spectacle into the spectacle itself.

[. . .] T V is pervasively ironic, forever flattering the viewer with a sense of his/ her own enlightenment. Even at its most self-important, T V is also charged with this seductive irony. On the news, for instance, the anchorman or correspondent is often simultaneously pompous and smirky, as if to let us know that he, like us, cannot be taken in. When covering politicians or world leaders, newsmen like Chris Wallace, David Brinkley, Harry Reasoner, Roger Mudd, and Sam Donaldson seem to jeer at the very news they report, evincing an iconoclastic savvy that makes them seem like dissidents despite their ever-readiness to fall in line. The object of the telejournalistic smirk is usually an easy target like 'Congress' or 'the Democrats', or a foreign leader backed by the Soviets, or an allied dictator who is about to lose his grip. Seldom does the newsman raise a serious question about the policies or values of the multinationals, the C I A, the State Department, or the president. Rather, the T V news tends to 'raise doubts' about the administration by playing up the P R problems of its members (P R problems which the T V news thereby creates): Can David Stockman be muzzled? Can Pat Buchanan get along with Donald Regan? Can George Bush alter the perception that he doesn't know what he's saying? Through such trivialities, the T V news actually conceals what goes on at the top and in the world, enhancing its own authority while preserving the authority of those in power, their ideology, their institutions.

Nevertheless, the telejournalists' subversive air can often seem like the exertion of a mighty democratic force. Certainly, T V's newsmen like to think that a jaundiced view is somehow expressive of a populist sympathy with all the rest of us;

and, of course, if we glance back through T V's history since the sixties, we will recall a number of thrilling confrontations between some potentate and a reporter bold enough to question him: Frank Reynolds putting it to Richard Nixon, Dan Rather talking back to Richard Nixon, Sam Donaldson hectoring Jimmy Carter or Ronald Reagan. Each time Ted Koppel sits before someone like Ferdinand Marcos, each time Mike Wallace interrogates some well-dressed hireling whose desk cannot protect him from that cool scrutiny, we sense a moment of modern heroism, as the newsman, with his level gaze and no-nonsense queries, seems about to topple one more bad authority for the sake of a vast, diverse, and righteous public – or republic, for there is something in this routine televisual agon that seems quintessentially American. We are, the T V news seems always to be telling us, a young and truth-loving nation, founded upon the vigorous rejection of the old European priests and kings, and still distrustful of all pompous father figures; and so those boyish skeptics who face down the aging crook or tyrant thereby act out a venerable ideal of American innocence.

All such moments dramatize a filial animus against the corrupt and presumptuous father. This family agon has become the definitive subtext of the T V news, now that the anchorman has evolved into a lad. Today's anchorman, in other words, is no longer a stolid papa, like Howard K. Smith, John Chancellor, or 'Uncle Walter' Cronkite, but a boy forever young and grave, like Peter Pan after a few years of business school. The earnest Brokaw, the bushy-headed Koppel, Rather in his collegiate sweater, look like only slightly weathered members of some student council, making those whom they interrogate – the generals, C E O's, and heads of state – seem automatically as shifty and decrepit as each probing telejournalist seems young and good.

However trivial his questions, then, the newsman, just by virtue of his looks and placement, always comes across as the heroic representative of a rising generation. Once we step back and look at T V whole, however, the newsman's stance seems less impressive. As we shall see, the assault on the bad father figure goes on and on throughout T V today, not out of any conscious moral program, but as a consequence of T V's self-fulfillment. Like the disappearance of T V's documentary gray, or T V's vestiges of cinema, the now routine subversion of the father is an expression of T V's impending unity. Seemingly progressive, the televisual animus against the Dad of old is, in fact, a device that works not to enlighten but to paralyze us. But before we speculate on the effects of T V's antipatriarchalism, we must first trace its rise; for early on, T V wass not yet wholly turned against the father, but was revealingly divided into two contradictory biases. We can best begin to grasp the closure of this critical division by recounting the long decline of Dad throughout the history of the sitcom.

At first, Dad seemed to reign supreme in sitcom country – or at least in its better neighborhoods. On the bulk of those shows set in the suburbs, Dad's authority around the house appeared to be the whole point of the spectacle. It was this implied paternalism that made most of those 'comedies' so unamusing: Dad's status was, back then, no laughing matter. Despite their laugh tracks and bouncy themes, the real spirit of those shows was expressed in their daunting titles: *Make Room for*

Daddy and *Father Knows Best* were simple threats. And those shows featuring Dad's wife or kids were also tellingly named, with half titles that took Dad's point of view, expressing his permanent exasperation at the foibles of his underlings: *Leave It to Beaver* (to Screw Things Up), *My Little Margie* (Needs a Punch in the Mouth), and *I Love Lucy* (in Spite of Everything).

Although the early sitcoms provided, now and then, a memorable moment of wild farce (usually the work of Jackie Gleason or Lucille Ball), they were, it seems, calculated to induce not laughter but anxiety. As the apparent ruler of the world, Dad, pushed around by no one, somehow deflated all of his inferiors – and all were his inferiors. Since we almost never saw him working, we had no sense that there was any class above his own; and he had no competition in the class below him. On those old sitcoms set among the proles, the husband and provider like Riley or Ralph Kramden wasn't competent enough to lord it over anyone, but was himself, in fact, the eternal jerk, a hapless fatso doomed to live in squalor, always trying to rise above it, always ending up worse off, not only just as poor but 'in the doghouse' too. Every one of his efforts at transcendence was necessarily ill advised, earning a weary put-down by 'the wife', who, ever yearning for new appliances but thoroughly convinced of her husband's hopeless impotence, could do nothing but look disgusted, arms akimbo.

In his well-appointed suburban home, on the other hand, Dad was subject to no such snideness, but was himself the ironic judge of all below him. He kept his underlings in line by setting an impossible example of self-possession, probity, and sound judgment – the virtues of small business. While the T V lawmen of the West enforced the peace with ropes and guns, Dad policed his indoor territory far less obtrusively, armed only with his pipe and elbow patches. And yet, for all the homeliness of Dad's appearance, his authority was far more awesome than that of any quick-shooting sheriff. Confronted with some hint of independence, Dad didn't have to raise a fist, but could restore conformity just by manifesting his supreme Dadhood: the mild frown of disappointment, the bland and chilling summons to 'a little talk'. These methods were unfailing, and oddly terrifying, primarily directed against Dad's son, who was a permanent victim, like the sitcom prole. As we watched in dread, we always knew that young Ricky, Rusty, Bud, or Wally was going to try somehow to prove himself, to accomplish something on his own, and that the effort would backfire disastrously, leaving the poor schmuck shamed and lectured, 'taught a lesson', by his serene and ever watchful Dad.

Although the son was Dad's main victim, the early sitcom also held Dad's other underlings in place. Mrs Dad, for instance, was always trim, erect, and loyal, like a well-bred whippet; but even she sometimes made trouble, and had to be reminded how to roll over and play dead. And while Dad's daughter was usually a 'good girl', answering when her Daddy called for his 'princess' or his 'kitten', sometimes she too got a little fractious, sprinting upstairs to yelp into her tidy pillow, until Dad snapped her out of it with a lopsided grin and a little Understanding.

Today, of course, that old Dad-centered universe has become the biggest and easiest joke on television. Yesterday's paternalistic vision is now a standard object of burlesque on the specials, on *Saturday Night Live*, in the ads, and on the current sitcoms. Mere mention of 'the Beaver' is enough to inspire a gale of aggressive laughter, expressing the assumption that 'we' today are enlightened well past the point of the naive fifties – the days when everyone (we think) could still adhere to the belief that Dad's in his haven, all's right with the world. This assumption of superior worldliness, this ironic view of those authoritarian fantasies, not only deprecates those dated T V programmes, but also belittles the whole period in which they were produced. It was 'a simple time' (the laughter implies), whereas today, of course, things are complex, and we all know better.

In simply laughing off the early sitcoms, however, we overlook their true perniciousness, as well as their implicit critical potential. First of all, the early sitcoms did not serve to bolster any extant paternal authority within the middle class, but helped to conceal the fact that by the fifties such authority had all but vanished. Like the T V Westerns of the fifties, like many contemporary movies, and like many of the ads (both print and televisual) intended for the postwar man of the house, these shows negated the actual and increasing powerlessness of white-collar males with images of paternal strength and manly individualism. Yet by the time those first sitcoms were produced, the world of small business had long since been swallowed up, or superseded, by what C. Wright Mills called 'the managerial demiurge', and so the virtues of small business, personified by Robert Young's Dad, were in fact passé.[1] It was already necessary then (as it still is) to get by on 'personality' rather than through diligence and thrift, to negotiate with charm and savvy the subtle crosscurrents of an immense and impersonal bureaucracy. Dad, well known to his friends and neighbors, his milkman and his mailman, the high school principal and the policeman on the corner, was therefore utterly unlike the real white-collar workers in his audience. And Dad's real counterparts were no less insignificant around the house, now that the wife and kids were out shopping or bopping with their friends, taking their guidance not so much from father (who in real life could rarely be at home) as from the newspapers, the magazines, the movies, other wives and/or kids – and (more and more) from television, which was, in fact, a force inimical to fatherly authority despite its early, transitory moment of paternalism.

While the flattering images on those old shows concealed the truth about the father's plight, they also contradicted the prevailing bureaucratic trend with an inadvertent and unconscious protest. Dad did not control his little world, but only haunted it, as a specter from the early days of capitalism (as well as a vestige of the postwar propaganda meant to get the American woman out of the factory and back into the kitchen). Dad's impulses were opposed to the consumerist imperatives that now began to overrun our culture. First of all, he kept his precious family in one piece, an inviolate community despite the lures and pressures of the circumventing market. More importantly, he stood for prudence, thrift, sobriety, self-discipline, pennies saved and joys deferred, exemplifying the old ideal of self-denial that had sustained Our Way of Life since the seventeenth century and that now threatened to impede it in the twentieth. That Puritan ethos was a boon as long as workers only had to earn and try to save, laboring to produce commodities for an upper class of buyers. Since World War I, however, the market had demanded that those same workers also buy and buy, and so advertisers started to malign the ascetic attitude, requiring those lean saints to gorge themselves, to give up their grim old abstinence in favor of our grim new self-indulgence. (Hedonism has never been a possibility within this system.) The ad agencies campaigned, in short, to turn the uptight Pa into an open maw; and they succeeded, which explains why Dad was an anomaly throughout his reign, and why he was deposed so soon.

If, therefore, we take another, truly critical look at those old shows, we can now see that their intention was absurd: to represent a sturdy bourgeois Dad between the ads for Wheaties, Skippy, Bosco, Lucky Strikes, Good'n'Plenty, Jell-O, Winstons, and a thousand other goodies that aroused the very tots and teens whom Dad was meant to scare into submission. Thus, T V had most of its audience in a double bind. It wooed the wife and kids, and generally stirred its viewers' infantile desires, with all sorts of bright, delicious images; and yet it contravened its own allurements by giving lots of air time to the Great White Father, who seemed to stand against the universal splurging that T V constantly promoted.

Clearly, something had to give, and it would soon be Dad, the personification of an outmoded ideology and now an obvious drag on consumption. However, if we look at Dad more closely, we begin to notice that his fictitious power, even in its heyday, had already begun to slip in every case.[2] It was not just the fat and pop-eyed Ralph Kramden, ineffectually roaring in his dingy walk-up, who had lost control, nor only the timid Riley, humiliated every week by some 'revoltin' development' of his own devising, nor only Mr Gillis, Dobie's old man, rasping out sarcasms from his store-front and always wearing an apron. While these lower-class father figures were overtly impotent, their more successful brothers were, although a lot more dignified, also the occupants of a precarious status. A few of the less impoverished Dads were already broad jokes – Ricky Ricardo, screaming in bad English, and Vern Albright, Margie's shrill and fruity Dad. But even those most even-tempered fathers, those men as bland and decorous as manikins at Brooks Brothers – the men played all but interchangeably by Carl Betz, John Forsythe, Robert Young, and Hugh Beaumont – were so respectable, their living rooms and neighborhoods so calm and quiet, their domestic 'problems' so slight and easy to resolve, that their rule begins to seem preposterous, even a little eerie, as we perceive that each of them is not the lord and master of his various dependents, but surrounded by them, held captive in his sepulchral home. And, indeed, these Dads too were often 'taught a lesson', although they tended not to be disgraced by such enlightenment.

In any case, that paternalistic moment soon passed, as the significance of the demographics became obvious. Long before the rise of Norman Lear, T V began to champion Dad's wife and kids on programs now contrived to please the actual wives and kids who watched the ads. In flattering its most dedicated customers, the sitcom stuck Dad well off in the background so that he might not cast his shadow over T V's dazzling window show. By the mid-sixties, the titanic burgher of the early years was now remarkably reduced, whether a pleasant nullity, like the Dads of Patty Duke and Dennis the Menace, or a mere straight man, incredulous and dim, like Samantha's husband on *Bewitched* or the boyfriend on *That Girl*, or Larry Hagman, then colorless on *I Dream of Jeannie*. Of course, there were exceptions, like the tense and hostile Rob Petrie played by Dick Van Dyke, by far the most resentful of all TV Dads, forever struggling to regain his vanished potency by undercutting his pathetic wife Laura, who was not yet Mary Tyler Moore. Whenever Laura tried to prove herself, to accomplish something on her own, like trying her hand at writing children's books, or rediscovering her talents as a dancer, the effort would backfire disastrously, leaving her depressed and him meanly contented.

The sixties generally revealed that Dad's prerogatives were threatened – not by any rise in real authority among women, but by the rising influence of TV and its corporate advertisers. In the culture of consumption, a man's home is not his castle but a temporary storage unit for whatever togs, foods, and gadgets the corporations have lately packaged or repackaged. Mom was clearly the foreman of this unit, the supervisor of most domestic purchases, and so, although still house-bound, still subservient, still obediently pretty, she now tended to appear as far more powerful than her predecessors. Jeannie was presented as a genie, Samantha as a witch, and yet it was not the supernatural realm that actually empowered these characters, but the commercial promise of household technologies. These figures were mere comedic extensions of the knowing housewife displayed in a million ads – the woman made magically adept by Brillo and Bab-O, vacuum cleaners and carpet sweepers, room fresheners and TV dinners, and who was thereby made to seem far superior to the very husband whom she still served and on whom she still depended.

The new sitcom was an expression of this contradiction, and yet concealed it under lots of desperate laughs. Dad, who in the fifties usually answered to no one, was now presented as an underling, like Jeannie's 'master', an Army major pushed around by senior officers, or Samantha's husband, an account executive in an ad agency, or Rob Petrie, a TV writer forever struggling to placate his celebrity boss. Blatantly cowed by those above him in the corporation, Dad now relied on Mom's advanced consumeristic acumen and/or was outwitted and upstaged by his precocious children, who were also his betters by virtue of their expertise as shoppers. In this transitional period, the only Dad who did not come across as a browbeaten hysteric was the wooden Fred MacMurray on *My Three Sons*, and his semi-dignity was possible only because his TV family was a bizarre, all-male preserve, his 'sons' anachronistically subdued, his 'wife' no prim and clever female but a dour old man wearing bangs and an apron.

Between Dad's wife and bosses, there was always an implicit understanding: both they and she were eager to see Dad swallow his yearnings and strive for another raise. This complicity carried over into the commercials, wherein the wife, sharing a little secret with the advertiser, would tip a wink, when hubby wasn't looking, into the camera, thereby demonstrating that her heart belonged to Procter & Gamble, General Mills, Johnson & Johnson, and other such suitors. Here was the beginning of TV's pseudo-feminism, which now pervades prime-time. The series and the telefilms today are invariably calculated to stroke the female viewers in some way, presenting a heroine who is untrammeled, plucky, confident, 'assertive', always in the right, and therefore not to be suppressed by any of the lecherous, pig-eyed males who keep trying to pick her up, slobber on her, rape her, or who succeed in raping her. Thus, the female audience today is flattered with the same formulaic and dishonest fantasy that was used to calm male viewers thirty years ago: 'You are more powerful than ever.' Or, to invoke a more familiar reassurance: 'You've come a long way, baby!'

If we compare this post-sixties pseudo-feminist exhortation with the fifties' pseudo-patriarchalist fantasy, we must observe that women are now far more exquisitely oppressed than their fathers used to be – more oppressed by the very mechanism that keeps telling them they are liberated. Whereas the older fantasy was in part transcendent, sustaining a belief in manly independence from the system, the modern fantasy entails no tolerance at all for any of the traits or pursuits that were formerly considered feminine: TV discredits and detests the power to nurture, derides all household talents, represses the possibility of an ardent female sexuality, and otherwise continues to promote the multinationals' assault on individual capacity. What TV does to women in the very act of seeming to exalt them is to turn them into cool young men, energetic and sarcastic, running their own businesses, or working for the corporation, always wearing suits and carrying major credit cards. It is not women who emerge triumphant in this fantasy, but the very system that degrades and underpays them – women are defeminized, and yet, strangely enough, never free from the requirement that they remain impossibly good-looking at all times. On TV, women are free only to conduct themselves with the same aggressiveness that men must also use in order to keep making it; and it makes no difference – is, indeed, more disturbing for the fact – that these TV images of women are, as often as not, devised by women, who regard this fantasy as most progressive. 'There are no woman doormats on this series,' says Esther Shapiro in defense of *Dynasty*, which she co-produces. 'The women are not victims. They can have the same villainy as the men.'[3]

In the early seventies, this development was nearing its fulfillment, just as Dad's demotion was complete, and now represented as a stroke of liberation. As usual, the lower-class father figure was presented as a joke, but now his subversion appeared politically correct. Archie Bunker was a butt, not because he was an over-reaching loser, like Ralph Kramden, but because he was socially unenlightened – sexist, racist, militaristic, a nexus of reactionary attitudes that allowed his juniors and his viewers to deride him in good conscience. All TV's prole father figures have been thus depicted and subverted throughout the seventies and eighties. Although generally lovable, the raunchy Schneider on *One Day at a Time* is still at heart a sexist pig, given to swaggering, at which the cool Romano women always smirk demurely. Mel on *Alice* is another such male ignoramus, much bossier than Schneider, but no more with-it, giving the waitresses in his employ a good many opportunities to roll their eyes behind his back.

On the post-sixties sitcom, however, it is not just the working-class father figure who is thus further deflated, but every would-be patriarch in every class. As we move beyond the level of janitors, short-order cooks, and factory workers, we find that the formula persists unchanged. Within TV's lower-middle class, the father figure is an object of amused contempt, if not ill-concealed impatience. Sauntering amid the laid-back detectives on *Barney Miller*, Inspector Luger is a joke precisely because he would be fatherly: older than everyone else, he presumes to offer solace and advice, wears a fedora, holds all the wrong opinions, and so his overtures provoke the usual grimaces of exasperation from all his hipper juniors. And on a slightly higher economic level, Stanley Roper of *Three's Company* and *The Ropers* is another elder butt, cranky and salacious, and given to rash actions that forever reconfirm the damning judgment of his wife, his youthful tenants, and his audience.

The reflexive ridicule of lower-class father figures no longer implies the exaltation of the bourgeois Dad. T V now undercuts all Dads together, in order to unite the other characters in a fleeting and invidious solidarity. On *Soap*, both Dads, one a prole and the other a wealthy businessman, are fools – the one high-strung and goofy, the other pompous and dishonest, their various mistakes and crimes occasioning frequent eye-rolling among their subordinates. The prole, however, is always a lovable incompetent, whereas the bourgeois is not even likable, but an ass so vain and selfish that – it is implied – his observers, both actual and fictitious, have a moral right, even an obligation, to despise him.

So it is with all the neo-Dads. Within each sitcom's middle-class milieu, anyone at all reminiscent of the early Dad – and there has always, until very recently, been at least one such scapegoat – becomes the object of the collective sneer. In the post-sixties sitcom, there is usually some fastidious jerk, ramrod-straight and buttoned to the neck; and/or some nervous, middle-aged wimp who disapproves of all the 'life' around him; and/or some pushy greaseball in outlandish clothes, who keeps trying to pick up all the women, or otherwise belittles them. Each of these butt types repeats, uncannily and in degraded form, some aspect of Dad's now defunct authority – his sense of propriety, his implied connection to the past, his (suppressed) masculinity, all of which recur as patently reactionary qualities. Thus, we have Clayton on *Benson*, Frank on *M*A*S*H*, Colonel Fielding on *Private Benjamin*, Les and Herb and Carlson on *WKRP in Cincinnati*, the boss in *9 to 5*, Dan Fielding on *Night Court*, and many others, regulars as well as supercilious-looking walk-ons. And outside the sitcom proper, the neo-Dad recurs endlessly as a major source of the comic relief, like Howard Hunter on *Hill Street Blues*, Craig on *St. Elsewhere*, Stanley Riverside on *Trapper John, M.D.*, and Higgins on *Magnum, P.I.*

Over the course of the sitcom's history, then, there has been an apparent reversal in the relationship between the master and his slaves. Each of these butts is a neo-Dad surrounded and subverted by his erstwhile inferiors – the wife, the kids, the colored – who now keep Dad in the same disgraced position that the Beaver or Bud Anderson once had to occupy; Dad is now the one whose every move results in his humiliation, Dad is the one who simply cannot meet the standard, which is now set by his previous victims, the sarcastic mass of women, children, employees. The patriarchal butt is nearly always childless, because these subjugated ironists stand for his children, jeering at the myth of his authority rather than upholding it. Although not as contemptuously treated as the outright butt, the Dad with children of his own is often still despised, albeit gently, undercut with tittering affection rather than with half-concealed hostility. Here we have Ted Knight, blustering adorably on *Too Close for Comfort*, or Dolph Sweet as the ever grumbling

'Chief' on *Gimme a Break*, or Tony Randall as the gibbering neurotic on *Love, Sidney*.

These butts and Dads are laughable to the extent that they presume to act like fathers. The only father figures who are not ridiculous are those who know enough to downplay their status and thereby blend in with the kids. Such Dads cannot be subverted because there is nothing in them to subvert. Michael Gross on *Family Ties* plays an exemplary cool Dad. Slim, glossy, affable, full of gentle wisecracks, this affluent ex-hippie, wearing earth tones and a tasteful beard, seems to be the child of his own children, who are as cynical as he is earnest in the sentimental moralism of 'the sixties'. Joel Higgins on *Silver Spoons* plays another Dad so boyish that he seems to be the son of his own son. A millionaire, he holds no job, and spends hours playing with elaborate toys.

The good Dad is non-authoritative even when he isn't thin and blow-dried. The placid Conrad Bain on *Diff'rent Strokes*, while sometimes capable of a pompous lecturette on ethics, is basically as hip and frisky as his two black sons and white daughter, despite his age and status as a super-rich patrician. Tom Bosley on *Happy Days* is another easy Dad, a seventies version of the fifties patriarch and therefore just as mild and insignificant as Dad once seemed crucial. Bosley looks like a homemade dumpling, or a nice bear in a cartoon, and therefore confronts us as the total modern opposite to the watchful hawk face of Robert Young.[4] And then there is the cuddliest and most beloved of T V Dads: Bill Cosby, who, as Dr Heathcliff Huxtable, lives in perfect peace, and in a perfect brownstone, with his big happy family, and never has to raise his hand or fist, but retains the absolute devotion of his wife and kids just by making lots of goofy faces.

T V, then, appears to have become enlightened. Whereas the early sitcom bummed us out with a gray authoritarian fantasy, today's T V comedy, so upbeat and iconoclastic, must represent a comic blow for freedom. Such, at least, is what the shows themselves would have us think. In the world according to Norman Lear and Susan Harris, the air is thick with liberal self-congratulation as the kids – both old and young, the black and yellow, brown and white – all blink and stare and roll their eyes in unison behind the back of some uptight neo-Dad, and every easy put-down touches off a noisy little riot of predictable applause. The mellow style of each successful neo-Dad implies the same rejection of the old paternal rule. Now the power appears to have been transferred downward and dispersed, according to some ideal program of egalitarian revolution. Our laughter at each butt, or with each cool new father, must therefore be the joyous laughter of emancipation from a tyranny that once required our stiff respect.

And yet power in the real world has not changed hands, but remains precisely in the same unseen and collective hands that have gripped it throughout this century. In turning against the early T V Dad, we merely turn against a superannuated figurehead, and only to the benefit of the very forces that invented him and that encourage us to keep on laughing at his memory. Once purified of Dad's stern image, T V was perfectly resolved to carry on the advertisers' long campaign for our absolute surrender, their effort to induce an incapacity far more profound than that of any bullied wife or son. Whereas Dad often had his little viewers feeling weak and childish, T V tempts all its viewers to remain as infants, with itself the electronic teat that gives us everything we need: 'We do it all for you.'

On T V, the serious father appears only in frightful caricature, as a 'child abuser' or provincial brute. There seems to be no middle ground between such nightmarish aggression on the telefilms and the bantering inconsequence of the friendly sitcom fathers. Certainly, today's good Dad will sometimes have a big maudlin reconciliation scene with his son (although seldom with his daughter), hugging the boy with tearful fervor after some estrangement or misunderstanding, but this routine effusion is always represented as a sign of healthy weakness on Dad's part. He's casting off his usual masculine reserve and 'getting in touch with his feelings'. Even his moments of unrestrained affection, then, demonstrate that Dad is at his best when *giving in*. And this suggestion of a radical capitulation carries over into those commercials where Dad today appears in his true colors: Tom Bosley pitching Glad bags for Union Carbide, Conrad Bain selling Commodore computers, Joel Higgins singing the praises of Prudential-Bache,[5] and Bill Cosby mugging expertly for General Foods, Ford, Texas Instruments, Coca-Cola, E. F. Hutton.

Cosby is today's quintessential T V Dad – at once the nation's best-liked sitcom character and the most successful and ubiquitous of celebrity pitchmen. Indeed, Cosby himself ascribes his huge following to his appearances in the ads: 'I think my popularity came from doing solid 30-second commercials. They can cause people to love you and see more of you than in a full 30-minute show.'[6] Like its star, *The Cosby Show* must owe much of its immense success to advertising, for this sitcom is especially well attuned to the commercials, offering a full-scale confirmation of their vision. The show has its charms, which seem to set it well apart from T V's usual crudeness; yet even these must be considered in the context of T V's new integrity.

On the face of it, the Huxtables' milieu is as upbeat and well stocked as a window display at Bloomingdale's, or any of those visions of domestic happiness that graced the billboards during the Great Depression. Everything within this spacious brownstone is luminously clean and new, as if it had all been set up by the state to make a good impression on a group of visiting foreign dignitaries. Here are all the right commodities – lots of bright sportswear, plants and paintings, gorgeous bedding, plenty of copperware, portable tape players, thick carpeting, innumerable knick-knacks, and, throughout the house, big, burnished dressers, tables, couches, chairs, and cabinets (Early American yet looking factory-new). Each week, the happy Huxtables nearly vanish amid the porcelain, stainless steel, mahogany, and fabric of their lives. In every scene, each character appears in some fresh designer outfit that positively glows with newness, never to be seen a second time. And, like all this pricey clutter, the plots and subplots, the dialogue and even many of the individual shots reflect in some way on consumption as a way of life: Cliff's new juicer is the subject of an entire episode; Cliff does a monologue on his son Theo's costly sweatshirt; Cliff kids daughter Rudy for wearing a dozen wooden necklaces. Each Huxtable, in fact, is hardly more than a mobile display case for his/her momentary possessions. In the show's first year, the credit sequence was a series of vivid stills presenting Cliff alongside a shiny Dodge Caravan, out of which the lesser Huxtables then emerged in shining playclothes, as if the van were their true parent, with Cliff serving as the genial midwife to this antiseptic birth. Each is routinely upstaged by what he/she eats or wears or lugs around: in a billowing blouse imprinted with gigantic blossoms, daughter Denise appears, carrying a tape player as big as a suitcase; Theo enters to get himself a can of Coke from the refrigerator, and we notice that he's wearing both a smart beige belt *and* a pair of lavender suspenders; Rudy munches cutely on a piece of pizza roughly twice the size of her own head.

As in the advertising vision, life among the Huxtables is not only well supplied, but remarkable for its surface harmony. Relations between these five pretty kids and their cute parents are rarely complicated by the slightest serious discord. Here affluence is magically undisturbed by the pressures that ordinarily enable it. Cliff and Clair, although both employed, somehow enjoy the leisure to devote themselves full-time to the trivial and comfortable concerns that loosely determine each episode: a funeral for Rudy's goldfish, a birthday surprise for Cliff, the kids' preparations for their first day of school. And daily life in this bright house is just as easy on the viewer as it is (apparently) for Cliff's dependents: *The Cosby Show* is devoid of any dramatic tension whatsoever. Nothing happens, nothing changes, there is no suspense or ambiguity or disappointment. In one episode, Cliff accepts a challenge to race once more against a runner who, years before, had beaten him at a major track meet. At the end, the race is run, and – it's a tie!

Of course, *The Cosby Show* is by no means the first sitcom to present us with a big, blissful family whose members never collide with one another, or with anything else; *Eight Is Enough, The Brady Bunch*, and *The Partridge Family* are just a few examples of earlier prime-time idylls. There are, however, some crucial differences between those older shows and this one. First of all, *The Cosby Show* is far more popular than any of its predecessors. It is (as of this writing) the top-rated show in the United States and elsewhere, attracting an audience that is not only vast, but often near fanatical in its devotion. Second, and stranger still, this show and its immense success are universally applauded as an exhilarating sign of progress. Newspaper columnists and telejournalists routinely deem *The Cosby Show* a 'breakthrough' into an unprecedented *realism* because it uses none of the broad plot devices or rapid-fire gags that define the standard sitcom. Despite its fantastic ambience of calm and plenty, *The Cosby Show* is widely regarded as a rare glimpse of truth, whereas *The Brady Bunch* et al., though just as cheery, were never extolled in this way. And there is a third difference between this show and its predecessors that may help explain the new show's greater popularity and peculiar reputation for progressivism: Cliff Huxtable and his dependents are not only fabulously comfortable and mild, but also noticeably black.

Cliff's blackness serves as affirmative purpose within the ad that is *The Cosby Show*. At the center of this ample tableau, Cliff is himself an ad, implicitly proclaiming the fairness of the American system: 'Look!' he shows us. 'Even *I* can have all this!' Cliff is clearly meant to stand for Cosby himself, whose name appears in the opening credits as 'Dr William E. Cosby, Jr., Ed.D.' – a testament both to Cosby's lifelong effort at self-improvement, and to his sense of brotherhood with Cliff. And, indeed, Dr Huxtable is merely the latest version of the same statement that Dr Cosby has been making for years as a talk show guest and stand-up comic: 'I got mine!' The comic has always been quick to raise the subject of his own success. 'What do I care what some ten-thousand-dollar-a-year writer says about me?' he once asked Dick Cavett. And on *The Tonight Show* a few years ago, Cosby told of how his father, years before, had warned him that he'd never make a dime in show business, 'and then he walked slowly back to the projects. . . . Well, I just lent him forty thousand dollars!'

That anecdote got a big hand, just like *The Cosby Show*, but despite the many plaudits for Cosby's continuing tale of self-help, it is not quite convincing. Cliff's brownstone is too crammed, its contents too lustrous, to seem like his – or anyone's – own personal achievement. It suggests instead the corporate showcase which, in fact, it is. *The Cosby Show* attests to the power, not of Dr Cosby/Huxtable, but of a consumer society that has produced such a tantalizing vision of reality. As Cosby himself admits, it was not his own Algeresque efforts that 'caused people to love' him, but those ads put out by Coca-Cola, Ford, and General Foods – those ads in which he looks and acts precisely as he looks and acts in his own show.

Cosby's image is divided in a way that both facilitates the corporate project and conceals its true character. On the face of it, the Cosby style is pure impishness. Forever mugging and cavorting, throwing mock tantrums or beaming hugely to himself or doing funny little dances with his stomach pushed out, Cosby carries on a ceaseless parody of some euphoric eight-year-old. His delivery suggests the same childish spontaneity, for in the high, coy gabble of his harangues and monologues there is a disarming quality of baby talk. And yet all this artful goofiness barely conceals an intimidating hardness – the same uncompromising willfulness that we learn to tolerate in actual children (however cute they may be), but which can seem a little threatening in a grown-up. And Cosby is indeed a most imposing figure, in spite of all his antics: a big man boasting of his wealth, and often handling an immense cigar.

It is a disorienting blend of affects, but it works perfectly whenever he confronts us on behalf of Ford or Coca-Cola. With a massive car or Coke machine behind him, or with a calculator at his fingertips, he hunches toward us, wearing a bright sweater and an insinuating grin, and makes his playful pitch, cajoling us to buy whichever thing he's selling, his face and words, his voice and posture all suggesting this implicit and familiar come-on: 'Kitchy-koo!' It is not so much that Cosby makes his mammoth bureaucratic masters seem as nice and cuddly as himself (although such a strategy is typical of corporate advertising); rather, he implicitly assures us that *we* are nice and cuddly, like little children. At once solicitous and overbearing, he personifies the corporate force that owns him. Like it, he comes across as an easygoing parent, and yet, also like it, he cannot help but betray the impulse to coerce. We see that he is bigger than we are, better known, better off, and far more powerfully sponsored. Thus, we find ourselves ambiguously courted, just like those tots who eat up lots of Jell-O pudding under his playful supervision.

Dr Huxtable controls his family with the same enlightened deviousness. As widely lauded for its 'warmth' as for its 'realism', *The Cosby Show* has frequently been dubbed 'the *Father Knows Best* of the eighties'. Here again (the columnists agree) is a good strong Dad maintaining the old 'family values'. This equation, however, blurs a crucial difference between Cliff and the early fathers. Like them, Cliff always wins; but this modern Dad subverts his kids not by evincing the sort of calm power that once made Jim Anderson so daunting, but by seeming to subvert himself at the same time. His is the executive style, in other words, not of the small businessman as evoked in the fifties, but of the corporate manager, skilled at keeping his subordinates in line while half concealing his authority through various disarming moves: Cliff rules the roost through teasing put-downs, clever mockery, and amiable shows of helpless bafflement. This Dad is no straightforward tyrant, then, but the playful type who strikes his children as a peach, until they realize, years later, and after lots of psychotherapy, what a subtle thug he really was.

An intrusive kidder, Cliff never fails to get his way; and yet there is more to his manipulativeness than simple egomania. Obsessively, Cliff sees to it, through his takes and teasing, that his children always keep things light. As in the corporate culture and on TV generally, so on this show there is no negativity allowed. Cliff's function is therefore to police the corporate playground, always on the lookout for any downbeat tendencies.

In one episode, for instance, Denise sets herself up by reading Cliff some somber verses that she's written for the school choir. The mood is despairing; the refrain, 'I walk alone . . . I walk alone'. It is clear that the girl does not take the effort very seriously, and yet Cliff merrily over-reacts against this slight and artificial plaint as if it were a crime. First, while she recites, he wears a clownish look of deadpan bewilderment, then laughs out loud as soon as she has finished, and finally snidely moos the refrain in outright parody. The studio audience roars, and Denise takes the hint. At the end of the episode, she reappears with a new version, which she reads sweetly, blushingly, while Cliff and Clair, sitting side by side in their high-priced pajamas, beam with tenderness and pride on her act of self-correction:

> My mother and my father are my best friends.
> When I'm all alone, I don't have to be.
> It's because of me that I'm all alone, you see.
> Their love is real. . .
>
> Never have they lied to me, never connived me,
> Talked behind my back.
> Never have they cheated me.
> Their love is real, their love is real.

Clair, choked up, gives the girl a big warm hug, and Cliff then takes her little face between his hands and kisses it, as the studio audience bursts into applause.

Thus, this episode ends with a paean to the show itself (for 'their love' is *not* 'real', but a feature of the fiction), a moment that, for all its mawkishness, attests to Cliff's managerial adeptness. Yet Cliff is hardly a mere enforcer. He is himself also an underling, even as he seems to run things. This subservient status is manifest in his blackness. Cosby's blackness is indeed a major reason for the show's popularity, despite his frequent claims, and the journalistic consensus, that *The Cosby Show* is somehow 'colorblind', simply appealing in some general 'human' way. Although whitened by their status and commodities, the Huxtables are still unmistakably black. However, it would be quite inaccurate to hail their popularity as evidence of a new and rising amity between the races in America. On the contrary, *The Cosby Show* is such a hit with whites in part because whites are just as worried about blacks as they have always been – not blacks like Bill Cosby, or Lena Horne, or Eddie Murphy, but poor blacks, and the poor in general, whose existence is a well-kept secret on prime-time TV.

And yet TV betrays the very fears that it denies. In thousands of high-security buildings, and in suburbs reassuringly remote from the cities' 'bad neighborhoods', whites may, unconsciously, be further reassured by watching not just Cosby, but a whole set of TV shows that negate the possibility of black violence with lunatic fantasies of containment: *Diff'rent Strokes* and *Webster*, starring Gary Coleman and Emmanuel Lewis, respectively, each an overcute, miniaturized black person, each playing the adopted son of good white parents. Even the oversized and growling Mr T, complete with Mohawk, bangles, and other primitivizing touches, is a mere comforting joke, the dangerous ex-slave turned comic and therefore innocuous by campy excess; and this behemoth too is kept in line by a casual white father, Hannibal Smith, the commander of the A-Team, who employs Mr T exclusively for his brawn.

As a willing advertisement for the system that pays him well, Cliff Huxtable also represents a threat contained. Although dark-skinned and physically imposing, he ingratiates us with his child-like mien and enviable life-style, a surrender that must offer some deep solace to a white public terrified that one day blacks might come with guns to steal the copperware, the juicer, the microwave, the VCR, even the TV itself. On *The Cosby Show*, it appears as if blacks in general can have, or do have, what many whites enjoy, and that such material equality need not entail a single break-in. And there are no hard feelings, none at all, now that the old injustice has been so easily rectified. Cosby's definitive funny face, flashed at the show's opening credits and reproduced on countless magazine covers, is a strained denial of all animosity. With its little smile, the lips pursed tight, eyes opened wide, eyebrows raised high, that dark face shines toward us like the white flag of surrender – a desperate look that no suburban TV Dad of yesteryear would ever have put on, and one that millions of Americans today find indispensable.

By and large, American whites need such reassurance because they are now further removed than ever, both spatially and psychologically, from the masses of the black poor. And yet the show's appeal cannot be explained merely as a symptom of class and racial uneasiness, because there are, in our consumer culture, anxieties still more complicated and pervasive. Thus, Cliff is not just an image of the dark Other capitulating to the white establishment, but also the reflection of any constant viewer, who, whatever his/her race, must also feel like an outsider, lucky to be tolerated by the distant powers that be. There is no negativity allowed, not anywhere; and so Cliff serves both as our guide and as our double. His look of tense playfulness is more than just a sign that blacks won't hurt us; it is an expression that we too would each be wise to adopt, lest we betray some devastating sign of anger or dissatisfaction. If we stay cool and cheerful, white like him, and learn to get by with his sort of managerial acumen, we too, perhaps, can be protected from the world by a barrier of new appliances, and learn to put down others as each of us has, somehow, been put down.

Such rampant putting-down, the ridicule of all by all, is the very essence of the modern sitcom. Cliff, at once the joker and a joke, infantilizing others and yet infantile himself, is exemplary of everybody's status in the sitcoms, in the ads, and in most other kinds of TV spectacle (as well as in the movies). No one, finally, is immune. That solidarity of underlings enabled by the butt's incursions lasts no longer than whatever takes or gags the others use against him. Once he leaves, disgraced afresh, each performs his function for the others, the status of oaf, jerk, or nerd passing to everyone in turn. Even the one who momentarily plays the put-down artist often seems a bit ridiculous in the very act of putting down the momentary loser. The butt's temporary assailant – the deadpan child, the wry oldster, the sullen maid – may score a hit against the uptight and boorish victim, but then perhaps the attacker him/herself is a bit *too* deadpan, wry, or sullen, and therefore almost as much laughed at as laughed with.

On the sitcom, in fact, one is obliged to undercut oneself along with everybody else. Such routine auto-subversion is effected through the sitcom's definitive form of monologue, a device which might be termed the Craven Reversal. For instance, one of the boys is being menaced by some giant thug. Although clearly frightened, the boy (who might be middle-aged) suddenly draws himself up and delivers a brave, indignant speech along these lines: 'You can't push me around like this! We're living in a *free country*, and I have *rights*! I'm not going to let some *bully* try to *impose his will* through *sheer physical force*!' and so on, until the bully growls, or flexes his muscles, or stands up from his chair to tower over the idealist, who immediately crumbles, quickly babbling, 'On the other hand, there's always room for compromise!' or something similar. Or a girl sees a celebrity, gets all fluttery, but tells herself she's being childish, must have pride, collect herself, until the famous person says 'Excuse me ...' and the girl collapses into fawning self-abasement. However the Reversal is set up, it always represents the same brief, pointless struggle: someone tries to overcome his nature, rise above his circum-stances, hold out against whatever TV says cannot be resisted, and that little effort fails predictably, as the would-be hero/ine contains him/herself for the greater glory of TV.

In short, the point of TV comedy is that *there can be no transcendence.* Such is the meaning of Dad's long humiliation since the fifties, and the meaning of every gratuitous and all-inclusive moment of derision. Because he would have stood out as an archaic model of resistance to the regime of advertising, Dad was, through the sixties and the seventies, reduced from a complicated lie to a simple joke. Lately, he has been regressing even further, for his parodic image has begun to disappear entirely from the sitcom's universe. Equal in their foolishness, the community of sitcom characters can now maintain the derisive pace without an overt vestige of the early Dad, for each can play the Dad merely by presuming to stand out for just a moment. Therefore, on *The Facts of Life, Golden Girls, Kate & Allie, Who's the Boss?* and other Dadless shows, even when no Dad-like visitor intrudes, there is no shortage of contemptuous asides or knowing glances, because one or another of the children, girls, or women will always somehow try too hard, come on too strong, put up some kind of front, or otherwise set herself up for her inevitable come-uppance from the others, each of whom will get hers too, sooner or later.

Through this subversive process, the sitcom betrays the self-destructive tendency of the social Darwinist ideal – that jungle ethic which has always given aid and comfort to the well-fixed champions of laissez-faire, and which is now respectable again, and highly influential, through the mediation of the Reagan mechanism. The aggression that motivates or undercuts each sitcom character in turn reflects the real aggression that pervades the corporate state, wherein every man and woman must 'look out for Number One'. And yet these apparent struggles for pre-eminence do not create heroic individuals, or permit any individuality at all. On the sitcom, what seems like a relentless effort on the part of each to triumph over all the rest is an effort not at self-definition or self-promotion, but at self-cancellation. The aim of each is merely to survive as yet another particle of the watchful and ironic mass.

And yet, despite this pervasive irony, the sitcom (like T V generally) is filled with maudlin intervals. Often there will come a sudden Tender Moment, when the ironists collectively break off from their snide gags and sarcastic looks. During this sentimental cease-fire, which is usually inserted just before the final 'pod' of commercials, a hush falls, the synthesizer plays some violins, and everybody goes sincere, until two of the combatants merge into a hug and the studio audience heaves a reverent sigh. This routine show of warmth might seem like a departure from the ironic norm; and yet that 'warmth' serves exactly the same purpose as the irony which it ostensibly opposes.

Each 'warm' climactic moment, first of all, seems intended to make up for the derision that precedes it: 'Hey, deep down, we're very *caring!*' the moment shouts at us. We are invited to believe that all the prior nastiness was really motivated by a lot of love, and so the sitcom's barbs and jeering are exempt from criticism. Conversely, the maudlin moment is apparently to be mitigated by the irony surrounding it: as soon as things get heavy, someone usually restores the caustic atmosphere by turning mean or acting like a jerk, so that the mawkishness seems to have been retracted. Alternately cloying and mean-spirited, then, the sitcom is nevertheless preserved against objection to these defects, since it seems too cool to be so corny, and yet too warm to be so cool.

In its tear-jerking phase as through its general irony, the sitcom functions to suppress all critical response. Whether it seeks to sneer along with us or tries to get us all choked up, its aim is to inhibit any independent thought, to preempt any negative reaction. Dad, the figure of our potential waywardness, is therefore the primary victim not only of the sitcom's ironies, but also of the sitcom's sentimental outbursts. When the music rises and the characters get teary-eyed, Dad is either broken down or driven out. If he doesn't give in and 'feel' along with everybody else, earning a big hand for his disintegration, he offsets the general bathos by demonstrating that he's much too frigid or obtuse to deal with it. His exclusion makes the others' sensitivity seem all the more acute, and also frequently provides the opportunity for that mean laugh which must immediately follow, and subvert, the ritual of pseudo-sympathy. Thus are the sitcom's passages of 'feeling', although seemingly anomalous, impelled by the same hostility that motivates the wisecracks and the rolling eyes.

Perfectly settled and enclosed, the sitcom world is now even more cloistral than it was back in the fifties, when Dad's kingdom, filmed rather than videotaped, included a front lawn and other antiseptic outdoor areas. Ricky and David, Bud or Wally could at least leave the house at times, to stroll or bicker mildly out on those sepulchral grounds. Today, each set, while far more colorful than Dad's gray neighborhood, is nevertheless more of a prison, excluding nature absolutely.[7] Now there are no more yards or trees, but only the usual bright living room or kitchen, as hermetic, up-to-date, and well equipped as the air-conditioned offices and studios where all these shows and ads are planned and sold. Here the only character who would ever think of opening a window, going for a walk, or contemplating other worlds is the occasional 'weirdo', the stereotypic 'space cadet', like the Reverend Jim on *Taxi*. Otherwise, no mind leaps up to any heaven. All here are earthbound, housebound, all but chairbound in a world of gratuitous and interminable jeering.

And this evocation of the chair brings us down to the discovery of that new creature who has displaced Dad as the sitcoms' basic hero. By implicitly extolling the fixed posture of ironic looking-on, T V exalts, in place of Dad, Dad's opposite: a figure not at all opposed to T V's sway, but in fact the very object of T V's triumph. It is, in short, T V's own full-time viewer whose 'power' T V now reflects and celebrates. Through its 'comic' apparatus, the sitcom persistently derides all tension, all uptightness, because such a state contains the possibility of waywardness, resistance, of a self impenetrable by T V; and the sitcom ridicules this state by playing it repeatedly against a spectatorial slackness, the same attitude of passive irony that the viewer exemplifies to the precise extent that he or she laughs along.

So the sitcom's endless round of sarcasms has served to promote T V itself. The ironist appears to see right through whatever pretense or dishonesty, pomposity or inhibition he confronts – exactly like T V itself, whose vision is, at base, so ruthlessly incisive. Moreover, the sitcom ironist comes across as so superior and hip because he imitates the sort of viewer that T V has finally produced for itself – not a credulous and ardent fan, but a jaded devotee, distrustful of those screaming images, yet somehow unable to give up half-watching them.

Of course, it is not only the sitcom that reflects T V's habituated viewer. T V today is almost unified by its self-reflection. The contemptuous underling who rolls her eyes behind the back of her ex-husband, mother, daughter, boss, or closest friend has analogues throughout the other genres. The talk show host, for instance, is a figure of the ideal viewer. As we watch T V's images, so does he sit and look on at his parade of guests, evincing a boyish wryness against which all too-demonstrative behavior seems comic, especially when he glances our way with a look that says, 'Can you believe this?' He is a festive version of the anchorman, with an air of detached superiority that is enabled by his permanent youthfulness, and by his middle-American calm and plainness. Johnny Carson of Iowa, like his heir apparent, that supreme ironist, David Letterman of Indiana, always seems somehow above the excesses of either coast, even as he brings them to us. Although ostensibly more highbrow than these stars, Dick Cavett of Nebraska – now on cable – seems another such teenaged ironist from the Great Plains. (The mobile and earnest Phil Donahue, although another plain Mid-western lad, is an incongruous T V star, his show a throwback to the public forum or 'progressive' high school course.)

T V's heroics are now also reflective of the viewers who cannot help but watch them. This has been evidenced in a negative way by the extinction of the T V Western, whose heroes were too self-sufficient, its locales too spare and natural, to survive in an ad-saturated atmosphere. T V now permits the Western only in the form of burlesque, whether as sitcoms like *Best of the West* or in parodic commercials.[8] Today, the solemnity of the old T V cowboys has evolved into the spectatorial cool of the new T V cop: Sonny Crockett is at once the descendant and the antithesis of Davy Crockett. An exemplary voyeur, the T V cop demonstrates his righteousness through the hip judgmental stare with which he eyes the many hookers/pimps/drug dealers/hit men/Mafia dons/psychotic killers/oily lawyers who flash and leer so colorfully before him. The history of T V's cops, in fact, is a history of disgusted looks, from the outraged glower of *Dragnet*'s Sergeant Friday to the more laid-back jeering gazes of the cops today – the casual smirk of Detective Hunter, the sarcastic glances that create the sense of solidarity at Hill Street Station, the deadpan looks of incredulity exchanged by Cagney and Lacey. Like us, the T V cop seems to deplore the bad guys even as he keeps on watching them; and T V's latest cop-hero is not only an adept voyeur, but is himself also a slick visual object, derived from the imagery of advertising. Indeed, his 'heroism' is entirely (tele)visual and consumeristic. We see him as 'the good' because he knows how to shop for clothes. Pre-eminently with-it in their tropical pastels, Crockett and Tubbs of *Miami Vice* are two observers of an underworld as seamy and repulsive, with its high-strung felons black and brown and yellow, as these two cops are smooth and chic. The eponymous bodyguard of *The Equalizer* is yet another well-armed and contemptuous onlooker, as stately and impassive as the connoisseur in an ad for scotch, and routinely angered by the many scummy types who, ill-dressed and misbehaving, cross his sight.

T V's reflection on the knowing viewer is a cynical appeal not only to the weakest part of each of us, but to the weakest and least experienced among us. It is therefore not surprising that this reflection has transformed the children's shows along with the rest of T V. Today the slow and beaming parent figures of the past – Fran Allison, Captain Kangaroo, Miss Frances, Mr Wizard – recur to us like lame old jokes; and the only current survivor of the type, the very easygoing Mr Rogers, has been the object of hip satire by, among others, Eddie Murphy on *Saturday Night Live*, and J. Walter Thompson for Burger King. The old children's shows were hardly free from commercialism; often the parent figure would engage in shameless huckstering, advising his 'boys and girls' to 'ask' for the sponsor's latest item. Although often disingenuous, however, the parental guise of the early hosts comprised a subtle barrier to the corporate exploitation of the very young, because that guise was based on the assumption that the child should be regarded as an innocent – fanciful and trusting, in need of some protection from the world that would absorb him all too soon. Such a child would, if respected, be off-limits to the market forces. That child's capacity for play and make-believe also might impede the corporate project, since his or her delight in such free pleasures would, if universally indulged, make trouble for Mattel, Hasbro, Coleco Industries, and other giant manufacturers of games and toys.

In order to prevent this hardship, TV now urges its youngest viewers to adopt the same contemptuous and passive attitude that TV recommends to grown-ups. The child who sits awed by He-Man, the GoBots, the Thundercats, or G.I. Joe is not encouraged to pretend or sing or make experiments, but is merely hypnotized by those speedy images; and in this trance he learns only how to jeer. The superheroes wage interminable war, and yet it is not belligerence *per se* that these shows celebrate, but the particular belligerence that TV incites toward all that seems non-televisual. The villains are always frenzied and extremely ugly, whereas the good guys are well built, smooth, and faceless, like the computers that are pro-grammed to animate them. Empowered by this contrast, they attack their freaky enemies not just with swords and guns, but with an endless stream of witless personal insults – 'bonehead', 'fur-face', 'long-legged creep', and on and on. Like TV's ads, these shows suggest that nothing could be worse than seeming different; but TV now teaches the same smug derisiveness even on those children's shows without commercials. For example, *Sesame Street* – despite its long-standing repu-tation as a pedagogical triumph – has become, in the eighties, merely one more exhibition of contagious jeering. The puppets often come across as manic little fools, while the hosting grown-ups come across as wise and cool – a marked superiority which they express through the usual bewildered or exasperated looks. Thus, the program's little viewers learn how to behave themselves – i.e., as viewers only. They are invited not to share the puppet's crazed exuberance, but only to look down on it; and so they practice that ironic posture which the show advises just as unrelentingly as it repeats the primary numbers and the letters of the alphabet.

As this flattery of the viewer now nearly unifies TV, so has it, necessarily, all but unified the culture which TV has pervaded. The movies now repeat the formulaic subversions that have served TV, debunking the heroics of the past through parodies of the Western, the Saturday matinee, the spy thriller, and yet preserving and intensifying the most hostile impulses of that defunct heroism: sadism, xeno-phobia, misogyny, paranoid anti-communism, each enacted graphically, and yet with a wink that tells us not to take it too seriously, however much we might like it. Even the less overtly bellicose films are, more often than not, merely televisual, despite the greater cost and scope of their images: *Ghostbusters*, *Beverly Hills Cop*, and *Back to the Future*, to pick just a few exemplary blockbusters, are each little more than a series of broadly subversive confrontations between some ludicrous butt and the cool young star(s). From TV, American film has now absorbed a stream of ironists – Chevy Chase, Bill Murray, Martin Mull, Michael Keaton, Tom Hanks, Steve Martin, Michael J. Fox, and others, some brilliant, some mediocre, but all used to make a smirking audience feel powerful. This archetype of boyish irony has spread beyond the silver screen, having become, in the eighties, through TV, the very paradigm of national leadership. Ronald Reagan, that low-key and aged lad, deftly quoting movie dialogue, and otherwise half jesting at his own theatricality, is yet another sly pseudo-insurgent, forever seeming to stand off, on our behalf, against those grand, archaic entities that menace him and all the rest of us – the 'evil empire' based in Moscow, 'the bureaucrats' and 'special interests' here at home.

Throughout T V, these figures recur seductively as our embattled fellow viewers; and yet these seeming dissidents only serve, like Dr Huxtable, to bolster a corporate system that would make all dissidence impossible. Of course, through their commercials, these corporations too pretend to take our side (while taking sides against us), defusing our rebelliousness by seeming to mimic it: A T & T advises us, through the soft-spoken Cliff Robertson, to reject its big, impersonal competitors, as if A T & T were a plucky little mom-and-pop enterprise; Apple likens I B M to a totalitarian state, as if Apple Computer Inc. were a cell of anarchists; G E depicts a world of regimented silence, its citizens oppressed and robotized, until the place is gloriously liberated by a hip quartet bearing powerful G E tape players, as if that corporation were a hedonistic sect and not a major manufacturer of microwave ovens, refrigerators and – primarily – weapons systems.

T V is suffused with the enlightened irony of the common man, 'the little guy', or – to use a less dated epithet – the smart shopper. Thus, T V has absorbed for its own purposes an ancient comic stance that has, throughout the history of the West, hinted at the possibility of freedom. Countless old scenes and stories have assured us that aggressive power cannot withstand the wry gaze and witty comment of the observant ironist, whose very weakness thereby seems the source of a latent revolutionary strength. Through such a stance, Diogenes embarrassed Alexander, Jesus discomfited the Pharisees; and in scores of comedies from Plautus through the Restoration and beyond, in hundreds of satires from Juvenal well into the eighteenth century, the servile fop or lumbering bully seems to be deflated by the sharp asides of an independent-minded onlooker.

Such spectatorial subversion of the powerful, or of those who have clearly given in to power, recurs throughout the European literary canon – but it was in America that this device became especially widespread, as the familiar comic weapon of a nation of iconoclasts. Here the spectatorial irony took on an overtly democratic force through the writings and performances of our most celebrated humorists: Artemus Ward, Josh Billings, Mr Dooley, 'Honest Abe', Mark Twain, Will Rogers. Through mastery of the native idiom, and by otherwise projecting 'an uncommon common sense', such ironists were each adept at seeming to see through, on behalf of decent fellows everywhere, all pomp, hypocrisy, convention, and whatever else might seem to stink of tyranny.

The history of this subversive irony has reached its terminus, for now the irony consists in nothing but an easy jeering gaze that T V uses not to question the exalted, but to perpetuate its own hegemony. Over and over, the spectator recurs within the spectacle, which thereby shields itself from his/her boredom, rage, or cynicism. T V deflects these (potentially) critical responses onto its own figments of the enlightened Other, and therefore seems itself to be enlightened, a force of progress and relentless skepticism. Yet the televisual irony now contravenes the very values which the older irony was once used to defend.

First of all, TV's irony functions, persistently if indirectly, to promote consumption as a way of life. Whereas the native humorists spoke out from an ideology of individualism, TV's cool tots appear to us as well-dressed hostages, branded with the logos of Benetton, Adidas, Calvin Klein. The self is an embarrassment on TV, an odd encumbrance, like a hatbox or a watch fob. TV's irony at once discredits any sign of an incipient selfhood, so that the only possible defense against the threat of ridicule would be to have no self at all. In order not to turn into a joke, then, one must make an inward effort to become like either – or both – of those supernal entities that dominate TV: the commodity and the corporation. These alone are never ironized on TV, because these alone can never lapse into the laughable condition of mortality. The corporation is, by definition, disembodied; the commodity-as-advertised, a sleek and luminous portent of nonhumanity. Both seem to gaze back at us from within the distant future, having evolved far beyond our weaknesses and fear: TV's irony derives from that contemptuous gaze, which threatens even the most blasé actors, the most knowing spectators. Through its irony, in short, TV advises us not just to buy its products, but to emulate them, so as to vanish into them.

And TV's irony facilitates an atmosphere of endless war. With its fresh egalitarian bias, the early irony was fundamentally humane, as the works of Lincoln and Mark Twain attest. The televisual irony, however, has merely enabled TV to regress into a continuous scene of brutal domination, by seeming to obviate all critical reaction (whether moral or aesthetic) to such modern barbarism.

Even as it flatters us for our powers of discernment, TV struggles to enforce our constant half attention by assaulting us relentlessly with violent distractions. Despite its pose of deference to the audience, TV's assumption is that the viewer is precisely as edgy, fickle, and dim-witted as TV would make everyone, and so the spectacle now comes to us shattered into a sequence of harsh fragments, overcharged and unrelated: gunshots, punches, screams, explosions, crashes, squealing tires, things and bodies hurtling, hurting, every audiovisual contusion further heightened by the efficient bangs and blaring of the synthesizer. The need to keep us half-engrossed has produced a spectacle of easy cruelty. The definitive image of prime time (beyond the sitcoms) is that nightmarish simulation of pursuit which also recurs throughout the so-called 'splatter movies': a nervous, tasty-looking woman walks alone down some dark hallway or deserted street, stalked by the hand-held camera.

Yet such overt sadomasochism is only one component of TV's assault, for TV is violent not only in its literal images of carnage and collision, but in its automatic overuse of every possible method of astonishment. Here we might mention the extreme close-ups, high contrasts, flaring colors, rapid cutting, the stark New Wave vistas, simulations of inhuman speed, sudden riots of break dancing. Yet such a catalog of tricks alone would miss the point, because TV's true violence consists not so much in the spectacle's techniques or content, but rather in the very density and speed of TV overall, the very multiplicity and pace of stimuli; for it is by overloading, overdriving both itself and us that T V disables us, making it hard to think about or even feel what T V shows us – making it hard, perhaps, to think or feel at all.

T V's irony inhibits any critical response, or any other strong reaction, to this brutalizing process. It would be uncool to object, or otherwise to take it hard. Thus, the experience of T V today is doubly terroristic. There is, first of all, the outright mayhem and derision – people ridiculed and/or beaten, burned, shot, knifed, raped, drowned, or blown up, cars crashing into cars, houses, plate-glass windows, cars run off the road and blowing up, cars driving over cliffs and blowing up, or just blowing up, or blowing people up, or running people down. And this explicit depiction of destruction also implies, appeals to, and is protected by a cruelty more refined: the cold thrill of feeling ourselves exalted above all concern, all earnestness, all principle, evolved beyond all innocence or credulity, liberated finally out of naive moralisms and into pure modernity. We all know that we see through it all, and therefore can enjoy it as if not fascinated by it. T V's cop shows, telefilms, and wrestling matches are preserved in their debasement by this assurance that we've seen so much that none of this can bother us. Such is the implicit assurance of the images themselves, and such too is the excuse advanced explicitly by T V's employees, who frequently exonerate themselves by claiming irony. 'This is basically a comedy', says George Peppard of *The A-Team*. 'We're doing send-up.' According to Glen A. Larson, executive producer of *Knight Rider*, the show is 'tongue-in-cheek', and works only because David Hasselhoff, the show's star, 'has that mischievous look in his eye that tells you, "Of course you're not going to believe this, but lean back and enjoy it anyway".'[9]

No matter how bad T V gets, it cannot easily be deplored or criticized as long as it manifests its own unseriousness. Yet the worst thing about T V is not its increasing badness. As long as we can still point out that something on T V is 'bad', we continue to invoke a number of traditional aesthetic standards. Such criteria are no longer relevant to T V today, which, increasingly self-referential, is less recognizable as something 'bad' as it turns more and more exclusively televisual. For all its promises of 'choice', T V is nearly perfect in its emptiness, all but exhausted by the very irony that it uses to protect itself from hostile scrutiny.

This explains in part why the early T V genres are now vanishing. Today the phrase 'T V genre' seems increasingly oxymoronic, for the T V spectacle has long since broken down or overwhelmed the old dramatic forms that once comprised it. At first, T V was, generically, as diverse as either of its parent media, radio and film. Shows like *I Love Lucy* and *The Honeymooners* preserved something of the mood and structure of the stage farce, and the spirit of vaudeville persisted in the live routines of Jack Benny, Milton Berle, Sid Caesar, Red Skelton. T V's many Westerns derived from the larger Westerns of John Ford and others, and its detective stories related, through Hollywood, to the novels of Dashiell Hammett and Raymond Chandler. T V's deliberate forays into the uncanny were similarly inspired by literary/cinematic antecedents: *The Twilight Zone* derived in part from science fiction, *One Step Beyond* and *Thriller* from the ghost story, and the shows produced (and sometimes directed) by Alfred Hitchcock were clearly reminiscent of his films. Early on, moreover, T V even included the sort of social realism that had marked the American stage since the Depression. Series such as *Playhouse 90*, *Kraft Television Theatre*, *Philco Television Playhouse*, and *Goodyear Television Playhouse* presented a number of plays of a type too topical and sobering to survive the rising influence of the advertisers – a deliberate (and brief) effort to use T V as an extension of the off-Broadway theater.

Of course, we ought not to exaggerate the aesthetic or social value of this generic conservatism. The fact that an early T V show referred to some prior body of novels, plays, or films need not mean that that show was any good. 'The Golden Age of Television' was hardly as luminous as its later eulogists tend to suggest. Furthermore, for all their obvious generic traits, a good many of those early shows were little more than cold war propaganda, scarcely veiled by the obligatory trappings of the Western or crime drama. However, even if many of its shows were badly done and/or politically loaded, T V back then was still not as oppressive and monotonous as it is today, because its range of generic categories sustained the memory of a pretelevisual moment. T V alluded to the act of reading, and to the act of joining others in an auditorium. The live pratfall, the somber Paladin, the haunted mansion, the lawyers fencing in a packed courtroom, the gray drama of a labor strike, Ralph Kramden mistakenly convinced that he's about to die, were among the images that pointed back and away from the very medium that was presenting them.

But T V now points largely to itself, and so genre has been all but superannuated. Throughout the virtual whole of any broadcast day, T V offers us T V and T V only, representing no action that does not somehow refer to, and reinforce, the relationship, or stand-off, between the bored, fixated viewer and his set. Whereas genre demands that both the viewers and the performers abide by its particular conventions for the story's sake, T V today automatically adapts whatever it appropriates to T V's own reflective project – not to mold a narrative, but only both to signal and appeal to the collective knowingness of T V's viewers and performers. The spectacle is an endless advertisement for the posture of inert modernity. Genre, therefore, is nothing but a source of campy touches – or the material for outright parody, the object of that relentless putting-down whereby T V subverts our pleasure in all prior forms of spectacle. Whatever was a source of pleasure in the past is now derided by and for the knowing, whether it's the Busby Berkeley musical affectionately mimicked in some 'special', or the silent movies derisively excerpted in the ads for Hershey or Toshiba, or the cowboy pictures lampooned by Philip Morris or Rich Little, or *The Towering Inferno* as parodied on *Saturday Night Live*, or *Dragnet* as parodied to sell the Yellow Pages, or *Mr Ed* as excerpted to sell tortilla chips, or the Mona Lisa as ridiculed to sell Peter Pan peanut butter. Through such compulsive trashing, the spectacle makes eye contact with the spectator, offering, in exchange for the enjoyment that T V cannot permit, a flattering wink of shared superiority.

Increasingly, T V is nothing but a series of assurances that it can never put one over on us. Those on T V collaborate with those who sit before it, in order to reconfirm forever our collective immunity to T V as it used to be, back when its stars and viewers were not as cool as all of us are now. Pat Sajak, the M C on *Wheel of*

Fortune, distinguishes himself from the sort of overheated game show host that was once common on T V: '"You've just won TEN THOUSAND DOLLARS!"' Sajak jabbers in unctuous parody, then adds, in his own more laid-back manner, 'I just can't do that.' Ruben Blades, schmoozing with Johnny Carson after a hot salsa number, complains of 'the stereotypes' that T V has imposed on Hispanics: 'Loot-sie! I'm home!' he shouts in mimicry of Desi Arnaz, then pleads suavely, 'Hey, gimme a break!', and the audience laughs, breaking into applause. And Susan Saint James, hosting *Friday Night Videos* with the two teenage girls who perform with her on *Kate & Allie*, has them giggling at her imitation of the heavy-handed acting she used to do on *Name of the Game*.

Such knowingness sustains the widespread illusion that we have all somehow recovered from a bout of vast and paralyzing gullibility; and yet we cannot be confirmed in this illusion unless we keep on watching, or half watching. Thus, the most derisive viewer is also the most dependent: 'Students do not take *General Hospital* seriously,' writes Mark Harris in T V Guide. 'They know it's not life; they say it's a "soporific"; they feel superior to it. But *General Hospital* is also necessary, indispensable.'[10] In short, our jeering hurts T V's commercial project not at all. Everybody knows that T V is mostly false and stupid, that almost no one pays that much attention to it – and yet it's on for over seven hours a day in the average household, and it sells innumerable products. In other words, T V manages to do its job even as it only yammers in the background, despised by those who keep it going.

And it certainly is despised. Everybody watches it, but no one really likes it. This is the open secret of T V today. Its only champions are its own executives, the advertisers who exploit it, and a compromised network of academic boosters. Otherwise, T V has no spontaneous defenders, because there is almost nothing in it to defend. In many ways at once, T V negates the very 'choices' that it now promotes with rising desperation. It promises an unimpeded vision of the whole known universe, and yet it shows us nothing but the laughable reflection of our own unhappy faces. It seems to offer us a fresh, 'irreverent' view of the oppressive past, and yet that very gesture of rebelliousness turns out to be a ploy by those in power. Night after night, T V displays a bright infinitude of goods, employs a multitude of shocks and teases; and the only purpose of that spectacle is to promote the habit of spectatorship. It celebrates unending 'choice' while trying to keep a jeering audience all strung out. T V begins by offering us a beautiful hallucination of diversity, but it is finally like a drug whose high is only the conviction that its user is too cool to be addicted.

Notes

1 C. Wright Mills, *White Collar* (New York: Oxford University Press, 1951), p. 77. This classic study should be read through carefully by anyone interested in finding out just what the fifties sitcom, and much of the decade's mass advertising, were intended – whether consciously or not – to deny.

2 My use of the epithet 'Dad' is determined, not by a T V character's paternity, but by his symbolic power as a figure of possible authority. Although childless, Ralph Kramden may still be deemed a Dad because of his relationship to us who watch him.

3 '*Dynasty* Creators Jump To Defend It', *New York Times*, 26 November 1984.

4 The trajectory of Robert Young's T V career offers some oblique corroboration of the historical argument offered here. Years after his service as T V's most intimidating Dad, Young returned to play the title role in *Marcus Welby, M . D .*, which ran from 1969 to 1975. Through the sixties and seventies, T V often allowed in its hospitals and clinics some of that fatherly authority which was now missing from the sitcom households. In this second paternal incarnation, Young played a father figure considerably more soothing than Jim Anderson had been. So soothing did Young seem, in fact, that he was hired, in 1977, by General Foods to appear as T V's pitchman for Sanka. Now there was very little left, in Young's persona, of that implied steeliness which had made *Father Knows Best* so disquieting. In the Sanka ads, he would usually appear as a sort of chuckling enforcer, keeping everyone mellowed out with plenty of decaffeinated hits. In any case, Young was, despite his tranquilizing function, ultimately still too Dad-like a figure for advertising in the eighties: General Foods dropped him in 1982, claiming to need 'less of an authority figure' for the campaign.

5 Higgins not only sings the praises of this particular advertiser, but also writes melodies for a number of other corporate clients, as a partner in a three-man jingle-writing company in Hollywood.

6 'Advertising', *New York Times*, 12 November 1985.

7 It is pertinent to mention here the disappearance, since the sixties, of the sitcom pastoral, exemplified by such shows as *Mayberry R.F.D.* and *Green Acres*.

8 T V's anti-patriarchal thrust has not only eliminated the cowboy, but has also darkened the image of the businessman: Dad's original vocation (insofar as one could ascertain it) has been denigrated along with Dad himself. On T V, one study pointed out in 1982, 'businessmen are cast as evil and selfish, social parasites'. Predictably, such characterization has been lamented publicly by prominent members of the business world. For instance, Herbert Schmertz, Mobil's vice president for public affairs, has warned that such depictions can do serious damage to American business interests. In January of 1984, Schmertz 'suggested', according to the *Times*, 'that exporting American television's "crazy-crooked businessman shows" helps fan foreign suspicions "of American institutions, particularly the multinational corporations"'.

Such warnings are unnecessary, since T V's 'crazy-crooked-businessman' has the quieting effect of making the faceless corporate presence seem all the more trustworthy and benign: Dow and Du Pont (for instance) seem perfectly well meaning and legitimate compared to J. R. Ewing. In any case, T V's automatic deprecation of all father figures – the businessman included – works to the ultimate benefit of Mobil and the other multinationals behind T V, for the reasons already given. See 'On T V and In Novels, The Bad Guy Sells', *New York Times*, 15 April 1984.

9 George Peppard made this remark on an instalment of *Evening Magazine* broadcast in December 1985. Glen A. Larson is quoted in 'David Hasselhoff of *Knight Rider*', *T V Guide*, 25 June 1983, p. 40.

10 'What T V Means to our College Students', *T V Guide*, 7 January 1984, p. 8.

VI

Hellivision: An Analysis of Video Games

GILLIAN SKIRROW

From *High Theory/Low Culture*, edited by Colin MacCabe
(Manchester: Manchester University Press, 1986)

Gillian Skirrow wrote this piece for Colin MacCabe's *High Theory/Low Culture* collection, and it is an exemplary demonstration of how a thorough grasp of the High Theory of the 70s can inform, without overwhelming, an investigation of a new entertainment medium. Skirrow manages to mount a challengingly critical argument without slipping into moralism or betraying condescension towards the video-game audience.

Her investigation is motivated by very down-to-earth worries about differential participation by men and women in computer technology. If video games are a major route into feeling good enough about computers to use them seriously, and if 'the pleasure of video games is gender-specific – women do not play them', then women are going to be disadvantaged in this field. So why should the pleasures of video games work overwhelmingly for men and not for women? Skirrow makes use of both psychoanalysis, specifically the theories of Melanie Klein, and more recent developments in feminist-oriented therapy (Eichenbaum and Orbach), to explore characteristic fantasy structures of the games.

Sometimes readers find Klein's views on the fantasy-life of the young child, in which a highly fearful and (hence) destructive set of reactions to the mother's body are in tension with subsequent worries about repairing imaginary damage, hard to take. But the recurrent motifs of video games, as Skirrow demonstrates, light up wonderfully (not to say chillingly) in a Kleinian light. This finding alone would make for fascinating reading; but it is the resourcefulness with which Skirrow can move so smoothly and so convincingly from this register of experience back to the broad currents of contemporary history and culture that makes her essay so satisfying.

M.A./J.O.T.

Dissection

In investigating popular culture the only way not to feel like a snooping health visitor, sniffing out whether someone's environment is fit to live in, is to examine some aspect or form of it which evokes passionate feelings in oneself. For me video games are both fetish and phobia, since at one level I am fascinated by the control involved in being able to relate to and interact with a text on the video screen, but at the level of the content of the games I am repelled. So in this chapter I want to dissect the games to take out their pleasures and, after the disembowelment, to try to read what the entrails predict for the future relationship between gender and uses of the new technology in both its popular entertainment and its business forms. For the pleasure of video games is gender-specific – women do not play them – and it seems important when studying popular culture to examine not only what pleasures arise at different historical periods, but for whom. The materiality of the relationship between text and spectator is nowhere clearer than in video games, where the spectator is also the performer, and performance involves learning a skill which will give the player an advantage over the non-player in the market for creative computer jobs as opposed to clerical, key-punching work. So in looking at the video games the study of effects and the study of pleasure will be the same thing.

History

The structure of video games nearly always conforms to a truncated version of the folk-tale form analysed by Propp: a lack provides the motivation for a hero to struggle with a villain which leads either to defeat for the hero (unusual in folk-tales but very common in video games) or to his victory and return. In computer circles, however, it is widely believed that the origin of video games lies in the war games which have been a popular form of entertainment since the seventeenth century. In war games the emphasis is not on an individual hero but on the environment in which a battle is to be fought. During the 1960s books of rules were published to use with war games which described a detailed environment to the players, usually set in one of four main periods: ancient, medieval, Napoleonic, or modern. Some games were still played with model armies, but board games were also developed, and – perhaps in tune with a general move towards the dramatisation of life – there evolved the role-playing game. One of the most successful of these games was *Dungeons and Dragons*, published by Tactical Studies Rules, which was a medieval fantasy. The environment was designed and presided over by a 'dungeon master' (Greimas's 'Destinateur'?) and each player could control one of the several characters: a fighting man, an elf, a wizard, etc. The fascination with a mythical, magical past, as evidenced by the popularity of J. R. R. Tolkien's *Fellowship of the Ring* published in 1954, and a general revival of interest in the occult, can partly be explained as a rebellion against modernity, but partly too it can perhaps be seen as an interest in representations of the almost-forgotten infancy – the magical past – of the individual. Even though the fantasy environments of role-playing games soon included spaces of the future, such as a post-nuclear metropolis or a spaceship, the way of functioning in these spaces was primarily magical – by answering conundrums, for example. Later these games were adapted for a single player, by being put into books as stories with a series of multiple choice questions and with the text as dungeon master. The major work in this form was *Tunnels and Trolls*, a version of which was devised for a mainframe computer.

The commercial development of the games for computer produced a splitting of the games into different categories. First on the scene were arcade games, the most memorable of which is *Space Invaders*, which focused on a real-time engagement with sheets of aliens. The skills called for in the arcade game are mainly fast reaction and good hand–eye coordination; the games' other attractions are their brilliant graphics, the laser precision of their weapons, and the very challenging targets which sometimes have unusual propensities, such as multiplying by splitting when hit. These games began to be installed in amusement arcades in 1975 and soon had the teenage generation addicted.

Meanwhile, listings for games which called for intelligence rather than physical skill were being published in computer magazines. These eventually found a commercial outlet as management or strategy games. Here the emphasis was on functioning in a technological environment and the games' intentions were apparently playfully didactic. For example, in such a game you might play the part of a ruler of a Third World country who – given so many acres of fertile land, so much grain in store, and so many people – has to balance the ponderables to last as many years as possible before being overtaken by famine or revolution.

The adventure game – with which we shall be mostly concerned in this essay – has evolved out of a mixture of all these categories, but its particular form has also been partly determined by its distribution system. The arcade game came into the home via games consoles, and their popularity led to games being developed for the home computer, which in turn led to an enormous expansion of the home computer industry. Ninety-five per cent of the software for home computers is now in the form of video games. But the games had to change, partly because the technology of the home computer was not adequate to the precision needed for a satisfactory arcade game, and partly because the owners of home computers were younger than the arcade frequenters and enjoyed a story framework for the battles.

So it was that the war game/folk-tale/comic strip combination became the dominant form through which children learnt computer literacy both at home and in computer clubs at school. But this history has not explained why this particular form of entertainment has captured the popular imagination to the extent of inspiring a feature film – *Tron* – and affecting the form of television commercials, popular music 'promos', and motifs and style in design in general, which, however short-lived it proves to be, had a very important effect at the time of the introduction of the new technology. Part of any account of the popularity of video games must be the fact that the games represent very powerfully the breakdown of boundaries characteristic of postmodern culture: boundaries between fantasy and science, between high-tech and primitivism, and between play and real life. But the boundary that I think best explains the games' attraction at this time, and particularly for boys and men, is that between anxiety and pleasure.

Industry

There is a lack of clarity about terminology in the production of video games which reflects an uncertainty about what kind of industry the games are. Sometimes the producing companies are called manufacturers, sometimes publishers, and sometimes producers, but the term that seems to be gaining the widest acceptance is 'software houses', with its overtones of domestic production.

The authorship of the games is similarly indeterminate. Often, boys write to a software house with a basic idea for which they are paid a fee. They are able to see themselves as authors or writers, certainly as creators, and earners too. There are also specialist writers of games, but the emphasis is often on the team of crafts-people, as in the film industry, who produced the game in its final form with graphics, music, and sound effects. To emphasise the 'glamour' angle, and at the same time apparently to undercut it with parody, the industry has set up its own festival, at Blackpool rather than Cannes, where the Golden Joystick awards are presented. The craft that is most suppressed in the publicity is the key one of the computer programmer.

In the texts of the games themselves uncertainty of origin is made into a virtue. The basic story is often realised through a pastiche of borrowings from other forms of popular culture. Inter-textuality is incorporated into the surprise mechanisms. For example, in the middle of one adventure game a monster called the Gambling Gorilla forces you into a game of *Play Your Cards Right*, an idea borrowed from a television quiz show. News and current affairs, in their media images, also form the subject of some games: *Harrier Attack* was very popular after the Falklands war, and games about political figures such as *Denis Through the Drinking Glass* and *The Tebbit* have had their moments. Euston Films' television series *Minder* has been made into a game, and films such as *Jaws*, *Death Race* and *Firefox* are reduced to their chase and battle sequences and marketed under the same title. Characters such as Spiderman from boys' comics also have their own adventure games. Other sources include books – especially Tolkien and science fiction, the confession and the diary; fruit machines – there is a game called *Jackpot*; sport – *Horace goes Skiing*, and many motor-bike games, car games, and adaptations of board games; toys – as in *Bear Bovver* (a horror version of the teddy bear's picnic), and *Tribble Trouble*; the circus – has an influence on the form of the games which are often a montage of attractions with an emphasis on oddities and the bizarre; graffiti – in the game *Painter* you are armed with a spray can and realistic squirting noises; music – 'popular' tunes such as 'High Noon' and 'The Yellow Rose of Texas' are one of the attractions of cowboy stories. There are also combinations of sources, for example, sport and science fiction merge in a game where you 'race your light cycle on the infamous grid'.

It has often been noted that the television screen blends together all the variety of material it transmits as 'television'. The games homogenise an even greater variety of sources, and yet there are some surprising absences from possible game ingredients. Most of the borrowings are from popular forms that appeal to boys – one might have expected some girls' comics to have been adopted. There are one or two games marketed as *Games for Girls*, but these are not adventures. One, for example, is a simple representation of horse-jumping, and another is remedial maths. It is interesting that popular children's adventure writers such as Enid Blyton or Arthur Ransome have not so far been adapted for the games market.

Apart from copyright problems it is likely that the familiar settings, relationships between groups of children and happy endings, do not adapt easily to a model of today's single hero waging a personal battle against overwhelming odds. The games market seems only interested in the very deadly or the very silly. The silliness often takes the form of parody, emphasising the self-conscious newness of computer technology and its potential power to upset existing practices and systems.

The games industry does not emphasise its own autonomy, but relies on realising familiar elements of popular culture in its own specific form. It recirculates meanings in such a way that the meanings simply seem to have arisen from the spirit of the times. Its image is not that of an industry making products for passive consumers, but of a people's technology which encourages and enables participation by all who wish to participate. The process of production is well understood by most of the consumers. Listings for games are printed in many magazines and books, and sheets of instructions for writing your own games are available. In this way the games seem to give a certain materiality to discourses about progress towards a dynamic, interactive, networking, high-tech culture. But at least half of the population is not playing along – so it remains an old boys' network.

Scene

It is interesting that the two most popular ways of using a television set other than to watch broadcast programmes – playing video games through a computer, or pop videos through a videocassette recorder – both apparently break with television's traditional role as world-window, undemanding of attention, having an illusion of real time, allowing us ordered glimpses into other people's lives and always with the tantalising possibility that the camera's scanning eye may pick up some exciting live event such as somebody's death or an embassy siege, and connect our aerial to it. Unplug the aerial and the spell of this particular liveness is broken. But when the real world is cut off from the set, television lets us see into, even go into, entirely other, magical worlds, where normal orienting boundaries are transgressed or effaced. This does not mean that our engagement with all these worlds is not one of liveness. Rather, the actual performance required of us in the video game is like being permanently connected to broadcast television's exciting live event.

Although the way that games and pop videos construct their respective worlds is very different, both attempt some kind of totalising experience which demands our undivided attention, temporarily eclipsing all other worlds. I shall examine later how this fits into contemporary discourses of holism, and the experience is also akin to what Lévi-Strauss identified as the 'totalitarian ambition of the savage mind' in contrast to the scientific thinking which aimed to divide the difficulty into as many parts as were necessary in order to solve it. As the explosion in information and technology in the last few years has made the possibilities of division seem infinite, the difficulties incomprehensible, and solutions remote, the popular imagination appears to have taken flight either into worlds like those presented by the pop videos where signs not anchored to meaning seem to suggest and encompass everything,[1] or into model environments like those of the video games where systems still have their own limited and understandable – though strange – internal coherence.

That the totalising experience presented by games is one of the reasons for their popularity is argued particularly clearly in *Gaming – the Future's Language*,[2] a book on role-playing games which claims that linear language no longer gives us information in the most helpful way – that we need to be able to grasp a whole system in a way which descriptions of its parts and their inter-relationships can never give us, but which a model, as in a game, can more easily represent. It is possible to see this concept – of modelling as a whole system – at work alongside the narrative patterns in individual television programmes too. The kind of dramatisation often used by *World in Action* or *Horizon* to demonstrate an issue of current affairs or human concern would be an example of this. Rather than facts being presented in series, a whole situation is shown in action.

In terms of individual psychology the search for knowledge through an experience of wholeness can perhaps be explained by this passage from the *Writings* of Melanie Klein: 'My experience has shown me that the first object of (the) instinct for knowledge is the interior of the mother's body, which the child first of all regards as an object of oral gratification and then as the scene where intercourse between its parents takes place, and where in its phantasy the father's penis and the children are situated.'[3] In relation to oral gratification, Beverle Houston has already proposed that the satisfaction promised by the broadcast output of television is the promise of endless consumption: 'in its endless flow of text, (television) suggests the first flow of nourishment in and from the mother's body, evoking a moment when the emerging sexual drive is still closely linked to – propped on – the life and death urgency of the feeding instinct'.[4] And she goes on to suggest how television may link the mother's body with the world's body for the viewer. Television's flow produces the idea that 'the text issues from an endless supply that is sourceless, natural, inexhaustible, and co-extensive with . . . as abundant, as plentiful as that which is already available to the viewer – psychological reality itself'. If the satisfaction which broadcast television offers is an apparently endless supply of sustenance, video games seem to aim more at satisfying the player's curiosity about the interior of the body from which the supply – and the player himself – originates: 'At the same time as (the child) wants to force its way into its mother's body in order to take possession of the contents . . . it wants to know what is going on and what things look like in there.'[5] Klein's usefulness to the study of video games is her extensive work with children and particularly her analyses of play using toys and other small objects as expressions of fantasies and experiences, and making the representational content of the play more revealing. In analysing the sexual development of boys, she found: '. . . the displacement of everything that is frightening and uncanny onto the invisible inside of a woman's body'.[6] So if it can be deduced from the video game's appeal to boys that these games may represent a journey into the 'maternal cave', it is not surprising to find that the environment down there is a hostile one.

The settings of the adventure games developed from the dungeons of role-playing games into two kinds of dystopia: the unnatural and the natural system. The unnatural system is perhaps the lesser threat, even though it includes such nightmare spaces as the *Catacombs*, where a maze materialises as you wander around it searching for treasure and a food supply before you starve to death or are eliminated by a passing monster; or the *Tomb of Dracula* where you have to ward off Dracula with a number of silver stakes while you steal his treasure from one of the many vaults; or the underground cavern in which you have to seek and destroy *The Orb* before it destroys the earth; or the spaceship *Snowball* with its cargo of deep-frozen humans, one of whom – you – is woken up to deal with an 'alien' situation which has developed in one of the 7,000 locations in the ship.

The other kind of dystopia, the natural or semi-natural system, can be set actually within the human body, such as the mouth (*Molar Maul*) or the bloodstream (*Fantastic Voyage*), but these are clinical and restrained adventures in comparison with the non-human natural environments of an island or a greenhouse or a pond. These are places which appear to be pleasant, harmonious self-regulating systems from the perspective of the passer-by, but in close-up reveal themselves to be red in the many teeth and claws that await your arrival on the scene. The blurb for *Savage Pond*, for example, explains that the tranquil waters of the village pond 'hide a world ruled by death and destruction – governed by the laws of nature. You play the part of a tadpole. . . .' The same kind of socialised biology can be seen in television nature programmes whose main function seems to be to show the savageness of the world without *us*, a savageness which, it seems to be implied, is just below the surface in 'man' too, and has to be controlled by civilisation. In video games it is cities which are good safe places which have to be defended, and the natural environment which is dangerous, evil and has to be escaped from. But what are we to make of this obsessively asserted difference between the civilised human world and the destructiveness of nature? One interpretation is that 'man' fears both his own destructiveness and a fantasised retaliation from the object of his destructive fantasies. Hence the obsessive anxiety with which he repeats the games, where the scene of the struggle is on a scale either so large ('you alone are left to defend the Galaxy') or so small ('you play the part of a tadpole') that the tragic and the comic merge into hysteria; fight it out in the womb.

Language

Tribble Trouble, *Dinky Doo*, *Boog-a-Boo* and *Super-Glooper* show that as far as marketing is concerned a playful, infantile, use of language is the name of the game. But although many names rely for their effect on the sound of words, there is no spoken language within the games. Sometimes a character may sing to you, as in *The Hobbit*, but this has no narrative power. The text communicates to the player only by writing, or by other-worldly sound effects, or by the movement of objects. The player communicates by typing in a telegraphic form of language. For example, a compound sentence such as 'draw sword and kill dragon then get gold and leave' would be the utmost in sophistication to be expected. Very often the player's only response is to simply touch a key or type one word, such as 'look'.

Although games using natural language may develop when or if home computers are made more powerful, it seems not unlikely that part of the attraction of the current games is their lack of facility with language and their consequent use of a different mode of expression, in which objects replace words as a form of communication. Todorov, in exploring the theme of 'the self' in literature of the fantastic, has noted what he calls 'a collapse of the limits between matter and mind' which is found also in madness, in drug experience and 'oddly enough', he says, 'in infants'.[7] As an example he illustrates the way that fantastic action often begins with figurative language: 'He curled himself into a ball and the ball rolled from room to room'. Melanie Klein notes: 'In its play, the child acts instead of speaking. It puts actions – which originally took the place of thoughts – in the place of words.'[8]

Although the players of video games are generally older than infants and not usually mad or on drugs, it seems that in certain situations, for example in the transference situation of psychoanalysis and in some kinds of games, infantile emotions and fantasies can easily be revived: '. . . I found it of great value from the clinical and theoretical point of view that I was analysing both adults and children. I was thereby able to observe the infant's phantasies and anxieties still operative in the adult.'[9] In the games, the magical value of objects often comes from the way they represent something which is usually expressed in language. For example – you are in a dark cave, the light you are carrying suddenly goes out and you are told that something slimy is encircling your legs. You type the command 'look' and are told that you see an octopus grasping your leg with its many tentacles ('hands'). Do you pick it up, or do you kill it? Your dilemma could be illuminated by your knowledge of the expression 'many hands make light work'.

Even objects assumed to be inert matter can and in many cases do, take on the qualities of life – a sword may pick itself up off the floor and put itself in your hand. And you can always use any object as a form of communication by hurling it at the addressee.

Quest

Most of the adventure games involve some sort of quest, but because the narrative coincides absolutely with the action, since the reader has become a performer, the usual structure of the quest, and indeed of narrative, is disturbed. Apart from the different position of the reader/performer the narratives resemble those of the exotic thriller, the travel story or science fiction or, more usually, a combination of all three, with a dash of the uncanny as well. Klein found that in the genres of story that particularly appealed to boys, there was also an emphasis on technology:

In many analyses of boys of the pre-pubertal period or sometimes even in the latency period most of the time is taken up with stories about Red Indians or with detective stories or with phantasies about travel, adventures and fighting, told in serial form and often associated with descriptions of imaginary technical inventions, such as special kinds of boats, machines, cars, contrivances used in warfare, and so on.[10]

She does not discuss the symbolism of the technical inventions, which is surprising considering the part they often play in male quests, but she does emphasise that the fantasy stories are about a search for knowledge in which organs of perception, tools of penetration and, presumably, means of transport can become equated with each other:

By means of the penetrating penis which is equated with an organ of perception, to be more precise, with the eye, the ear or a combination of the two (the boy) wants to discover what sort of destruction has been done inside his mother by his own penis and excrements and by his father's and to what kind of perils his penis is exposed here.[11]

The same equation seems to exist in the different levels involved in playing video games, where the performer is using the technology of the computer keyboard to transport a character who represents his own perceptions round a space which represents his mother's body to discover its dangers and to take away the treasures which it contains: '*The Knight's Quest* – the idea of this game is to guide a knight, who is your eyes and ears, around the country looking for the lost treasures of Merlin.'[12] Most stories begin with a lack which involves the hero going somewhere. But whereas 'quest' narratives have generally been concerned primarily with the hero's departure, his leaving home – and have often been interpreted as the adolescent male's process of separating himself from the family to find 'himself' elsewhere – in the games it is clear that the movement 'away from' stands in for a repressed 'movement towards' the mother's body. It has been pointed out that the irony of Oedipus's situation was that his journey was a return to his family trouble and not a movement away from it as he had thought.

If most quest stories are about a search for knowledge of the interior of the mother's body and the nourishment it contains, then there are at least two different objects of the quest: one at the level of the search for knowledge and one at the level of the fiction, which is an actual object such as lost treasures, or the Holy Grail. In most non-game stories the eventual finding of the actual object satisfies us as readers because it usually coincides with a resolution of all strands of the plot, and because we can identify with the hero's enjoyment of, for example, 'the nourishment of the Holy Grail (which) feeds the soul even as it sustains the body'.[13] In a game, however, we do not identify with someone else's satisfaction, we expect to experience it. So finding the actual object of the quest is invariably disappointing, except in the game which contained clues as to the whereabouts of real buried treasure, but then the satisfaction was outside of the game.

Since there can be no adequate reward for success the game has to be about lack itself – the desire to continue to play – rather than about a final satisfying resolution. Although there is a basic cause–effect structure, the enigmas that keep you playing are not to do with what the treasure will be like, but rather what the next environment will be like, and what will happen there. The events or adventures themselves do not seem to be related to each other by anything but time and place. The environment is important as a container of a variety of hazards – so description in the games is always part of the action – but the hazards do not have any logical connection with each other. For example, you may be in a room with two doors, one guarded by a monster and one unguarded. If you choose to avoid the monster and try to leave by the other door it may open onto a chute which drops you down five floors into a room which could be nearer or further from your destination and will contain its own set of hazards. There are no moral principles such as reward for taking the difficult path or facing up to problems. Obstacles are there only to reinforce desire. The performer is a believer in chance operations and the games progress by the mechanism of surprise rather than suspense, which is also characteristic of uncanny or 'marvellous' narratives in other media.

Unlike other quest narratives the games rarely end with a triumphant and heroic return. This is partly because the hero is not entirely heroic. His behaviour is often like that of a thief. If he gets away at all his return is an undignified flight, and there is rarely anyone to marry to round things off. Women are not there as rewards, they are the landscape, the scene in which the performance takes place. The fascination of video games is not related to resolution; rather it is to be looked for in the opportunities provided for repetition of a set of actions, performed with an almost neurotic compulsion.

Performer

One of the agreed criteria for evaluating a video game is its level of addictiveness. No doubt this is also a criterion among television programme controllers for evaluating series and serials, but in no other cultural form is repeatability of exactly the same experience given such explicit value as it is in games. It seems likely that the addiction is related to the fact that the person who plays the game has some physical participation in it, even if, or because, only at arm's length. It seems important to investigate the fascination of this repetition, not least because, according to some 'purist' accounts, one of the characteristics of popular culture has always been an element of participation, with a resulting awkwardness of the relation between narratives and popular culture. Perhaps the games, crossing the borderlines between story-telling and participatory sport, may be setting a new style for popular narrative.

In the games, 'audience' disappears as the distinction between 'doer' and 'viewer'. The viewer is in a separate space but appears to be in the position of co-creator, or subject to which everything else is the predicate. And yet the emphasis or at least all the interest, is in that predicate, the paranoiac environment. The performer himself has no character traits that are not causal – because he is adventurous, he has an adventure – and, needless to say, there is no development of character as the game progresses. It is the game that controls, as the 'dungeon master' or 'Destinateur', with the performer as only a function of its flow. You perform in it. It performs for you. It performs you. So the enigmas for the performer are of the order of 'where am I?' rather than 'who am I?'. The performer is also apparently a double or a split subject since the game is simultaneously in the first person (you in the real world pressing keys) and the third person (a character on the screen, such as a knight, who represents you in the world of the fiction). This is a different kind of split from that in a spectator watching a film, for example, where identifications can be with a variety of characters and positions. For the performer of a game the first and third person are almost totally identified, so there can be no suspense based on knowing more (having seen more) than the protagonist who represents you. 'Protagonist' is perhaps an inappropriate description since, as the function of the flow, the performer reacts rather than acts.

In the description of most games it is made clear that the performer is on the defensive: he is defending either the entire universe, or Watford or himself-as-tadpole, against destructive forces. Also clear, though sometimes contradictory, is that a kamikaze motivation is the rule rather than the exception. In arcade games you expect to be attacked by sheets of kamikaze aliens, but in the adventure games it is your own behaviour that is suicidal. This is frequently made explicit in the names of games and their software houses, for example, *Get Liquidated*, Kamikaze, Terminal Software. The unlikelihood of your survival seems in fact to be a criterion of a 'good' game, part of its addictiveness. It is quite frightening to try to give an explanation for the popularity of suicide, an explanation which must be in terms of a complex interweaving of many elements. But in relation to the games, however, these elements seem to include a reaction to the threat of nuclear war, a reactivation of infantile feelings triggered by the games, and partly, perhaps, the attractions of masochism. Masochism puts you, as the object of other people's sadistic or murderous intentions, at the centre of attention, which goes some way to shift the emphasis of the game away from the predicate and back to yourself as subject.

Having a nothing-left-to-lose position also overrides the necessity for you to have any other positions, values or ideas and so concentrates your mind on crisis management – a social skill not without its value in Britain in the 1980s. The crises are always *now*, in real-time, live. There are no flashbacks or flashforwards. The game is attached to the present and to reality through the person of the performer. But the first-person performer who presses the keys is actually also in liminal time. Within the game's time there is a close relationship between time and language. All language is performative, and there is no taking refuge in silence. Most situations have to be responded to immediately or they are overtaken by nasty events. This affects the player's time in the real world. Continuing to perform in the game, as in *The Arabian Nights*, is the same as continuing to live. When you stop you die, and the narrative stops too. You have no perspective from which to watch it to the end, you can only presume that the equilibrium reasserts itself, having expelled you.

So what is the pleasure in the repetition of this life and death performance? Melanie Klein argues that what causes the repetition compulsion in children's play is anxiety about an unreal danger directed towards the insides of their own bodies. We are concerned here not with how this anxiety arises, but how it is dealt with. In this, Melanie Klein's theory is informed by her practice in analysing children and her success in relieving their anxiety. According to her theory each sex has its own essentially different mode of 'mastering' anxiety. The boy, putting all his faith in the omnipotence of his penis-as-magic-wand (not surprising in a culture which values this object so highly) turns the danger from an internal to an external one and 'embodies' it as his father's penis inside his mother's body. The strategy is to go into battle with a similar weapon to that of the enemy, and in a theatre of war well away from his own insides.[14] Once having entered the mother's body in fantasy he risks the danger of being castrated by his father's penis, which is waiting for him in there, or of having his own penis prevented from retreating, and being shut inside his mother's body:

These phantasies contain such ideas that 'the penis, incorporated into the mother, turns into a dangerous animal or into weapons loaded with explosive substances'; or that her vagina, too, is transformed into an instrument of death, as for instance, a poisoned mouse-trap.[15]

However, if he performs well he will be able to destroy everything in sight and escape intact. After this he is often overwhelmed by a need to restore what he has destroyed, but doubts his ability to do this:

His fear of not being able to put things right again arouses his still deeper fear of being exposed to the revenge of the objects which, in his phantasy, he has killed and which keep on coming back again . . . it is not until a rather more advanced stage has been reached that its anxiety is also felt as a sense of guilt and sets the obsessional mechanisms in motion. One is amazed to discover that . . . the mastering of anxiety has become (the child's) greatest pleasure.[16]

But, of course, the anxiety can never be finally mastered by this mechanism.

The endeavour in this account is to show the centrality of the relationship of the infant to the mother's body; the fact that this is so clear in video games, is, I think, more important than the boy's use of the phallus–penis as a means of separating himself from his mother. Since, I believe, 'the masculine position' has not changed much since Melanie Klein was analysing her little boys crashing engines and cars together (and the male directors of silent films were putting the same scenes on the screen) it would be surprising if boys adopted any other mechanism for separating, and even more amazing if they were able to repudiate separation itself. Although it can be argued that society is (however slowly) beginning to de-centre men – through changing work patterns as much as through changing discourses of sexuality – it is still no surprise that men respond to this uncertainty by inventing things that, while seeming new, while seeming to offer a breakdown of boundaries, help them master anxiety by reasserting the old boundaries and differences.

Machine

As demonstrated by Melanie Klein's observations, and cultural forms such as the James Bond phenomenon, machinery seems to be a necessary part of male fantasy and performance. The camera that Vertov thought he was, seemed to offer a precision that humans could only envy and aspire to. The new generation of machines produces an even more ecstatic identification, for they offer a magical liberation from all kinds of rigidity, including the laws of time and space. Video games can use computer graphics to produce multi-perspectival representations, a fourth dimension, making our normal perceptions of time and space seem inadequate. Video-effects technology, now widespread in the commercials and music industries, seduces the viewer into identifying with an undefined future – represented by laser-light and processed sound – which has a relationship which needs to be explored with a present which is in some ways over-defined, and in other ways falling apart.

Not only has technology been incorporated into art, but the performance of a machine, like that of a person, is now no longer judged by what objects it can make, but what it can organise, what effects it can create. The structure of present technology is less important in the popular imagination than the more visible structure of the old mechanical machines were in their day. There is little fun in taking an integrated circuit apart, so the emphasis is now on the process of working with the machines rather than on understanding how they work. Behind all of which is the frightening fact that the machines of artificial intelligence are incomprehensible to the people who work with them, are out of touch with human reality, and therefore are, to all intents and purposes, out of control.

This power that the new technology is rightly feared to have may partly account for the carefully cultivated 'cuddly' image of the micro-computer. Posters selling them to the business world often use childlike motifs, such as cartoon figures from children's television programmes, to show how simple they are. Publicity for the video games themselves is usually so extreme in its death-and-destruction imagery that its obvious parody undercuts the fear. Some games incorporate an element of bathos: 'Find and destroy the Dictator's battle headquarters and save Watford'; and sometimes the scale of a game is that of a micro-world in which the protagonist is a tadpole, or a flea. All of which builds on the unspoken fear that the future of the world is indeed with the machines of artificial intelligence and if you can't lick 'em. . . .

Women and Fantasy

Feminist work has begun to enter debates about popular culture through studies of cultural forms which are popular with women, such as the 'woman's film' of 1940s cinema or television soap operas. This is a welcome complement to the emphasis on male pleasures given by studies of sport and crime fiction, but it still begs the question of why there should be such a clearly marked split along gender lines in popular cultural forms. This section tentatively suggests some psychoanalytical and cultural reasons why women's fantasies are different from men's and lead to a different kind of cultural activity.

The position of women has changed considerably since Melanie Klein's *Writings*, so it seems appropriate to augment her work here with observations and theory from more recent feminist psychoanalytical practice, and I have particularly drawn on that of Luise Eichenbaum and Susie Orbach at the Women's Therapy Centre in London. Both Klein and the more recent studies suggest that girls come to terms with their earliest anxiety in a different way from boys. The anxiety is still about an unreal threat to their insides, which in boys in our culture gets confused with anxiety about their different anatomy from that of the mother and their consequent need to separate, with the result that the boy projects his fear onto the mother's body and fights the Oedipal conflict in there with his penis. In girls the original anxiety is not overlaid by anxiety about differences, so the threat is not projected outwards and remains a threat to their insides. Klein suggests that the girl feels that her body is poisoned and for this reason needs good nourishment from the mother's body to make it well again. The observations at the Women's Therapy Centre also suggest that girls' and women's feelings of lack are usually about the need for nourishment. The therapists make clear that this in their view is in opposition to the penis-envy theory: 'We have found no evidence that the way women experience themselves as inadequate connects in any way with the fantasy of a penis or its transformation into a baby.'[17]

The frustration the girl suffers at never being able to get enough nourishment leads, according to Klein, to fantasy attacks on the mother's body using as weapons the faeces (represented by shiny things) and magical thoughts. But the mother's body, because of the anatomical identity with her own, which it also represents, is an uncomfortable setting for a war game, so in the girl's fantasy the emphasis is not on the attack but rather on the need to repair the damage the attacks have done. For women, then, the leading anxiety, obsession and therefore pleasure is about restitution. Melanie Klein notes that girls will pile up pieces of paper neatly in a box until it is quite full. The neatness and carefulness are because restitutive acts must adhere in every detail to the damage done in fantasy. She observed that drawing, sewing, making dolls' dresses or reading books were typical ways of reconstituting the mother's body, and therefore the girl's own. She maintains that giving birth to a baby is particularly satisfying because it signifies that the interior of the woman's body is unharmed and can produce good things, which in fantasy represents restoring a number of objects, even in some cases recreating a whole world.

Although it is not possible here to go into detail, it is important to note that Eichenbaum and Orbach argue very strongly that women's anxiety and their specific ways of dealing with it are culturally and historically produced and are mediated through the psychology of the mother and the effect of the social position of women on the mother's psychology. There is also nothing in Melanie Klein's observations – as opposed to her arguments – that suggests a biological essentialism about the way the two sexes deal with anxieties. She noted that girls do make attacks, and are not lacking in weapons when necessary. Similarly, boys do have a restitutive phase after an attack and will often build towns and villages with the toys. The implication is therefore that the pressures which produce and maintain a gendered split between activities of attack and those of restitution are cultural. The activities themselves then become part of the pressures which discourage women from projecting outwards and fighting for what they need, and which prevent men from recognising their restitutive needs except in sublimations such as do-it-yourself.

The obsessions in both sexes seem to start in response to a cultural pressure for separation. It has always been assumed that separation from the mother was more difficult for boys than for girls, because of the complication of the Oedipus conflict, but Eichenbaum and Orbach maintain that in fact separation is easier for the male gender because the anatomical differences make boundaries clearer. This may suggest that a fixed sexual identity is also easier for, and more important to, men since they are defining themselves *against* something. Later men then try to define women against their male otherness, but because women did not begin by defining themselves in difference, they may be less phobic about undefined sexuality, and this has implications for their preferred cultural forms.

Since our culture is dominated by male definitions of women, it is not surprising that in their most popular forms women's fantasies appear in the guise of romances or soap operas, where the preoccupation is with reconciliation – or lack of it in relationships. However, it is quite instructive to look at the more conscious fantasies of feminist fiction where women are renegotiating their identity. The most striking feature of these in the context of the above discussion is the emphasis placed on new worlds, often Utopian, or on new creatures with different or unclear sex/gender boundaries. But also interesting is the fact that if Greimas's model of the quest narrative is placed over these feminist narratives there are large passages which fall outside the model – usually passages in which nothing happens. This exercise also reveals that many of the narratives are reverse quests, often away from male culture, which is represented by civilisation and high technology, and towards the 'womb of nature', and either a primitive, artisanal culture, or complete disintegration.[18]

So, it is not surprising that video games and other forms of popular interest based on battles have little appeal for women. Video games are particularly unattractive since they are part of a technology which (unfortunately, in my view) is identified with male power, and they are about mastering a specifically male anxiety in a specifically male way. The obsessive activities of restoration which are performable, and have been in continuous performance by women for hundreds of years, such as knitting, sewing, looking after and talking about babies, similarly seem to have little appeal for men. It is perhaps for this reason that they have never been studied seriously as part of popular culture. So far men's need to project has led to their obsessions being amplified and made available to us all. It would take major cultural and material changes to shift the emphasis on to activities of restoration and this is perhaps partly why the separate development of a low-tech culture seems so appealing to many women at the present time. It seems to be the only opposition, however unrealistic.

Conclusion

> We must make allowance for the complex and unstable process whereby discourse can be both an instrument and an effect of power, but also a hindrance, a stumbling-block, a point of resistance and a starting point for an opposing strategy.
>
> Michel Foucault, *The History of Sexuality*, vol. 1, p. 101.

In trying to understand the relationship between gender and the micro-world of video games the discourse of psychoanalysis has been a helpful one, but in order now to look at the place of the games within the wider relationships between gender, technology, history and cultural forms, other discourses have to be brought in. The statement of Foucault which introduces this section suggests a framework for looking at this inter-relationship of discourses. It is fairly clear how discourse can be an instrument of power, but less obvious how it comes to be a point of resistance. Foucault proposes the idea of 'reverse' discourses. He demonstrates that a discourse which projects and amplifies itself enough also makes it possible for a reverse discourse to be formed and heard from the place which it addresses. A reverse discourse is not necessarily an oppositional one since it is constructed in the terms of the one that brought it into being, but it can be the starting point for an opposing strategy. So, for example, the nineteenth-century discourse which integrated the woman's body into the sphere of medical practice eventually produced a reverse discourse from women about their rights over their own bodies. This has helped women gain some control over their own fertility and sexuality, but it has also kept women's discourse preoccupied with the body and with sexuality, until recently, when the concern with body over individual reproduction and life has grown into an opposition to the technologies of mass destruction and, by extension, has reinforced an opposition to all technology. A recognition that the technologies of war are related to male anxieties and desires is summed up in the anti-nuclear slogan 'take the toys from the boys'.

The focus on the body, however, has also generated a discourse about wholeness – coming no doubt as well from women's anxieties about restitution – which has emphasised the integration of all systems of the body and denied separations between psychic and physical states. This has fed into already existing discourses about alternatives to western medicine, and indeed to western science and philosophy. So there is now a growing popular discourse of 'holism' which, if not reinstating an Aristotelian universe or Lévi-Strauss's 'savage mind', is certainly supporting religious intuitive thinking as against scientific ways of understanding. This discourse can be seen at work in the totalising representations of both the utopias of feminist fiction and the dystopias of video games. It also partly explains the blurring of borderlines, in both forms, between past, present and future. It is impossible to totalise the jumble of the present unless it is seen as the future of something past or 'the past of something yet to come',[19] or unless our brains could hold, process and access as much information as a powerful computer, and as rapidly. There is a fear, a fearful knowledge, which is scarcely to be recognised as real, that we are entering a time when a great deal of executive power will be realised through, if not transferred to, machines. Power will become unassailable, because invisible. With this knowledge of power come anxieties about exploitation and manipulation, about inability to separate oneself from it. To this fear video games are in many ways the predictable male response: the video screen makes the fear visible, but obliquely, for like the Medusa, it must not be directly confronted; the visibility of the fear allows it to be expressed but remains unspoken; the quest for the performer's destiny occupies the fantasy space in which infantile battles were fought in the mother's body and won; the male references in the intertextuality of the content of the games gives the male player a sense of familiarity which helps him over the strangeness of the new technology; the domestic image and setting of the home computer constantly remind the performer of his mastery and his power to switch the machine off, even if it does beat him at his own game. And as his own game seems to be the rehearsing of his own death, to lose is only to affirm his own resurrection. Foucault points out the irony that the forces which have power over life, now translated into the management of survival because of their capability of producing death on a global scale, can only be avoided by the individual's right to suicide. All aspects of life, particularly sexuality, being so closely scrutinised, death remains the only secret. However, as it is only in the fantasy of the video games that a single suicidal enemy is a real threat to a strong power, there seems little potential for a discourse from the position of death becoming an oppositional force to be reckoned with. On the evidence of the games the preferred male solution seems to be to bury themselves in the mother's body with their fantasy weapons and forget about the very real dangers in the world outside until these dangers manifest themselves as disputes about boundaries, as in the Falklands 'crisis', in which case they can be understood and dealt with by playing the war game, again.

If there is the possibility of a reverse discourse to the one that aligns the uses of technology with maleness, with domination and eventually with destruction, it has to come from the position where technology and women are addressed as the same thing, or as part of the same scenario, and has to take account of the part technology plays in male fantasy. While technology is seen as weapons to be used in the hellish battles within women's bodies, women will never be seen, or be able to see themselves as the users of technology: 'In the micro industry 99.9 per cent of customers are men, largely because the product is beyond the cerebral capacity of the weaker sex and also because it doesn't come in pretty colours.'

It is not of course just infantile fantasies that sustain opinions like that, found in the magazine *Computer Dealer*. Such opinions are supported by other discourses, but particularly those relating to sexuality.

Foucault believed that in the nineteenth century sexuality was constructed and used as one of the technologies of power, as power changed from being the power to inflict death to the power to manage and organise life and survival. I would argue that sexuality is now such an important form of control and so implicated in discourses of power and domination that technology itself has had to become sexualised in order for it to be apparently under control.

There is already a growing concern among educators about the lack of participation by women in the new technology, but so far this concern has only manifested itself in terms of an 'equal opportunities' issue. In order to help a reverse discourse to emerge, more work needs to be done on the relationship between a technologised sexuality and a sexualised technology.

Notes

1 E. Ann Kaplan, 'A Post-Modern Play of the Signifier? Advertising, Pastiche and Schizophrenia in Music Television', in Phillip Drummond and Richard Paterson (eds.), *Television in Transition* (London: BFI Publishing, 1985).

2 R. D. Duke, *Gaming – The Future's Language* (London: Sage, 1974).

3 Melanie Klein, *Writings* II (London: Hogarth Press, 1980), pp. 173–4.

4 Beverle Houston, 'Viewing Television: the metapsychology of endless consumption' (Paper given at the International Television Studies Conference, London, 1984).

5 Klein, *Writings* II, p. 174.

6 Klein, *Writings* II, p. 260.

7 T. Todorov, *The Fantastic* (New York: Cornell, 1975), p. 115.

8 Klein, *Writings* II, p. 9.

9 Klein, *Writings* III, p. 138.

10 Klein, *Writings* II, p. 81n.

11 Klein, *Writings* II, p. 245.

12 R. Bilboul, J. Durrant and M. Spencer, *The Good Software Guide* (London: Fontana, 1984), p. 25.

13 *The Holy Grail*, quoted in T. Todorov, *The Poetics of Prose* (Oxford: Blackwell, 1977). (Note the association with Mothering!)

14 Ronald Reagan's proposal for a real live performance of *Star Wars* seems to be based on the same strategy.

15 Klein, *Writings* II, p. 132.

16 Klein, *Writings* II, p. 169.

17 Luise Eichenbaum and Susie Orbach, *Understanding Women* (London: Pelican, 1985), p. 31, n.10.

18 For this information I am grateful to a workshop on 'The uses and applications of Greimas' model for the analysis of novels written by women', led by Kristien Hemmerechts at the Women's Writing Conference held at Manchester Polytechnic in September 1984. Greimas' model can be read in A. J. Greimas, *Sémantique structurale* (Paris: Larousse, 1966); and *Du Sens* (Paris: Seuil, 1970). There is an English translation/adaptation of these models given in J. Culler, *Structuralist Poetics* (London: Routledge & Kegan Paul, 1975). The novels studied in relation to the model were: M. Atwood, *Surfacing*; D. Lehmann, *Dusty Answer*; J. Rhys, *Good Morning Midnight*; M. Sinclair, *Life and Death of Harriet Frean*; and S. Townsend Warner, *Lolly Willowes*.

19 Fredric Jameson, 'Progress versus utopia, or can we imagine the future?', *Science Fiction Studies* no. 9 (1982).

VII

Video Replay
Families, Films and Fantasy

VALERIE WALKERDINE
From *Formations of Fantasy*, edited by Victor Burgin, James
Donald and Cora Kaplan (London: Methuen, 1986)

Why would anyone want to watch people watching television? This is the question trenchantly posed by Valerie Walkerdine in the following discussion; and if your first reaction is that such scrutiny is indeed rather intrusive and pointless, Walkerdine makes it clear how heavily such a judgment bears on all forms of audience research, but particularly on a British cultural-studies tradition which we are used to thinking of as 'on the people's side'.

Walkerdine's thinking grows out of the attempts made in the 70s to conceptualise the viewer as 'positioned' – by the text, but also by objective class membership, by the subjective way in which this translates into lived experience (Althusserian 'ideology'), and by gender–race–age–disability discrimination patterns. A retrospective study of the Positioning Metaphor is urgently needed, since it now seems to have been helpful and paralysing in roughly equal proportions. Given the scepticism felt within this tradition about other ('bourgeois') attempts to set up a predictive social science, Positioning Theory showed in its heyday a curious willingness to set itself up as potentially predictive. ('Feed the Text's Strategies and all the viewer's Positions into the Imaginary Computer, and we should be able to tell just what the viewer will make of the Text, and explain why he or she is so captivated by it or so resistant to it.') This now looks like a scientistic fantasy; it also shares with its enemy social-science modes a tendency to demean the *subjects* so confidently *placed* in their subject-*positions*, despite the caveats that were almost always entered about real people not being reducible to the positions on offer.

On the other hand, the Positioning Metaphor has the merit of focussing attention on how constrained any one of us is, and by what forces. Walkerdine's description of the Coles watching *Rocky II* involves an attempt to rethink the relationship between constrainedness and fantasy, both for the Coles and for herself as researcher/subject. The rethink involves doing justice to a form of viewing which initially strikes her – and, surely, as we read the transcript, us – as unsettling, even pathological. As she brings us to understand the forces shaping Mr Cole's commitment as (male) viewer to a 'fighting' ethos, alongside the forces shaping her (and our?) nervousness about this ethos, Walkerdine moves Positioning Theory a long way towards a sensitivity and generosity that its earlier formulations lacked.

M.A./J.O.T.

I am seated in the living room of a council house in the centre of a large English city. I am there to make an audio-recording as part of a study of 6-year-old girls and their education. While I am there, the family watches a film, *Rocky II*, on the video. I sit, in my armchair, watching them watching television. How to make sense of this situation?

Much has been written about the activity of watching films in terms of scopophilia. But what of that other activity, film theory, or, more specifically, what about this activity of research, of trying so hard to understand what people see in films? Might we not call this the most perverse voyeurism?[1] Traditionally, of course, observation – like all research methods in the human and social sciences – has been understood as, at worst, minimally intrusive on the dynamics and interaction unfolding before the eyes of the observer, who is herself outside the dynamic. My argument is that such observation, like all scientific activity, constitutes a voyeurism in its will to truth, which invests the observer with 'the knowledge', indeed the logos. The observer then should be seen as the third term, the law which claims to impose a reading on the interaction. This is offered as an explanation to which the observed have no access and yet which is crucial in the very apparatuses which form the basis of their regulation. In addition, the observer becomes the silent Other who is present in, while apparently absent from, the text. Clearly, I cannot escape the contradictions and effects of my own need here to produce a reading, an analysis, an account of what happened. But in order to insert myself explicitly into the text, I shall attempt to speak also of my own identification with the film I watched with this family.

My concern is therefore not just with the voyeurism of the film spectator, but also with the voyeurism of the theorist – in whose desire for knowledge is inscribed a will to truth of which the latent content is a terror of the other who is watched.

From this perspective, I shall explore, in a preliminary way, the relationship of families to television and video and, more particularly, the effectivity of the films they watch upon the constitution of family dynamics. Within film theory concepts from psychoanalysis do not seem to have been used to examine how specific films have been read in practice, nor how they produce their specific effects. Identification, for example, is often discussed in terms of the effectivity of representation as distorted perception – the viewer is accorded no status which pre-exists the film. Psychoanalysis is used, in the end, to explore the relations within a film rather than to explain the engagement with the film by viewers already inserted in a multiplicity of sites for identification.

The family I shall be discussing did not watch *Rocky II* as ideal, acultural viewers, for example, but in relation to complex and already constituted dynamics. And these dynamics cannot simply be reduced to differences of class, gender and ethnicity – although the question of how these enter into the divided relations of domestic practices is, nevertheless, central.

Such differences themselves exist within a regime of practices, in which 'fantasy' and 'reality' already operate in a complex and indiscernible dynamic.[2] In trying to understand the domestic and family practices in which adults and children are inscribed, therefore, I examine the play of discourses and the relations of signification which already exist. And I approach the viewing of the film in the same way, as a dynamic intersection of viewer and viewed, a chain of signification in which a new sign is produced – and thus a point of production or creation in its own right.

In discussing families watching films, I try to show how aspects of the filmic representations are incorporated into the domestic practices of the family. This explains the themes and emphases in my argument. First, there is the question of how to understand the act of *watching*. I shall describe the watching of families as a surveillant voyeurism, a 'will to tell the truth' about families which contains a set of desperate desires – for power, for control, for vicarious joining-in – as well as a desperate fear of the other being observed. Secondly, I want to challenge the 'intellectualisation of pleasures' which seems to be the aim of much analysis of mass film and television. In opposition to the implicit contrast between the masses narcotised by the mass fantasies produced by the consciousness industry and the intellectual unbefuddled by the opium of ideology, it seems to me that we should look at the desire for forms of mastery that are present in our own subjectification as cultural analysts before rushing to 'save' 'the masses' from the pleasures of imaginary wish-fulfilment. Thirdly, therefore, I stress the materiality of power and oppression. Politics, in other words, are central to the analysis.

Rocky II

The Coles are a working-class family. They live on a council estate and have three children – Joanne, aged 6, Robert, 9, and James, 13 – together with a large Alsatian dog, named Freeway.[3] I am seated in their living room. The video of *Rocky II* is being watched, sporadically, by the whole family. I sit there, almost paralysed by the continued replay of round 15 of the final boxing sequence, in which Mr Cole is taking such delight. Paralysed by the violence of the most vicious kind – bodies beaten almost to death. How can they? What do they see in it? The voyeuristic words echo inside my head, the typical response of shame and disgust which condemns the working class for overt violence and sexism (many studies show, for example, how much more sex-role stereotyping there is amongst working-class families). In comparison with a bourgeois liberalism it seems shameful, disgusting (key aspects of voyeurism) and quite inexplicable except by reference to a model of pathology.

I do not remember if I saw all of the film then. All I recall now is the gut-churning horror of constant replay. Much later, when beginning to do the work for an analysis, I hired the video of *Rocky II* and watched it in the privacy of my office, where no one could see. And at that moment I recognised something that took me far beyond the pseudo-sophistication of condemning its macho sexism, its stereotyped portrayals. The film brought me up against such memories of pain and struggle and class that it made me cry. I cried with grief for what was lost and for the terrifying desire to be somewhere and someone else: the struggle to 'make it'. No longer did I stand outside the pleasures of engagement with the film. I too wanted Rocky to win. Indeed I *was* Rocky – struggling, fighting, crying to get out. I am not saying that there is one message or reading here for all to pick up. On the contrary the film engages me as a viewer at the level of fantasy because I can insert myself into, position myself with, the desires and pain woven into its images. Someone else might have identified with Rocky's passive and waiting wife. But Rocky's struggle to become bourgeois is what reminded me of the pain of my own.[4] The positions set up within the film then create certain possibilities, but it seems to be the convergence of fantasies and dream which is significant in terms of engaging with a film.

One aspect of the popularity of Hollywood films like the *Rocky* series is that they *are* escapist fantasies: the imaginary fulfilment of the working-class dream for bourgeois order. And they reveal an escape route, one which is all the more enticing given the realistic mode of its presentation, despite the very impossibility of its realism.[5] Such are popular films then, not because violence or sex-role stereotyping is part of the pathology of working-class life, but because escape is what we are set up to want, whatever way we can get it. For the majority of women and men, the escape-route open to me, that of the mind, of being clever, is closed. It is the body which presents itself either as the appropriate vehicle for bourgeois wardship (all those women starlets, beauty queens and 'kept' women) or for the conquering champion who has beaten the opponents into submission.

What is important for me about watching a film like this is the engagement, the linking, of the fantasy space of the film and viewer. Watching *Rocky II*, to be effective, necessitates an already existent constitution of pains, of losses and desires for fulfilment and escape, inhabiting already a set of fantasy spaces inscribing us in the 'everyday life' of practices which produce us all. This does not imply a concept of a unitary subject, whose location in a 'social totality' determines the reading of a film, but rather a fragmented subjectivity in which signifying practices produce manifest and latent contents for the inscription of fantasy. Such wishes cannot be understood outside signifying activity – which is itself also discursive and involves aspects of power and regulation.

The magic convergence, therefore, is an act of signification, the fusion of signifier and signified to produce a new sign, a new place, desire leaping across the terminals, completing the circuit, producing the current. These multiple sites of my formation, these dynamic relations, are the diversity of practices in which power and desire inscribe me. The reader is *not* simply in the text, not then the spectator in the film, motivated simply by a pathological scopophilia. The *position* produced for the reader or spectator is not identical with an actual reader constituted in multiple sites and positions. Perhaps the 'desire to look' belongs with the film theorist and social or behavioural scientist who disavow their own engagement and subsume their own fantasies into a move into the symbolic, the desire for the mastery of explanation. Just as there is no 'reader' (simply and exclusively) 'in the text' nor is there a preformed subject whose experience is reflected, biased or distorted in the film. If fantasies of escape are what we are set up for, then any amount of cinematic fantasy posing as realism about the drudgery of our lives will not convince us to abandon our enticing fantasies.

There is, in this watching, a moment of *creation* – if it is effective and successful as a cultural product for the mass market whose desires it helps to form. There is certainly an aesthetic or a pleasure, and yet each of these terms is more redolent of an up-market art movie in which there are taken only to be acceptable, not nasty, pleasures. An aesthetic is cold. What I am talking about is red hot. It is what makes the youths in cinema audiences cheer and scream for Rocky to win the match – including many black youths, even though the Mr Big of boxing, whom he defeats, is black. It is what makes Mr Cole want to have the fight on continuous and instant replay forever, to live and triumph in that moment. And it is what makes me throb with pain.

Rocky II, like *Rocky I*, was a great box-office success. It brought in huge cash returns and Sylvester Stallone as Rocky was said to live out the part of the poor Italian-American who makes it in his 'real' life. The films tap into the classic working-class image of boxing as an escape-route for tough young men. Boxing turns oppression into a struggle to master it, seen as spectacle. In Stallone's later films this is transformed into a one-man defence of 'America' (against Russia in *Rocky IV*) and the 'forgotten heroes' of the Vietnam War in *Rambo*. Although it is easy to dismiss such films as macho, stupid and fascist, it is more revealing to see them as fantasies of omnipotence, heroism and salvation. They can thus be understood as a counterpoint to the experience of oppression and powerlessness.

Rocky II tells the story of a successful fighter who, after a successful career in the ring, tries to go straight. Despite his attempts to achieve respectability and a 'decent' lifestyle, he can find no way out of the misery of menial manual labour (working in an abattoir) except a return to boxing. Rocky is portrayed as a 'tryer', a 'fighter', a small man who beats the black, villainous Mr Big by dint of his perseverance, his 'sticking power'. The story thus engages the fight for the bourgeois dream of the small man who has 'brawn not brains'. Rocky's attempts to get a clerical job or to become an actor in television commercials are doomed because he cannot read. It is the woman he marries, the quiet girl, who equally struggles for him, who bears and nearly loses 'his' child, who like the good-enough bourgeois mother, teaches him to read. Yet, failing all else, in order to become respectable, he has to return to fighting and he has to fight to win, nearly killing himself in the process. The struggle to be respectable is therefore also to be able to 'provide for' and 'look after' a wife and child/ren who will not need to work, suffer or go short of anything. The film itself is replete with such fantasies. What is important for Rocky's story is the presentation of the *necessity* of fighting for survival. Certainly here the fight pays off and the hero wins. But it validates trying and fighting and therefore the singular effectivity of bodily strength and the multiple significance of 'fighting'. Understood in this way, 'macho-masculinity' becomes no mindless sexism, but a bid for mastery, a struggle to conquer the conditions of oppression, which remain as terror. It also throws into sharp relief the effects of the bourgeois mastery of the mind. These do not require the *overt* forms of physical violence or shows of strength, which are replaced by symbolic violence and displays of logocentric pyrotechnics.

Intricately tied in with the necessity for fighting, and therefore for aggression, is the necessity to protect a 'good woman'. The wife is both to be protected from other men (with more money and more glittering prizes?) and to be protected from the ' streets' – from being the bad woman, the whore, the tart. She has to be kept pure and virginal. In this respect Rocky is represented as a 'big man' at home. The sets are made especially small so that he looks giant-size and yet remains a 'small man' in the outside world: a man who has to fight and to struggle therefore 'to be' the big man at home. This shift is especially significant for Mr Cole.

As well as being portrayed as bodily big at home and small outside and in the ring, Rocky is also presented as an outer spectacle, hiding inner pain. Rocky is a public hero who provides good entertainment. 'The crowd' and the 'public' do not see the inner suffering and struggle which produce this entertainment; only his wife does. In the opening minutes of the film, when Rocky has won a match after almost being beaten to death, he screams 'Adrienne, Adrienne', like a desperate child; her protector is in reality dependent upon her. Against a musical crescendo on the soundtrack they slowly struggle to reach each other. Finally, when he is safe in her arms, they say 'I love you' to each other. This shot is held for several seconds, before a cut to the titles for *Rocky II* – this narrative image provides the lead-in from, and flashback to, the first film.

Fighting, as a key signifier in the film, is related to a class-specific and gendered use of the body (as against the mind). Masculinity as winning is constantly played across by the possibility of humiliation and cowardice (that he is 'chicken'): Rocky's body is constantly presented as beaten, mutilated and punished. The film always presents this body as spectacle and triumph, triumph over and through that mutilation, which is the desperate fear which fuels it. Although such a reading of masculinity is now common within film analysis[6] it is the *class-specific* aspects of this masculinity that are important. Physical violence is presented as the only way open to those whose lot is manual and not intellectual labour, and another aspect of this classed masculinity is the wardship of a woman who does not have to work (like a man) but whose domain is the domestic.

The fantasy of the fighter is the fantasy of a working-class male omnipotence over the forces of humiliating oppression which mutilate and break the body in *manual* labour. Boxing as a sport is a working-class-specific development of fighting, in which young poor men break their bodies for prize money. It is a classic working-class spectacle in that sense, in which the boxer's mutilation provides the sport for the spectators. What is to be won is both the symbolic conquering of oppression and monetary gain – although of course, young men are as exploited in boxing as anywhere else.

Echoes of upward mobility recur throughout the film, and not just in Rocky's attempts, despite his wife's protests, to display the 'proletarian flash' of cars, jewellery and clothes. Particularly significant is the way his attempts at respectability are seen to be thwarted by his failure at school. Asked what he was thinking about in the last round of his fight as he is loaded into an ambulance, he replies, 'I don't know – that I should have stayed at school or something.' His interview for a clerical job goes like this:

Interviewer   How far did you go in high school, Mr Balboa? Do you have a criminal record? Would you be interested in manual labour?

Rocky	Well, I've got nothing against honest manual labour, it's just that I'd like to see if I can make a living sitting down, like you're doing over there.[7]
Interviewer	Can I be honest? No one's going to offer you an office job; there's too much competition. Why don't you fight? I read somewhere that you're a very good fighter.
Rocky	Yeah, well, when you're punched in the face five hundred times, it kind of stings after a while.

And at a later interview, he is told:

> Hey, look, pal, you've got to be realistic. You've got no high school diploma, no qualifications. Wouldn't you be better with a good paying menial job?

'Adapting to reality' is presented as the most punitive of options, for it condemns him to a life of misery and poverty. It is bourgeois dreams which provide a way out, and the body which is the vehicle, given an absence of 'brains'. Constantly, the 'assurance' of a secure gender, and class identity is subverted by Rocky's terror, struggle and failure – in fighting and reading for example. A coherent identity, a sense of having 'made it', is presented as a sham, not anything easily achieved.

Meanwhile Adrienne works and suffers in silence, having got a job in a pet shop to help out. She gives birth prematurely through overwork and goes into a coma. No wonder that Rocky needs to box, because he is saving her from death through overwork. She is a key figure: she simultaneously prevents Rocky from boxing and spurs him on to win. The struggle is thus also a specifically gendered struggle, in which positions relating to domestic and waged work are played out.

The Coles

I have chosen to explore the term 'fight/ing/er' because it figures centrally in the *Rocky* films, not as a celebration of masculinity in a positive sense, but as something Rocky is 'driven to', a last resort.[8] I now want to consider how 'fighting' enters as a relation into domestic discursive practices and produces a certain effectivity with respect to the family members, linking this to my presence as an observer and thus to the monitoring of pathology (correct language for example) and to moral regulation.

Let me begin by outlining briefly how the observation was experienced as my surveillance of them. When I entered the house for the first recording, Mr Cole shouted to his daughter, 'Joanne, here's your psychiatrist!' I had never mentioned psychiatry, let alone psychology, and yet it was evident to him that I was monitoring normality/pathology. In addition to this, on several occasions he made reference to the monitoring of 'correct language'. Joanne would at first not wear the microphone and Mr Cole was quite clear that, if nothing was said into it, 'they' would think she had nothing to say. Quite.

> Do you know you're wasting the tape, you are missy. Gonna go back to school and say what did Dodo do at home? And they'll say 'nothing'. Here's the proof – a blank tape.

In addition, he tells his daughter to 'do nothing, just act normal' and yet tries to encourage her to speak by saying 'The rain in Spain falls mainly on the plain' or 'How now brown cow' (phrases often used in elocution lessons, of course) into the microphone. On other occasions, moral regulation centres around dichotomy 'rude vs. respectable' behaviour.

How did the family watch *Rocky II*? I shall begin with the final, bloody rounds of the boxing match at the end of the film. At this time Mr Cole (F), Joanne (J), or Do, and her brother, Robert (R), were watching, together with the 3-year-old child of a friend, called Jonas. Mrs Cole (M) was in the kitchen, working, and 13-year-old James was elsewhere in the house. I reproduce below an annotated transcription of the sequence.[9]

Rocky II, the video

000

Fight scene, possibly the 15th round.

R: (untranscribed)

F: Watch, watch. Cor he ain't half whacking him, ain't he, Do?

Watch here.

010

F tells J to go and ask M to make some tea. J goes to the kitchen. M's friend is with her – Scottish accent – with her young child. They talk about karate.

050

J is back in the TV room. She brings in the doughnuts. Film is on in the background.

J goes out again. She talks to M in the kitchen.

090

J is back in TV room. There is general conversation going on, 'Do you want a doughnut', etc. J is not saying much.

M's friend comes in with younger child.

112

J is sitting on the settee, eating a bun.

115

No-one is saying much.

118

F: Hey, watch this, Rob.

R: Does he kill him?

F: Watch.

125

F pauses video or winds back to the closing round, because M is handing out the tea and cakes.

Rocky fighting championship round, pitched against huge black opponent. Things aren't looking good. Rocky is taking a beating. The crowd is going wild, cheering, shouting.

Rocky is in his corner with his trainer, Chris, who is warning him.

ROCKY: I know what I'm doing.

CHRIS: Listen. You're getting killed out there.

ROCKY: It's my life.

Both fighters are in their corner with coaches. They are both badly beaten.

The commentator favours Rocky's opponent. He says 'All he has to do is stay awake to steal the title.'

R: Mum, hurry up.
F: You ready?
M: What?
F: We've yet to see the end of this.

R: This is the 5th round.
F: Fifteenth, watch it.

There is talking in the background. M asks R to get something for her (?her slippers). R is put out.

R: Dad, stop it for a minute.
F: Ohhh, June.
M: Well, I wasn't to know. I thought you'd stopped it just for me.
F: No, we didn't stop it just for you. He's been trying to watch it.

The video is stopped again and wound back to the 15th round.

145
M and F are talking.

148
Getting ready to switch video back on
F: Are you ready? (? to R or M).

149
Video is switched on.

This is the 15th round again. Rocky takes lots of punches from opponent. Then he fights back for a bit.
The crowd is shouting and cheering. Who for?
Both fighters are in a bad way – no one seems to be winning at the moment.

J talks about Jonas.

J: He's got all jam down him.

155
Everyone is quiet, all watching the film.

Rocky begins to punch opponent who is too weak to retaliate
by this time.
Both men's faces are a bloody
mess. They both stagger round
the ring, exhausted, but Rocky
just has the upper hand.

161
F asks J if she likes her cake.

The crowd chants 'Rocky,
Rocky'.

Suddenly the film switches to
slow motion.

F hands round custard tarts.

172
R: They both fall down.

There is slow, dramatic music
Rocky and his opponent fall.

All the while Rocky's wife has
been watching the fight at home
with her brother.

All very quiet in T V room.

175
Author and M talk about cakes.

She seems to feel every punch
herself, she looks distressed.
Her brother is enjoying the
fight, cheering and jumping up
and down. Rocky's wife gasps
'Oh'. She has her hands up to
her face.

179
F says something to R about the film (untranscribed).

In the ring everyone is shouting
for Rocky and opponent to get
up. The crowd is still going
wild. Rocky's coach is yelling
for Rocky to get up.
Rocky just about manages to
stagger to his feet before the
countdown ends.
Film cuts to wife and her
brother at home. They are both
jumping up and down with joy.

185
Child (unidentified) talking.

190

Crescendo of triumphant
music.

Rocky's face is a bloody mass as
he accepts the prize.
He is very emotional.
He speaks to the T V cameras.

ROCKY: Thank you, thank you, I can't believe this is happening.

Rocky says that this is the greatest moment of his life, 'apart from when my kid was born'.
He begins to cry.
He says to his wife at home 'I did it'.

We see her crying as she quietly says 'I love you, I love you.'

M and author are talking.

199
R: (? to F) I've gotta see, err *Rocky I*.
F: So have I. You saw *Rocky II* today.

201
F: (untranscribed) . . . after the last film (laughs).
M(?): They're only messing.

208
There is much triumphant cheering and music.
End of film.

M: He says to Paul (untranscribed) . . . no, he said you're *Rocky II* and I'm (untranscribed) . . .
F: Paul said that? (laughs)

214
Turn over to television.

I would like to pick up several points from this. First, there is the specific way in which a videotape is watched. This differs from the fascinated concentration of the spectator in the darkened cinema, and also from the way that television is often used as a backdrop to domestic routines. The video has been deliberately selected and hired. More important, because – as here – it can be stopped and replayed, it allows for more overt connections to domestic practices and relations. Thus, secondly, Mr Cole is able to point excitedly to the fighting – once to Joanne ('he ain't half whacking him . . .'), later to Robert. Thirdly, Mr Cole both 'sends out for' tea from Mrs Cole, who has to service the family, and also emphasizes that they have not stopped the video to replay it for her. She is told in no uncertain terms that 'we didn't stop it just for you', but for Robert who's 'been trying to watch it'. The fighting (linked to control of playback on the video machine) is in this way most clearly presented as masculine, and something from which women are excluded.

The theme of fighting came up many times in my recordings and interviews with the family. Fighting is the key term for Mr Cole in particular. He sees himself as a 'fighter' – against the system and for his children, whom he also encourages to fight. In my second recording, he urged Robert and Joanne to fight each other, telling Joanne to give as good as she gets: 'Well, bash him hard . . . You've been told, you whack him as hard as him.' Mr Cole also commented to me: 'It's surprising really, they're like this at home, but in school, if someone's whacked her, she's crying for about an hour after.'

In an interview with me, Mr and Mrs Cole also referred to Joanne as a tomboy, relating this to fears for her femininity. As Mr Cole observed: 'Obviously, she plays with dolls . . . (untranscribed) with any luck . . . (untranscribed) . . . she might get married and away we go . . . if we can find somebody.'

This concern for her future in terms of femininity is cross-cut by issues about class, in which fighting is a key term. When I commented that Joanne is quiet at school, Mr Cole saw the solution in terms of standing up for herself: 'Well, I think she needs to have a good row with one of the kids in school, give them a good hiding', adding that the two boys were 'the same, until they started like'. The fear would disappear if she could 'hit just as hard or harder'.

Other aspects of Mr Cole's relation to Joanne are salient here. His nickname for her is 'Dodo'. In this instance, although 'Dodo' might relate to an infantile mispronounciation of Joanne (Jo-Jo: Dodo), it also has links with infantilisation and death. Dodo, says Mr Cole, is an extinct bird. Dodo is therefore an anachronism, something which no longer exists (a baby?) but which is kept alive in Mr Cole's fantasy of his daughter as dependent. It may also keep alive for Mr Cole a feminine which is opposite from, and Other to, himself.

Mrs Cole revealed her own reticence and similarity to Joanne when I questioned her about her own activities as a shop steward for NUPE. 'Well, I wouldn't have done it, not less I got roped into it,' she says; and 'I think if I had to stand up there and talk in front of a whole load of people I'd crack . . .' Mr Cole systematically encourages and undermines her, commenting that 'we're not talking about thousands of people'. He, conversely, is on the executive of the local Labour Party. He also 'fights for his children'. Mr Cole is the 'big man' at home. He 'talks for' his wife and systematically stops her talking. He is the 'fighter'. Like Rocky, he is a 'big man' at home who is 'small' and has to 'stand up for himself' in the world outside. Mr Cole is physically very small and the necessity for a fighting masculinity might therefore relate here to a terror of femininity (invested in Dodo?).

Two incidents illustrate this combativeness. The first was the Coles' successful struggle with their local education authority to get the elder son, James, into a prestigious school. The other was their campaign for the removal of asbestos from their daughter's school. For Mr Cole 'The point of fact is though, as any layman knows, asbestos kills'; unlike other parents and teachers he would not put education above physical health and life. The Coles were the only parents to keep their daughter home until the asbestos was removed – the only ones who 'had enough fight'. According to Mr Cole: 'We're Evil . . . We like to go against the system . . . I think they've got a little black book on me somewhere.' Indeed, the Coles are not liked by the school, for whom their fighting is perceived as 'trouble-making'. The notions of fighting stressed by the Coles also make Joanne's 'nurturant' teacher see her as a problem child.

Here the signifier 'fighting' enters into a different relation as it forms for the teacher a characteristic of combative and troublesome parents. It is read as a threat to her position and therefore relates to her reading of the Coles and her own fears of professional powerlessness. Joanne, for her part, stresses the need to 'work hard' and not to 'jaw'. She is largely silent in her interview with me and wants to go and 'get on with her work'.

Mr Cole also encourages his sons to fight and had Robert tell me a story of how he was banned from the school coach because he 'beat up' another boy. In addition, during one recording, he stopped the play-fight between Robert and Joanne with 'no fighting downstairs, eh? . . . Yes, sir, I'll kill you'. At the end of the recording, because of my presence, James managed to go off swimming without really getting permission. Mr Cole's response was, 'Wait till this lady goes, you've had it.' Here, 'fighting' is both an aspect of a bid for power over the body and yet a desperate struggle in relation to it. Fighting can be turned into a celebration of masculinity, but its basis is in oppression. This should also be understood, as in Rocky, as the desperate retreat to the body, because the 'way out', of becoming bourgeois through the mind is not open to Mr Cole.

Talking (saying 'the right thing', surveillance) is also crucial to aspects of power and regulation. As in *Rocky*, it establishes the place of the body and its place in relation to class and gender. Always there is a sense of surveillance of what is said, what can be said outside my hearing, its wrong and pathologised character, as well as the silence and silencing of Mrs Cole and Joanne, the combative talk and fighting. Fighting and power/powerlessness therefore seem to me especially related to an experience of oppression and present a picture of the very 'failure' in covert regulation, the reasoned/reasoning avoidance of conflict which is the object of psycho-educational discourse and which therefore pathologises them.[10] Although Mr Cole stressed his concern that Joanne should fight (like the boys), fighting remains an aspect of a gendered practice. It is the masculine body which is invoked even when Joanne fights, as a 'tomboy'. Mrs Cole's only role in this is to service. She performed domestic labour throughout the recordings and very rarely spoke. Mr Cole 'ordered' cups of tea and stressed that he likes times when his wife is on holiday best because 'she bakes every day'. Robert picks up Mrs Cole's status as a 'servant' in relation to Joanne, at one point calling her his 'slave'.

Fighting enters into the Cole's domestic practices as a relation in a way which is totally consonant with its presentation in *Rocky II*. That relation was crystallised in the watching of the film and the repetition of the final round. In terms of 'forwards' movements therefore, I am placing the relations of signification within history, and within an experience of gendered and class-specific lived oppression. Fighting is a key term in a discourse of powerlessness, of a constant struggle not to sink, to get rights, not to be pushed out. It is quite unlike the pathological object of a liberal anti-sexist discourse which would understand fighting as 'simply' macho violence and would substitute covert regulation and reasoning in language as less sexist.

It is in this way that I am aiming to demonstrate the *fixing* of fighting in that lived historicity – the *point de capiton*. I am stressing too that 'fight/ing/er' as a relation is quite specific in its meaning and therefore *not* co-terminous with what fighting would mean in, for example, a professional middle-class household where both the regulation of conflict and the relation to oppression are quite different. This is an argument *against* a universalism of meaning, reading and interpretation.

However, having examined the manifest content in which the relations of signification are historically fixed, this is not all there is. If we are to explore the latent content, it is necessary to ask what is suppressed/repressed/forgotten beneath the term? The working-class male body is a site of struggle and of anxiety, as well as pleasure. Mr Cole is a very small man. Fighting is a way of gaining power, of celebrating or turning into a celebration that which is constituent of oppression. Power in its manifest content covers over a terror of powerlessness, an anxiety beneath the pleasure.

Mr Cole is afraid of being 'soft', of a femininity lurking beneath the surface. This is referred to while the family watch the musical film *Annie* on video. It is seen as a 'women's film', and its fantasies, its dancing and singing, are constantly held up for ridicule. It is as though Mr Cole cannot bear to be seen (by me?) as liking such a film, as having passive, romantic fantasies. In this analysis, masculinity as fighting is a defence, a defence against powerlessness, a defence against femininity. The backwards movement can be articulated in relation to several points. The fear of being watched or monitored (counterpointed by my voyeurism), the expectation of female servicing (when his wife is at home), the *struggle* to fight against a fear: all these suggest that fighting represents a triumph over, repression of, defence against, the terror of powerlessness. This powerlessness, as in *Rocky II*, is presented as the humiliation of cowardice – of the man who cannot work, fight, protect women, and who is therefore feminised. Latent beneath Mr Cole's conscious self-identification as a fighter may lurk the fear of a small man whose greatest fear is his cowardice and femininity. It is this which has to be displaced by projection on to, and investment in, others (his wife, Joanne) who can be the objects of his protection and for whom he fights.

In psychoanalytic terms, such a reading keys into the necessity for – but also the fraudulence of – the phallus as a sign of power. Whether one finds in this an Oedipal struggle or an omnipotent, pre-Oedipal one, might be a point of dispute. However, my aim is not to suggest that the historical 'fighting' is really about a psychic relation. Far from it. It is to demonstrate the centrality of sexuality and power in the lived historicity of current struggles and the interminable intertwining of present and past, of material conditions and psychic relations. What is being fought for and fought against by Mr Cole can therefore be understood as having a manifest and latent content. But, since Mr Cole's (childhood) anxieties were and are produced in specific historical conditions, it is quite impossible and indeed dangerous to separate the one from the other.

[. . .]

Fantasy and Intellectualisation

How finally are we to come to terms with the voyeuristic social scientist? The 'space' of observation, I would argue, like that of watching videos, is a fantasy space in which certain fictions are produced. One effect of these fictions is to constitute a knowledge, a truth that is incorporated into the regulation of families. At the same time, the 'claim to truth' designates the social scientist as an expert in the bourgeois order which produces this intellectuality. But it also, I have suggested, hides the fear that motivates it. The masses must be known because they represent a threat to the moral and political order; the theorist/voyeur expresses shame and disgust at the 'animal passions' which have to be monitored and regulated – and which she cannot enjoy. This logic of intellectualisation is evident in many studies of audiences. I therefore want to consider how the fantasies and fictions embodied in academic accounts as well as in films are inscribed in the daily lives of ordinary people.

Modern apparatuses of social regulation, along with other social and cultural practices, produce knowledges which claim to 'identify' individuals. These knowledges create the possibility of multiple practices, multiple positions. To be a 'clever child' or a 'good mother', for example, only makes sense in the terms given by pedagogic, welfare, medical, legal and other discourses and practices. These observe, sanction and correct how we act; they attempt to define who and what we are. They are, however, criss-crossed by other discourses and practices – including those of popular entertainment, for example. This multiplicity means that the practices which position us may often be mutually contradictory. They are also sites of contestation and struggle. We never quite fit the 'positions' provided for us in these regulatory practices. That failure is, in Freudian psychoanalysis, both the point of pain and point of struggle. It shows repeatedly that the imposition of fictional identities – or socialization – does not work.[11]

What I am proposing here is a model of how subjectification is produced: how we struggle to become subjects and how we resist provided subjectivities in relation to the regulative power of modern social apparatuses. This model rejects the old image of the masses trapped in false consciousness, waiting to be led out of ideology by radical intellectuals. Rather, I would argue, these two categories form a couple defined and produced in relation to each other. The modern bourgeois order depends upon a professional intellectual élite which 'knows' and regulates the proletariat.[12] One side effect of the creation of this 'new middle class' has been that some of its radical members, having themselves achieved social mobility through the route of higher education, claim that it is *only* through rationality and intellectualisation that the masses can see through the workings of ideology and so escape its snares.

The audience for popular entertainment, for example, is often presented as sick (voyeuristic, scopophilic) or as trapped within a given subjectivity (whether defined by the social categories of class, race and gender or by a universalised Oedipal scenario). What is disavowed in such approaches is the complex relation of 'intellectuals' to 'the masses': 'our' project of analysing 'them' is itself one of the regulative practices which produce our subjectivity as well as theirs. We are each Other's Other – but not on equal terms. Our fantasy investment often seems to consist in believing that we can 'make them see' or that we can see or speak *for* them. If we do assume that, then we continue to dismiss fantasy and the Imaginary as snares and delusions. We fail to acknowledge how the insistent demand to see through ideology colludes in the process of intellectualising bodily and other pleasures.

It was in opposition to that approach that I tried to make sense of Mr Cole's self-identification as a fighter. I argued that fighting relates not only to masculinity, but also to lived oppression, to the experience of powerlessness and the fear of it. The implication is that we should stop being obsessed by the illusory tropes of an oppressive ideology, and that we should start to look at fantasy spaces as places for hope and for escape from oppression as well.

Asked why they read romantic fiction, the women Janice Radway spoke to said that it helped them to escape from the drudgery of servicing their families – and thus to cope with it. They read at quiet moments (in bed, in the bath) when they could recall the tattered dreams of their youth and long for someone to love them as they wanted to be loved. Their reading was therefore double-edged: not only a way of coming to terms with their daily lives, but also an act of resistance and hope. It is this question of the hope and pleasure that women invest in romantic fiction, which Radway brings out very clearly, that I want to dwell on. But I depart from Radway's analysis, because she remains caught up with the idea that these readers might move 'beyond' such romantic notions; she also rejects psychoanalytic explanations for failing to engage with the specificity of readers' lives.[13] That seems to underestimate both the material and the psychical reality of these women's servitude and the pain of their longing for something else.

The danger with such approaches to the study of the audience, however radical in intent, is that their insistence on the transcendence of ideology through the intellectualisation of pleasure(s) can itself become part of a broader regulatory project of intellectualisation. This seems to be implicit, for example, in the description of a course for women about women and/in the cinema.[14] When the students were encouraged to deconstruct the codes of representation in various types of film, some found it difficult because it meant giving up, or supplanting, the pleasure they had previously felt in watching movies. Similarly, in many media studies courses in schools, children are asked to analyse popular television programmes. What concerns me is how these women, children, whoever, are being asked to deal with their previous enjoyment of such things – a pleasure shared with family, friends and their general social and cultural environment. It seems that they are being left little room for any response other than feeling stupid, or despising those who are still enjoying these 'perverse' pleasures.

What this typically academic emphasis on rationality and intellectualisation can overlook are the specific conditions of the formation of pleasures for particular groups at a given historical moment. Rather than seeing the pleasures of the 'masses' as perverse, perhaps we should acknowledge that it is the bourgeois 'will to truth' that is perverse in its desire for knowledge, certainty and mastery. This is the proper context in which to understand the *desire* to know the masses, the voyeurism of the (social) scientist. The crusade to save the masses from the ideology that dupes them can obscure the real social significance of their pleasures and, at the same time, blind us to the perversity of radical intellectual pleasures. The alternative is not a populist defence of Hollywood, but a reassessment of what is involved in watching films. This becomes part of the experience of oppression, pain and desire. Watching a Hollywood movie is not simply an escape from drudgery into dreaming: it is a place of desperate dreaming, of hope for transformation.

Popular pleasures produced in/under oppression can be contrasted with the more cerebral pleasures of discrimination or deconstruction. These ultimately derive from the scientific project of intellectualisation, the Cogito, which culminates in the scientific management of populations, the power/knowledge of the modern social order. The intellectualisation of pleasures, in other words, is linked not just to the desire to know but also to the project of controlling nature. This has had as its other and opposite a fear of the powers of the unknown, the animal, the unlawful, the insane, the masses, women, blacks. These 'others' became objects to be known and thus civilised and regulated. There exists among the bourgeoisie a terror of the pleasures of the flesh, of the body, of the animal passions seen to be burning darkly in sexuality and also in violent uprisings. No surprise then that the regulation of children's consumption of the modern media focuses so obsessively on sex and violence.

In the end then the 'problem' of popular pleasures – the Coles' enjoyment of *Rocky II* – turns out to lie not (only) with 'the masses' but (also) with the fears and desires of the bourgeois intellectual. The desire to know and to master conceals the terror of a lack of control, a paranoia which is the opposite of omnipotent fantasy, a megalomania. These I have called perversions to point up the way in which they project their own terror of the masses on to the masses themselves. It is this projection that motivates the desire to rationalise the pleasures of the body, to transform them into pleasures of the mind. This body/mind dualism valorises mental labour as genius or creativity and denigrates the servicing and manual work which make them possible – the labour of the masses and their terrifying physicality. It is in this context of the mental/manual division that the physicality of *Rocky*, expressed so clearly in its violence, should be placed.

I have tried to establish the difference between the 'cold' aesthetic of high culture, with its cerebral and intellectualised appreciation, and the bodily and sensuous pleasures of 'low' cultures.[15] What is most important is to understand the different conditions in which these pleasures – and their associated pains and hopes – are produced. In the oppressive conditions of the bourgeois order 'animal passions' are regulated, the 'rising of the masses' is feared, the individual is defined in terms of brain or brawn, the only way out offered is through cleverness, guile, making it, working, trying. And so embourgeoisement is the only dream left in all those desires for, and dreams of, difference . . .

Notes

This analysis would not have been possible without the work and insights of Helen Lucey and Diana Watson of the Girls and Mathematics Unit, University of London Institute of Education. Many of the arguments are developed in my 'On the regulation of speaking and silence', in C. Steedman, C. Urwin and V. Walkerdine (eds.), *Language, Gender and Childhood* (London: Routledge & Kegan Paul, 1985); V. Walkerdine, *Surveillance, Subjectivity and Struggle* (Minneapolis: University of Minnesota Press, 1986); and *The Mastery of Reason*, in press; V. Walkerdine and H. Lucey, *Final Report of Grant No. C/00/23/0331/1 to the Economic and Social Science Research Council*, 1985; and V. Walkerdine, H. Lucey and D. Watson, *The Regulation of Mothering* (working title) (Cambridge: Polity Press, forthcoming). I would also like to thank Philip Corrigan, Dick Hebdige and David Morley for helpful comments and criticism.

1 Foucault has documented this in relation to a 'will to truth' in which production of a knowledge has real effects in the surveillance and regulation of the Other. I add the dimension of *voyeurism* to this perverse will to truth because it allows us to explore the fears and fantasies present in this watching, classifying surveillance – the desire to *know* the Other and therefore to have power over, to control, to explain, to regulate it. This claim to certainty and truth becomes not normal, but profoundly perverse. It is linked with disgust and with shame: shame at watching – desire to see how 'the other half lives' – and the vicarious excitement in that which is forbidden to the bourgeois researcher and in which s/he profoundly desires to engage but must only monitor, watch, describe and moralistically criticise and prevent. (cf. Sigmund Freud, *The Standard Edition of the Complete Psychological Works* vol. VII (London: The Hogarth Press and the Institute of Psychoanalysis, 1962), pp. 156–7.

2 In that sense I shall argue that the 'truths' which create the modern form of sociality are fictions and therefore themselves invented in fantasy. The 'real' therefore becomes a problematic category which I shall deal with only by reference to 'veridicality', on the one hand, and cultural forms and practices, on the other. That is, both scientific and cultural practices produce regimes of meaning, truth, representation in which there are particular relations of significa- tion. What is important in respect of these is the production of a *sign* – i.e. how we enter as 'a relation' and how in actual social practices and cultural forms we become 'positioned'. The concept of positioning relies upon the importance attached to signifier/signified relations. In addition, we can utilise the concept of fantasy to understand our insertion within other 'dramas'. In this respect then the mode of analysis is similar, and also potentially allows an examination of fantasies inscribed in *both* the imaginary and the symbolic.

3 Freeway is the name of an extremely small dog in the television series *Hart to Hart*. Using it as the Alsatian's name is therefore something of a joke.

4 That pain of becoming bourgeois through work: a route opened to working-class women, perhaps for the first time in the post-war educational expansion. See my 'Dreams from an ordinary childhood', in L. Heron (ed.), *Truth, Dare or Promise* (London: Virago, 1985).

5 The dramatic butchery of the fights in the *Rocky* films would be impossible under the existing laws of amateur and professional boxing. Kathryn Kalinak makes a similar point about the impossibility of the escape route through dance presented in *Flashdance*; the heroine is simply much too old to take up a a classical ballet career. See '*Flashdance*: the Dead End Kid', *Jump Cut* no. 29 (1984), pp. 3–4.

6 See, for example, S. Neale, 'Masculinity as spectacle', *Screen* vol. 24 no. 6 (1983).

7 The term 'pencil-pusher' for a man with a clerical job was (at least in my family) a term of both abuse and envy. It was what everyone wanted, because it was easy, but it could not count as real work, because it did not involve heavy manual labour.

8 This reading reflects my own identification with *Rocky II*, but it is also evident in an account of reactions to the film among members of a C S E Media Studies class; see A. Brookfield, 'Reading *Rocky* films: versions of masculinity', in *Working Papers for 16+ Media Studies* (Clwyd County Council, 1985). Brookfield describes the working-class youths' identification with Rocky but, 'although the narrative framework was structured around a "success story", the group challenged some aspects of the representation of success. In discussions of aspects of social class within the film the boys tended to adopt an oppositional stance towards the "American Dream" ideology. In doing so they picked up as relevant to their lives an element present in the lyrics of the theme music to the film. These suggest that poverty brutalises and makes it necessary to take to the streets and kill to survive.' (p. 88) I would take issue with Brookfield's assumption that 'the [Rocky] films address a wide and differentiated audience, who will bring a variety of readings to them; these different readings are based on different assumptions about "mascu- linity"; in general, students' readings of the films remained within a dominant framework'. (p.

85) This implies precisely the notion that I have criticised, namely that working-class masculinity is always lived as class specific, in relation to the body and the mental/manual division of labour. These are not therefore in any simple sense 'different assumptions about masculinity'.

9 The numbers refer to the counter on the tape recorder, and therefore provide a record of the passage of time during the recording. 'Untranscribed' refers to utterances which were inaudible and could therefore not be transcribed.

10 See Walkerdine, 'On the regulation of speaking and silence'.

11 J. Rose, 'Femininity and its discontents', *Femininist Review* no. 14 (1983,) p. 9.

12 For a discussion of intellectuals, see Philip Schlesinger, 'In search of the intellectuals: some comments on recent theory', *Media, Culture and Society* vol. 4 no. 3 (July 1982).

13 Radway's rejection seems to rest on an equation between psychoanalysis and a purely formalist account of how texts 'position' subjects. Although there have been occasional attempts at just such a synthesis, at a theoretical level the equation is misleading. It seems to me that psychoanalysis might open up a way of engaging with the reality of women's fantasies, pleasures and desires as they read the novels.

14 S. Clayton, 'Notes on teaching film', *Feminist Review* no. 14 (1983).

15 P. Bourdieu, *Distinction: A Social Critique of the Judgement of Taste* (London: Routledge & Kegan Paul, 1984), chap. 1.

INDEX OF NAMES

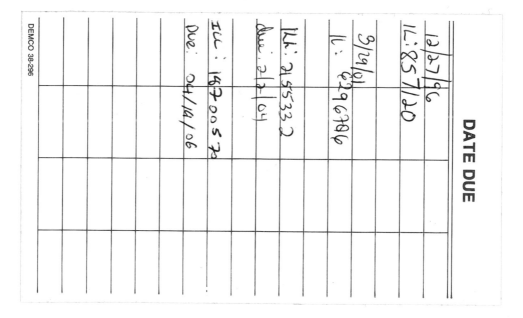